The American Peace Society

Also from Westphalia Press

westphaliapress.org

The American Peace Society

A Centennial History, 1828-1928

by Edson L. Whitney

WESTPHALIA PRESS
An imprint of Policy Studies Organization

Westphalia Press
An imprint of Policy Studies Organization
1527 New Hampshire Ave., NW
Washington, D.C. 20036
info@ipsonet.org

ISBN-13: 978-1-63391-545-9
ISBN-10: 1-63391-545-X

Cover design by Jeffrey Barnes:
jbarnesbook.design

Daniel Gutierrez-Sandoval, Executive Director
PSO and Westphalia Press

Updated material and comments on this edition
can be found at the Westphalia Press website:
www.westphaliapress.org

THE
AMERICAN
PEACE SOCIETY
A CENTENNIAL
HISTORY

The
American Peace Society

A Centennial History
(Third Revised Edition)

By

Edson L. Whitney

With a Foreword by

Theodore E. Burton

Washington, D. C.
The American Peace Society
March, 1929

TABLE OF CONTENTS

TO

Dr. and Mrs. Arthur Deerin Call

BECAUSE OF THEIR FAITHFUL EFFORTS TO PROMOTE
THE AIMS OF THE AMERICAN PEACE SOCIETY; BECAUSE
OF THEIR UNTIRING ENERGY IN GATHERING AND PRE-
SERVING SUCH RICH MATERIAL RELATING TO ITS
HISTORY; AND BECAUSE OF THEIR INVALUABLE HELP
WITHOUT WHICH IT WOULD HAVE BEEN IMPOSSIBLE
FOR HIM TO PREPARE THIS ACCOUNT — THIS VOLUME
IS AFFECTIONATELY DEDICATED BY

The Author

MAY 8, 1928

PREFACE

THE following account of the American Peace Society during the first century of its existence is offered as a contribution to economic and social history. In the early days the society took the initiative in the peace movement. In fact, the history of the peace movement in this country to the close of the last century is practically the history of the American Peace Society. To-day its main office is to advise and instruct, for the movement has expanded to such an extent as to be incapable of control by any one organization.

The account contains no arguments in favor of peace or in criticism of war. It is not a panegyric of the society or of any one connected with it. It is a plain description of the organization of the society, its aims, the methods it has used to influence governments to adopt something in place of war, and the progress it has made in expanding idealism into actuality. It is based mainly upon the records of the society and its printed publications.

The records of the society are contained in four volumes,—the first covering July 7, 1835 to October 13, 1854, the second Jan. 17, 1855 to May 13, 1896, the third May 13, 1896 to Nov. 28, 1919, and the fourth Dec. 26, 1919 to the present. These records include the meetings of the executive committee, the board of directors, and of the society, with occasional accounts of the action of special committees and the officers. The records previous to July 7, 1835 are not in the possession of the society.

All important acts of the society, with annual reports of officers, are related in the Advocate of Peace and its predecessors. Besides the records and the magazine, old letters in the possession of the society, the publications of other peace societies in Europe and America, and a few other publications have been examined, as the biographies of William Ladd, Elihu Burritt, Charles Sumner, Andrew Carnegie, and a few other noted men who have been connected with the society. A history of these other peace organizations has not been included in this account except in so far as they have been connected with the history of the American Peace Society.

E. L. W.

WASHINGTON, D. C.
1928

THE American Peace Society is one hundred years old. It is of importance that its history should be told. It pleases me to find that this is done and with such fulness. Through years yet to come, others concerned to know of the development of the historic peace movement will turn to these pages with interest and profit, for the work of the American Peace Society has been a very worthy contribution to right thinking in a field where informed judgments are peculiarly a fundamental need of the world.

Theodore E Burton
President, American
Peace Society.

Washington
April 21, 1928

THE AMERICAN PEACE SOCIETY

A Centennial History

Chapter I

EARLY PEACE SOCIETIES

THE organized peace movement may be said to have had its origin in the Napoleonic wars. True, many individuals before that time had spoken of peace and advocated peace, but in no case had they obtained any large following. The ancient religions—Christianity, Buddhism and Hindooism—taught peace. The ancient writers—Homer, Euripides, Cicero, Seneca, Tacitus, Plutarch — were critical of war. The testimony of the early Christian Fathers—Justin Martyr, St. Irenæus, Clement of Alexandria, Tertullian, Athanasius, St. Gregory, St. Augustine, Celsus, Origen and St. Cyprian—and the later reformers—Wiclif, Erasmus, Luther, John Wesley, Bacon, and Jeremy Bentham—was to the same effect. The Quakers and the Mennonites preached peace as a part of their religion, and the Holy Alliance, to keep the peace, was formed in 1815 by Alexander of Russia, influenced to some extent perhaps by the Grand Design of Henry IV. of France, drawn up two centuries before. The teachings of these writers were not without effect. At least four peace societies—three in the United States and one in England—were formed during the years 1815 and 1816.

The first of the group was founded in New York City. David Low Dodge, a Presbyterian merchant living in Hartford, had his attention called to the subject of peace in 1804. On his removal to New York, two years later, he undertook a systematic study of the question. Coming to the conclusion that war was wrong, he published anonymously in 1809 a tract entitled "Mediator's Kingdom not of this World." Three literary men replied to this in a pamphlet entitled "The Duty of a Christian in a Trying Situa-

9

tion," which Dodge answered in a pamphlet entitled "Remarks on the Pamphlet Entitled The Duty of a Christian in a Trying Situation." From that time Dodge became an advocate of the cause of peace.

In 1810, Dodge met others holding views similar to his own. Together they discussed the best way to propagate their doctrines. Two years later about forty men met in the parlor of Dodge's house and organized the first peace society in the world; but due to the war threats then current a second meeting was not held. At the close of the war, Dodge published a book containing 130 pages entitled "War Inconsistent with the Religion of Jesus Christ." August 16, 1815, twenty men gathered together and formed the New York Peace Society[1] to discourage war and promote peace. Membership therein was open to "any person of good moral character who receives the Bible as the rule of his faith and is approved by the board of directors." New members were admitted only with the consent of all the old members. By 1819, the society had a membership of seventy and was spending two to three hundred dollars a year in the interest of the cause.

The formation of the second society was due to Rev. Noah Worcester, who was born in Hollis, N. H., Nov. 25, 1758. Worcester served in the Revolutionary War, was pastor of churches in New Hampshire for nearly thirty years, and moved to Brighton, now a part of Boston, in May, 1813, where he became editor of the Christian Disciple. For some years his thought had been turning to the subject of peace. He prepared a small book on the subject, but he was unable to find a publisher willing to print it. At Christmastime, in 1814, before the formation of the New York society however, he finally printed it anonymously, under the title, "A Solemn Review of the Custom of War." In this influential essay he suggested the formation of peace societies to combat the evils of war. The little book fell into the hands of some Quakers in Warren County, Ohio, who were so impressed with the horrors, devastation and grief there depicted that, Dec. 2, 1815, they formed the "Society for Promoting Peace." This Ohio society was divided into four branches, and at the end of a year it had one hundred members and had published three thousand copies of tracts relating to war and peace.

---

[1] The articles of association are given in the Friend of Peace, Vol. II, No. 1, pp. 30, 31.

The third society was formed in Boston, through the direct efforts of Noah Worcester. At the annual convention of the Congregational ministers of Massachusetts in the spring of 1815, Dr. Worcester moved the appointment of a committee of five "to consider whether it is expedient for this convention to adopt any measure, or measures, or if any what, to correct the public mind on the subject of war." The committee as appointed consisted of Noah Worcester, William Ellery Channing, President Kirkland of Harvard, John Foster of Brighton, and Dr. Osgood of Medford. These five with others, including the governor and lieutenant governor of the state, several professors of Harvard College, two judges, and ministers of several denominations, twenty-two men in all, met in the study of Dr. Channing, Dec. 28, 1815, and there signed the constitution of the Massachusetts Peace Society. Officers were elected Jan. 11, 1816, with Lieutenant Governor William Phillips, president; Hon. Thomas Dawes, vice president; Deacon Elisha Ticknor, treasurer; Thomas Wallcutt, recording secretary; and Noah Worcester, corresponding secretary. Levi Hedge, Drs. Abiel Holmes, Daniel Sharp, Henry Ware and W. E. Channing were among the trustees and counsellors.

At the next annual meeting of the minister's association, May 29, 1816, Dr. Channing delivered a vigorous sermon against war, and the committee, appointed the year before, gave a report in harmony with the sermon. The convention adopted the report[1] and many members joined the recently organized Massachusetts Peace Society.

Thus three peace societies had been formed within a period of about four months, each ignorant of the formation of the others. Other societies followed. At the close of the year 1819, seventeen independent societies had been formed in Maine, Vermont, Massachusetts, Rhode Island, New York, Pennsylvania, Ohio, Indiana, Kentucky, North Carolina, and Georgia. By 1828, their number was fifty. In 1820 there was formed the Female Peace Society of Cincinnati, the first of a series of such societies composed entirely of women.

The idea was not confined to the United States. Dr. Bogue, head of the Missionary Seminary in Gosport, in England, called attention to the question of peace in October, 1813, and published an

---

[1] The report and an address on the subject are printed in the Friend of Peace, No. 5, pp. 27-33.

article upon the subject in his "Discourses on the Millenium," which was later sent out as a tract.

In the following spring, on the invitation of a Friend, William Allen, several men met at his house in Plough Court, Lombard Street, London, for the purpose of carrying out the ideas suggested in Dr. Bogue's tract. Each member was asked to draw up a plan of procedure, and June 6, 1814, three came together, voted to form a society to circulate tracts and diffuse information tending to show that all war is inconsistent with the interests of mankind and is contrary to the spirit of Christianity. There the matter rested for a time.

In the Philanthropist for July, 1815, was printed a letter dated April 17, 1815, signed "A Friend of Peace," suggesting the formation of a society for the purpose of spreading information on the subject of war. The writer outlined a plan with observations respecting the questions to be discussed. June 1, 1816, William Allen again called a group to found a committee to complete the organization. The next meeting was held June 14, when, after learning of the formation of the Massachusetts Peace Society, they completed the organization of their society giving it the name of the "Society for the Promotion of Permanent and Universal Peace," to oppose war of any kind and to extend information on the subject of war.

This "The Peace Society" of London, still in existence, is the oldest of the peace societies agitating against the institution of war. Its early supporters were mainly Friends. Its activities have been confined chiefly to the formation of a peace sentiment, giving of public lectures, conducting through its secretary correspondence relating to war and peace, and forming branch societies of which there were forty by 1826. In the earlier years it issued tracts most generously. In the first year, the society circulated 46,000 of them. In 1820, 150,000 were issued, translated into German, Spanish, Dutch, French and Welsh, and sent to foreign countries, as well as to the kings of France and Spain. At the annual meeting in 1839 it was announced that the number of tracts issued to date was 967,000. In 1818 the society sent a set of tracts to the Prince Regent and another to the Czar of Russia, and the next year 5,000 copies to the fair at Leipzig. It aided in organizing independent societies in Scotland, Ireland and Nova

Scotia, and began the publication of its journal the "Herald of Peace," in January, 1819.

As a result of the promiscuous distribution of these tracts, *La Société des Amis de la Morale Chrétien et de la Paix* was organized in Paris, Dec. 20, 1821, at the house of S. V. S. Wilder, a former member of the Massachusetts Peace Society and later a director of the American Peace Society. Through its peace committee the society carried on correspondence for years with the American and British societies and various persons in Germany and Switzerland. The society was composed of many persons of note,—the king and his son the Duc d'Orleans, Guizot the historian, Casimir-Perier the prime minister, and nearly all the members of his cabinet.

The Geneva Peace Society, Switzerland, the second peace society formed on the continent of Europe, was established Dec. 1, 1830, by Comte de Sellen, a member of the sovereign council of Geneva. He had been interested in the inviolability of human life and had had his attention called to the subject of peace through a stray copy of the Herald of Peace that came into his hands.

The Massachusetts Society was the most active of the American societies. Worcester and Channing, Trinitarian and Unitarian ministers, worked together harmoniously, Worcester as corresponding secretary and Channing as counsellor. During the first year of its existence the society received the approval of the Massachusetts Convention of Congregational Ministers and of the General Association of Massachusetts Proper. Beginning in 1818, it founded branch societies, the plan being to have one in every town in the state and one in every state that did not have a state society. These were to be used as agencies for the distribution of tracts. Twelve such societies had been formed by the close of 1819—eight in Massachusetts, three in New Hampshire, and one in Connecticut—and an average of three or four, were formed each year, during the next decade. The membership of a branch society was generally between ten and twenty.

At the close of the first year the Massachusetts society had 130 members, of whom fifty were ministers. At the close of the second year it had 304, of whom eighty had fought in the Revolutionary War. At the end of the third year it had 550 members, and in 1819, at the end of the fourth year, it had 882. Among the members of the society in addition to those already mentioned were Levi Hedge,

Levi Frisbie, Joseph McKean, Simon Greenleaf, Henry Ware, and Isaac Parker, all professors at Harvard, Abiel Holmes, father of Oliver Wendell Holmes, Francis Parkman, the historian, Ezra Ripley, John Tappan, Lewis Tappan, Samuel Parkman, Epes Sargent, Josiah Quincy, Thomas Vose, Dr. T. M. Harris, Jonathan Phillips, Eliphalet Kimball, David Reed, Dr. Charles Lowell, Caleb Strong, Christopher Gore, C. J. Parker, and Alden Bradford, at the time all well known residents of Boston and vicinity, and John T. Gilman, ex-governor of New Hampshire. The president and thirty-three delegates in the convention called to revise the constitution of the Commonwealth of Massachusetts in 1820 were members of the society.

Worcester wrote letters to President Jefferson, Oct. 18, 1815, and to President Adams, Jan. 23, 1816, inviting them to become members of the society. Adams replied Feb. 6, 1816, approving the idea of peace but refusing to join the society because "universal and perpetual peace appear to me no more nor less than everlasting passive obedience and non resistance. The human flock would soon be fleeced and butchered by one or a few. I cannot therefore sir be a subscriber or a member of your society."[1]

Jefferson replied Jan. 29, 1816, thanking him for the documents and expressing approval of the peace ideas. His letter closed as follows: "I retire therefore from the question with a sincere wish that your writings may be effective in lessening this greatest of human evils, and that you may retain life and health to enjoy the contemplation of this happy spectacle." Later, however, he wrote another letter under date of Nov. 26, 1817, in which he stated that he favored the abolition of war though he despaired its abolition. Continuing, he wrote: "The enrolment you propose of my name in the records of your society cannot be unacceptable to me."[2] It is needless to say that he was elected an honorary member of the society at its next meeting.

At about the same time, Prince A. Gallitzin of Russia was elected an honorary member; and on June 8, 1819, Hon. Elias Boudinot of New Jersey, president of the American Bible Society, Thomas Chalmers, the British anti-slavery advocate, and others.

April 9, 1817, a letter was sent to the Czar of Russia, enclosing

[1] The letter and reply are printed in Vol. I, Number 4, of the Friend of Peace, pp. 24-26.
[2] The earlier letter to Jefferson and his reply are printed in the Friend of Peace, Vol. I, Number 3, pp. 21-24, and his second letter in Number 11, p. 24.

a copy of each of the publications of the society as a token of esteem, to which he replied July 4, 1817, with thanks.[1]

The society was supported mainly from membership fees. These and money received from the sale of publications amounted to about one thousand dollars a year. Occasionally a bequest or gift came, such as one hundred dollars from Rev. Henry Jefferies, chaplain of the East India Company, in June, 1822. According to the constitution of the society its funds were to be used "for the diffusion of light on the subject of war and in cultivating the principles and spirit of peace." In furtherance of this object, Noah Worcester, the corresponding secretary, in 1816, established a magazine entitled the "Friend of Peace," which appeared at irregular intervals as the editor had material and means to publish it until 1828, when fifty numbers had been issued. The earlier numbers contain many articles explaining the position of the society, while the later contain many items of interest showing the progress of the movement. The numbers bear no date of issue. Volumes I, II, and III consisted of twelve numbers each, volume IV of fourteen numbers and four appendices. Each number of the first two volumes contained forty octavo pages, except numbers 5 and 11 which contained 36 pages, while the numbers and appendices of the last two volumes contained 32 pages each.

Tracts based on morality and the teachings of the Bible, appealing mainly to the intellect, were issued in abundance; in 1816, 4820; in 1819, 16,149; in 1828, 27,500. They were circulated everywhere. During the first five years of the society's existence some were sent to Nova Scotia, New Brunswick, France, Holland, and Russia. Through Congregational and Baptist missionaries they were sent to San Domingo, Great Britain, Gibraltar, Bombay, Ceylon, Singapore, Tahiti, Hawaii, and South America. Thirty-eight complete sets of all the publications of the society were sent to the New England colleges. In 1823, copies were sent to all officers of the Federal government and to each state and territorial governor. In 1817, an address was made to the Masonic fraternity as Christians, and a memorial was sent to the Massachusetts legislature requesting them to pass a resolution favoring peace.

The society was organized by religious men and was main-

---

[1] The correspondence is given in the Friend of Peace, Vol. I, Number 10, pp. 24-27.

tained by religious men, many being Quakers and ministers, and they naturally turned to professing Christians for support. In 1816, letters were sent to the various assemblies and meetings of ministers in the United States urging them to use their influence for peace. As a result the Methodist Reformed church conference in New York in 1817 assumed the character of a peace society and seven religious denominations declared against war. The Vermont convention of Congregational churches passed resolutions in favor of peace, in September, 1819. The African Baptist Association in Philadelphia formed itself into a peace society in 1823. As a result of the influence of the society, letters appeared in the daily and weekly newspapers relative to the merits of peace and war, and articles on the peace movement are to be found in the leading magazines of the time.

Chapter II

ORGANIZATION OF THE AMERICAN PEACE
SOCIETY

But the time had come for the formation of a national society, one that should coordinate the work of the various societies and command the respect of the world as did the London Peace Society. Worcester recommended the formation of such a society, but felt unable to carry his suggestion into effect. The society was actually formed by William Ladd on whom the mantle of Worcester fell.

William Ladd was born in Exeter, N. H., May 10, 1778, the oldest son of a merchant in that town. He prepared for college at the academy there and graduated from Harvard College in 1797, at the age of nineteen. For fifteen years he led a roving life, as a sea captain, sailing first his father's and later his own ships, as a merchant in Savannah, Georgia, and as a cotton planter in Florida. On the death of his father in 1806, Capt. Ladd returned to Portsmouth and again sailed the ocean until the War of 1812. Two years later, reputed to be worth about $80,000, he settled in Minot, Maine, on a five hundred acre farm that had formerly belonged to his father. Soon after he united with the Congregational church of that town and became interested in various questions of a religious and philanthropic nature—missions, Sunday schools, temperance, slavery,—to all of which he gave liberally of his means.

Ladd's attention was first called to peace societies in 1819 by Rev. Jesse Appleton, president of Bowdoin College. The reading of Worcester's "Solemn Review" soon after further impressed the subject upon his mind. After examining some copies of the Friend of Peace and some tracts published by the Massachusetts Peace Society, which were given him by a friend to whom they had been sent, he said[1]: "I became convinced that war is an evil which might be banished from civilized society and that it is the duty of every man to lend a helping hand to bring about so desirable an event. I felt it a duty which I owe to God and my fellow-creatures

[1] In his Essays of Philanthropos on Peace and War, p. 7.

to do something to hasten the glorious era when men shall learn war no more." He felt that the custom of war rested wholly upon public opinion, which must needs be changed.

Ladd undertook the task of effecting that change. Beginning July, 1823, he wrote a series of thirty-two articles on peace and war, for the "Christian Mirror," a religious paper printed in Portland, Maine, and started a second series of thirty-seven articles in the same paper in 1825. Each series was later reprinted in one volume. In 1824 he joined the Massachusetts society, and the next year established six branches for it. He established a peace society in Minot in the same year, and Feb. 10, 1826, revived the Maine Peace Society which had been established Jan. 31, 1817, and which had been very active for a time. In 1818, this Society had sent a memorial against privateering to President Monroe, but, by 1822, had ceased to function. Ladd became corresponding secretary of both the Maine and the Minot societies. He delivered addresses before other societies. One, the annual address before the Massachusetts Peace Society, Christmas, 1825, attracted wide attention, being reprinted and published in England.

Ladd watched the peace societies of foreign lands. He corresponded with the London Society in 1824 and later became a member of it, receiving copies of all its publications. He studied its workings and became convinced that the movement in this country needed a directing head to give tone, unity and strength to the existing societies, one central society, preferably in New York as the metropolis of the country, to which all other societies should be auxiliary and make their reports. It was his idea that the society in turn should make a consolidated report, publish books and tracts to be circulated by the auxiliaries, keep an agent in the field to visit, aid and encourage the local organizations, and spread peace principles and organize new societies wherever advisable.

At the reorganization of the Maine society, Ladd laid his plan before it; whereupon that society voted "that it is expedient to take measures for the formation of a national peace society."[1] A similar vote was passed by the Portsmouth, N. H., Peace Society, which had been organized Nov. 19, 1818, and now reorganized by Ladd, and by the Massachusetts Peace Society at its annual meeting Dec. 25. 1826. All three societies appointed Ladd as their agent to confer with the societies in New York and Phila-

[1] Hemmenway, Memoirs of William Ladd, p. 230.

delphia, and to organize a national society, if such should prove to be feasible.

Ladd was not able to take up the work until the next year. In January, 1828, he visited New York and Philadelphia, stopping and organizing societies at many places on the way. His reception in both cities was discouraging.

The New York society had ceased holding meetings in 1822, though Dodge its founder, who had carried on correspondence with Ladd for four years, was trying to keep it alive. At a meeting in April, 1825, it had been voted to reanimate the society; but in the following January it was reported to be fifty dollars in debt. On his arrival in New York, Ladd was told by the officers of the society that it was dead and could give him no help. He refused however to be discouraged. He talked and lectured in the city for two weeks. He stated that "they might as well throw snow balls into the crater of Vesuvius in the hope of extinguishing it as to expect to cool me," and again, "Retreat does not belong to my vocabulary." In Philadelphia he was better received. The Pennsylvania society which had been formed in December, 1822, by Rev. Henry Holcombe, D. D., pastor of the First Baptist Church, had been recently revived. It met him cordially, and Feb. 18, 1828, approved his plan.

The organization meeting was held in New York at the home of David L. Dodge, May 8, 1828, two days before Ladd reached his fiftieth year. On that day, with David Low Dodge as chairman, Congregationalists and Unitarians from New England, Presbyterians from New York, Baptists from Pennsylvania, and Quakers from various states met and formed the American Peace Society. The constitution, which had been drawn up by Worcester, after consultation with Ladd, and after it had been shown to and approved by the Massachusetts, Pennsylvania and other societies, was adopted with a few alterations. Whereupon Dodge wrote in the minutes of the New York society: "May, 1828, The New York Peace Society Resolved to be merged in the American Peace Society, the members however not to be considered as members of the latter without signing the Constitution, which in fact was a dissolution of the old New York Peace Society formed 16 August 1815, and the American, May, 1828, was substituted in its place." Hence arises the question whether 1815, instead of 1828, is not the date of the founding of the American Peace Society.

The constitution was not long. Omitting the preamble, it read as follows:

I. The object of the society shall be to diffuse light respecting the evils of war, and the best means for effecting its abolition.

II. The funds of the society shall consist of annual subscriptions, life subscriptions, donations of individuals and contributions of auxiliary societies and Christian churches and congregations.

III. The payment of five dollars or more annually shall entitle any person to membership; the payment of twenty dollars shall constitute a minister a member for life; any person who shall pay thirty dollars at one time shall be a member for life, and any donor of fifty dollars or more shall be an honorary member of the society. Every annual subscription must be paid on or before the twenty-fifth of December of every year.

IV. Every subscriber shall be entitled to receive annually such publications as the society shall make the vehicle of its communication. Auxiliary societies, churches and congregations shall be entitled to the value of two thirds of their contribution in the tracts or periodical publications of the society at the wholesale prices. Any religious society that shall make its minister or any other member of it a life subscriber shall in like manner be entitled to receive two thirds of the value of the money it shall pay into the treasury and females who shall form associations to aid the society shall be entitled to the full value of the money which they may contribute in tracts or periodical works of the society when required.

V. The business of the society shall be conducted by a board of twenty directors who shall have power to supply such vacancies in their number as may occur by death or resignation; to appoint such officers, agents or assistants as they may deem necessary; to appoint their own meetings and special meetings of the society directing as to time and place; and to manage the funds and all concerns of the society and to add to their numbers.

VI. At the annual meeting the directors and treasurer shall exhibit their report and the directors shall be chosen for the ensuing year who shall appoint the time and place of the next annual meeting.

VII. The presiding officer of the society or any person having his proxy together with the secretary and three other members shall constitute a quorum to do business.

VIII. Auxiliary societies shall be entitled to be represented at the meetings of the society by one delegate for each year of which they may pay ten dollars or more to the funds of the society. Should they pay sixty dollars they shall be entitled to be represented by two delegates, and auxiliaries paying one hundred dollars or more shall be entitled to add one member to the board of directors, and also to send one delegate to the meetings of the society for every hundred dollars paid.

IX.   The object of the society shall never be changed; but in other respects the foregoing articles may be amended, and others added at any regular meeting which shall be duly notified, provided three fourths of the members present shall concur in the amendment or amendments of the article or articles proposed to be added.

The society immediately issued a circular letter prepared by Ladd giving a history of the peace movement to date, explaining the objects of the national society, and inviting all interested in the movement to join and help.   According to the circular the object of the society was to collect and diffuse light on the subject of peace and war by printing and distributing useful tracts on the subject, to issue a periodical publication edited by an appointee of the board, to convey the society's communications to the public, to give information about foreign peace societies, and news concerning the diffusion of pacific principles, to show war in its deformity, to search for the cause of war, to portray the consequences of war, to teach followers the precepts of the gospel of peace, to bring about a pacific spirit among Christians, a disgust for war, a relish for peace, and lessen the cause and frequency of war, to soften its horrors, to deprive tyranny of its tools, to increase the number of non-combatants by the force of public opinion, to give greater security to lives and property, to abolish paper blockades, to lessen the number of articles termed contraband of war, to abolish privateering, to establish the principle that free ships make free goods, and thus dry up many fruitful sources of war, and force public opinion to abolish impressment and conscription.   One sentence should be quoted in full as illustrative of the views of Ladd: "We hope to increase and promote the practice already begun of submitting national differences to amicable discussion and arbitration; and finally of settling all national controversies by an appeal to reason, as becomes rational creatures and not by physical force as is worthy only of brute beasts and that this shall be done by a congress of Christian nations whose decrees

shall be enforced by public opinion that rules the world. * * * Then
wars shall cease." This platform of Ladd is still today the platform of the American Peace Society.

Ladd believed the prospects for peace to be good. He believed
in using the methods adopted by the various philanthropic and
benevolent societies of the day, in speaking and printing, in distributing tracts, forming auxiliary societies, and in religion; in
other words by the creation of a healthy public opinion against
war, depending for its creation on Christianity and philanthropy,
economics, patriotism, arts and sciences, with piety, prayer, and
service. The platform of the society was thus very broad. Most
of the existing peace societies opposed war of any kind, defensive
as well as offensive. But the American Peace Society omitted all
reference to defensive warfare, preferring to leave that to be considered after offensive warfare had been abolished.

On this subject the circular read: "We believe the custom of war
to be contrary to the principles of the Christian religion, subversive
of the liberty of mankind and destructive to their happiness; a
horrible custom which every one is called upon to do what he can
to abolish. These truths we hold to be undisputed, and they are
the foundation of our society. Nevertheless we draw no dividing
or distinguishing line. We do not as a society agitate the question
whether defensive war can be carried on on Christian principles.
We receive into our communion all who seek the abolition of war
whether they hold to the lawfulness of defensive war or condemn
all war in every shape—whether they allow a latitude of construc-
tion to the injunction of our Savior or take the exact and strict
letter of them. We endeavor to avoid all doubtful disputations
and to walk peacefully with all who will walk with us, whether they
go further or not so far as the majority of the society, and we
open the columns of our periodical publication to all who choose
fairly and candidly to investigate the subject of defensive war, but
hold ourselves responsible for nothing which appears on our pages
which is not expressly authorized by this board." Further on he
said, "We are not confined to any sect or denomination of Christians, but ask the countenance, the encouragement and the support
of all. Neither have we anything to do with the fluctuating politics
of the day."[1]

[1] The circular is printed in full on the first seventeen pages of the first
number of the Harbinger of Peace, May, 1828.

The society was distinctively religious. Its work was to rest on the intellect and the Bible. However it did not refuse the help of any one. It admitted to membership all who sought the abolition of war, philanthropists, economists, scientists, patriots, Christians, conservatives or radicals. Worcester showed his faith in the organization by paying into its treasury thirty dollars and becoming its first life member.

Chapter III

IN NEW YORK CITY

THE society opened correspondence immediately with the London and Paris societies and in 1831 with the Geneva Peace Society. This correspondence related to what the societies had done, described plans for the future and contained words of encouragement and mutual consolation. Plans for an energetic campaign were immediately prepared. The country was divided into two departments: The eastern, consisting of New England; and the southwestern, consisting of the rest of the United States. As it was intended to have the American Peace Society the central society in the country, the Massachusetts society with twelve other state and local societies having a thousand members in all, immediately became its auxiliaries, and vigorous attempts were made to establish new ones. Five were formed during the first year, ten the second, and three the third, mainly in New York and New England. By May, 1832, the total membership of the society was 1454. Several new societies were formed afterwards, but few of them as auxiliaries, and no serious effort seems to have been made to retain even those that had already affiliated with it.

The annual meetings of the society were held in May, the month in which other benevolent and religious societies met. At the first annual meeting in 1829, eight delegates were present, representing Maine, Massachusetts, New York, Windham County, Conn., Hartford, and Orange County, N. C., societies. David L. Dodge presided; Capt. Ladd acted as secretary. As in all subsequent meetings the annual report of the board of directors, written by the secretary, was read and directed to be printed in the society's magazine. The completeness of this and subsequent reports, and the full account of the doings of the society recorded in its magazine, cause the loss of its records previous to 1835 not to be so seriously felt. All the reports given in New York were written by Ladd, except the sixth which was written by R. M. Chipman.

The annual meetings in New York City were held in various places; the first, May 13, 1829, at the Presbyterian church in the Bowery; the second and ninth at the Baptist meeting house on Nassau Street; the third, fourth and fifth at Clinton Hall, 129 Nassau Street; the sixth and seventh at Chatham Street Chapel, and the eighth, May 12, 1836, at the Tabernacle Church. David Low Dodge presided at the first meeting in 1829; Rev. John Codman, D. D., of Dorchester, at the second and the Hon. S. V. S. Wilder at the rest. The fourth meeting was held at ten o'clock in the morning; the others at three, four, or half past four in the afternoon.

The number of directors elected in 1828 was twenty-two; in 1829, forty, increasing to fifty-two in 1834; seventy-one different men in all. Among these might be mentioned: Eleazar Lord, Anson G. Phelps, David L. Dodge, John Griscom, LL. D., Lewis Tappan, Hugh Aikman, S. V. S. Wilder, Rev. L. D. Dewey, D. E. Wheeler, Esq., Prof. J. C. Rostan, and Rev. George Bush, of New York; William Ladd, Minot, Maine; Rev. Asa Mead, Brunswick, Maine; Hon. Stephen Longfellow (father of Henry W. Longfellow), Portland, Maine; Governor John T. Gilman, Exeter, N. H.; Hon. James Sheafe, and Hon. Nathaniel A. Haven, Portsmouth, N. H.; John Tappan, Esq., Hon. Heman Lincoln, Rev. Charles Lowell, D. D., (father of James Russell Lowell), J. B. Blanchard, Esq., Dudley A. Tyng, Rev. Howard Malcolm, Boston; Rev. Noah Worcester, D. D., Brighton, Mass.; Prof. Simon Greenleaf, Cambridge; Rev. Ralph Emerson, D. D., and Rev. Ebenezer Porter, D. D., Andover, Mass.; Rev. Francis Wayland, D. D., Moses Brown, Nicholas I. Brown, and John Griscom, Providence; Rev. T. H. Gallaudet, Hartford, Conn.; Matthew Carey, Philadelphia; Judge Thomas S. Grimke, Charleston, S. C., and Dr. Stephen B. Cleaveland, Cincinnati.

The directors were elected at the annual meeting. The practice was for a nominating committee to be appointed early in the meeting, and to make a report before the meeting adjourned. All available members who had served for a year were generally renamed as their own successors. Occasionally there was a nomination from the floor, and the nominees were elected by a viva voce vote.

The Executive Committee consisted of from five to ten persons chosen by the directors from their own number and resided for the most part in New York City. It was this body that directed the work of the Society.

All the officers and committees were appointed annually by the directors who held a meeting for this purpose at the close of the annual meeting. During the first year only one officer was appointed, William Ladd, who, after the declination of Noah Worcester because of his age, held the office of Secretary and performed the duties of Treasurer. In 1829-30, he was Corresponding Secretary of the Eastern District and Editor; 1830-31, Secretary for Foreign Correspondence and Editor; 1831-32, General Secretary; 1832-35, General Agent. Rev. Alexander G. Fraser, 1829-30, was Recording Secretary and Corresponding Secretary of the Southwest District. Rev. L. D. Dewey, 1830-31, was Recording and Domestic Secretary and, 1831-35, Recording Secretary. Prof. J. C. Rostan, 1831-33, was Secretary for Foreign Correspondence. D. E. Wheeler, 1831-33, was Secretary for Domestic Correspondence. R. M. Chipman, 1833-34, was Corresponding Secretary, followed by Rev. George Bush, 1834-35. The position of Treasurer was filled by David L. Dodge, 1829-30, Hugh Aikman, 1830-34, and J. K. Moore, 1834-35.

Noah Worcester was the first life member of the Society. The number of life members increased slowly year by year. There were seven at the end of the first year, fifteen at the end of the second, nineteen at the end of the third, twenty-four at the end of the fourth, thirty-one at the end of the fifth, and thirty-seven at the end of the sixth, including such persons as John Tappan, Dr. Charles Lowell, Capt. Ladd, Thomas S. Grimke, President Allen and Prof. Upham of Bowdoin College, Dr. Howard Malcolm, Rev. E. S. Gannett, President Tyler of the Theological Seminary at East Windsor, Conn., Prof. Mussey of Dartmouth College, President Wayland of Brown University, and J. T. Blanchard.

The list of honorary members began at the second annual meeting with the election of Robert Marsden, chairman, and Thomas Hancock, M. D., honorary foreign secretary of the London Peace Society; Comte de Sellen, the organizer of the Geneva Society in 1833, and Hon. Judge Campbell of Ceylon in 1835.

The subsequent annual meetings were similar to the first, except that instead of discussing the amendments to be made to the constitution, they discussed the resolutions to be passed and transacted any other business that came before them.

The income of the society was small and insufficient to carry out the plans made at the outset. The income, expenditure and balance on hand for each of the first seven years were as follows:

Year ending May	Income	Expenditure	Balance on hand At end of year
1829	$ 618.08	$547.69	$ 70.39
1830	—.—	495.85	140.17
1831	537.17	331.95	205.22
1832	234.00	279.94	159.28
1833	274.42	149.92	283.78
1834	642.78	893.94	33.37
1835	1139.13	605.43	567.07

The work of the society was carried on in the office at slight expense. Ladd acted as its general agent, travelled extensively in its cause, gave lectures, circulated its publications, carried on its operations, issued its appeals and paid its deficits. But one field agent received any pay and that was Rev. Asa Mead of East Hartford, Conn., who for three months in the spring of 1830 travelled in the interests of the Society from Maine to New Jersey, delivered forty addresses, spoke to 20,000 persons, preached peace in the pulpit on Sunday, organized societies at Newark, N. J., and Troy, Utica, Rome, Auburn and Whitesboro, N. Y., and started seven others, receiving from the society $198.59 for his services. No further agents were appointed until 1833 when Rev. Prof. Bush of New York, Rev. Mr. Malcolm of Boston, and Rev. Mr. Rowland of Exeter, N. H., served as agents of the society without pay and presented the cause as they had opportunity. During the following year, Rev. G. C. Beckwith acted as volunteer agent for the society, preaching ten sermons in four cities, and raising some money. In the report of his work he said: "I feel confident that it would be very easy for a suitable man devoting his whole time and energies to the business, to raise funds sufficient to sustain extended and efficient operation."[1] During the same year Capt. Ladd travelled 1300 miles in the cause of peace, delivered forty addresses, wrote numerous essays for the newspapers, kept up an extensive correspondence, and collected $962.26 for the society.

Ladd gave $200 each to eight or ten educational institutions in 1831 and 1833, including Dartmouth and Colby colleges and

[1] American Advocate of Peace, June, 1835, p. 223.

Andover and Bangor seminaries; and Howard Malcolm the same amount to the Newton Theological Institution, the income from which, twelve dollars a year, was to be given in prizes to students writing the best essays on the subject of peace. Several story books were published teaching peace ideas suitable for Sunday School use.

Ladd believed in tracts. During the first year the society distributed 26,000 tracts. Rev. Mr. Malcolm while agent of the society placed tracts on board 730 vessels entering the port of Boston during winter of 1833-34. During the year 1834-35, a set of the tracts published by the London Peace Society was sent to the mission stations throughout the world and the society bought the stereotype plates of the "Solemn Review," after the Massachusetts society had reprinted 10,000 copies of it. Five hundred copies of the Friend of Peace for distribution as seemed best were received from Worcester in 1831.

When Worcester at 79 years of age had discontinued his magazine—The Friend of Peace—the fear was expressed that the cause of peace might be left without a periodical. "At that juncture" to use the words of Ladd, "I solemnly pledged myself to the society and to the friends of peace in general that, if God spared my life and health, there should be a peace periodical whether I were assisted by others or not."[1] Immediately after the organization of the American Peace Society he started the Harbinger of Peace, a monthly duodecimo paper of 24 pages, edited by himself and published for the American Peace Society, from May, 1828, through April, 1831. About 1500 copies of each number were printed, or upwards of 50,000 in all. The first and last numbers were printed in New York. Intermediate numbers were printed at Portland, Maine, Portsmouth, N. H., or Boston, wherever Ladd happened to be at the time. The magazines when printed were sent to New York and distributed from there. This proved to be a very unsatisfactory arrangement; so Ladd, who felt unable to move to New York, prepared the material and sent it to a New York printer to publish. But preparing a magazine in Maine and having it printed in New York, 350 miles away, with an irregular mail twice a week between the two places, did not prove satisfactory. At the end of the first year Ladd prevailed upon McElrath and Bangs, printers and booksellers, to publish the material furnished, and he appointed an assist-

---

[1] Calumet, March and April, 1835, p. 101.

ant editor to read proof and answer correspondence in New York. But the latter soon left the city. In May, 1830, at the end of a year, McElrath and Bangs declined to continue the arrangement, and Rev. L. D. Dewey, an ardent friend of peace with office at 17 Ann Street, agreed to superintend the publication from the end of the second year.

The Boston friends were dissatisfied with the size of the magazine. It seemed small to them and did not look respectable. Several offered to contribute to it when an editor should be secured residing where it was published. Several proposed to move it to Boston and place it in more able hands. Ladd wanted to be relieved of the work, and the board of directors thought it should continue to be printed in New York. Accordingly it was decided to increase the number of pages in an issue to 32 octavo size, thus doubling the material in a number, the expense of publishing to be reduced by issuing it bi-monthly. The time also seemed appropriate to change the name of the magazine. Calumet, the new name, was explained to mean the pipe of peace smoked by Indians on the conclusion of a treaty, and presented as an offering of peace to those with whom they wished to live in friendship, being equivalent to the olive branch of the Greeks, and symbolic of the time the American Peace Society was endeavoring to bring to pass. The first number of the Calumet was dated May and June, 1831, and the last, four years later, March and April, 1835. The first eighteen numbers were paged continuously and called volume I; the last six, volume II. A title page and index were prepared for volume I. The title page reads "The Calumet, New Series of the Harbinger of Peace, but under the Direction of the American Peace Society, 1831-34, New York. Published by L. D. Dewey."

With Dewey, acting as recording secretary of the society and superintending the printing of the magazine, was soon associated D. E. Wheeler acting as editor and Secretary for Domestic Correspondence, both working part time and serving without pay for the love of the cause. Ladd, however, though he withdrew from the editorship, was associated with these two men as a publishing committee and continued to furnish most of the material printed in the magazine until a stroke of paralysis, May 9, 1833, two days after the annual meeting of the society, brought his activities to a close for a year. The magazine had more than paid expenses, and as the society had a surplus of $283.78 they hired a divinity student in

New York City, R. M. Chipman, to devote half of his time to the paper and to act as editor, for which he received $300 for his year's work. Then he withdrew.

Ladd, unable to attend the next annual meeting, offered in a letter to the society to give $300 a year so long as necesary for at least five years to help support a suitable person as corresponding secretary and editor of the society's publications and another person to give a part or all his time as a traveling and preaching agent to lay the cause of peace before the churches, making this offer with the understanding that others would make up the amount to $2,000 a year. An appeal for funds was made. Rev. George Bush assumed charge of two numbers of the magazine when the funds became exhausted. Ladd advanced between two and three hundred dollars and again assumed the editorship for four numbers, when he laid down his "burthen which had oppressed" him for seven years, as he expressed it, and the Calumet came to an end.

Both the Harbinger of Peace and the Calumet were full of interest. They contained stories, poems, heavy and light articles, tracts, letters, extracts from the correspondence with other societies, news of peace and war, notices of the society, and accounts of meetings held in the interest of peace. Ladd's work on these magazines had been a labor of love. He received no salary as editor and paid the deficit on the magazine. Articles on peace also appeared in the newspapers and periodical press from time to time. The Phi Beta Kappa address at Bowdoin College in 1833 was given by Rev. William Allen D. D., president, on the subject of peace.

Though philanthropic and economic arguments for peace were used and the impoverished condition of Europe was carefully described in the magazine, the society felt that fundamentally the question was a religious one and that it could best be extended through the efforts of the church. On the motion of Ladd, the General Conference of Maine, June 29, 1829, voted to "approve the objects of the American Peace Society and to recommend them to the serious attention of Christian churches." A similar resolution was passed by the General Association of New Hampshire Sept. 1, 1829, and the General Convention of Vermont later.

Therefore it seemed advisable to seek the aid of religious bodies directly. At the annual meeting of the society in May, 1831, it was resolved "That this society request the prayers of all Christians of every denomination, that God would be pleased to smile on their exertions, to promote peace on earth and good will to man." This resolution was extensively circulated among religious bodies with the result that on March 20, 1832, three Congregational churches in Portland held a united prayer meeting to implore God's blessing on the exertions of the society. Resolutions favoring the cause of the society were passed by the Lincoln County Conference of Maine, Aug. 20, 1833; the General Association of New Hampshire, Sept. 18, 1833, and Oct. 3, 1834; the Piscataqua Association at Hampton, July 16, 1833; a convention of Congregational ministers in Boston, May 30, 1833, and the Evangelical Consociation of Congregational Churches of Rhode Island in June, 1833. May 29, 1832, the conference of Baptist ministers in Boston resolved "all war utterly inconsistent with the spirit of the Gospel," as did the Lincoln County Conference in Maine, Aug. 20, 1833. Resolutions favoring the abolition of war were passed by the New England Conference of Methodist churches in Boston, June 14, 1833, the General Association of Congregational Churches of New Hampshire, Sept. 18, 1833, the Piscataqua Association of Congregational Churches, July 16, 1833, the General Conference of Maine at Bath, June 24, 1834, and the New Hampshire General Congregational Association, Oct. 3, 1834.

At the annual meeting of the society in May, 1832, it was resolved "That the Board of the American Peace Society invite the ministers of the Gospel of every denomination to preach one sermon a year on war and peace." The next month the General Conference of the Congregational Churches of Maine, representing 166 churches, recommended that prayers for peace be made annually at Christmas time and that ministers be requested to preach on that occasion. The next year the society passed two resolutions: "That the American Peace Society request of all ministers of the Gospel who are friendly to the cause of universal and permanent peace to preach upon that subject on the Sabbath next preceding the 25th of December, annually, or on the 25th," and on the motion of Ladd, "That the American Peace Society request all churches favorable to the cause of peace, to appoint a prayer meeting to pray for God's blessing on the exertions of this society on or near the 25th day of December, annually, and to take up a collection at that meeting in aid of the funds of the society." Ladd reported that for the year ending May, 1834, the contributions for the society taken at prayer meetings amounted to $87.89, and for the year ending May 1835, $311.41. Recommendations that a peace prayer meeting be held or a peace sermon be preached annually in December, near the 25th of the month, one or the other or both, were passed by various religious bodies; the General Conference of Congregational Churches of Maine, June, 1832; the Congregational ministers in Boston, May 30, 1833; the Evangelical Consociation of Congregational Churches of Rhode Island, June, 1833, and 1834; the Lincoln County Conference, Maine, Aug. 20, 1833; the General Association of Congregational Churches of New Hampshire, Sept. 18, 1833 and Oct. 3, 1834; the Piscataqua Association of Congregational ministers, July 16, 1833; the York and the Hancock and Waldo conferences of Maine; and the Dutch Reformed Classes of Poughkeepsie in the fall of 1833.

In 1830, many ministers preached on peace as requested. In 1833, sixty-seven ministers agreed to preach one peace sermon each year. In 1834, 205 ministers actually preached such a sermon at the close of the year, in 1835, 525.

Chapter IV

AT HARTFORD

On his way to New York Ladd had stopped at Hartford, Conn., and there delivered a lecture on peace, Jan. 10th, 1828. On his return he organized a society there Feb. 29, 1828, with 102 members. His lectures produced a profound impression upon one of his hearers, James Watson by name, a native of East Windsor, Conn., born in 1774, and in 1828 a merchant and importer in Hartford, a religious man, and for the preceding ten years greatly interested in the temperance movement. Watson now threw himself whole-heartedly into the peace movement. At the first annual meeting of the Hartford society, March 18, 1829, he caused it to resolve itself into the Peace Society of Hartford County with himself as its agent and his store the repository for the publications of the society. In its interest he drove to remote places in the state where he addressed the people and scattered tracts, arousing considerable interest in the question of peace.

In the year 1831, with a membership of 305, the society sent 1038 copies of the "Solemn Review" to 409 ministers of the state of Connecticut, to the members of the legislature of the same state, to the president, vice president, members of the cabinet (except the Secretary of War), senators, representatives in Congress, the justices and other officials of the Federal courts, the judges of the state superior court, the governor of each state, ten bishops, and presidents of twelve colleges, and circulated 400 copies of Mead's address made at the preceding annual meeting of the society. Watson himself during the same year went to every neighborhood and personally distributed 996 copies of the society's publications and about fifty other tracts.

The next year, 1832, Watson united the three societies of the state into a state society with Rev. T. H. Gallaudet, the founder of the school for deaf and dumb in Hartford, as secretary, and with a vice president in each county. At their first annual meeting held in New Haven Sunday evening, May 6, 1832, an address was delivered by Hon. Thomas S. Grimke of Charleston, S. C., in the presence of the state legislature in session at the time. Grimke, born of a French Huguenot family at Charleston, Sept. 26, 1786, was a graduate of Yale and a judge in his native state. He was a very religious man and greatly interested in the temperance reform. He delivered an address May 9, 1827, that attracted the attention of Ladd who called his attention to the subject of peace. Following his address on the Bible at the Phi Beta Kappa meeting at Yale in 1830, Dr. Hubbard, ex-secretary of the Windham County Peace Society, gave him a copy of Hancock's book on peace. Grimke soon became a strong speaker against war of any kind. He became a director of the American Peace Society and delivered the address before the Connecticut Peace Society as previously stated. This address attracted great attention and 300 copies of it were printed and distributed by the society, copies being sent to the president, vice president, members of the cabinet, and both houses of Congress.

Two agents were appointed in the summer of 1832 who with Watson visited all existing societies in the state, delivered addresses before them, supplied them with peace tracts and publications, and within eighteen months a peace society existed in each of the eight counties of the state, all urged to take an active interest in the cause of peace and to enter into correspondence with one another and with the state society.

On May 11, 1832, the trustees recommended to the directors of the American Peace Society the publication of a 64 octavo page quarterly at one dollar a year, to be entitled the American Advocate of Peace and edited by an able man who should devote all his time to this work at an "honorable compensation." The trustees also recommended that the American Peace Society appoint a vice president in each state who should try to establish a state society with county or district societies wherever practicable and that every peace society in the country should become an auxiliary of the American Peace Society. This was an ambitious program which for financial reasons the national society felt unable to adopt at the time.

Whereupon Watson, on his own responsibility, in June, 1834, started such a magazine himself, dignified in character, ably edited and entitled as suggested—the American Advocate of Peace. To its publication he gave his thought. Copies of it were sent to all members of Congress, judges of the United States courts and several officers of the Federal government, as long as the magazine was issued by the Connecticut society. Watson offered to supply the American Peace Society with the new quarterly at a reasonable rate; but the offer was not accepted because it meant the relinquishment of Calumet, and it was feared that such an act would cause the American Peace Society to appear to be an auxiliary of the Connecticut society.

A year later however, it seemed better to have one good magazine than two poorer ones. So, to use the words of Ladd in his farewell article: "I have made a visit to Hartford, and finally, after considerable diplomacy, have concluded a treaty, by which we are to relinquish the Calumet, after the present number; and the American Advocate of Peace is to be published at Hartford, for the American Peace Society, and now I hope the society will ratify the treaty."[1] The Advocate was to be sent free to ministers who preached a peace sermon yearly, or took up a contribution in favor of peace, to members of the board of directors, honorary members, life members and annual subscribers to the society.

Ladd's closing words in the Calumet should be repeated: "My labors in the publishing and editorial departments of the American Peace Society have come now nearly to a close; though I hope and trust, that being freed from the care of the periodical, I shall have more leisure to extend my operations as general agent, should the society again entrust me with the agency. I feel more encouraged than ever in the good cause, more willing to make sacrifices, both of time and money. The signs of the times show, that the principles of peace have taken root in the church of Christ, which is our main dependence, though we should by no means depreciate the labors of those, who advocate the cause of peace, from motives of philanthropy and a desire to promote the temporal interests of their fellow-men. I take this opportunity to render my sincere and hearty thanks to all who have aided me in the good cause. That the blessings pronounced upon the peacemaker, by the Prince of Peace, may descend and rest upon them, is the fervent prayer of their devoted servant and fellow-laborer."

The Calumet ended with the number for March, 1835, with a gasp of relief. The last four numbers had been prepared by Ladd only with the greatest difficulty. The first of the four had contained an appeal for help. The second repeated the appeal. In the third,

[1] Calumet, March and April, 1835, p. 164.

Ladd said "We publish another number of the Calumet, which we have been influenced to do, chiefly by the desire of paying a tribute of respect to our lamented friend and brother in the cause of peace, the late Hon. Thomas Smith Grimke," who had died Oct. 12, 1834. The fourth number contained the announcement of the change in the magazine.

The March number of the American Advocate of Peace contains this statement: "With this number the Advocate completes its first year. The work will continue to be published as heretofore at Hartford, by Mr. Watson, but will be put out for the American Peace Society. The care of the journal will hereafter devolve upon Mr. Francis Fellowes, whose excellent contributions to our pages the past year, will be a sufficient warrant to our readers for the ability with which it will be carried on by him." Francis Fellowes was Secretary of the Connecticut Peace Society.

In all, eleven numbers of the magazine were issued, the first appearing June, 1834, and the last bearing the date December, 1836. The individual numbers of the magazine are entitled "Advocate of Peace," but the title page of volume I and the cover pages of volume II are entitled "American Advocate of Peace." Volume I includes the first eight numbers, June, 1834 to March, 1836, and carries a title page and an index. Volume II includes three numbers, June, September and December, 1836. The title page of volume I is inscribed: "Conducted by C. S. Henry, Hartford, William Watson, For the Connecticut Peace Society." The cover of the numbers of volume II substitutes "Francis Fellowes" for "C. S. Henry," and "For the American Peace Society," for "For the Connecticut Peace Society," and the last number issued substitutes "Printed by P. Canfield," for "William Watson." Volume I contained 386 pages quarto size, the pages of the individual numbers varying from 46 to 56. Each number in volume II contains 48 pages. Three thousand copies of the magazine were printed, of which the American Peace Society took seven hundred.

At the same time, May, 1835, by vote of the society at its annual meeting, the executive officers of the American Peace Society were moved to Hartford, where the society expected to profit from the help of the corps of able men Watson had rallied around him. Though the Connecticut Peace Society continued to remain independent of the American Peace Society and never affiliated with it, the change introduced several new persons into the central society.

Ladd continued to hold the position of General Agent. Rev. T. H. Gallaudet became Corresponding Secretary, Francis Fellowes Recording Secretary, David Watkinson Treasurer the first year and William Watson the second, all except Ladd residents of Hartford. The executive committee also was composed of Hartford men who met generally once a month always at Watson's home or office.

While most of the former directors continued to remain with the society there were added to the board Hon. William W. Ellsworth, Francis Fellowes, William Watson, Rev. C. S. Henry, Melvin Copeland and several other residents of Hartford; Prof. T. C. Upham, Rev. John W. Chickering and President Allen of Bowdoin College; President Lord, D. D., of Dartmouth College; Hubbard Winslow and Amasa Walker of Boston; Rev. A. P. Peabody, Portsmouth, N. H., and later professor at Harvard College; Rev. R. W. Chipman, Harrington, Conn.; Thomas Cock, M. D., New York City; and Calvin E. Stowe, Professor at Lane Theological Seminary, Cincinnati. Professor Stowe preached a peace sermon in the chapel of the seminary on the last Sabbath in December, 1834, and later organized a peace society in the seminary. William Watson sent Henry Barnard to a meeting of the London Peace Society. The first of a series of bequests made to the society was made by the Hon. Benjamin Tallmadge of Litchfield, Conn., in 1835, $250 in amount.

The activities of the society otherwise continued as before, but on a somewhat increased scale. Rev. George C. Beckwith was employed to travel and preach in the interest of the cause for nearly a year. Rev. Guy C. Sampson of North Goshen, Conn., visited Vermont. Rev. Henry C. Wright traveled 1943 miles and delivered 60 lectures in New York state. Rev. William Ely of Mansfield spent three months in Tolland County, Conn., from August to October, 1835, where he tells us he spoke in some church each Sunday and spent twenty-four days in a house-to-house canvass, explaining the objects of the society, endeavoring to interest the people in the work, leaving tracts, and receiving gifts for the society. During the year ending May, 1836, Ladd travelled 2000 miles, delivered 70 lectures, formed two societies and collected $120.67.

Tracts continued to be distributed including 3,000 copies received from the London Peace Society. Ladd purchased several publications and distributed them freely. The society issued two tracts:

"A Solemn Appeal to Christians of all Denominations," and "The Duty of Females to Promote the Cause of Peace." Several books on the subject of peace appeared. Prof. Thomas C. Upham of Bowdoin College, one of the directors of the society, issued a Manual of Peace, containing 408 pages, in 1835, which was reissued several times during the next forty years. The American Tract Society issued a prize essay entitled "The Duty of Christians with Respect to War." Efforts to get societies to affiliate with it or to form new auxiliaries ceased, though several new societies were formed in churches and educational institutions. In May, 1837, eight ladies' peace societies were reported, of which one, the Essex County Olive Branch Circle at Salem, Mass., held a fair April 26 of that year, the first ever held for the benefit of the cause of peace, and sent the American Peace Society one hundred dollars, the proceeds from the sale.

The resolutions passed by the society at its annual meeting in May, 1836, were in the main, repetitions of those passed on preceding occasions and included a recommendation that peace sermons be preached annually in December, and that the annual concert of prayer with a collection for the society be observed. Two of the resolutions are here given in full: 2. Resolved, That we regard the manner in which our late difficulties with France have been settled, as indicating a change in public sentiment highly auspicious to the cause of peace, and as proving the practicability of some system by which all disputes between civilized and Christian nations may be adjusted without a resort to the sword; that the King of England deserves the thanks of this nation and the world, for the generous tender of his services as mediator to prevent the needless effusion of blood; and that an address in behalf of the friends of peace in these United States be sent by the American Peace Society to his Majesty William IV expressive of the admiration and gratitude we feel for an act so magnanimous and so honorable to a Christian monarch. 7. Resolved, That the exigencies of our cause require, for the present year, ten thousand dollars; that an effort be made, in reliance on God, to raise five thousand dollars as the lowest sum that will sustain the enlarged plan of operations contemplated by the society; and that the friends of peace be earnestly desired to cooperate in carrying this resolution into effect.[1]

---

[1] The resolutions are printed in full in the American Advocate of Peace, June, 1836, p. 42.

The address called for by the latter part of the first resolution here given was written by Ladd, and sent through the London Peace Society. A deputation of that society presented it to Lord Palmerston, then prime minister, who in his reply said: "The king has been very much gratified by the friendly and approving expressions contained in the address of the American Peace Society."[1]

Religious bodies continued to pass resolutions against war and to recommend the preaching of peace sermons at Christmas time, as the Massachusetts Conference, October, 1835; General Conference of Maine, June 21, 1836; General Association of Connecticut, June 24, 1836; Methodist Conference, Mass., July 12, 1836. In December 1834, 535 ministers preached such sermons; in 1835, 700 pledged themselves to do the same, and in 1836, 998.

During the year and a half the society had been in Hartford, it had prospered. William Watson was its mainstay. Late in October, 1836, he went to New York and Philadelphia to lay the objects and claims of the society before the friends of the cause in those cities and to solicit their renewed cooperation. Returning home he contracted a fever and died Nov. 13 at the age of 63.

[1] The letter of Ladd dated Feb. 10., 1837, and the reply of Lord Palmerston dated May 22, 1837, are given in the Advocate of Peace, December, 1837, pp. 183, 184.

Chapter V

TO BOSTON

The death of Watson was a severe blow to the society. There seemed to be no reason why the offices should remain longer in Hartford, a town at that time with less than ten thousand inhabitants. Therefore, when the Massachusetts Peace Society renewed the invitation it had made in 1830 and gave assurance that a place in Boston was awaiting their coming, the society at its last annual meeting held in New York in May, 1837, voted to accept the invitation and to move to that city, where the cause of peace had found such staunch friends in the earlier days.

The same year the society underwent a reorganization. A new constitution, as suggested by the Executive Committee, Dec. 14, 1835, and prepared by William Ladd, George C. Beckwith and Dr. Thomas Cock of New York, was adopted, reading as follows:

I. This society shall be designated the American Peace Society.

II. This society being founded on the principle that all war is contrary to the spirit of the Gospel shall have for its object to illustrate the inconsistency of war with Christianity, to show its baleful influence on all the great interests of mankind, and to devise means for insuring universal and permanent peace.

III. Persons of every Christian denomination desirous of promoting peace on earth and good will towards men may become members of this society.

IV. Every annual subscriber of two dollars and every donor of five dollars shall be a member of this society.

V. Twenty dollars paid at one time shall constitute any clergyman or his wife, and thirty dollars any other person member for life; and fifty dollars shall make the former, and one hundred dollars the latter an honorary member for life.

VI. The chairman of each corresponding committee, the two highest officers of every auxiliary contributing to the funds of this society and every minister of the Gospel who preaches once a year on the subject of peace and takes up a collection in behalf of the cause shall be entitled to the privileges of regular members.

VII. All contributors shall be entitled within the year to one half the amount of their contributions in the publications of the society.

VIII. The officers of this society shall be a president, vice presidents, directors, secretaries, treasurer, and an executive committee of not less than five with power to fill their own vacancies and transact the general business of the society. The board of directors whose chairman shall be the same with the executive committee shall consist of not less than twenty, six besides the chairman or his proxy constituting a quorum and shall have power to supply vacancies in any office of the society and direct all its operations till successors are chosen.

IX. The society shall hold an annual meeting at such time and place as the board of directors may appoint to receive their own and the treasurer's report, to choose officers and transact such other business as may come before them.

X. The object of this society shall never be changed; but the constitution may in other respects be altered on recommendation of the executive committee or any ten members of the society by a vote of three-fourths of the members present at any regular meeting.

Articles V, VI, and VIII underwent slight changes at the annual meeting in 1839 to read as follows:

V. The payment of twenty dollars at one time shall constitute any person a life member and fifty dollars a life director.

VI. The chairman of each corresponding committee, the officers and delegates of every auxiliary contributing to the funds of this society and every minister of the Gospel who preaches once a year on the subject of peace and takes up a collection in behalf of the cause, shall be entitled to the privileges of regular members.

VIII. (First sentence unchanged.) The board of directors shall consist of not less than twenty who shall have power to supply vacancies in any office of the society and direct all its operations until successors are chosen. The vice presidents shall also be ex-officio directors and the president, secretary and treasurer, ex-officio members of the executive committee.

The original constitution, following the lead of the London society, had placed the control of the society in the hands of directors with power to appoint all officers. The new constitution, more democratic in character, placed the control in the hands of the society

who elected the officers and necessary committees. During the first
five years after the removal of the society to Boston, its annual meetings were held in the Marlboro Chapel at 3 P. M. The reading of
the report of the directors, and the discussion of the resolutions
following, were open to the public, but the election of officers took
place in executive session.

At the election of officers in 1837, Ladd was made President, after
the refusal of S. V. S. Wilder of New York to serve. Ladd at first
refused to accept the position, but later combined it with that of
General Agent and held both until his death. Rev. George Cone
Beckwith was elected Corresponding Secretary. Beckwith was born
in Granville, N. Y., Jan. 3, 1801, graduated from Middlebury
College in 1822 and Andover Theological Seminary in 1826. He
became successively pastor of the First Congregational Church at
Lowell, professor in Lane and Andover Theological Seminaries, and
pastor of the High Street Congregational Church in Portland,
Maine. There he became acquainted with William Ladd and
interested in the subject of peace. He delivered addresses upon the
subject. He was a director of the American Peace Society from
1833 to 1835; then its agent. In 1837, on the recommendation of
Ladd he was elected its corresponding secretary, working first under
the direction of Ladd, and, after the latter's death, carrying the
burden of the society upon his own shoulders for upwards of thirty
years. Thomas Thompson Jr. served as Recording Secretary, 1837-
1839; Edward Noyes, 1839-40; and J. P. Blanchard, 1840-41.
James K. Whipple served as Treasurer and Depositary, 1837-41.

Among those who served as Vice President between the years 1837
and 1840, were S. V. S. Wilder (‡) and Anson G. Phelps (‡), New
York, Hon. Gerit Smith, Peterborough, N. Y., Hon. Theodore
Frelinghuysen, Newark, N. J., Hon. William W. Ellsworth,
Hartford, Conn., Hon. Thomas W. Williams, New London, Conn.,
Rev. Francis Wayland, D. D., LL. D. (‡), Providence, William E.
Channing, D. D., Hon. Jonathan Phillips, Hon. Richard Fletcher,
John Tappan (‡), Rev. Charles Lowell (‡), Hon. Amasa Walker (‡),
Boston, Prof. Simon Greenleaf (‡), Harvard College, S. E.
Coues, Esq. (‡), Portsmouth, N. H., and Hon. J. Loomis, Mont-
pelier, Vt.

Among the new directors were Samuel Lord, Portsmouth, N. H.,
Baron Stowe, Ezra S. Gannett, Charles Sumner, and Edward Noyes,

‡Had formerly served as directors

Boston; Rev. Samuel J. May, Scituate, Mass.; and Rev. Henry Ware Jr., Cambridge, Mass., while of the earlier directors who continued through these years were Lewis Tappan and Dr. Cock of New York; Rev. Howard Malcolm, Boston; Hon. Stephen Longfellow, Portland; Alvan Stewart, Utica; Prof. Upham, Bowdoin College; Prof. Peabody, Portsmouth, and Prof. Calvin E. Stowe of Cincinnati. Among members of the executive committee, which held its meeting in the Eagle Bank, were Amasa Walker, Charles Sumner, J. P. Blanchard, Charles Noyes, Howard Malcolm, Ezra S. Gannett, and Rev. J. W. Parker. In 1839 David L. Dodge was added to the list of honorary members and the names of Amos G. Phelps, Gerit Smith, Isaac S. Lloyd, Rev. George C. Beckwith, Hon. Thomas W. Williams, and Thomas W. Tolman were added to the list of life directors by reason of the payment of one hundred dollars each to the society.

Several resolutions were passed by the society in 1837, similar to those passed at former annual meetings. One similar to the seventh passed in 1836 was as follows: "Resolved, That the aspect of the times, the smiles of Heaven on our efforts during the past year, and the unexpected preparation of the public mind for appeals on this subject, call upon the friends of peace for much greater exertions in this cause, and make it desirable that at least ten thousand dollars should be raised this year for the support of lecturers and the circulation of publications on peace."

Considerable discussion arose as to the proper statement of the object of the society. As originally written its objects were "to diffuse light respecting the evils of war and the best means of effecting its abolition." Many members thought that this statement should be more specific; and, as most of them were opposed to war of any kind, defensive as well as offensive, and some societies had refused to join the American Peace Society until its constitution took a decided stand on the question, they caused the new constitution of 1837 to contain a clause relative to this matter, as before stated. Ladd said that the society had but one object,—to prevent war between nations, and thus expressed himself: "We shall denounce none merely for not coming fully up to our views; but we shall urge all to follow faithfully the light they have." Nevertheless, some who were thorough believers in defensive war withdrew from the society, notably, President Allen of Bowdoin College. To have its position better understood, the society adopted five resolutions explaining that the article was merely declaratory of its general object, that it referred to national wars, whether defensive or not, but did not apply to individual self-defence; that no one need take any pledge in order to join the society, and that membership was open to any one who desired the extinction of war whether he agreed with the principle of the article or not.

Towards the end of the year 1837, William Lloyd Garrison announced that he proposed to give the "Liberator" a wider range and to discuss the subject of peace in connection with the abolition of slavery. This was but a short time before Lovejoy was killed at Alton, Ill., while defending his property. In spite of the non resistance views held by Garrison and his followers, the abolitionists with practical unanimity approved the course of Lovejoy in arming himself to protect his press. As many of the peace advocates were abolitionists also, this led to a division of opinion among them.

Following the Lovejoy incident, came the peace convention in Boston, on the 18th, 19th and 20th of September, 1838. This convention was under the direction of Rev. Henry C. Wright, George Benson and William Lloyd Garrison, men zealous for slavery reform as well as greatly interested in the cause of peace. They had requested the American Peace Society to call the meeting. The society, however, kept aloof from the scheme and had no more connection with it than to send to its members invitations prepared by the committee in charge. Being interested in it as a peace convention, Ladd with others from the society attended it in order to prevent the introduction of topics having no connection with peace and voted "No" on the question of organizing. However the convention was in the hands of its friends and they organized the New England Non Resistance Society, opposing capital punishment, imprisonment of wrong doers, and war, and favoring the abolition of human government and resistance to any government by force. They pledged themselves not to take the oath of allegiance to any government, act as legislators, judges, or jurors, hold any civil office, or exercise the right of suffrage. Although the American Peace Society disclaimed all connection with the movement, the fact that for many years peace was on the program of both societies led many to believe that the objects of both were identical, and to charge the American Peace Society with being opposed to the government and therefore disloyal.

The last number of the American Advocate of Peace was issued at Hartford by the American Peace Society, in the spring of 1837, after the death of Watson. On its removal to Boston the society bought from the heirs of Watson the unsold copies of the first ten numbers of the magazine—10,920 at 1½ cents each and 254 bound volumes at 30 cents—and in June, 1837 began the publication of a new magazine of 12mo size under the title of "Advocate of Peace," without funds, subscribers, or contributors, and with an edition of 2,000 copies, increasing the next year to 3000 copies. It appeared quarterly for a year, monthly for a year, bimonthly for three years, and then monthly again. The first number was prepared by Ladd. In it he stated that he contemplated no special change in the work except to make it more strictly the organ of the society and to chronicle the efforts made in the direction of peace both in thought and in deed. He intended to pursue a liberal course and to open the pages to a fair discussion of both sides. The first few copies of the magazine were in form similar to the magazine published in Hartford,—three or four set articles in each number followed by a few items of news—but with more news about the society than formerly. Soon however it began to recount the progress of the peace movement and to discuss important topics connected with the cause, paying more attention to news and discussions and less to essays. That is, it became more newsy and less literary, designed for the mass of intelligent people. It tried to obtain reports from all societies that their activities might become known through publication in its pages. The first year of publication in Boston was a heavy expense to the society because of the small number of paying subscriptions. From this time until after the Civil War it was the only peace periodical, except Quaker papers, published in this country.

The character and plans of the society were not changed by the removal to Boston. In the first number of the magazine Ladd wrote: "Our principles are known; and for the defence and propagation of these principles, we shall plant ourselves upon the word of God. * * * It is with us a question not so much of policy as of conscience. It is a branch of our religion. It belongs to the higher ethics of Christianity. The argument from expediency is very strong; but the argument from Christian duty is irresistible. Here is the pivot of this cause. If peace be not an enterprise strictly evangelical, its principles a part of the Gospel, its duties an element of our religion essential to the full and perfect development of Christian character, we are prepared to abandon it forthwith for work more appropriate to our high and holy calling."[1] And this view dominated the American Peace Society for many years after the death of Ladd.

To bring about this change in public sentiment Ladd advocated the use of moral influence, the pen and the tongue, the press and the pulpit, the church, the family, the Sabbath school, the secular school, and the college. An example of Ladd's views was shown during the winter of 1837-38, following the removal of the society to Boston when the executive committee conducted a course of lectures on peace, delivered in the Odeon. The lectures were well attended, and it is probably a great loss to the cause that for financial reasons all of the lectures were not printed. The speakers were Ralph Waldo Emerson, whose address is preserved as his Essay on War, Amasa Walker, Rev. William E. Channing, D. D., Rev. Henry Ware Jr., D. D., William Ladd, Rev. Rufus P. Stebbins and Rev. Samuel J. May.

Ladd as general agent was very busy in the interests of the society. During the year ending May, 1837, he travelled 2737 miles and delivered 65 lectures; during the year 1837-38, he travelled 2770 miles and delivered 143 lectures. During the year 1838-39 he was engaged in preparing the volume of essays on the congress of nations. He lectured but little until the trouble with England over the northeastern boundary early in 1839 caused him to tour the country in the interest of peace. He spoke in Vermont before both colleges, the legislature and the General Association of Congregational Churches, and in nearly every important town in the state; then in Troy, Albany, New York City, Philadelphia, Washington; stopping in New York City, Boston, and Portsmouth, to write for the press. September 30, 1840, he started on a western tour, speaking during the winter in Springfield, Troy, Albany, Schenectady, Utica, Syracuse, Auburn, Canandaigua, Rochester, Geneva, Lockport, Niagara Falls, and Buffalo. After delivering forty-nine addresses illness caused his return home.

In his work he was ably supported by Rev. George C. Beckwith, who superintended the correspondence, the periodical, and the other publications of the society and spent much of his time in the office. making short trips away from the city as opportunity offered. During the year ending May, 1837, he travelled 5000 miles, mainly

[1] Advocate of Peace, June, 1837, pp. 3, 4.
[2] Printed in the Advocate of Peace, February, 1924, p. 92.

in New England, delivering on an average four lectures a week besides writing fifty articles on peace for the newspapers. During the year 1837-38, he travelled 3700 miles and delivered 170 lectures.

In addition to these two men, who gave their whole time to the society, several others were engaged for shorter periods of time. Thus, during the year ending May, 1838, Rev. George Trask lectured extensively in New Jersey, Pennsylvania, and Ohio, and three Andover theological students spent their spring vacation lecturing for the cause. One of them, Rev. John Lord, later the well known historian, travelled for the society 34 weeks, covered 1350 miles, and delivered 143 lectures in 1839.

In the summer of 1840, Rev. Wm. H. Dalrymple acted as agent for a time and in the fall of 1840, Rev. D. O. Morton, a life member of the society, visited the West for the cause, and a number acted as local agents in different parts of New England. During the year 1840-41 Prof. Alpheus Crosby of Dartmouth College and several settled pastors represented the society. It was estimated that the gratuitous incidental services of pastors as local agents equalled the services given by the regular agents.

During these years the society continued its publication and dissemination of tracts and books. It distributed twenty thousand copies of two tracts, fifteen hundred copies of a third, one thousand copies of the "Solemn Review," 50 copies of Thrush's book on war, one thousand copies of Dymond's Essay on War, between three and four thousand back numbers of The Harbinger of Peace, and Calumet, and twelve thousand copies of the Friend of Peace; in all, over forty thousand books and tracts, besides fourteen thousand publications received from the London peace society. Few were paid for, thus keeping the treasury of the society perpetually empty. During the year 1837-38 the society received $100 from the trustees of the Obadiah Brown Book Fund of Providence, for stereotyping books. With this sum it stereotyped four tracts and Hancock's "Peace."

When the trouble arose with England over the northeastern boundary of Maine early in 1839, Beckwith by direction of the executive committee issued an appeal to the people urging calmness and a settlement of the question by negotiation and not by arms. A copy was sent to over fifty news-papers, but not one in five printed it, and every paper in Maine ignored it.[1] Still the society felt

[1] A copy appears in the Advocate of Peace, May, 1839, pp. 275-79.

that public attention was being called to the subject of peace more extensively and more effectively than before.

From 1836 to 1841 the reports of the treasurer were not published in the magazine or the records, so that exact financial figures for those years can not be given. The agents in the field collected what they could out of which they paid their expenses and turned the remainder over to the society. Ladd and Beckwith invariably paid their own travelling expenses. Ladd announced that the collections for the year ending May, 1837, were $2,724.51, more than all the contributions to the society during the first seven years of its existence; for 1838, $3635.78; for 1839, $3356.54; and for 1840 about $3000.00, at which time the society was $1500 in debt, due to a large extent to inability to collect money following the commercial crisis of 1837. An appeal was therefore made to all friends of peace for funds to enable the society to continue its work and to put at least ten agents in the field. This appeal was made from time to time for several years until the society finally worked its way out of debt.

No attempt was made to have new societies become auxiliaries, and few of those recognized as auxiliaries sent any report to the parent society. The only request made of an auxiliary was that it help the national society financially as much as possible. Two sentences inserted in the constitution of the Lowell Peace Society, organized by Beckwith in January, 1838, were suggested as worthy of incorporation in the constitution of all peace societies, as follows: "The object of this society shall be to promote the cause of peace by cooperating with the parent society. Any person may become a member of this society by paying an amount sufficient to procure the periodical of the parent society." Beckwith organized the Vermont State Society as an auxiliary, Aug. 16, 1837. The Maine and New York societies had ceased their activities on their merger into the American Peace Society. The Connecticut society ended with the death of Watson. The Massachusetts society ceased its activities soon after the removal of the American Peace Society to Boston. Alone of the New England state peace societies that of Rhode Island remained active.

Resolutions were passed by the highest religious bodies connected with the leading denominations in New England approving the work of the society, promising their support, and favoring the preaching of at least one peace sermon by their ministers a year, preferably at

Christmas time, the resolutions being frequently passed after an address by Ladd, Beckwith or other representative of the society. The number of ministers who pledged themselves to preach at least one peace sermon a year was by June, 1837, upwards of a thousand, and Ladd reminded them that the society would gladly receive a contribution at that time, even offering to send the Advocate of Peace for a year to every one contributing a dollar. April 11, 1837, forty-eight students at the Andover Theological Seminary promised to present the cause of peace at least once a year to the congregations over which they might be placed.

On the whole the society never regretted its removal to Boston, for there they found a larger number of more able and devoted friends, and the income of the society increased in amount. By May, 1840, the number of life members had increased to 220.

Chapter VI

PEACE ESSAYS

THE directors of the American Peace Society felt at first that the various local societies should spend their time in sowing the field and spreading the gospel of peace, but that the national organization should engage in some constructive movement, in the formation of some definite program, and make an effort to win people to that. In studying history it was found that the cause of peace had been helped 'by the formation of loosely constructed leagues, such as the Amphictyonic Council and the Achaean League in Greece, the Hanseatic League in Europe, the Swiss confederation of 1308 and the diet in the old German Empire—and that the more practical suggestions that had been made by writers during the preceding century—such as those of Henry IV, Penn, St. Pierre, and Rousseau—looked toward the formation of a league of a similar character. Furthermore, during the preceding two centuries fifty international congresses had been held in Europe, each called to settle questions by arbitration. Though there is nothing to show that any society before the founding of the American Peace Society had thought upon the subject, Ladd had become very early a convert to the idea of a congress of nations, and, as he said at the organization of the American Peace Society, he had enlisted until "a congress of nations for the abolition of war shall be founded or I shall cease to breathe."

In the circular letter, the work of Ladd, adopted by the society on the day of its organization, May 8, 1828, appears this statement: "We hope to increase and promote the practice already begun of submitting national differences to amicable discussion and arbitration and finally of settling all national controversies by an appeal to reason, as becomes rational creatures, and not by physical force, as is worthy only of brute beasts, and this shall be done by a congress of nations, whose decree shall be enforced by public opinion."[1]

[1] In Harbinger of Peace, May, 1828, p. 10.

50

To arouse general interest in the subject of peace as well as to ascertain the defects in such a plan, the board of directors, May 14, 1829, at the close of the first annual meeting, offered a prize for the best dissertation on the subject of "A Congress of Nations for the Prevention of War," to be submitted by May 1, 1830, later extended to Jan. 1, 1831, the winner to receive honorary membership in the society, a gold medal, or thirty dollars in cash, as he chose. But the response was not very encouraging. Only two presented papers at the appointed time, one of whom withdrew his essay from competition and had it printed in the Harbinger of Peace,[1] the first essay on a congress of nations printed in America.

It was felt that the smallness of the prize accounted for the few essays offered. So, May 1, 1831, the offer was renewed, the time extended to April, 1832, and later to the following December, and the amount of the prize increased to fifty dollars. A month later, two friends in New York, names never disclosed but understood to have been Rev. L. R. Dewey, the editor of the Calumet, and Origen Bacheler, one of the board of directors of the society, but with no authority from the board of directors or executive committee offered through the magazine two prizes, a first of five hundred dollars and a second of one hundred dollars, for an essay, forty to one hundred and twenty pages in length, the title to be "A Congress of Nations for the Amicable Adjustment of National Disputes and for the Promotion of Universal Peace without Recourse to Arms."

This time the number of essays submitted was larger,—37. They were looked over by a committee who selected seven and sent them to the committee on award consisting of the eminent jurist Joseph Story, and to William Wirt of Virginia and John McLean of Ohio, respectively attorney general and postmaster general under Presidents James Monroe and John Quincy Adams. The committee reported, April 29, 1833, "that five of the essays possessed very high merit; and that their merit is so nearly equal, and yet of so distinct a character, that injustice would be done by awarding the highest prize to any one, to the exclusion of the others."[2] They therefore suggested that the six hundred dollars offered in prizes be equally divided among the five writers and that the essays be published for general distribution.

[1] For January, 1831, pp. 193-223.
[2] Calumet, May and June, 1833, p. 414; Prize Essay on a Congress of Nations, p. iv.

This the donors of the prize were unwilling to do. Learning that the judges were unanimously of opinion that no one essay was superior to the others, they, without ascertaining the names of the writers, renewed their offer for the best essay upon the subject, slightly changed to, "A Congress or Court of Nations for the Amicable Settlement of National Differences and the Abolition of War." The essays were to be submitted by June 30, 1834, and to be between sixty and one hundred and fifty pages in length, the manuscripts to be the property of the society. The amount of the prize offered was increased to one thousand dollars, which might be divided between two essays if of equal or nearly equal merit. By June 24, 1834, thirteen manuscripts had been received, one in Latin, and sent to a new committee consisting of John Quincy Adams, ex-president of the United States, Chancellor Kent of New York, and Judge Grimke, of South Carolina. Daniel Webster was later substituted for Judge Grimke who had died in October, 1834.

This committee did not report until February, 1837, shortly before the removal of the society to Boston, and then in the following words, each member of the committee having selected a different essay for the prize: "The referees to whom were submitted by the Secretary of the American Peace Society the several essays offered for the premium of one thousand dollars are of opinion that among the essays submitted there is not one so decidedly superior to all the rest as not only to be worthy of the prize, but exclusively worthy; and as the essays were submitted on that condition, the referees do not make any award in the case."[1] They recommended an equal division of the prize between the three writers selected. Though the society had in 1834 appointed Ladd and Blanchard a committee to select other judges well versed in the law of nations, in case this committee should fail to bring in an award, nothing was done, for the donors withdrew their offer and the essays were returned to their writers.

The society was in a quandary as to what to do. It had not offered the prizes, but it had allowed its paper to be used as a medium of publicity to the offer of the prize, and it felt in a manner responsible for keeping some one out of his prize. Furthermore, it was felt that some of the essays possessed great merit. Thinking that the authors should not lose their reward nor the world the benefit of their labors, the executive committee, Mar. 7, 1838,

[1]Prize Essays on a Congress of Nations, p. v.

authorized Ladd to select for printing the five essays showing most merit, and voted that the writers of these essays be paid one hundred dollars each, half in cash and half in books, that the price of a volume be set at two dollars and a half and that they be published on receipt of sufficient subscriptions to pay for two thousand copies, inasmuch as the society was without funds to publish them itself. As soon as the London Peace Society learned of this it ordered 250 copies of the peace essays, and they were ordered printed.

Several of the essays had been withdrawn by the writers and three or four had been printed. Ladd examined thirty-five essays of both lots, all that he could obtain. He found that "the previous committee were judicious in advising a distribution of the prize." He selected the five he considered to be the best, none of which seems to have been taken from the second group of essays, and upon the request of the society added a sixth written by himself which gave his own views and what he found relevant in the rejected essays. It is worthy of mention in this connection that every essayist referred to the congress of nations as a single body with legislative and judicial duties. Ladd seems to have been the first to divide it into two distinct bodies, "a congress with legislative powers to settle points of international law; a court to apply this code and adjust such cases as might be referred to them,"[1] public opinion to be the executive; and diplomacy to be entirely separated from the judiciary.

The volume appeared in the spring of 1840. It contained 700 pages. The first essay was by John A. Bolles of the Boston bar. The second was signed Hamilton, the writer unknown. The third was by Charles B. Emerson of Boston. The fourth was by Thomas C. Upham, Professor of Mental and Moral Philosophy in Bowdoin College. The fifth was by Origen Bacheler, the writer of the petitions to Congress from the New York Society described in the next chapter, a director of the American Peace Society, and one of the reputed donors of the prize. The sixth was by Ladd, so satisfactory that the London Peace Society issued an edition of twenty thousand copies for circulation in Great Britain. The essays were paged separately and serially, and several of them were bound individually in stiff covers. In addition to the essays the volume contained a preface, giving an account of the essays, and several appendices consisting of documents bearing upon the subject. These essays

---

[1] *Advocate of Peace*, October, 1838, p. 97.

anticipated every essential principle embodied in the Hague conferences and the international court, more than a half century later.
Ladd assumed all pecuniary responsibility connected with the
issuance of the book.

Copies were sent to the president of the United States and each
member of his cabinet, the governors of the several states, each
ambassador in Washington except the British, to every cabinet in
Europe, and to each of the American republics. The ambassadors
in Washington acknowledged receipt of the volume, and all, except
those from Spain and Austria, promised to send them to their home
governments. The copy to Queen Victoria was sent through the
London Peace Society with a personal letter written by Ladd in
June, 1840, to which the Queen replied through Lord Palmerston,
Sept. 3, 1840, with thanks, saying that she "has nothing more at
heart than the preservation of peace and the promotion of harmony
and friendship among nations."[1] A member of the London society presented a copy to the library of each college of Oxford
University and to the Duke of Wellington. The single essay by
Ladd was sent by the London society to editors of magazines and
newspapers throughout England, to Louis Philippe, King of the
French, and to each of his ministers, to the King of Belgium, to the
library of the University of Bonn, to members of each branch of
the British Parliament and to the judges of England. John Quincy
Adams in a letter to Ladd said that the "publication of the five
dissertations and the distribution of them among the princes and
rulers of nations will awaken and keep alive the attention both of
Europe and America to the subject."[2]

[1] Ladd's letter and Lord Palmerston's reply are printed in the Advocate of
Peace, April, 1841, pp. 279, 280.
[2] Prize Essays on a Congress of Nations, p. vi.

Chapter VII

A CONGRESS OF NATIONS

WHILE the society was at no time ready to define the exact form a congress of nations should take, it was very desirous to have the idea accepted by the world generally. It did not confine itself to essays. It believed in practical work as well. It is proper to insert here a letter from John Marshall, Chief Justice of the United States Supreme Court, dated Sept. 12, 1832, in reply to one from Ladd: "The whole spirit of the Sacred Volume inculcates peace. The human race would be eminently benefited by the principle you advance. The religious man and the philanthropist must equally pray for its establishment. Yet I must avow my belief that it is impracticable."[1]

At the time the society offered its first peace prize in 1829, Thomas Thompson Jr., a member of the Massachusetts Peace Society and after 1837 a director of the American Peace Society, with the approval of the former society, circulated in Boston and vicinity a petition in favor of a court of nations[2] and within a year obtained twelve hundred signatures to it. Whereupon the American Peace Society, acting upon a suggestion from the Massachusetts Peace Society, issued the following statement: "We the undersigned, convinced of the great advantages and blessings which an abolition of war and the reference of all international disputes to a court of nations would confer upon mankind, heartily concur in recommending a suitable reference of this subject by the peace societies to the attention of congress as soon as such reference shall be found practicable and convenient."[3]

The society circulated many thousand copies of this paper. It was said that nine out of every ten persons to whom it was presented signed it. Within two years, 1454 papers were returned to the

[1] The latter is printed in full in the Calumet, November-December, 1830, p. 290.
[2] Printed in the Advocate of Peace, November and December, 1845, p. 124.
[3] Printed in Prize Essays, etc., pp. 588, 589.

society from Maine, New Hampshire and Vermont containing several thousand names, including those of a lieutenant governor, a state treasurer, a state secretary, 29 senators, 34 representatives, 8 judges, 37 lawyers, 4 college presidents, 32 professors, 381 college students, 44 medical students, 33 principals of schools and academies, 39 physicians, 75 clergymen, 582 merchants, 3 generals, and 57 persons who had served in the Revolutionary War.

Through the effort of the society a convention of Congregational ministers in Massachusetts, May 28, 1830, voted that peace societies be recommended to call the attention of Congress to the advisability of nations referring international disputes to a court of nations. This caused Ladd to introduce the following motion at the annual meeting of the American Peace Society in 1832, which was passed: "Resolved, That the time has arrived when preparations for a congress of nations for the amicable adjustment of national disputes should be commenced, and that the friends of peace should make vigorous efforts for the accomplishment of this object."[1] The Connecticut Peace Society at its meeting the next month passed a similar resolution, and at its annual meeting in June, 1834, it urged the American Peace Society to continue what it had begun.

At the 1834 session of the Legislature of Massachusetts, a motion was introduced recommending a court of nations for the securing of permanent peace. Finally, Feb. 6, 1835, a very mild petition signed by Thomas Thompson Jr., and William Ladd, stating that a large portion of the community had suggested that the peace societies request Congress to devise suitable means to refer all international disputes to a court of nations, to be established in such manner as the various nations might adopt, believing that some system of arbitration should supersede an appeal to arms, and requesting the legislature to consider the matter and take such steps "as may appear best adapted to promote the end in view," was presented to the Senate of the General Court of the Commonwealth of Massachusetts by Hon. Sidney Willard, a member of that body.[2] The special committee consisting of Sidney Willard, Daniel Messinger and Ephraim Hastings, to whom the petition was referred by the Senate, recommended that the legislature pass a resolution favoring the establishment of some mode for the amicable and final

[1] Calumet, May and June, 1832, p. 195.
[2] The petition is printed in the Calumet, March and April, 1835, pp. 203, 204; Prize Essays on a Congress of Nations, pp. 641, 642.

adjustment of all international disputes.[1] The Senate adopted
the report by a vote of nineteen to five. However, the lateness of
the session prevented its consideration by the House.

Thompson, who was managing the petition with the legislature,
was confined to his house by sickness during the year 1836, and,
therefore, nothing was done that year. But in 1837 he presented a
petition[2] to the Massachusetts Legislature, the executive committee of the Massachusetts Peace Society doing the same,[3]
requesting that body to express an opinion on the advisability of
the government uniting with others to establish a congress of
nations. These petitions were presented to both houses and by
them, Feb. 18 and Feb. 20, 1837, were referred to a joint committee. This committee presented an extended report, April 4,
1837, with four resolves annexed, denouncing war, approving the
institution of a congress or a court of nations as the best practical
method of adjusting disputes between nations, recommending that
the president of the United States open negotiations with other
governments with a view to effecting the same, and that the governor
of the commonwealth transmit a copy of the report and resolutions
to the president of the United States and to the governor of each
state suggesting that the latter invite the legislature of his own
state to cooperate in favor of the resolution.[4] The report and
resolutions were adopted by the Massachusetts Senate by a vote of
thirty-five to five and by the House unanimously.

Thompson again laid the matter before the legislature of Massachusetts at its session in 1838. The resolutions recommended by
the committee at the preceding session in favor of a congress of
nations were passed unanimously in a slightly changed form by the
House and with but two dissenting votes in the Senate, and the
governor was instructed to lay them before Congress and the executive of each state.[5]

It will be noted that the work with the Massachusetts legislature
was done under the direction of the Massachusetts Peace Society,

---

[1] The report is printed in Calumet, ibid. pp. 205, 206; Prize Essays, pp.
642-45.

[2] Prize Essays, pp. 645-48.

[3] Prize Essays, pp. 648-50.

[4] The resolutions are printed in the Advocate of Peace, June, 1837, pp. 21,
22; the full report and the resolutions are printed in Prize Essays, pp. 651-59.

[5] The report of the joint committee with the resolutions is printed in the
Advocate of Peace, August, 1838, pp. 68-70. The resolutions alone are in the
Prize Essays, p. 660. The resolutions of 1837 and 1838 are printed in the
Advocate of Peace, February, 1903, p. 32.

for the American Peace Society was not established in Boston until well into the year 1837. Indeed the American Peace Society showed a disinclination to interfere with the work undertaken by its auxiliary. Its agents however were speaking upon the subject. Ladd secured in a short time the names of nearly a thousand petitioners for a congress of nations. He laid the matter before the legislature of Maine in the winter of 1838, and began work at the same time with the Vermont legislature.

The society had been waiting for the sanction of the Massachusetts legislature before carrying the subject to the American Congress. But in May, 1837, when the national society was moving from Hartford to Boston, a new society was organized in New York to promote the adjustment of international difficulties by arbitration and establishment of a congress of nations for this purpose. By the end of the year it had a membership of five hundred with an agent in the field. It held public meetings weekly for four or five months in the various churches of the city. It took advantage of the vote by the Mexican congress, May 20, 1837, authorizing its president to refer its differences with the United States to a friendly power for arbitration, to send a petition to Congress requesting it to join with Mexico in settling the differences between the two nations and to propose to the various governments of the world that they cooperate in the establishment of an international board of arbitration or congress of nations to which should be referred as an invariable rule of action such international disputes as could not be amicably adjusted by diplomacy, and also that it should prepare a code of international law.[1] Copies of the petition were sent to forty peace societies for signature.

The American Peace Society and its auxiliary the Vermont Peace Society cooperated with the New York Peace Society in obtaining signatures to the petition. Many of these found their way to Congress. Six petitions with 608 signatures were sent to the House of Representatives by the New York society, one by Ladd with 540 signatures from Maine, one by the Vermont society with 143 signatures, one signed by 135 members of the Massachusetts legislature. Some petitions were sent to Henry Clay in the Senate and others to Congressman Evans of Maine, to Caleb Cushing and to John Quincy Adams of Massachusetts. The petitions were viewed

[1] The Petition is printed in Peace Essays, pp. 661-65. The part relating to the congress of nations is printed in the Advocate of Peace, November, 1838, pp. 185-87.

by the majority of the House of Representatives with no little aversion "as abolition petitions or petitions against the annexation of Texas in disguise."[1]

The first of these petitions received by Adams contained thirty-five names. He introduced it into the House where it was referred to the Committee on Foreign Relations, as were the later petitions as received. Adams caused the petition to be printed. Both he and Henry Clay spoke on the subject and declared their aversion to war with Mexico. Her proposal to arbitrate was conditionally accepted and the dispute referred to the King of Prussia as arbitrator. The result was that war with Mexico was averted for a time. The Mexican minister in appreciation of the act sent one hundred dollars to the New York Peace Society, thanking them for their instrumentality in preventing war between the two countries.

Legare, Chairman of the Committee on Foreign Relations in the House, reported on these several petitions in a long and able document, showing sympathy with the petitioners and frankly discussing the conditions. He stated that the committee concurred in the benevolent objects expressed, that the spirit of the age was with them, but that he did not believe that a reform so fundamental could be brought about except by a gradual progress of civilization. He recommended the memorialists "to persevere in exerting whatever influence they may possess over public opinion." In other words the committee felt that the object was a desirable one but that the present was not the time to undertake a reform of this radical character.[2]

Ladd was greatly pleased with the result. He had expected Congress to ignore the petition. But that John Quincy Adams and Henry Clay should speak in advocacy of peace and that Legare should write so sympathetic a report exceeded his expectation. He felt that the time was ripe for a forward movement. He urged all ministers, auxiliaries and friends of peace to send petitions to John Quincy Adams, Henry Clay or others in Congress. He prepared a short form of petition which he circulated freely, many copies of which found their way to Congress during each session for several years thereafter. He filled the Advocate of Peace with articles in favor of a congress of nations. The executive committee of the society Oct. 24, 1838, sent a lengthy memorial and petition for a

---

[1] Statement by Adams, Prize Essays, p. 593.
[2] The report is printed in Prize Essays, pp. 666-78. Extracts from it are printed in the Advocate of Peace, November, 1838, pp. 139-41.

congress of nations to both houses of Congress,[1] and the New York Peace Society did the same.[2]

Rev. John Lord spent some time in Vermont, and with the aid of the Vermont Peace Society did yeoman service in that state. Beckwith spent two months in the western part of Massachusetts and Connecticut, where he started nearly thirty petitions. Ladd secured from the Congregational ministers of Maine a license to preach and occupied every pulpit open to him from Maine to the District of Columbia, frequently speaking three times on Sunday. His sermons were generally an hour and a half in length. The petitions secured like the other petitions were sent to the Committee on Foreign Relations, which, as this was the short session of Congress, made no report on them.

During the campaign in 1839, Ladd when in Washington personally interviewed President Van Buren, the members of his cabinet and several congressmen on the subject of the congress of nations. The president was favorable to the scheme but felt that it would be unwise for the United States to call on the governments of Europe until they had been sufficiently enlightened on the subject to receive the proposal with favor. He highly approved circulating the prize essays among the sovereigns and statesmen of Europe and America.

In 1839-40, after the subsidence of the feeling over the northeastern boundary question, the society sent another petition to congress[3] urging that body to call a congress of nations to arbitrate questions that could not be settled diplomatically. It was not expected that any immediate good would result from this petition but it was felt that keeping the matter continually before Congress would eventually cause attention to be paid to it. At the same time acting upon the request of the American Peace Society, Sept. 20, 1838, the London society which had always been friendly to the plan though it had taken no action on the question presented a petition to Parliament in its favor, April 12, 1839.[4]

Sept. 30, 1840, Ladd started on a western tour in the interest of the society, a work that he had long contemplated. He went through New York state as far as Buffalo. He was far from well

---

[1] Printed in the Advocate of Peace, January, 1839, pp. 184-89; Prize Essays, pp. 679-85.

[2] Printed in Prize Essays, pp. 685-93.

[3] Printed in the Advocate of Peace, February, 1840, pp. 118-20; Prize Essays, pp. 694-96.

[4] Printed in Prize Essays, pp. 699, 700.

and spent four weeks in bed at Canandaigua. His legs troubled him considerably and he often sat while preaching, at times pleading the cause from his knees. His illness increased, and after an absence of six months, during which time he had spoken nearly every night and often three times on the Sabbath, he started for home. On his way he stopped with friends in Portsmouth, N. H., where he died April 9, 1841, at the age of 63 years.

Chapter VIII

GENERAL PEACE CONVENTION OF 1843

THE future of the society looked dark. The old leaders in the movement were going or gone. Ladd, the founder, the organizer, the editor, the preacher, the president, the main support of the society from its birth, was gone. Noah Worcester, the founder and corresponding secretary of the Massachusetts Peace Society, had died in Brighton, Oct. 31, 1837. William Ellery Channing, in whose study the Massachusetts Peace Society had been organized, long a staunch supporter of the American Peace Society, died in the spring of 1843. Henry Ware, an early disciple of Worcester and long director of the American Peace Society, died Sept. 22, 1843. David L. Dodge, founder of the first New York Society, died April 23, 1852. It had been frequently said that the American Peace Society was a one man society and that it would end with the death of Ladd; but Beckwith, with the help of J. P. Blanchard, who had been the corresponding secretary of the Massachusetts Peace Society from 1830, a director of the American Peace Society since 1831, a member of its executive committee from the time of its removal to Boston, and elected its recording secretary in 1840, kept the society alive.

At a special meeting of the society, Oct. 13, 1841, Samuel E. Coues of Portsmouth, N. H., a nephew of Ladd by marriage and a vice president of the society since 1839, was elected president. Lewis T. Stoddard, a director and member of the executive committee since 1837, was elected recording secretary, and Josiah P. Blanchard was transferred to the office of treasurer with the title of "general agent" at a salary of $100 a year, to transact the business of the society at a permanent home office, to care for the office, tracts and books, act as its local representative and superintendent and collect funds in Boston and vicinity. In November, 1842, the depository was located at 13 Tremont Row, moved in March, 1845, to 22 Cornhill, five months later to 60½ Cornhill and the following November to 21 Court Square.

The death of Ladd had removed the chief financial support of the society. For years he had given it from one to two thousand dollars yearly or its equivalent. In gratitude for his services, the society erected in the cemetery of Portsmouth, N. H., where he was buried, a plain, simple, and modest monument to his memory with the inscription: "William Ladd, Born May 10, 1778, Died April 9, 1841. Blessed are the peacemakers, for they shall be called the Children of God." On the opposite side of the monument is the following inscription made several years later: "Sophia Ann Stidolph, Widow of William Ladd, Died Dec. 29, 1855, Aged 75 Years."

Ladd had made the society his residuary legatee, after bequeathing about $2000 to relatives and others and providing his wife with an allowance of sixty dollars a month during her life. But this money did not provide for the present. It was necessary to obtain money immediately and from other sources. One of the resolutions passed at the annual meeting in June, 1841, following Ladd's death was: 8, That a special appeal be made for funds to meet the crisis to which the death of our president has brought the cause, and to give it a new and lasting impulse. For several years an appeal was made annually for $5000 a year to support the magazine and an editor, to publish tracts, and to pay the expenses of a secretary and agents in the field. Nevertheless at its annual meeting in May, 1843, the society was reported to be $2515 in debt.

During the year 1841-42, the society did more publishing than before. It issued new editions of its nine stereotyped tracts, of Dymond on War and Hancock on Peace, republished 2000 copies of an able article in the Democratic Review, and stereotyped the principal part of Upham's book on peace, selling 800 copies to the London society and 100 to the Rhode Island Peace Society. Articles appeared in the Democratic Review, Boston Courier, and New York Journal of Commerce pleading the cause of peace. A series of articles continuing for four months was prepared by some friends and printed in ten religious papers.

Beckwith in addition to conducting the correspondence of the society continued to travel in the interest of the cause in New England and New York, preaching three times on Sunday. In the year ending May, 1843, he travelled between five and six thousand miles, visiting all towns of importance in New England and New York. Coues travelled considerably in the interest of the society and without expense to it. Blanchard as opportunity offered travelled to towns within a hundred miles from Boston. In the year 1841-42, he travelled upwards of five thousand miles. Rev. D. O. Morton, a life member of the society, continued in the field for a year, 1841-42, making frequent trips in northern New England. He was followed for a year by Rev. F. N. Miller who made frequent trips from his home in Portsmouth into northern New England at $600 a year. In 1843, the custom of appointing agents in several large towns to serve without pay was adopted. Twelve such were appointed that year to serve in New England, New York and Philadelphia and to make occasional trips to near-by towns.

Thus the cause lived and the directors were able to say in their annual report, May, 1842: "In spite of every obstacle and discouragement we have held on the even tenor of our way, and extended rather than curtailed our operations. We have had in service more persons than heretofore; we have raised for the cause nearly as much money as in any former year and more than in the year immediately preceding; we have spread before the community a larger number of publications than usual, and have also set at work some other agencies that promise in the end results of great and lasting importance."

In the summer of 1841, Joseph Sturge, of Birmingham, an English philanthropist and president of the London Peace Society, while on a visit to the United States, met several of the friends of peace in Boston, July 26th, and there laid before them a suggestion that had already been discussed in London, that a general convention be held in London to be attended by delegates from all the peace societies in the world for the purpose of exchanging views as to the best methods of promoting universal peace among the nations of the earth by a concert of action and to devise means to bring such action about. Judge William Jay of New York, son of the maker of Jay's treaty in 1794, and author of a recent book on peace and war, had suggested that until the nations were ready to accept a congress of nations a clause might be inserted in all conventional treaties made between nations mutually binding the parties to submit all international disputes to the arbitration of some one or more friendly powers. The meeting passed two resolutions to refer both suggestions—holding a convention and adopting Jay's plan—to the executive committee of the American Peace Society for decision or correspondence and consultation with the friends of

peace in this and other countries.[1] This action was endorsed
by the society at its annual meeting in May, 1842, when it passed
the following resolution: "That this society deems it very desirable
to have a general conference of the friends of peace from different
countries held at London as soon as practicable and that the
London Peace Society be requested, should they concur in this
recommendation, to select the time and make the requisite arrangements."[2]

Sturge on his return to London placed these resolutions before the
London society which, at a meeting held Sept. 15, 1841, expressed
approval of Judge Jay's suggestion and the holding of a general
conference at an early date,[3] and referred the matter to a committee for consideration. After extensive correspondence, an open
conference was held. Of five to six hundred invited, seventy met in
London, May 14, 1842, and after an interchange of views voted to
hold a world convention to deliberate upon the best means to
promote permanent and universal peace.[4] A committee was
appointed to determine the time for holding the convention and
make arrangements for it. In June, 1842, it was resolved that the
peace convention should follow that of the Anti Slavery Society in
1843.

The program, principles, object, and business of the convention
were determined Feb. 17, 1843, and a subcommittee on arrangements
appointed. An effort was made to notify all likely to be interested
in a convention of this character. Circulars were sent to all the
correspondents of the London society in Great Britain urging them
to appoint delegates to the convention. The leading newspapers
and periodicals of the country gave a notice of the meeting. Copies
of the circular and of Jay's book on war and peace were sent to
every member of Parliament, to the ambassadors from foreign
nations in London, and to the judges in the realm. Notices were
sent to the West Indies, Toronto and Montreal, and in French to
the members of the French society and to friends of peace in several
cities in France, Switzerland, Germany, Belgium, Holland, Sweden,
and Spain, as well as to the leading journals on the continent.
Similarly the American Peace Society sent notices throughout the
United States.

[1] Printed in the Advocate of Peace, October, 1841, p. 67.
[2] Ibid., June, 1842, p. 148.
[3] Ibid., October, 1843, p. 110.
[4] Ibid., October, 1843, p. 110.

The convention held its sessions in Free Masons' Hall, Great Queen Street, for three days, opening Thursday, June 22, 1843, and ending with a rousing public meeting on Monday, the 26th. It was the greatest event in the peace movement to date. It was reported in all the leading London papers. It was not popular but consultative and deliberative in character. Its object was to deliberate as to the best means to promote permanent and universal peace. It was composed of the officers and committee of the London Peace Society, of persons specially named by that committee, the seventy who had been present at the conference in May, 1842, delegates elected by peace societies, religious bodies, philanthropic, literary or scientific institutions, and persons elected at public meetings of towns or districts specially convened for this purpose.

Of 334 delegates appointed, 292 were from Great Britain including all the English leaders in the peace movement with several members of Parliament, six from the continent of Europe and 36 from the peace societies of the United States. Eighteen Americans actually attended, including the following eleven members of the American Peace Society: Rev. G. C. Beckwith, Rev. Jonathan Blanchard, Rev. H. N. Kellogg, Rev. Joshua Leavitt, Rev. Amos A. Phelps, Stephen P. Andrews, Isaac Collins, Dr. Thomas Cock, John Tappan, Lewis Tappan, and Amasa Walker; besides Rev. Robert Baird, D. D., Secretary of the Foreign Evangelical Society, New York City, J. W. C. Pennington, Hartford, and Arnold Buffum, Cincinnati. In attendance at the meetings, but as visitors and not as delegates were Hon. Richard Cobden, Hon. Joseph Hume, and Hon. W. Ewart, members of Parliament.

About 150 were present at each session. Christian sentiment and feeling were strong. The deliberations were conducted in a serious and orderly manner. Sittings were opened, as had been those of the antislavery convention, which had immediately preceded this one, by silent prayer. The sessions commenced at ten in the morning and four in the afternoon. Propositions and resolutions were submitted in writing to the secretaries not later than the close of the sitting previous to that in which it was proposed to introduce them and amendments were submitted to the chairmen in writing. The secretaries acted as a committee of arrangements.

At the opening session Secretary Jefferson of the London society read the statement of the origin and object of the convention, the means that had been used to assemble it, the rules for conducting its business, and the principles on which it was called,—"That war is inconsistent with the spirit of Christianity and the true interest of mankind." This principle was taken as admitted and was not discussed at the convention.

Charles Hindley, M. P., was elected president of the convention. One half of the six vice presidents were vice presidents of the American Peace Society,—John Tappan, Boston, Amasa Walker, Professor in Oberlin College, and Thomas Cock, M. D., New York City. Beckwith, secretary of the American Peace Society, acted as one of the secretaries. Letters of regret at their inability to be present were read from Hon. James C. Birney, S. E. Coues, Rev. Alpheus Crosby, Rev. William E. Dixon, Hon. William Jay, Rev. Howard Malcolm, Anson G. Phelps, Rev. Charles Spear, Rev. Calvin E. Stowe, Rev. Thomas C. Upham, S. V. S. Wilder, Hon. Thomas W. Williams, appointees of the American Peace Society, W. H. Y. Hackett and Marcillus Bufford of the New Hampshire Peace Society, William Dawes, H. C. Taylor and Hamilton Hill of the Oberlin College Peace Society, John Howland, president of the Rhode Island Peace Society, and from delegates appointed from Amsterdam, Basle, Frankfort, Geneva, Paris, Stockholm, and Toronto.

Two papers were read: one by Rev. John Burnet of London on "The Essential Sinfulness of War", referred to a committee of nine of whom Walker and Blanchard were members; and the other by H. T. J. Macnamara, who had recently received the prize offered by the London society for the best peace essay, on the "Best Practical Means of Carrying out Pacific Principles," advocating particularly the adoption of Judge Jay's plan immediately and Ladd's later when feasible. Each paper was referred to a committee which after revising it reintroduced it into the convention, where it was discussed, and with changes finally ordered to be printed as part of the convention proceedings. Four other papers were read including one on Preparation for War, prepared by J. P. Blanchard and read by Beckwith, the only paper presented by an American.

In addition to several minor resolutions adopted at different times during the progress of the convention, ten resolutions designed to embody the results of their deliberations were introduced by a committee on resolutions, consisting of Rev. A. A. Phelps, Lewis Tappan, Amasa Walker and two others representing the London

society. Among other matters these resolutions thanked Macnamara for his paper and recommended its publication; recommended all governments to adopt the principles of arbitration for
the adjustment of all international differences and the introduction
into all international treaties of stipulation providing for this mode
of adjustment; recommended a congress of nations to settle the code
of international law, and a high court of nations to interpret and
apply that law as one of the best practical modes of settling international disputes; recommended that friends of peace adopt
measures for the diffusion of the principles of peace among all
classes of the community in order to produce a public opinion that
will ensure the permanent prevention of war in every country;
recommended that when symptoms of the approach of war appear,
the peace societies should enter a protest against such threatened
war and try to secure the preservation of peace; recommended that
peace societies endeavor to effect a regular organization of the whole
country by the establishment of county, district and town branches
of the parent society; recommended that the local societies use the
local press and introduce the knowledge of peace principles into public schools, institutes and the like and by encouraging "the formation
of societies or associations among the working classes;" and recommended the preparation of suitable addresses to children and the
circulation among them of interesting tracts and books that would
inculcate peace ideas. The convention also went on record as
opposed to military education in schools and colleges, the manu-
facture of weapons of war and preparations for war and closed by
thanking the London society for making the arrangements for the
convention.

Thus the two suggestions of Ladd and Jay that had led to the
calling of the convention were unqualifiedly adopted. Aside from
the withdrawal of two persons who were unable to agree with the
convention relative to asking the government to end war, there was
no divided vote on any important matter. The kindest and best of
feeling prevailed throughout.

At the public meeting held in Exeter Hall, the Strand, the
following Monday the attendance was about two thousand. Charles
Hindley, M. P., presided. Seven resolutions were passed after discussion: "That war is inconsistent with the spirit of Christianity
and the true interest of mankind," that a continuance of the opium
traffic was to be lamented; that the cordial cooperation of all

Christians be invited to diffuse the principles of peace; that the aid of women in the cause was desirable; that governments be urged to use arbitration in future international disputes; that the meeting held with alarm the employment of military force to preserve tranquillity in Ireland; and that the thanks of the meeting be presented to Charles Hindley, M. P., for his kind and able attention to the business of the convention.

On the motion of the Marquis de la Rochefoucauld-Liancourt an address to the governments of the civilized world was prepared by the committee on arrangements in which the following paragraph appears: "The convention is of opinion that one of the greatest securities against the recurrence of international warfare would be the recognition of the principle of arbitration, and the introduction of a clause into treaties, binding themselves to refer all differences that may arise to the adjudication of one or more friendly powers; and it earnestly recommends the adoption of this practice."[1] This address the London society was requested to forward to all the governments of the civilized world. A committee consisting of Lewis Tappan of New York, representatives from the Paris and Brussels societies, the chairman, secretary, and the treasurer of the London society and others, introduced by John Bowring, M. P., presented the address on July 1st, to Sir Robert Peel, the prime minister of England. He received the committee very courteously and promised to place the address before the other members of the cabinet.

July 5th, four persons, including Lewis Tappan again, after an introduction by Dr. Bowring, M. P., presented a second copy to the King of Belgium who at the time was visiting in London. The King replied in strong terms expressing his approval of the principle of arbitration. July 20th, a committee of five, including Beckwith, Cock, and Walker, introduced by Guizot, the prime minister, presented a copy to Louis Philippe in his palace at Neuilly. He welcomed them and gave them a pleasant reply in which he said, "I think the time is coming when we shall get rid of war entirely in all civilized countries. They are beginning to learn more wisdom."[2] In the following January the American Peace Society sent to Louis Philippe an address replying to the sentiments thus expressed by him and requesting him to urge all nations to adopt arbitration

[1] The address in full is printed in Proceedings of the First General Peace Convention, p. 32; and Advocate of Peace, October, 1843, p. 123.
[2] Quoted in Advocate of Peace, November, 1843, p. 125.

as a means for settling differences between them.[1] June 14, 1844, this address was presented to him at the palace of the Tuileries by a deputation including Marquis de la Rochefoucauld-Liancourt and Rigaud, foreign secretary of the London society. After an introduction by the Marquis, the King thanked them for it, stated that he saw no need of war and hoped that it might come to an end.

While in Paris, May 7, 1844, Rigaud formed a new peace society, the Société de la Paix de Paris, which very graciously elected Judge Jay as honorary president and Beckwith and Blanchard as honorary members. In March, 1844, Rigaud visited Brussels. There he sent a French translation of the resolutions of the peace convention to each senator and member of the Belgian lower house, left one hundred copies with the peace society at Brussels and sent an equal number to the society at Mons. Then he interviewed Canon Clementi, the auditor of the pope's nuncio, Monseigneur Pecci, then in Brussels, and gave him a copy of the memorial addressed to the Pope, with translated copies of the resolutions. These the auditor promised to send to the Pope. From there he went to Amsterdam and sent the king of the Netherlands a copy of the "Proceedings of the First General Peace Convention" together with the resolutions in French and a copy of the letter to the Prince of Orange, Prince Alexander, the council of state, the cabinet, and each member of both houses of the States General.

Eventually, thirty-four governments received the address or were apprized of the proceedings of the peace convention.

[1] Printed in Advocate of Peace, July, 1844, p. 225.

Chapter IX

PROGRESS OF THE SOCIETY

Following the London convention, the prospect of peace in America seemed fairly bright. From the first, the religious press of the country had been in sympathy with the movement. In 1843, a series of articles on peace prepared by friends of the movement appeared in thirty religious papers. The following year a plan, suggested by Henry Dwight of Geneva, N. Y., was matured to write short pithy articles, called olive leaves of peace, to be sent broadcast to a thousand papers in the United States, Canada, and Great Britain. This was actually done by Burritt in the pring of 1846 through what he called the Olive Leaf Mission. Copies of a short article on the subject of peace were printed on slips of paper surmounted by a dove with an olive leaf in its bill and periodically sent to every newspaper in the country with the request that it be printed, which was done by about two hundred papers on the average. Then the New York Commercial Advertiser and the New York Tribune took an interest in the subject. In 1847 the North American Review contained an article on the congress of nations by Rev. Mr. Dewey of New York.

The Advocate of Peace continued on its way. It remained unchanged for a year. Beginning June, 1842, it became a monthly with occasional double numbers devoted to news almost entirely served in short pithy articles in a popular style. In January, 1847, it again resumed the bi-monthly form because of lack of funds. An edition consisted of six or eight thousand copies with an occasional issue of ten or twelve thousand. During 1846, a copy of each issue was sent to each member of Congress.

Beckwith wanted to issue two papers, one a large able dignified quarterly for the educated classes and the other a weekly with facts, anecdotes, brief racy articles, believing that in this way all classes would be satisfactorily cared for. This idea was carried out for a short time by Burritt, who in April, 1846, started a small

bi-weekly paper entitled the Bond of Brotherhood. It contained
short articles, items and paragraphs on the subject of peace and
war. It was designed for gratuitous circulation among passengers
on the cars and boats. It was printed at a cost of $3.50 per
thousand and it was hoped that organizations of various kinds
would be interested enough in the plan to buy copies in large
bundles and distribute them. Ten thousand copies of the first two
numbers and twenty thousand of the third and fourth were printed
and actually distributed on the cars in Worcester and Fitchburg,
Mass., and on canal boats in Syracuse and Rochester, N. Y.

In the fall of 1843, the society sent to every mission station
established by American Christians the Advocate of Peace and
copies of Upham's, Hancock's, and Dymond's books on war and
peace; and at the same time copies of the same books and the prize
essay to the libraries of the colleges and professional schools of the
country. In 1846, it sent 1600 volumes to ministers in the West
for their own use and many more tracts for distribution among the
people.

The society possessed but few tracts of its own. At the request
of the executive committee Beckwith undertook the task of preparing, stereotyping, and publishing a full series of them. By
1846, he had stereotyped sixty-four tracts, containing more than
six hundred pages of extracts from more than twenty authors, published more than six thousand copies of them, and raised funds
sufficient to defray the expense of their publication.[1] Two thousand sets of these tracts were combined into volumes under the
title "The Book of Peace," and sent to many public and college
libraries, editors, men of business and influence in the country and
to every foreign missionary from America.

In 1847, the society published a comprehensive work on the
subject of peace containing 252 pages, a manual or encyclopaedia
on the subject, to be circulated among the families of the land, and
issued four thousand copies of it within a year. Copies were sent
to each member of Congress and the cabinet the next year. In
1848 an edition of four thousand copies was printed and sent to
Christian ministers and Sabbath schools in the Mississippi valley.

Hitherto the time at the annual meetings had been occupied in
discussion by those present. Many of these discussions consisted of

---

[1] The titles of these tracts and other publications of the society with a brief
description of each are given in Advocate of Peace, November, 1854, pp. 171-76.

the delivery of prepared speeches which were printed in full in the magazine. Coues limited the discussion and in its place gave an address at the meeting held at Marlboro Chapel, May 23, 1842. For the next nine years the annual meetings were held in the evening following an address by some one of note. In 1843, the address was by Rev. Dr. Andrew P. Peabody; in 1844, by Walter Channing, M. D.; in 1845, by Hon. William Jay. The addresses were given in the Central Church on Winter Street, attended by large audiences and subsequently printed in pamphlet editions for general distribution.

Blanchard's duties in the office prevented his lecturing at any distance from Boston, but he made frequent trips to towns not far away. Coues continued his labors speaking in various places in northern New England. Beckwith, after his return from Europe was engrossed with the general operations of the society and for some months did not travel far from Boston. In the latter part of January, 1844, he went to Washington and delivered the address of the London peace convention to President Tyler to whom he was introduced by Hon. A. K. Parris, comptroller of the treasury and a former governor of Maine. The president received the memorial with expressions of pleasure and spoke feelingly in the interest of peace. Later in the spring Beckwith spent two months and a half in New York, where in April a new New York Peace Society was organized as an auxiliary of the American Peace Society. Beckwith made later trips to New York, Philadelphia, and Albany, districts which he cultivated yearly for a few years.

Aside from Beckwith and Blanchard, the society had an agent or two in the field a good deal of the time. Rev. Aaron Foster, a brother-in-law of Beckwith and a Presbyterian preacher, during 1844, visited Washington where he obtained sympathetic expressions about peace from many public men, and labored in central New York for a year and later rendered occasional service to the society. Rev. E. W. Jackson, a Methodist minister, visited twenty Methodist conferences of ministers during the summer of 1845, going as far south as Richmond, Va., and returning through western New York. For a while in 1846, Rev. Cyril Pearl, a Congregational minister, worked in Maine; and at various times during the years 1846, 1847, and 1848, Rev. William H. Dalrymple, a Baptist clergyman, worked in Massachusetts.

Through the efforts of the secretary and these agents, several religious organizations at their annual meetings passed resolutions favorable to the cause of peace and to the efforts of the society. Probably the most notable peace event in the year 1845 was the Fourth of July address by Charles Sumner, a director of the American Peace Society, before the city authorities of Boston. It was an eloquent oration pleading for peace as the "true grandeur of nations." It created a profound impression at the time, and many thousand copies of it have been printed and circulated by peace societies all over the world. It is said that Charles Sumner's interest in peace dated from the time he heard an address on the subject by William Ladd in Park Street Church. Sumner's address was followed the next year by an address before the Phi Beta Kappa Society at Harvard, which, though not professedly on the subject of peace, plead the cause from beginning to end. These two addresses, one popular and the other scholarly, placed the matter of peace before all classes of people.

The society had for some time paid little attention to the formation of auxiliary societies; but at its annual meeting in May, 1842, it resolved: "That it is expedient to form auxiliary societies in New York, Philadelphia, and other large cities and towns in the United States, and that the executive committee be authorized to form them in such places as they may think best,"[1] and after the passage of the resolution by the London convention the next year, in favor of the formation of such societies, the society urged their organization in the United States, requesting however that the parent society be informed of such establishment.

Following the resolution adopted in London that the friends of peace in each country petition their rulers to adopt arbitration as a stipulated substitute for war, the society prepared a circular explaining the object of the plan and sent a copy of it under date of Sept. 28, 1843, to the governor of each state, requesting that the subject be brought before each legislature for such action as seemed best.[2] Accompanying it were copies of the Advocate of Peace containing an account of the convention, and a copy of the December number was sent to every member of each legislature in the country.

Ladd's plan to bombard Congress with petitions for a congress of nations was continued. The society was without funds to carry

[1] Printed in Advocate of Peace, June, 1842, p. 159.
[2] Ibid., December, 1841, p. 80.

on the winter of 1841-42 as formerly. However, it prepared a form of petition[1] and urged all friends of peace to copy it with any modifications desired, have it signed by as many persons as possible, and send it to some member of Congress. Ministers and principals of educational institutions were especially urged to cooperate. In this way many thousands of petitions reached Congress, but no attention was paid to them. In the fall of the year 1841, J. L. O'Sullivan, a member of the New York Assembly from New York City, offered a lengthy resolution in that body condemning war, recommending a congress of nations as the best way to end war, requesting the government to endeavor to bring such a congress into existence, and that the president be advised of this resolution.[2] The peace society in London with its thirty or more auxiliaries and the independent peace societies in Scotland and Ireland were in sympathy with the plan.

At the same time the society prepared a blank form of petition which it circulated among the friends of peace, requesting them to obtain signatures and send a copy to the president, another to the secretary of state, and a third to some member of the senate requesting that there be inserted in all future treaties made between the United States and other nations a clause agreeing "to settle whatever differences or disputes may arise between them by a reference in the last resort to some third party mutually chosen."[3]

The society held a public meeting in the Masachusetts Hall of Representatives, Feb. 8, 1843, at 7 P. M., for the discussion of subjects relative to the cause of peace. Beckwith prepared the resolutions and presented them with explanatory statements,[4] and later petitioned the Massachusetts legislature to pass resolutions favoring a congress of nations to decide international disputes and to send a copy thereof to Congress with instructions to our senators and representatives to bring the subject to their consideration. Jan. 31, 1844, the committee of the House to whom the petition had been referred reported favoring the petition and recommending that the governor notify Congress in the manner indicated in the petition.[5] The bill however failed of passage and the society

[1] Printed in the Advocate of Peace, July, 1844, p. 224.
[2] Ibid., December, 1841, p. 80.
[3] Ibid., October, 1841, pp. 67-69.
[4] Ibid., December, 1843, p. 142.
[5] The report and resolutions are printed in Advocate of Peace, April, 1844, pp. 190, 191.

requested the governor to urge the Massachusetts senators in Congress to take the petition with them to Washington.

Inspired by the act of Mr. Hindley, the chairman of the London peace convention, who, Mar. 11, 1844, had presented to the House of Commons forty-three petitions in favor of measures calculated to insure the maintenance of peace, the American Peace Society prepared a campaign for the year 1845, five members of the society without any special authorization voluntarily agreeing to hold a series of peace conventions in the middle and western parts of the State of Massachusetts. These volunteers were Coues, the president, Blanchard, the treasurer, Aaron Foster, an agent, Amasa Walker, a vice president, and Elihu Burritt of Worcester. They had meetings in Worcester, North Brookfield, Westfield, Springfield, Cabotville, Chicopee, Massachusetts, and in Hartford, Conn., December 10 to 17. Two meetings were held daily the first four days. Sermons and addresses were delivered by local friends. In general the meetings were poorly attended, but full accounts of them appeared in the Boston, Worcester and local papers.

Then they started to bring the question of arbitration and a congress of nations before Congress and the state legislatures by means of petitions, the press, and meetings. In February, 1845, the New York Peace Society sent a petition to the New York legislature requesting that body to pass a resolution in favor of stipulated arbitration and a congress of nations and to transmit such resolution to the legislatures of other states and to Congress with instructions to our senators and congressmen to use their best endeavors to bring the subject to the favorable consideration of the general government.[1] The society earnestly urged the friends of peace in New Hampshire, Rhode Island and Connecticut to send petitions to their legislatures which were about to meet, with a letter to some member of the legislature requesting his special attention to the subject.[2]

In the fall of 1845, Gov. Slade of Vermont, who had received one of the circulars of the society, referred to it very favorably in his message to the legislature, urging consideration of the request,[3]

---

[1] The petition is printed in Advocate of Peace, May, 1845, pp. 58, 59.
[2] A suggested form of petition is printed in Advocate of Peace, December, 1844, p. 288, and in a revised form for May, 1845, p. 60.
[3] The part of the message relating to peace is printed in Advocate of Peace, November and December, 1845, pp. 132, 133.

and one branch of the legislature passed a resolution therefor. At the same time the society prepared an elaborate petition to Congress, the first since the death of Ladd, requesting the introduction among nations of substitutes for war and circulated it for signatures throughout the country. Peace meetings were held in various towns in New England, addressed by the leaders in the movement, and many petitions were signed and sent to Washington to be presented after the subsidence of the excitement over Oregon and Texas.

These activities were a great expense to the society. Its income was not large. In spite of the advance by Coues of $781.31 in 1841 and $300 in 1843 on account of the bequest by Ladd, and of his payment of $338.80 toward the expenses of the delegates to the London convention, and $400 received from the sale of Ladd's farm at Minot, and the bequest of $1000 by Henry Ware in September, 1843, and of an equal amount by Horace Appleton Haven of Portsmouth, N. H., Oct. 22, 1842, the society found itself sinking further and further into debt. In May, 1843, the indebtedness was $2515.35; 1844, $3636.35; and 1845, $4328.82. A payment of $4700 on account of the legacy of Ladd reduced the debt in 1846 to $1749.16. A few months later it had risen to nearly $3000, but by rigid economy in 1847, the debt was reduced to $17.12, and that was soon extinguished.

During these years the treasurer's report showed the following:

For year ending May	Receipts	Expenditures	Balance
1842	$2878.51	$2862.44	$ 79.36
1843	2418.60	4854.66	2515.35
1844	3273.55	4394.48	3636.35
1845	4540.59	5232.47	4328.82
1846	5859.36	3280.29	1749.16
1847	3387.31	3404.43	17.12

In 1846, Beckwith collected in addition $2029.61, which he spent for debt reducing purposes.

The number of vice presidents during these years varied from twenty-five to thirty. Among those who were elected in addition to those previously mentioned were Rev. Andrew P. Peabody, then of Portsmouth, N. H., Rev. Howard Malcolm, then President of Georgetown College, Georgetown, Ky., Samuel Greele, Esq., and

Robert Waterston, Boston, Rev. Calvin E. Stowe, then of Lane Theological Seminary, Cincinnati, and Henry Dwight, Geneva, N. Y. Of new members of the executive committee which varied from ten to twenty members a year, may be mentioned Louis Dwight, Charles Brooks, James L. Baker, Elihu Burritt, E. W. Jackson, Hubbard Winslow, William C. Brown and John Field.

Chapter X

OREGON AND TEXAS

THE time for the presentation of the petitions never came. The Oregon question took up the attention of the society. With the London Peace Society it passed resolutions protesting a resort to arms. In February, 1846, a memorial signed by Beckwith and the executive committee of the New York Peace Society was sent to the president urging him to have the difficulty over Oregon settled amicably. A series of meetings was held in the larger towns and cities of the New England states where peace addresses were made.

Three days after the annual meeting, in May, 1845, several friends of peace held a meeting for an interchange of views. At this meeting Elihu Burritt acted as secretary. Burritt was one of the most unique, picturesque and interesting characters that ever appeared in the peace movement. A descendant of William Burritt, who settled in Stratford, Conn., in 1651, he was born in New Britain, Conn., Dec. 8, 1810, the youngest of five sons. For several years he followed the trade of a blacksmith. Though his schooling had been slight, he had a wonderful command of English and a remarkable memory. He was extremely versatile. He studied mathematics, Latin and French when resting from his work at the anvil. He later studied other languages, twenty in all, taught in an academy in a neighboring town, became a commercial traveller for a manufacturer in New Britain and then a merchant himself just before the commercial panic of 1837, in which he lost all his property. Then he went to Worcester where he resumed his earlier occupation as blacksmith, devoting his spare time to study.

By this time he was familiarly spoken of as "The Learned Blacksmith," a name that stayed with him through the rest of his life. In 1841, he began to write and lecture. He made a lecture tour to New York, Philadelphia, Baltimore, and Richmond, returning to his anvil during the summer. He became interested in the anti slavery movement and then in peace. Without having heard of

Worcester or Ladd or talked with any advocates of the cause, he prepared and delivered a lecture on peace in Tremont Temple, Boston, and then found himself claimed as a co-worker of the American Peace Society. He returned to Worcester and in the fall of 1844 started a weekly paper called "The Christian Citizen," devoted to the anti slavery cause, peace, temperance, and similar movements. He was a speaker at the peace meetings held in the western part of Massachusetts, in December, 1844, and the fall of 1845, and was elected a member of the executive committee of the American Peace Society at its annual meeting in May, 1845.

Burritt now came to the aid of Beckwith, who for seven years had borne the brunt of the burden, carrying the society on his shoulders, preaching Sundays, lecturing week days, visiting ecclesiastical bodies and colleges, conducting the correspondence of the society, writing for the press, and editing, circulating, and obtaining subscribers to the Advocate of Peace. June 23, 1845, Elihu Burritt was elected editor of the Advocate of Peace from the following September. Beginning with the first of January, 1846, he took charge of it for one year. He was to conduct it as the organ of the society, to be allowed to retain the profits if any, and to return it to the society on demand. He edited the paper through the year 1846 as a monthly containing short articles by various writers, with a few pages of news notes at the end of each number. The title was changed to "Advocate of Peace and Universal Brotherhood," the first number bearing the statement, Vol. I, No. 1, and appearing from Worcester, Mass. As an adjunct to the American Peace Society, the Worcester County Peace Society was formed Feb. 17, 1846, with Amasa Walker, president, Elihu Burritt corresponding secretary, and an agent appointed to visit every town in the county to present the cause of peace.

Though the Oregon question was satisfactorily settled, the Mexican war nearly disrupted the society. It was the first international war in which the United States had been engaged since the founding of the peace societies in 1815. The war was unpopular in New England. The requisition of the president upon the governors of these states for troops was but feebly responded to. Several members of the society took the position that the war was wrong, that the action of the United States in plunging into it was unconstitutional, that the society should take a position of opposition to the government, and demand the dissolution of the union, and block its efforts to bring the war to a satisfactory conclusion. To many this sounded like treason.

One of the resolutions presented at the annual meeting in May, 1846, by those who felt that the phraseology of the constitution endorsed their views, was as follows: "That all good men should repudiate the doctrine which requires us to support our government, right or wrong, in any war it may choose to undertake; and he who aids or sanctions any war which he deems wrong, becomes confederate with its crimes, and violates the plainest precepts of Christianity, and of common morality."[1] As Burritt put it: "The foundation principle of the constitution of the American Peace Society asserts the entire uncompromising opposition of all war to Christianity, we could not retain any official relation to that society for a moment after one jot or tittle of this vital principle had been abated. We could not keep rank for a moment with peace advocates of defensive wars."[2]

This resolution and the view expressed by Burritt were in strict conformity to Section 2 of the constitution stating the object of the society, and if enforced would exclude from membership moderate friends of peace, who had been welcomed in accordance with the resolutions of 1839. After long discussion, however, at an adjourned meeting, a substitute resolution was passed by a vote of about ten to one as follows: "That as citizens of the world, as friends of mankind, or as followers of Christ, we are for peace, opposed to war. We will do all in our power to promote peace and to oppose war; and we call upon all Christians, upon all friends of man, upon all men, to lift up a voice for peace, distinctly, decidedly, and unalterably."[3] The Society also voted, because of the connection of many members of the society with such matters, to devote itself strictly to the single object of abolishing international war, and to keep entirely distinct from the question of anti government, capital punishment, and other extraneous subjects.

Accordingly at the meeting of the executive committee, in June, 1846, one month after the annual meeting, Burritt, with S. E. Coues, the president since 1841, Blanchard, the treasurer since 1841, Thomas Brown, recording secretary, 1842-44, James L. Baker, recording secretary, 1844-46, Walter Chaning, E. W. Jack-

---

[1] Printed in Advocate of Peace, June, 1846, p. 130.
[2] Printed in Advocate of Peace, December, 1846, p. 275.
[3] Ibid., June, 1846, p. 137.

son, Benjamin D. Peck, and Amasa Walker, members of the executive committee, and others, withdrew from office.

The radicals had gone. The duty of reconstructing the society fell upon the moderates. Coues had paid all deficiencies during his term of office. With no money in the treasury and in debt, several of the members proposed a suspension of operations. But Beckwith, the only officer left in the society, had seen as dark days for the society before. He again came to its rescue. He reorganized it. He held himself responsible for the payment of all its bills. For four years he raised the money to pay the bills, acted as executive secretary. Dec. 16, 1846, Theodore Frelinghuysen of New York, a vice president of the society since 1839, was elected president, L. T. Stoddard was elected treasurer. The other vacancies were left unfilled.

A committee was appointed to draw up a new constitution, suitable for moderate friends of peace and based on the terms adopted by the general peace convention held in London in 1843, "regarding war as inconsistent with Christianity, and the true interests of mankind, the sole object of this society shall be to seek its abolition and promote universal and permanent peace."[1] The society announced that membership was open to any one willing to work for the entire abolition of war, that it was in accord with the principles adopted by the London Peace Society, and would circulate the best publications printed by that society, or written by Bogue, Worcester, Channing, Dymond, Upham, Coues, Hancock, Grimke, Ladd, or Sumner, recognized by everybody as orthodox leaders in the peace movement, and made strong efforts to rally together all friends of peace.

In October, the draft of a revised constitution was submitted for consideration. The old constitution however remained unchanged, as it was felt at the annual meeting in May, 1847, that any action in changing it might be misconstrued. Furthermore, Ladd in his will had expresed a desire that the constitution should not be changed; and many feared that a change might endanger his legacy to it, or bring about a controversy that might result in injury to the society. Accordingly, the society satisfied itself with merely reaffirming the resolutions of 1846.

Burritt continued the magazine until the end of the year when he returned it to the society. Aside from the 500 copies taken by

---

[1] Advocate of Peace, March and April, 1847, p. 88.

the American Peace Society, the circulation of the magazine had not been large, and it had been conducted at a loss. Beckwith again assumed its editorship, publishing it as a bi-monthly, resuming the old name of Advocate of Peace, and printing 2000 copies of each number.

Meanwhile the society was not idle. July 20, 1846, immediately after the declaration of war with Mexico, Beckwith, as correspond- ing secretary of the society, sent a letter to President Polk earnestly entreating him to end the war as soon as he could by recalling the American troops from Mexico, and then to offer to adjust the trouble by arbitration. This was followed by another letter seven days later urging him to accept the offer of Great Britain to mediate in the matter. A petition urging that measures be taken to end the war was sent to Congress, Dec. 7, and introduced into the House of Representatives Dec. 15, by Hon. Charles Hudson.[1] All persons desirous of having the war brought to an end immedi- ately were urged to petition Congress to that effect. Twenty-five hundred printed forms of a petition were sent to half as many individuals with the request that they obtain as many signatures to them as possible and send them to Congress. Several were so sent, the number unknown. To aid in creating the proper senti- ment, peace meetings were held in Boston in February, and in Ports- mouth in March, 1847, the former addressed by J. P. Blanchard, Rev. James Freeman Clarke, Charles Sumner, Theodore Parker and others. In December, 1847, the society sent another petition to Congress to end the war, followed in the spring of 1848 by petitions from thousands of others, one signed by nine thousand Quakers and another signed by three thousand Unitarians.

December 1, 1846, the society offered a prize of five hundred dol- lars for the best essay of from 150 to 250 pages in length on the war with Mexico, its origin, progress, and the whole sweep of its evils to all concerned, to be submitted within four months after the close of the war. The essays, twelve in number, were sent to the judges in November, 1848. In April, 1849, it was announced that the committee, consisting of Rev. W. W. Jenks, Baron Stow, and Prof. Simon Greenleaf of the Harvard Law School, had awarded the prize to Rev. Abiel Abbott Livermore, pastor of the Unitarian Church, in Keene, N. H. Another contestant was Judge Jay, who

---

[1] Copies of these communications are printed in Advocate of Peace, Febru- ary, 1847, pp. 16-19.

had his essay printed at his own expense, donating the stereotype plates thereof to the American Peace Society. Six thousand copies of it were disposed of within two months of the date of publication with the aid of the society and seventeen thousand by the end of the year, upwards of three thousand dollars being donated by friends to pay the cost of gratuitous distribution.

The essay by Livermore was printed at the end of the year and seven thousand copies distributed. Copies of both volumes were sent to the members of both houses of Congress and to the legislatures in the free states.

February 24, 1848, the society was incorporated by special act of the legislature of Massachusetts in order to be able to hold property and receive legacies and obviate the difficulties accompanying voluntary associations. The act was short and reads as follows: "Samuel Greele, John Tappan, Simon Greenleaf, their associates and successors, are hereby made a corporation by the name of the American Peace Society, for the promotion of national peace, with all the powers and privileges, and subject to all the duties, restrictions and liabilities set forth in the 44th chapter of the Revised Statutes. Section 2. The said corporation may take and hold real and personal estate, the net annual income of which shall not exceed the sum of three thousand dollars."

Chapter XI

THE PEACE CONGRESSES

At the London peace conference in 1843 it had been voted to hold another convention at a time and place to be determined by the London society, after communicating with the societies in Europe and the United States. Five years passed by, however, before such a congress was called. During this time the London society was actively at work spreading the peace idea on the continent, and the American Peace Society was equally as busy at home. In 1844, Beckwith suggested the formation of a universal peace society for the world, with a central committee at London;[1] but the society was too busy at home to get the plan actually under way.

At the annual meeting of the American Peace Society, May 26, 1845, on motion of Amasa Walker, it was "Resolved, That the American Peace Society cordially invite the friends of peace throughout the world to assemble by their delegates in the city of Boston on the last Wednesday of May, 1846, or at such time as may be deemed expedient on consultation with the friends of peace in other countries to hold a second general convention for the promotion of permanent and universal peace."[2] But the warlike feeling existing between England and the United States over the Oregon question prevented the resolution being carried out.

In the fall of 1845 when the feeling over the Oregon question was very tense, Joseph Crosfield, a merchant in Manchester, England, wrote in the Manchester Times an appeal to the merchants of England suggesting writing and not fighting and urging the transmission of friendly international letters to the merchants of America; thus recalling the action of citizens of Manchester, Leeds, and other cities in 1841 when, fearing a general European war, they had sent friendly resolutions and addresses to France.[3] The sugges-

[1] The plan is outlined in Advocate of Peace, May, 1844, pp. 193-203.
[2] Printed in Advocate of Peace, June, 1845, p. 62.
[3] A copy by one of the citizens of Manchester is printed in Advocate of Peace, December, 1841, p. 84.

tion was well received. Public meetings were held in several cities. The inhabitants of Boston, the citizens of Worcester, and Manchester, England, sent letters to Boston, Worcester, and New York, in America, while the citizens of Plymouth, Rochdale, and Margate, and the manufacturers and merchants of Huddersfield sent letters to Americans generally. These were answered by citizens of Plymouth, Mass., Portsmouth, N. H., and other cities in the same words of kindness,[1] and good will as the original letters.

These letters were sent through Burritt, then editor of the Advocate of Peace and by him forwarded to their respective destinations. Copies of them were reprinted as olive leaves and sent to all newspapers in the country. From this Burritt got the idea of a universal brotherhood to promote political and social improvement, to abolish war and the war spirit, which he introduced into the Advocate of Peace in March, 1846, page 19, and incorporated as a department of the magazine in April, 1846. The name of brotherhood was taken from a speech delivered by George Bancroft in Philadelphia, in 1842, in which he used the expression " the Brotherhood of Nations."

Out of this Burritt created the League of Universal Brotherhood, July 29, which, with the approval of his English friends, he launched at the general temperance convention in London, Aug. 5, 1846, to which he went as a delegate June 16, eleven days after his withdrawal from the American Peace Society. He had intended to remain in London only three months, but the growth of the League was so rapid that he remained there for three years. Through the aid of Joseph Sturge, who was interested in all philanthropies as well as peace, he began the publication of "The Bond of Brotherhood," as an exponent of the objects of the new association, which was formally organized in London, May, 1847, with headquarters at Birmingham. It soon had a membership of twenty thousand persons who had signed a pledge[2] avowing the strongest doctrines of peace, and this in the face of the strong warlike feeling existing at the time.

This was an age of congresses and world conventions. Such had recently been held in Italy, Germany, and England in the interest of science, temperance, anti slavery, and prison reform. Following

[1] Copies of several of these friendly letters are printed in the Advocate of Peace, March, 1846, pp. 73-79, and May, 1846, pp. 123-27.
[2] A copy of the pledge is printed in the Advocate of Peace, October, 1846, p. 243; Elihu Burritt, by Charles Northend, pp. 26, 27.

the civil war in Switzerland in 1847 and in the midst of the revolutions which followed one another in quick succession the next year, Burritt—but let us quote his own words: "It was in Manchester, the day after the revolutionary outbreak in France—Feb. 24, 1848—that in conference with a few individuals of that city, it was resolved to try the experiment of holding a little upper-room meeting in Paris, of such friends of peace from different countries as should be disposed to attend it. At that time we dared not aspire to call the proposed meeting a peace convention, but a peace conference."[1]

The opportunity for starting such a movement seemed very favorable since the new regime in France had raised as its banner: "Liberty, Equality, Fraternity." Burritt immediately went to Paris where he conferred with prominent men in regard to the proposed convention. He found the idea sypmathetically received. On his return to England a week later he made arrangements for delegates to the convention. May 29, he secured a resolution from the League of Brotherhood in favor of the plan.

In August, Burritt issued a circular explaining the character which the convention should assume and suggested topics that were proper for consideration at such a gathering. He obtained the promise of the London Peace Society to unite with him in the demonstration provided nothing was done inconsistent with broad Christian ground, and all questions of a political nature should be avoided. August 14, he went to Paris to make final arrangements for the meeting. But due to the political excitement there at the time he reluctantly came to the conclusion that it was neither prudent nor practicable to attempt to hold the convention in that city. Accordingly he went to Brussels, where with representatives from the London society a meeting was arranged with M. Rogier, the prime minister, who after understanding their plan expressed himself as willing to help them in every way, gave them letters to M. Visschers, a well known Belgian philanthropist, who formed a committee to act with the English delegation.

Arrangements were made and the meeting opened Sept. 20, for three days, as originally planned. About three hundred persons attended the meetings. One hundred thirty came from England. They met in London, Sept. 19, went by special boat to Ostend where they were welcomed by the mayor, alderman and

---

[1] Elihu Burritt, by Charles Northend, p. 89.

citizens of the town. They proceeded to Brussels by a special train ordered by the Belgian government. But two delegates represented the United States—Burritt and Henry Clapp of Cincinnati.

The meetings were at the Salle de la Société de la Grande Harmonie, which was finely decorated for the occasion. Visschers, the chairman of the provisional committee, was chosen president of the congress, Burritt a vice president, and Henry Clapp a secretary. The meetings of this and succeeding congresses, as had been done at the convention at London in 1843, were opened by silent prayer.

Four papers were read, three written by Englishmen and the other by Burritt, "On the Propriety of Convoking a Congress of Nations, the object of which shall be to form an International Code, in order, as far as possible, to settle on a Satisfactory Basis, Moot Questions, and generally to secure Peace." The discussion of these papers was by members of parliament, ministers, and university professors, from France, Belgium, Holland, England, and Turin, followed by an address by the President of Liberia.

Among the resolutions framed was one to adopt proper measures to abolish war and to settle international troubles by arbitration, one for a congress of nations, one for universal disarmament, and one for another conference to be held when and where it might seem to be proper.[1] The congress closed with a reception.

Ratification meetings followed in London, Birmingham, Manchester, and other cities in England. A deputation of five, including Burritt, waited upon Lord John Russell, prime minister of England, October 30, told him about the congress, the objects they had in view, and presented him with an address from the congress, delivered by Visschers the president of the congress. Lord John Russell received the deputation with courtesy, expressed his interest in preserving peace, and his approval of the congress. Addressing himself to Burritt he said in regard to stipulated arbitration, "If the United States should make such proposal to the British government, it would be taken into their most serious consideration."[2]

The success of this congress encouraged the League of Brotherhood and the London Peace Society to plan for another and larger one to be held at Paris in 1849. To carry out the plan they elected

[1] The resolutions are printed in Advocate of Peace, July, 1849, pp. 110, 111.
[2] Quoted in Advocate of Peace, January-February, 1849, pp. 16, 17.

a joint committee representing the two societies; but the work of preparation for this as well as for the succeeding congresses was left to Burritt, as the secretary of the League, and Richard, as the secretary of the peace society. In connection with the campaign of Cobden to urge Parliament to make an arbitration treaty with the powers of Europe, one hundred and fifty meetings were held in England during the winter of 1848-49, at each one of which references were made to the proposed meeting in Paris.

Burritt obtained a subscription of five thousand pounds, opened communication with Francisque Bouvet and Ernest Lacan, both of whom had attended the Brussels congress and approved holding the meeting in Paris. Through their influence several men of prominence in Paris became interested in the matter. Together Burritt and Richard went to Paris April 18, 1849, to make preliminary arrangements for the congress. There with the aid of Bouvet and Visschers, the president of the Belgian congress of the year before, they secured approval of Victor Hugo, well known author, Athanase Coquerel, eloquent Protestant preacher, Emile de Girardin, most important political editor in France, Horace Say, councillor, Frédéric Bastiat, noted political economist, the Abbé Deguerry, Lamartine the poet statesman, Wolowski, member of the national assembly, and Viscount de Melum a philanthropist, who agreed to act on the committee of organization to complete the necessary arrangements for the congress.

They returned to London, May 8, and opened correspondence with the American Peace Society to secure the presence of a large delegation from America. Circulars were issued throughout Great Britain, June 26.[1] Another trip was taken to Paris, July 5, when final arrangements were made and the cooperation secured of De Tocqueville, Minister of Foreign Affairs, who obtained from Dufaure, Minister of the Interior, authority to hold the assembly.[2]

The convention lasted from Aug. 22 to 24, 1849, and is generally considered to have been the most successful convention in the series, though the cartoonists made fun of it and the magazines and newspapers of the time spoke of it critically and sneeringly. The convention consisted of delegates appointed by peace societies, branches of the League of Brotherhood, churches, public meetings

[1] A copy is printed in Report of Proceedings of the Second General Peace Congress, pp. 4, 5.
[2] The letter of authorization is printed in ibid., p. 6.

called for the purpose of electing delegates, officers and representatives of religious, philanthropic, civic, municipal and literary organizations and individuals accepted by the committee.

Naturally the largest delegation came from England, representing all the important benevolent societies in the kingdom. Six hundred and seventy persons from all parts of the kingdom led by Cobden occupied two special trains to Dover, and two steamers from there to Boulogne, where they were met by crowds, with a reception by the town authorities and an address by the mayor. The government very kindly dispensed with passports and exempted their baggage from custom house examination. Aside from the English delegation, there were twenty from the United States, twenty-one from Belgium, about one hundred from France, and about thirty from other countries, including one each from Montreal, Halifax, and Guatemala. The meetings were held in the Rue de la Chaussée d'Antin, the hall seating two thousand persons, and several of the meetings taxed the hall to its full capacity.

Victor Hugo, with Coquerel on his left and Deguerry on his right, presided at the meetings and gave the most eloquent address of his life, first using an expression frequently heard since,—the United States of Europe.[1] Nine vice presidents were appointed, including Cobden and Hindley from England, Hon. Charles Durkee, M. C. from Wisconsin, Amasa Walker, member of the Massachusetts legislature, and Visschers from Belgium. Four secretaries were appointed, including Richard and Burritt. The minutes of the meeting were kept in English and French. Letters were received from the American Peace Society, the archbishop of Paris, who was made honorary president of the congress, from Chevalier, Professor of Political Economy in the Collége de France, Tissot and Thierry, members of the French Academy, Béranger, the poet, Dufaure, minister of the Interior, Lacrosse, minister of Public Works, Ferdinand de Lesseps, builder of the Suez Canal, Saint-Hilaire, member of the National Institute of France, Molina, minister from Costa Rica, six German cities, professors in universities of Bonn, Königsberg, Utrecht, Jena, Prague, and Cologne, and many others.

Papers were read on international arbitration and on a congress of nations by Burritt, which were thoroughly discussed by the congress. Resolutions were passed requesting nations to submit to

[1] The address is printed in the Report, pp. 10-14; in Advocate of Peace, November, 1849, pp. 136-40.

arbitration all differences that arise between them, to call their attention to the necessity of a general and simultaneous disarmament, in favor of a congress of nations, against loans and taxes for the prosecution of wars of conquest, for the improvement of international communication, to eradicate international hatreds, and directing an address to be made to all the nations.

Every courtesy was shown the delegates. And the cordial thanks of the congress were voted to the French government by the congress. De Tocqueville, minister of Foreign Affairs, held a reception in honor of the congress at which were present members of the diplomatic corps and the national assembly. Lacrosse, minister of Public Works, opened to the visitors the national palaces, museums, and public establishments in Paris and the fountains of Versailles and St. Cloud. The English delegates gave a public breakfast to the Americans in the old Tennis Hall at Versailles where Cobden presented each American delegate with a New Testament in French. The responses were made by Burritt, Dr. Allen, ex-president of Bowdoin College, Rev. James Freeman Clarke, Congressman Clapp and Amasa Walker.

A week following the congress, Sept. 1, a delegation of ten, including Victor Hugo, Visschers, and Hindley, met Louis Napoleon, the President of the French Republic, presented him with a copy of the resolutions passed at the congress and urged upon him the advisability of a reduction of armaments. The president expressed his concurrence with the views of the congress, but said that their execution must be deferred to some more seasonable opportunity, for the condition of Europe at the time presented obstacles to their execution. Throughout the fall many ratification meetings were held in England and the United States. Those at London, Birmingham and Manchester were attended by audiences of from five to seven thousand persons including deputations from France and Hungary.

At Paris it had been decided to hold the next congress in Germany, Frankfort, if possible, a city near the border line where Talleyrand had planned a peace congress under the direction of Napoleon, and in a country without peace societies or even any peace sentiment. Strong efforts were made in the United States to arouse interest in this next congress. On Washington's birthday, 1850, Charles Sumner as chairman, and Amasa Walker and Burritt as secretaries of the peace congress committee for the United States circularized the country urging every state, town, congressional district, church, literary and religious body to elect delegates to the congress.[1] During the winter Burritt personally spent two months visiting eighteen states, from New England south to Washington and west to Missouri and Wisconsin, for the purpose of securing delegates to the Frankfort congress.

Burritt returned to England May 15, and the next month he and Richard, as the secretaries of the peace congress committee, went to Frankfort by way of Paris and Brussels where they were encouraged by the hopeful spirit displayed. At Frankfort they secured the sympathy and cooperation of Dr. Varrentrapp, who formed a local committee of nine in Frankfort, consisting of ministers of the French Reformed, Lutheran and German Reformed churches, president of the Jewish Industrial College, inspector of a Catholic School, a banker, a member of the Frankfort senate, a physician, and a professor at Heidelberg, thus representing all classes and interests. They easily secured authority from the Frankfort senate to hold the meetings and obtained from the Lutherans the use of their church, St. Paul's, for the occasion. Visschers, Richard, and Burritt visited the principal cities of Germany where they were well received by professors, ministers, authors and editors, who displayed great interest in the principles and projects of peace.

The London society held no meetings to secure delegates, but issued a circular outlining their plans. Visschers issued a circular from Brussels and Garnier another from Paris, both in French, and the committee at Frankfort a third in German. Peace Societies, leagues of brotherhood, local bodies of various kinds were requested to send delegates. Nearly a thousand such were elected. The English delegates—five hundred in number—as before went in a gates from the United States.
American Peace Society resulted in the presence of thirty-six delebody. They passed through France, Belgium, and Prussia without passports or an examination of their baggage. The efforts of the
The congress was held for three days, Aug. 22-24, 1850. The meetings were presided over by Herr Jaup, ex-prime minister of Hesse Darmstadt. Eight vice presidents were elected including Visschers of Belgium, Cobden and Hindley from England, Rev. Dr.

[1] A copy of the circular is printed in Advocate of Peace, March-April, 1850, pp. 201-03.

Hitchcock, president, and Rev. Dr. Hall, professor in Amherst College. Eight secretaries were also selected including Dr. Varrentrapp for Germany, Richard for England, Burritt and Prof. C. D. Cleveland of Philadelphia for America. As before, all meetings were opened with silent prayer. Letters were read from Victor Hugo, Bastiat, Say, Baron von Humboldt, the scientist, Abbé Deguerry and others.

No papers were read, but speeches were made on the resolutions introduced by Cobden, Hindley, Sturge, and Richard from England, President Hitchock, E. H. Chapin, Artemus Bullard and Burritt from the United States, Girardin, Garnier, and Coquerel from Paris, Dr. Bodenstedt from Germany, Visschers from Belgium, Madonao from Piedmont, Ledderstedt, Swedish consul at the Cape of Good Hope, Drucker from Holland, George Copway, an Indian chief from the United States, and others. The discussions were carried on in three languages, thus making the proceedings somewhat tedious. Resolutions were passed against war, duelling, and granting loans to belligerents, favoring arbitration, non intervention and disarmament, and calling a congress to form a code of international law.[1]

As at Paris, the public buildings and institutions were opened to the delegates and the hospitality of the city accorded them for which the delegates unitedly expressed their thanks. Before separating, the English delegates presented each member of the Amrican delegation with a copy of the Bible printed in German for which Henry Garnett of New York replied for the delegation.

As a side issue to the convention it might be mentioned that it received a formal request from Schleswig-Holstein to mediate in its dispute with Denmark. The convention voted that it did not have the power to act in a mediatory capacity. Three members, however, Burritt, Sturge and Frederick Wheeler, on their own responsibility went to the seat of conflict. They were well received, but events rendered attempted arbitration proceedings useless.

It was decided to hold the next congress in connection with the World's International Exhibition of the Industry of all Nations to be held at London in 1851, the first of its kind, where it was hoped that the question of international peace might gain new followers. A conference of the friends of peace was held in London, Nov. 28, 1850. The old peace congress committee was reappointed and the

---

[1] The resolutions are printed in Advocate of Peace, November-December, 1850, p. 292.

work of preparation was carried on strenuously. Extensive correspondence was carried on with fellow laborers in France, Belgium and the United States as to the best plans to adopt for making the convention a success.

Following the Frankfort convention, Burritt revived the olive leaf system used in the United States. He arranged with forty papers in Paris, Copenhagen, Stockholm, Vienna, Madrid, Germany, Holland, and Italy to publish monthly "an olive leaf for the people." A column and a half of paragraphs taken from standard authors relative to peace, at a cost of about six dollars each, paid for by groups of ladies of which two years later there were 112 in England and ten in the United States. Through these olive leaves Burritt advertised the congress. The London society prepared several publications in French, German, and Italian and circulated them on the continent as widely as possible. Visschers distributed circulars of invitation in Belgium, Garnier in France, Varrentrapp in Germany, and the American Peace Society in the United States, all urging as many to attend the congress as possible. At its annual meeting in May, 1851, the latter named society voted to take a more active part in the congresses than heretofore, to recommend that they meet biennially instead of annually, that the congress be under the general management of a central committee appointed by the various national societies, and that the next congress be held in the United States.[1]

The London society sent a special circular to the clergy in London and elsewhere asking their sympathy and prayers and requesting them to preach on the subject of international peace on the Sunday before the congress met. Meetings were held and delegates were elected, representing civic, religious, philanthropic and literary societies. June 17, 1851, Cobden introduced a motion into Parliament to prevent rivalry in warlike preparations in time of peace.

The congress met July 22-24, 1851, in Exeter Hall, the largest in London, with a seating capacity of four thousand. The hall was frequently filled to capacity. Twelve hundred delegates were present, including all the British peace leaders and twenty members of Parliament, including John Bright, Brotherton, and Ewart; sixty, including Horace Greeley and Beckwith, from sixteen of the Amer-

---

[1] The resolutions are printed in Advocate of Peace, July-August, 1851, p. 112.

ican states; thirty-eight from Germany, a large delegation from France, and representatives from Belgium, Holland, Sweden, Norway, Austria, Italy, Spain, and Guatemala.

The congress was called to order by Richard. Sir David Brewster, the eminent scientist, founder of the British Association for the Advancement of Science, and a member of the London society, presided. Eight vice presidents were elected including Cobden and Hindley from England, Visschers from Belgium, Hon. E. Jackson and Judge Niles from the United States. Nine secretaries were elected including Burritt and Beckwith from the United States and Richard from England. As before, all sessions were opened with silent prayer. Letters were received from Count Dumellis, president of the Chamber of the Department of Turin, Victor Hugo, Girardin, Garnier, Coquerel, Bouvet, Carnot, St. Hilaire, from France, Bodenstedt and Jaup from Germany, Leone Levi, Leigh Hunt, and Thomas Carlyle from England, and from the governing officials of Sheffield, Dunfermline and Turin. The presence of fifteen workingmen from Paris produced a profound impression upon the congress.

As at Frankfort, no set papers were read; but resolutions were presented and discussed, a set speech being delivered by the mover of each resolution. Beckwith talked upon the subject of stipulated arbitration. Burritt spoke again for a congress of nations, known by that time as the American plan. Visschers of Belgium, Cobden of England, Cormenin, Bouvet and Coquerel spoke on the various resolutions introduced. Resolutions were passed against war, standing armies, interventions, and loans for war use, and in favor of arbitration and the preparation of a code of international law.[1] Individual receptions were given by Hindley, Cobden, and Sturge, and a final reception to all the foreign delegates by the English delegates.

And here ended the first series of peace congresses, for though it was voted at London to hold another congress in 1852, at that time all the energies of the friends of peace in England were vainly spent in an attempt to prevent an increase of armaments in both France and England. The proclamation of the second empire toward the close of the year 1852, and the outbreak of the war between Russia and Turkey the next year led to the Crimean war which the London

---

[1] The resolutions are printed in the Advocate of Peace, September-October. 1851, p. 137.

society tried in vain to prevent. It held peace conventions at
Manchester, Jan. 27, 1853, and Edinburgh, Oct. 12 and 13, 1853,
attended by Cobden, Richard, Bright, Sturge, and several members
of Parliament, the latter convention being presided over by the Lord
Provost of the city.

Chapter XII

STIPULATED ARBITRATION

WHILE Burritt and the London society were holding these congresses, others were trying to put their teachings into effect. Cobden who had been appointed by the congress at Brussels in 1848 to urge the British Parliament to make an arbitration treaty with the powers of Europe, held many meetings in London during the following winter where the question in all its phases was thoroughly discussed. As a result more than one thousand petitions containing two hundred thousand names reached the House of Commons, praying for the adoption of stipulated arbitration by that body. On the motion in that house that Parliament request the Queen to direct the Secretary of State for Foreign Affairs to enter into communication with other states and invite them to concur in treaties to settle disputes by arbitration,[1] eighty-one votes were cast in its favor, thus showing that a large minority of the English people were thinking favorably upon the subject.

While Cobden was discussing the question in London, Francisque Bouvet, one of the vice presidents of the Brussels convention, introduced a proposition into the French Chamber, Jan. 8, 1849, directing the French government to propose to the governments in Europe and America that they unite in calling a congress to sit in Constantinople, May 1, 1849, to discuss the question of proportional disarmament, the abolition of war, and the substitution of arbitration therefor.[2] It was referred to the Committee on Foreign Affairs which in an elaborate report expressed itself as in favor of the idea but refused to recommend it on the ground that the disturbed condition of Europe rendered the calling of such a congress inexpedient at that time.

Following Bouvet by eight days, Congressman Amos Tuck of New Hampshire introduced a resolution into the House of Representatives directing the Committee on Foreign Affairs to inquire

[1] The motion is printed in Advocate of Peace, July-October, 1849, p. 113.
[2] The proposition is printed in ibid., 112, 113.

into the expediency of authorizing the Secretary of State to open correspondence with foreign governments on the subject of procuring treaty stipulations for the reference of all future disputes to arbitration on the establishment of a congress of nations.[1] Immediately, a joint committee was appointed by the American Peace Society and the League of Brotherhood to urge upon Congress the necessity of considering the resolution. It was hoped to be able to make a demonstration so strong that Congress would be compelled to pay attention to the request. An address to the public was issued urging help in this matter.[2] A big meeting was held in Park Street Church, March 28, which adopted resolutions in favor of a congress of nations, but because of the lateness of the session it produced no particular impression upon Congress.

During the next eight years every session of Congress received petitions from the society and its friends requesting that attention be paid to this subject. On the election of Zachary Taylor as president of the United States, Beckwith wrote him, Dec. 1, 1848, suggesting that stipulated arbitration or a clause binding the nation to settle its international differences by an umpire be introduced into every future treaty made by the United States, that a congress of nations composed of diplomatic delegates from different states be called to frame a code of international law to be binding on all nations, and that a high court of nations be established with power to interpret and apply the code. He called attention to the statement of Lord John Russell, premier of Great Britain, made Oct. 30, 1848, a month before, to a deputation from the Brussels congress.[3] Whether influenced by this letter or by the general feeling on the subject, President Taylor, in his inaugural address, said that the government ought "to exhaust every resort of honorable diplomacy before appealing to arms." This was followed by the address of Charles Sumner at the annual meeting of the society, in May, 1849, so generally considered his masterpiece in favor of a congress of nations and a high court of judicature.[4] Five thousand copies of it were printed and circulated immediately, and later at the seventy-fifth anniversary of the battle of Bunker Hill, Edward Everett referred feelingly to the question of peace.

[1] The resolution is printed in Advocate of Peace, May-June, 1849, p. 70, and July, 1849, p. 112.
[2] Partially printed in Advocate of Peace, May-June, 1849, pp. 52, 53.
[3] Letter printed in full in Advocate of Peace, January, 1849, pp. 3-6.
[4] Printed in Advocate of Peace, July-October, 1849, pp. 73-125.

The time seemed propitious to bring the attention of Congress to the subject. Accordingly, the society sent a petition to Congress, December 18, 1849,[1] urging the consideration of a congress of nations or of international treaties as a means to avoid war, and printed in its journal a form of petition which it urged all friends of peace to send to both houses of Congress.[2] It was desired to have copies sent from every state in the union.

A convention was held in Rutland, Vt., Feb. 14, 1850, which adopted a resolution requesting the representatives in Congress to press the matter of a joint resolution for peace measures as energetically as possible,[3] and urged sending petitions to Congress to carry out the suggestion contained in the resolution. Later in the year the Vermont legislature passed a resolution requesting their representatives in Congress to urge the president to propose to all nations the establishment of permanent boards to settle international disputes and directing the governor to notify governors of all other states of the resolution.[4]

At the next session of Congress a new petition of the society, dated November, 1850,[5] backed by several hundred other petitions received by Senator Robert C. Winthrop of Massachusetts, was by him formally laid before the Senate, Dec. 16, 1850, and referred to the Committee on Foreign Relations. Gov. Foote of Mississippi, chairman of that committee, brought in a report, Feb. 5, 1851, declaring it proper and desirable for the government to secure in treaties a provision referring misunderstandings to umpires before resorting to war.[6] Beckwith spent a month in Washington, in the interest of the petition. He took the report of the committee to the president, the cabinet, and some of the foreign ministers resident in Washington, finding them all to be in favor of the proposition. The lateness of the report however, made it impossible for it to be considered at the short session of Congress.

Encouraged by the reception of these petitions, the society determined to work for stipulated arbitration as the one thing most likely to be obtained. They urged every one in the country to send two petitions to Washington, one to his representative in the House

[1] Printed in Advocate of Peace, November-December, 1849, p. 154.
[2] The form of petition is given in ibid., p. 155.
[3] The resolution is printed in ibid., March-April, 1850, p. 203.
[4] The resolution is printed in ibid., January-February, 1851, p. 29.
[5] Printed in ibid., March-April, 1851, pp. 50, 51.
[6] A copy of the report is given in ibid., March-April, 1851, pp. 52, 53 and July, 1853, pp. 312-314.

and the other to his senator,[1] requesting the insertion of an arbitration clause in every treaty hereafter to be made by the United States. Dec. 3, 1851, the society sent in its petition,[2] and local petitions from all over the country flowed in a stream to Congress throughout its session of 1851-52; but no action was taken on them. However, the continued agitation was bringing forth fruit. In 1852, the Free Soil Party at its convention in Pittsburgh placed a plank in its platform as follows: "That we recommend the introduction into all treaties hereafter to be negotiated between the United States and foreign nations of some provision for amicable settlement of difficulties by a resort to decisive arbitration."[3]

In the fall of 1852 the society prepared a volume on "Stipulated Arbitration as a Feasible and Effective Substitute for War," a copy of which it sent to each governor and legislator in the New England states. Beckwith followed it up by personally interviewing these members, seeking their aid in obtaining favorable action on a new petition for stipulated arbitration which was presented to each house of Congress in December, 1852. As a result of his efforts, the legislatures of five of the New England states took favorable action on the petition and passed resolutions accordingly—Vermont,[4] in the fall of 1852, Rhode Island,[5] in January, 1853, Maine,[5] in March, Massachusetts,[6] in April, and Connecticut,[7] in June. The New Hampshire legislature referred the resolution to the next legislature.

The petitions sent to Congress in December, 1852, by the society and others from all over the country in response to the request of the society, were by the Senate referred to the Committee on Foreign Relations. Judge Underwood, of Kentucky, chairman of that committee made a long and elaborate report[8] to the Senate, Feb. 23, 1853, on the memorials, recommending the adoption of the following resolution: "Resolved, That the Senate advise the president to secure, whenever it may be practicable, a stipulation in all treaties

---

[1] Form of petition is given in Advocate of Peace, December, 1851, p. 187.
[2] A copy is printed in Advocate of Peace, January, 1852, pp. 14, 15.
[3] Printed in ibid., October, 1852, p. 158.
[4] A copy of the petition of the society to the legislature with a copy of the report of the special committee is printed in Advocate of Peace, January, 1853, pp. 216-18; the report alone in ibid., July 1853, p. 315.
[5] The resolution is printed in ibid., July, 1853, p. 316.
[6] The report and resolution are printed in ibid., pp. 316-20.
[7] The resolutions are printed in ibid., August, 1853, pp. 329, 330.
[8] Printed in ibid., April, 1853, pp. 257-67.

hereafter entered into with other nations, providing for the adjustment of any misunderstanding or controversy that may arise
between the contracting parties, by referring the same to the decision of disinterested and impartial arbitrators, to be mutually
chosen." But again, due to the lateness of the session, no action was
taken on the report.

At the instance of the society the state associations of Congregational churches in Massachusetts, Maine, Rhode Island, Connecticut,
and Vermont, during the summer of 1853, passed resolutions in
favor of stipulated arbitration.[1]

Then the society suggested that a clause be inserted in the fishery
treaty, at the time pending between England and the United States,
binding both parties in case of misunderstanding to submit the
matter in dispute to an impartial arbitrator. Shortly before leaving
office President Fillmore and Secretary of State Everett, after an
examination of the question, stated their willingness to insert such a
clause in the treaty; whereupon the London society sent a deputation to Lord Clarendon, the British Secretary for Foreign Affairs,
and persuaded him to instruct the British minister in Washington
to the same effect.

This led the society to redouble its efforts with the new administration. At the opening of Congress, Dec. 1, 1853, it sent a petition
to each house again urging the adoption of the principle of stipulated arbitration and requested all the friends of peace throughout
the country to send similar petitions to that body. At the same time
preparation was made to lay the matter before the president
directly. The society requested thousands of ministers in more than
twenty states of the union to circulate petitions, and, after
obtaining a reasonable number of signatures, to send them to an
agent of the society, one having been appointed in each state, who
would prepare a memorial to be sent with the petitions to the
president, requesting him "to propose to all nations with whom we
have intercourse a provision in our treaties with them for referring
to the decision of an umpire all misunderstandings that they be satisfactorily adjusted by amicable negotiations."[2] It was thought
that these state memorials would attract the attention of the

[1] The resolutions are printed in ibid., August, 1853, pp. 327-29.
[2] As suggested in a form of the petition given in Advocate of Peace, November, 1853, p. 370.

president and cause him to see that the more intelligent citizens of the country were in favor of arbitration.

November 23, 1853, one week before sending the petition to Congress, the society sent its petition to the President, expecting the state petitions to follow as soon as they were prepared. In this petition the society urged that the President consider favorably this proposed substitute for war and "more especially that in the important treaty now pending between Great Britain and the United States you will propose to the British government the insertion of a provision for referring to the decisions of umpires all future misunderstandings that can not be satifactorily adjusted by negotiation."[1]

Two treaties followed, one June 30, 1854, with Mexico relative to the transit of persons across the Isthmus of Tehuantepec in which the principle of arbitration was to be applied to future misunderstandings, and the other, Sept. 11, 1854, with Great Britain relative to the New Foundland fishery question, providing for arbitration in disputes that might arise there under, but not to other misunderstandings in the future. Thus the five year campaign of the society had brought some results, though it had not obtained all it wanted, —arbitration in all disputes of every kind that might arise in the future. At the session of Congress, opening in December, 1854, the society renewed its campaign urging the friends of peace wherever living to send petitions to Congress asking that a clause for stipulated arbitration be inserted in all future treaties made.[2]

Again, in December, 1855, and December, 1856, similar petitions were sent to Congress, only to be ignored. The financial panic of 1857 and the consequent reduction in income to the society, together with the disturbed political condition over the Kansas situation, resulting in the predominance of the slavery question, caused the executive Committee, Nov. 24, 1857, to vote it inexpedient to continue the petitions to Congress for the present.

The society, however, was greatly interested in the Treaty of Paris, made Mar. 30, 1856, at the end of the Crimean War, feeling that its basic work, supported as it had been by Burritt in Europe, was in part responsible for certain provisions inserted in that treaty. Due to the insistence of the British delegates supported by a committee of the London society—Hindley, Sturge, and Richard—who

---

[1] A copy of the petition is printed in Advocate of Peace, January, 1854, pp. 13, 14.

[2] The form of petition is given in ibid., December, 1854, p. 189.

visited Paris and urged the insertion of an arbitration section in the treaty, a clause was inserted recommending the powers to refer to arbitration certain causes of difference that might arise in the future, thus recognizing the principle of arbitration. The insertion of other clauses abolishing privateering, a neutral flag to cover enemy's goods, requiring blockades to be effective to be binding, and declaring free ships to cover free goods except contraband of war, must have been due to the facts and views so long diffused by the friends of peace.

Chapter XIII

A DECADE OF PROGRESS

THE finances of the society had never been in good condition. In the earlier years the society had generally ended each year in debt, which Ladd had usually paid. At his death he left one thousand dollars to pay the debts of the society. For the next five years Coues had tried to pay the deficits, and when he stopped in 1846, the society was three thousand dollars in debt. Thereupon, Beckwith, who for upwards of a year had raised his own salary, now agreed to act as financial collector for the society in connection with his duties as corresponding secretary and editor.

An outline of the method of procedure adopted by this agreement is as follows: No debts to be contracted without adequate means to pay them; no measures to be undertaken, no expenses to be incurred, and no money to be paid out except in execution of the votes of the executive committee; no bills to be paid until approved by a committee on bills; for all liabilities incurred under the direction of the committee, the corresponding secretary acting as financial agent was to be held personally responsible. The entire income of the society was appropriated first to pay the expenses thus incurred and if this should be insufficient in any one year, the secretary or financial agent was to be allowed time to raise the necessary funds and to complete any measures undertaken by him in pursuance of the votes of the committee. The secretary was to receive and disburse the money of the society and lay before the committee a quarterly report of all receipts, disbursements, and outstanding liabilities. The committee therefore held quarterly meetings to survey and adjust the financial concerns of the society. Agents of the society received a stipulated compensation and were instructed to render quarterly accounts of their receipts and expenditures. The secretary laid all vouchers before the committee for inspection and then passed them to the treasurer for preservation. The annual reports of the treasurer were submitted to auditors.

All questions of importance were commonly referred to sub committees for investigation.[1] It will thus be seen that the secretary was personally responsible for all bills of the society. He collected and disbursed all funds, presenting vouchers and receipts therefor to the treasurer after their approval by the executive committee.

Beckwith kept the expenses down for the first two years after the plan had been adopted, when a change in procedure was proposed. It was desired to have all money collected turned over to the treasurer immediately and paid out by him on order of the committee. Beckwith objected to this plan since it rendered him unable to pay bills already contracted, and accordingly he ceased to make any collections. At the end of three months, November 15, 1849, the society found itself one thousand dollars in debt and the new plan was therefore abandoned. Beckwith again undertook the task of collector with the result that at the annual meeting in May, 1851, the treasurer reported all bills paid.

But Beckwith's financial policy was not satisfactory to certain members of the society, and at the annual meeting just referred to, a committee of twelve, representing four religious denominations, was appointed to investigate the criticism of their financial system and the further charge that the society was being run by one man. An attempt to elect a new set of officers failed, and, to quote from the record, "the meeting became a scene of wild confusion and uproar, until it was announced by a member of the society that the police had been sent for."[2]

At the next annual meeting the committee of twelve reported in favor of continuing the old system with slight modifications.[3] The old board of officers was reelected, the former policy continued, and at the annual meeting, May 29, 1854, all back indebtedness was reported paid. The executive committee appointed a standing committee on publications in addition to the committee on bills and on advice. William C. Brown, the recording secretary, was appointed office agent to take care of the depository and to attend to office details, thus releasing Beckwith for editorial and field work, whose salary was raised from $1200 to $1600 a year, Sept. 17, 1852.

The reports of the treasurer from 1847 to 1860 are as follows:

[1] As outlined in Advocate of Peace, June-July, 1852, pp. 122, 123.
[2] Advocate of Peace, July-August, 1851, p. 123.
[3] For the report see Advocate of Peace, June-July, 1852, pp. 119-22. An explanation by the executive committee of their method of procedure appears on pp. 122-24.

Year ending May 1	Receipts	Expenditures	Balance on Hand
1847	$3387.31	$3404.43	$ 17.12[1]
1848	4011.91	3936.18	74.73
1849	3697.48	3680.62	16.96
1850	6187.35	6204.31	9.77
1851	3394.09	3241.42	162.44
1852	2121.64	1965.22	156.42
1853	3248.75	3240.49	164.68
1854	5157.43	5051.25	270.86
1855	5074.70	4771.47	574.09
1856	4172.38	4629.34	117.13
1857	4157.27	4218.67	55.73
1858	2822.33	2762.38	93.18
1859	4670.20	4619.43	163.95
1860	3267.35	3223.02	208.28

[1] Deficit.

In this table, as in all financial tables in this volume, the amounts given in each year in the column headed "Receipts" do not include the balance on hand at the beginning of the year.

Following the resignation of Coues in 1846, Theodore Frelinghuysen was elected president of the society in December. He served only until the next annual meeting when he was succeeded by Anson G. Phelps, who served for one year only. William Jay of New York, son of John Jay, and the author of the plan for stipulated arbitration, served as president from 1848 until his death in 1858. President Francis Wayland of Brown University served as president from 1859 to 1861. J. P. Blanchard, who resigned as recording secretary in October, 1841, was succeeded by Lewis T. Stoddard to May, 1842, Thomas Drown, 1842-44, and James L. Baker, 1844-46. No one was appointed in 1846. William C. Brown served from 1847 to 1870. J. P. Blanchard served as treasurer from 1841 to 1847, and John Field from 1847 to 1870. Among others who served the society before the Civil War, some of whose names have not been previously mentioned were Hon. Samuel Fessenden of Portland, Me., and J. P. Fairbanks of St. Johnsbury, Vt., as vice presidents; and Charles Brooks, Rev. A. L. Stone, John A. Andrew, Thomas Gaffield, Rev. Alpheus Crosby, H. H. Leavitt, Benjamin Greenleaf, and George W. Bosworth as directors, all of Boston.

Lord Ashburton was elected an honorary member in 1842, John Bright and Rev. Titus Coan honorary vice presidents, May 28, 1855. Among the life directors, in addition to those whose names were formerly given as joining in 1839, were J. P. Blanchard, Samuel E. Coues, Henry Dwight, Samuel Appleton, James Arnold, Moses Grant, William Ladd, William Jay, Jonathan Phillips, Amasa Walker, and J. E. Worcester, the lexicographer.

The annual meetings of the society were held in the Central Church on Winter Street from 1843 to 1848, and in Park Street Church from 1849 to 1861. They followed the public meeting in the auditorium of the church from 1843 to 1853, when they reverted to the former practice of meeting in the afternoon at three o'clock and by so doing having more time to consider the business of the society. The speakers at the public meetings during these years were as follows: Rev. Orville Dewey, D. D., 1848; Charles Sumner, 1849; Rev. A. L. Stone, 1850; Rev. R. W. Clarke, 1851; Rev. Frederick Huntington, 1852; Judge William Jay, 1853; Rev. William H. Allen, LL. D., 1854; Hon. William Jay, 1855; Rev. Warren Burton, 1856; Rev. Rufus P. Stebbins, 1857; Hon. Gerit Smith, 1858; Rev. George B. Cheever, D. D., 1859; Rev. Samuel J. May, 1860; Elihu Burritt, 1861.

Until his breakdown, Oct. 22, 1855, Beckwith spent considerable time in travel, frequently covering five thousand miles in a year. For several years he spoke on the average thirty-eight times a week. For four years following his sickness in 1855, he spent his time quietly in Boston, his editorial work for nearly a year being performed by Blanchard at no expense to the society. By 1859, he had recovered his health sufficiently to be able to do a large part of his work.

After the society was out of debt it felt that it ought to place some agents in the field; and from 1852 until the outbreak of the Civil War it had two lecturing agents out all the time; in 1855-56, five, and in the following year, six, most of them discussing the question of stipulated arbitration. Among the more prominent agents were Rev. William Potter who, in 1853-54, travelled in Alabama, Tennessee, and Kentucky, where the inhabitants heard peace preached for the first time; Rev. Henry Snyder who, in 1853-58, travelled mainly in western New York; Thomas H. Palmer who in

1853-54, travelled through Vermont and neighboring states at his own expense; Rev. A. C. Hand, who, in 1854-56, travelled through Wisconsin and Illinois, and Rev. William W. Crane who, in 1855-58, travelled in Michigan. In 1857, Rev. Charles S. Macreading, a Methodist clergyman in Milwaukee, served as agent so acceptably that the executive committee, Nov. 8, 1858, appointed him a general agent to give all his time to the interests of the society. By the terms of the contract made with him he was to receive all the money he collected up to eight hundred dollars a year, and one-half of that raised between eight hundred dollars and twelve hundred dollars. All above the last named amount was to go to the society.

Besides these travelling and preaching agents the society through its committee on advice commissioned several preachers in various parts of the country to act as local agents, that is, to advertise the society, hold public meetings in its interest, speak for it, obtain an occasional collection for it, circulate its petitions, and interest as many in the peace movement as possible. These agents worked in the vicinity of their residence at no expense to the society. Besides making the objects of the society known in many places, they occasionally benefited the society financially. The number of such agents began to increase in 1852. In the next year they numbered twenty; but with the society's decrease in activity, the number had fallen to ten in the year 1858.

In this connection should be mentioned the efforts of Rev. Dr. Titus Coan, a missionary of the American Board, located at Hawaii. He was in communication with the society from 1848 until his death, Dec. 2, 1882, at eighty-two years of age. He had received one of the sets of tracts and a copy of the Book of Peace sent to missionaries by the society, following 1846. April 24, 1848, he sent to the society one hundred dollars, the gift of a native church at Hilo. Several subsequent gifts, varying from twenty-five to one hundred dollars, came from the same congregation at various times. In return the society sent him occasional bundles of its publications which were distributed among seamen in vessels touching that port. In the spring of 1855, the Hilo church offered the society one hundred dollars toward a prize of five hundred dollars for a history of the Crimean War, even offering to pay the whole amount of the prize if it were not possible to obtain the necessary funds from others. The society, however, declined the offer, feeling that the subject was one of more interest to the London society.

Resolutions for mutual and simultaneous disarmament of all nations were first passed by the society at the annual meeting in May, 1859,[1] following the action of the London society in attempting to bring the question before the people of England. These resolutions were taken to England by Hon. Amasa Walker and by him laid before the London society.

By the year 1852, the society found its stock of tracts greatly depleted. Recognizing their value in the campaign then started, they reprinted all their tracts and books in editions of from one to five thousand each. During the year 1852-53, they stereotyped several new tracts and reprinted about fifty old ones in editions of from one to twenty thousand each, and continued reprinting and stereotyping tracts until the outbreak of the Civil War. In 1854, they reprinted four thousand copies of Charles Sumner's address before the society in 1849, with an appendix containing in full Judge Underwood's report to the Senate on stipulated arbitration in 1854.

Advocate of Peace continued to be printed in editions of thirty-five hundred to four thousand copies each, a bi-monthly, 1847 to 1851 and from August, 1856 to December, 1868. Between those dates it was issued as a monthly. With the number for March, 1857, the title became "The Advocate of Peace."

In the fall of 1853, Thomas A. Merrill, a vice president of the society, and for fifty years pastor of the Congregational church at Middlebury, Vt., offered through the American Tract Society, of which he was president, five hundred dollars for the best essay on "The Right Way or the Gospel Applied to the Intercourse of Individuals and Nations." This prize was won two years later by Rev. Joseph A. Collier, Pastor of the Reformed Dutch Church of Geneva, N. Y.

The yearly prayer meeting, the Christmas sermon in the interest of peace, and the concert of prayer with the annual contribution for the society continued to be observed up to the Civil War. The little trouble between the United States and Great Britain over Central American matters in the winter of 1855 and 1856, though it was lightly treated in this country, was considered very seriously by the friends of peace in England, who felt that another war between the two nations was imminent. Peace addresses, following the example of a decade before, were sent by the British Congregational and

[1] Printed in The Advocate of Peace, August, 1860, p. 5.

Baptist unions to their sister churches in America, and by several British cities and towns to various cities here.[1] The League of Brotherhood took up the matter. Addresses were sent by members of the English Olive Leaf circles to corresponding circles in the United States. One sent by the citizens of Manchester, May 17, 1856, and containing 31,641 signatures was sent to Beckwith and by him laid before the city governments of Boston, July 14, 1856, and New York City and Philadelphia later, and printed in one hundred newspapers in the country.[2]

The society did not heartily sympathize with the efforts made in Europe for liberty or for popular government, which in general met with failure, due, as the society believed, to the lack of religious or moral principles shown by the leaders of the movement. Reformers abroad found the church tied to the old system and naturally became atheistic, thus causing the feeling in this country to be lukewarm towards the attempt to put into effect a theory with which they were in the heartiest accord. Thus the society took no part in encouraging the attempts at political reform made in Europe. Kossuth, however, was recognized as a Christian man, and the churches and the society gave him a warm welcome on his visit to America in 1851.

[1] Those from Edinburgh and Glasgow are printed in Advocate of Peace, May, 1856, pp. 76-78.
[2] Printed in Advocate of Peace, August-September, 1856, pp. 119, 120.

Chapter XIV

CIVIL WAR

In the report of the directors to the society, May 26, 1856, attention was called to the fact that the agents of the society "reported special obstruction to our cause from the pending controversy between freedom and slavery in Kansas." The report further stated: "The public, as well as our own co-workers should learn to look upon questions of this sort as not lying fairly within the range of our legitimate field. It should ever be borne in mind that our distinct and sole mission is to do away with the custom of war, or the practice of nations settling their disputes by the sword. * * * * It is no part of our work to say precisely how disputes between individuals, or local parties under a government, shall be adjusted. * * * * The friends of peace think themselves advocates of freedom and right; but by what specific means these shall be secured in a contest like the one now pending, it is not the province of this movement to prescribe, any more than it is of the temperance or of any other cause."[1]

Following the reception of this report, the society adopted the following resolution: "That the great issue now pending in Kansas, an issue pregnant with vast and far-reaching results, illustrates the vital importance of having the mass of every people thoroughly imbued with such principles and habits of peace as shall lead them to settle all their domestic, as well international controversies without violence and blood."[2]

The society made no comment upon the steady movement toward war, except for the earnest plea of the executive committee issued in January, 1861, and sent to more than five hundred leading papers throughout the country, to consider the questions at issue in a sane manner and to avoid the evils sure to follow from an appeal to the sword. Yet it was not unprepared for the blow

[1] Advocate of Peace, June, 1856, p. 88.
[2] Ibid., p. 82, Resolution 12.

when it fell. Soon after the fall of Fort Sumter, the officials of the society met for an interchange of views. The results then reached were expressed in several articles appearing in the Advocate of Peace for March and April, 1861. In one of these articles, entitled "Peace at Home"[1] are the following statements: "The principles of peace are needed everywhere, no less at home than abroad; and, while our cause restricts itself to the single purpose of doing away the custom of International war;[2] we have long supposed it would be found in time quite as necessary among ourselves as in our intercourse with other nations. This necessity is now upon us much sooner, and in a worse form, than any one could well have deemed possible. Indeed, it has come very like a clap of thunder in a cloudless sky. Of our thirty-three states, six have suddenly raised the flag of rebellion under the soft equivocal name of secession, set at defiance the constitution and laws of the general government, appropriated to their own use all the national property within their reach, and erected themselves into a separate independent slave-holding confederacy, confessedly established for the support, perpetuity and extension of slavery. * * * * To the friends of peace, then, what is the obvious and imperative lesson of the hour? Wake anew to the claims of peace as a leading, paramount question of our country and the age. Cling to your principles more fully, more persistently than ever."

In an article on "The Right of Revolution,"[3] appears the following: "This dogma is claimed by nearly all advocates of government by the people as self evident and undeniable. We are not aware that the peace society has ever had occasion to express its views respecting it; but in our editorial capacity, we have ventured, at the hazard of some severe criticism, to call in question its truth and assert its direct contrariety to the teachings of the New Testament."

In an article entitled: "Rebellion Actually Begun," in the May-June, 1861, number of the Advocate of Peace, the society stated its position as follows:[4] "We trust our friends will, first of all, bear ever in mind that peace is always loyal. It is not possible for a

---

[1] Advocate of Peace, March April, 1861, pp. 199-202.
[2] In one of its early tracts entitled "Sketch of the Peace Cause" appears practically the same statement. The society "concerns itself solely with the intercourse of nations for the single purpose of abolishing this practice of war.
[3] P. 202.
[4] P. 258.

peace man to be a rebel. We may dislike the government over us and seek to change it, but never in the way of violent resistance to its authority. We cannot for a moment countenance or tolerate rebellion. All our principles and habits require us to sustain the government in every proper, legitimate effort for the enforcement of law, and the condign punishment of offenders. The cause of peace was never meant to meet such a crisis as is now upon us. It belongs not to peace, but to government alone; and all that can be required of us, is that we prove ourselves loyal citizens. The issue belongs not to peace men, but to rulers, as a question of authority, right and power. Our government put the issue on the proper ground, by calling for the power needed to enforce the laws against an organized and armed rebellion. It is not strictly war, but a legitimate effort by government for the enforcement of its laws and the maintenance of its proper and indispensable authority. The principle is the same with that which quells a riot in one of our cities, or seizes an assassin or incendiary, and brings him to condign punishment. We should be tender of human life; but we must ever keep ourselves on the side of the government against all wrong doers. If the Christianity of Paul would not let him resist by violence even the despotism of Nero himself, it surely becomes every peace man to throw his entire influence against the gigantic crime of attempting to overthrow the freest and best government on earth, in order to establish upon its ruins an oligarchy of slaveholders for the extension of slavery over a continent."

In the annual report of the society, May 27, 1861, the following words are used:[1] "Stand by the government in every way not forbidden by your principles. No peace man can ever be a rebel or lend the slightest countenance to rebellion. True it is not ours, as a peace society, to say what shall be done with rebels, but it is ours, as loyal citizens, to stand firmly by the government and render such aid as we consistently can in executing its laws, and bringing offenders to condign punishment. The government may not be right in all respects, but no peace man can consistently refuse to uphold its authority, or fail to throw his influence against the gigantic crime of attempting to overthrow the best government on earth."

Twelve resolutions were adopted at the meeting, ten of them relating to the Civil War. Three of these, showing the position of the society to be exactly as described in the report, were as follows:

---

[1] *Advocate of Peace*, July-August, 1861, p. 269.

8. "That the cause of peace, restricting itself to the single object of doing away the custom of war, the practice of nations settling their disputes by the sword, has never attempted, because outside its proper sphere, to decide how an oppressed people shall vindicate their rights; how murder, or any other offense against society, shall be punished; or in what way government shall deal with a mob, an insurrection, or an organized rebellion."

9. "That the peace society, while regarding questions like these as beyond its legitimate province, has ever been, as it ever must be, loyal to government, a steadfast supporter of its just authority, and in favor of having its laws duly enforced as indispensable to the public safety and weal."

11. "That * * * * we approve as proper and wise under the circumstances, the efforts of our executive committee, in their appeal last January, to dissuade our people, both South and North, from all thought of settling the issue before them by a resort to arms, and to rely only on the peaceful expedients provided in our constitution and laws expressly for the purpose." These views did not differ from those of Ladd and Worcester expressed in 1837, as mentioned in Chapter V.

The society was placed in an awkward position. Its peace principles led it very generally to be denounced as unpatriotic, a charge which it felt to be unwarranted. It protested its loyalty to the government. It refused to consider the Civil War to be a war, but an attempt on the part of the government to maintain its authority over its subjects, acting as a parent with a disobedient child or a teacher with an unruly pupil.

It felt it should take some action, just what it could not decide. In the fall of 1861, it sent a letter to the London Peace Society stating its difficulties and seeking advice, only to receive a reply that they could not say what they "would do in a moment of extreme temptation,"[1] which gave the society no satisfaction whatever. The desire of the society was thus stated:[2] "What we want is a clue to our duty in the case now upon us. Generalities, however true, will not suffice. We wish to know precisely what we ought to do now and here." A letter of suggestion from the London society in

[1] The Advocate of Peace, August, 1862, p. 130.
[2] The Advocate of Peace, August, 1862, p. 130.

September, 1862, with the reply of Beckwith, Oct. 10, 1862, shows the feeling of utter helplessness in the matter.[1]

The society quietly continued its meetings through the war, but on a diminished scale. Its resolutions, its office, its tracts, its magazine, though reduced to an edition of two thousand copies, continued as before; but lectures on the subject of peace were suspended. The society requested the general concert of prayer, preaching, and contributions at Christmas time to be observed, and answered the more radical element as best it could.

Its views were not changed at the end of the war. In the report of the directors read at the annual meeting, May 29, 1865, are these words: "We find in the sad and terrible experience of these four years no reason to change any part of our principles or our policy, but much to confirm our belief of their essential correctness, wisdom, and necessity,"[2] and again repeated "a due enforcement of law, whether against one offender or a million, we regard as a proper and necessary measure of peace, * * * It is only a legitimate indispensable enforcement of law against its wholesale violation. Our government in the present case has attempted nothing more than such enforcement. * * * * The sole question agitated through all these years of blood has been whether our laws should be enforced against those who violate them, or whether these wholesale transgressions shall be allowed to trample all lawful authority under their feet with impunity."

At the annual meeting of the society after receiving the report containing the expressions above recited, it was resolved to adhere to the distinction heretofore made between the enforcement of law and the ordinary operations of war, that the society had nothing to do with the future condition and policy of the government, that the difficulties that might arise as a result of the war should be settled by peaceful measures, and that the civil government was in duty bound to execute the law against evil doers.

[1] Printed in the Advocate of Peace, November-December, 1862, pp. 169-76.
[2] The Advocate of Peace, May-June, 1865, p. 264.

Chapter XV

RECONSTRUCTION

At the close of the war the society again took up its work. It planned new editions of its books, and the appointment of agents to agitate the question of peace and promote a general circulation of its publications. Its view of the necessity of calling a congress of nations remained unchanged, as appears from the following resolution passed at its annual meeting, May 29, 1865: "Resolved, That the progress of our rebellion has disclosed anew the uncertainty and inadequacy of the so called law of nations as a rule of duty, an arbiter of disputes, or a regulator of intercourse between nations; and for this reason, as for many others, the cause of peace is imperatively needed to obtain such a congress and high court of nations as shall secure for them in time a system of legal, peaceful justice, analogous to what every civilized community has provided for its own members."

A group of radical peace men including some members of the American Peace Society who were greatly dissatisfied with the position it had taken in declaring that a civil war was not war, met in Boston, Dec. 12, 1865, under the leadership of Rev. Adin Ballou, called a peace convention in Boston, March 14 and 15, 1866, and prepared to revive and reorganize the New England Non Resistance Society of 1838, which had come to an end with John Brown's raid. Blanchard was chairman of the convention and Amasa Walker was an adherent. At Providence, May 16, 1866, they organized the Universal Peace Society, later known as the Universal Peace Union, planning to have branches in every country. Their headquarters later were in Philadelphia where they became incorporated, April 9, 1888. Beginning in 1869, a camp meeting was held nearly every year at Mystic, Conn.

The Union kept closely in touch with the European societies, having leaders of many of them on its roll of vice presidents, including such persons as Leone Levi of the London Peace Society,

116

Pratt of the International Arbitration and Peace Association, Burt of the Workingmen's Peace Association, Couvreur, Passy, Desmoulins, Lemonnier, Potonié, and Godin of France, Geiger of Frankfort, Vigano of Milan, Mancini of Rome, Van Eck of The Hague, Groegg of Geneva, Marcoartu of Spain, and Bajer of Copenhagen. Branches were formed in several states which were more or less active according to circumstances. Rev. Alfred H. Love was its president during most of its existence. It issued a monthly magazine and prepared many petitions in the interest of the several objects that it represented. At first, the relation between it and the American Peace Society was that of mild criticism. But after a few years their relations became more friendly, and they frequently worked together harmoniously in order to obtain the consummation of their common desires.

Another society which worked in harmony with the American Peace Society was founded at about the same time,—the Peace Association of Friends in America. This society was organized at Baltimore in November, 1866, and united with other bodies November 20, 1867. It soon became very active, holding conventions, having lecturers in the field, and printing and circulating much peace literature. It cooperated with the American Peace Society, many of whose publications it bought and distributed. For a while the headquarters of the society were at New Vienna, Ohio; but they were early moved to Richmond, Indiana, from where they issued their magazine, the Messenger of Peace. It was incorporated Feb. 22, 1894. William G. Hubbard was president and Daniel Hill secretary for many years, and both were long on the roll of officers of the American Peace Society, the former for forty-six years.

In view of the many criticisms made of the course pursued by the society during the war, a few of the leading friends of peace met in the office of the society, Jan. 17, 1867, and after considering the criticisms offered, voted to approve its course in not interfering with questions concerning the relations between governments and their subjects, to approve the methods adopted by the society in the past, to recommend the insertion of an arbitration clause in future treaties made by the government, and a reduction in large standing armies, to approve the establishment of an international court and a congress of nations, and to recommend that friends of peace contribute liberally toward aiding the society to prosecute its work.[1]

At the following session of Congress the society sent to both houses a petition in favor of calling a congress of nations and of considering some plan for a mutual cessation of armaments. The deputation that carried the petition to Washington was very well received, but the time was not sufficiently far removed from the war to enable the question to be considered. In fact, it was not until well into the year 1868 that the society began to make any progress. Steps had been taken the year before to send out lecturers, but no arrangements had been completed because of the doubt whether the popular feeling was such as to permit a presentation of peace claims. In that year, however, the Advocate of Peace was sent free to three hundred Young Men's Christian Associations, then being organized in the larger cities of the country. In 1869, it was sent also to all the leading colleges and theological seminaries of the country, to one thousand of the leading newspapers of the country and to many ministers and laymen believed to be interested in the cause. The circulation of the magazine increased fivefold to nine thousand copies a month. Tracts continued to be used. In 1867, new editions of twenty tracts were issued and four new ones stereotyped. In 1868, fifty-one were stereotyped and five books reissued. In 1870, copies of "A Plea with Ministers for the Cause of Peace" were sent to ten thousand ministers in the country.

After due consideration a western department was opened at Chicago, Oct. 29, 1868, under the direction of Rev. Amasa Lord, who during twenty years of connection with the American Bible Society had shown great zeal and self denial in his work. He was given a salary of fifteen hundred dollars a year and his traveling expenses. At the same time, the executive committee adopted rules relative to agents,—to be commissioned by the executive committee, salaries to be limited to the amount of their collections, society publications to be given them at half price, and quarterly reports of their collections to be made to the society.

Lord was very active. He introduced a system of colportage, lecturers, preachers, and agents to obtain subscriptions to the magazine. He urged the cooperation of ministers and Christians generally. He established depositories of publications in many western

[1] The letter calling a conference is printed in the Advocate of Peace, January-February, 1867, pp. 206, 107; the resolutions adopted on pp. 209, 210.

states and scattered the tracts and books of the society throughout the West. Within a year, twenty-five lecturers, twenty-three lecturing agents and ten local agents had been appointed covering the states of Ohio, Indiana, Illinois, Michigan, Wisconsin, Minnesota, and Iowa. And in the following year their number was increased. Though the cause was new to this section it met with but little opposition. Ministers cooperated with the agents and helped them arrange for meetings. They met with discouragement however at the indifference shown and the small amount of contributions received.

Nevertheless, during its first year the department became nearly self sustaining and might soon have become entirely so had Lord been permitted to continue the work as he had planned it. But on Feb. 18, 1870, he was called to Boston to take charge of the Boston office, as Beckwith, who had been in poor health since the preceding July, was daily becoming weaker and rapidly approaching his end.

Beckwith died May 12, 1870, from heart disease, caused from prolonged overwork. He was nearly seventy years of age, having been born Jan. 3, 1801. For thirty-five years, half of his life, he had been connected with the society, two years as an agent, thirty-three years as corresponding secretary, and for most of that time editor of the Advocate of Peace. He had been instrumental in causing the removal of the society from Hartford to Boston. He had been a co-worker with Ladd for many years, and had jumped into the saddle on the latter's death. As will appear later, he was the financial savior of the society. In truth, it may be said that the history of the society during its forty-two years had been directed by Ladd and Beckwith, both zealous in its cause, and both devoting their lives and their money to its support. Beckwith believed in the final triumph of the peace movement. He never faltered in his work, supporting the society in times of greatest need and, during the war, almost single handed. He served on a small salary and gave nearly all of it back to the society every year. He was interested in every good cause and contributed also to missions, the temperance enterprise, and the anti-slavery movement. He rejoiced in the success of each. Like Ladd, Beckwith was a man of moderate means and was not obliged to work for a living; like him also, he made the society a residuary legatee after the death of his wife.

For a time, Beckwith's mantle fell upon Lord, already well broken into the work. The day after Beckwith's death, Lord was appointed acting corresponding secretary with a salary of fifteen hundred dollars a year and travelling expenses. Lord spent much of his time in Chicago. For a time in 1870 and 1871, Rev. S. Hopkins Emery acted as assistant secretary and editor of the Advocate of Peace, being followed Jan. 1, 1871, by the Rev. Howard C. Dunham, who in thirty-two days as agent had addressed eight congregations and several Sunday schools, made two hundred and fifty calls, obtained several subscribers to the Advocate of Peace, and collected $180 in cash at an expense of $65.

Lord inaugurated many changes. He placed advertisements on the cover of the magazine. He offered premiums for new subscribers, a peace photograph for one subscriber, a volume containing fifty-two interesting stories for children for two subscribers, and Lindley Murray's "The Power of Religion" for three subscribers. At his suggestion the last two pages of the Advocate of Peace from August, 1870, to November, 1871, were devoted to children, under the title of the Child's Advocate of Peace; and, beginning January, 1872, this was succeeded by a four page paper for children called the Angel of Peace. He prepared brief articles on the subject of peace and war and sent them to nearly five thousand periodicals published in the United States. He prepared some peace envelopes containing pictures, Scripture passages, and stating the objects of the society. During the next few years many thousands of these envelopes were sold, the price being fifteen cents for twenty-five and $3.33 per thousand. He had twelve new tracts stereotyped, the Book of Peace republished, a book for children printed, and Sumner's lecture on the Franco-Prussian Duel published, of which twenty-five hundred copies were distributed by the society.

In January, 1871, he issued an appeal to ministers and others, inviting them to become life members or directors of the society in return for twenty or fifty dollars' worth of services, the value to be set by the worker and the work to consist of securing insertion in newspapers of brief paragraphs original or selected, relating to peace and war. One hundred and two topics were suggested as subjects for articles, while the society offered to furnish articles already written and documents to aid in preparing new articles if desired. He prepared a plan whereby one could deposit with the society occasional amounts of money receiving as interest thereon divers publications of the society, with the understanding that the sums so deposited should become a donation to the society if their return was not requested by the donor during his lifetime. He extended the agency plan, endeavoring to have an agent in every community. To carry out these plans he asked for a contribution of ten thousand dollars a year, and—he got it.

Outside matters demanded his attention too. August 25, 1870, the directors of the society passed nine resolutions immediately after the outbreak of the Franco-Prussian War, denouncing standing armies and armaments and the existing war system, and urging ministers, statesmen, and citizens generally "to join in a general and earnest endeavor to create such a public sentiment as shall imperatively demand a general disbandment of the armies of the world."[1] This was followed the next month by a joint address of the American Peace Society and the London society to the friends of peace, urging the prevention of the spread of the war and on the close of the war to favor the taking of measures that will "place the peace of the world beyond the reach of the personal ambition of individuals or the capricious impulses of popular passion."[2]

Later in the year when the question over the Alabama claims became acute, the executive committee prepared a petition requesting Congress to discourage all measures tending to involve our nation in a war with Great Britain, to reduce standing armies, to favor the introduction of a provision in all treaties for arbitration of questions which the contracting parties can not amicably adjust, and to secure an early proposition by our government to others to unite in the establishment of a Congress or court of nations to settle international disputes.[3] Copies of this petition were circulated throughout the country and returned to the society with twelve thousand signatures. These petitions with a memorial to Congress, dated Jan. 2, 1872, urging the adoption of arbitration as a practicable means to settle differences between nations as evidenced by the adoption of the Treaty of Washington, which had been ratified May 8, 1871, and suggesting that the United States initiate measures for the establishment of a permanent system of international arbitration by the adoption of a high court of arbitration, were presented to Congress by Senator H. B. Anthony

---

[1] The address in full is printed in the Advocate of Peace, September, 1870, p. 282.

[2] The resolutions are printed in ibid., September, 1870, p. 285.

[3] The petition is printed in ibid., January, 1873, third page of cover.

from Rhode Island, accompanied by an address endorsing the society and commending the object of the memorial.[1] On his motion both were referred to the Committee on Foreign Relations.

But Lord was only acting as corresponding secretary, and at the end of the year, May, 1871, Beckwith's successor was elected— Rev. James Browning Miles, born in Rutland, Mass., Aug. 18, 1822; a graduate of Yale in 1849 and for a time a tutor there, since Jan. 2, 1855, he had been pastor of the First Congregational Church of Charlestown, Mass. Lord returned to Chicago, July 1. Early in the fall his health failed, and in December, he became seriously ill, resulting in his resignation as western secretary, May 27, 1872. Later in the year Leonard H. Pillsbury was appointed his successor with headquarters at Manhattan, Kansas.

Thus during the three and a half years, Oct. 29, 1868, to May 27, 1872, that Lord was connected with the society, he saw it awaken from its slumber following the Civil War. During his time he saw six prominent officials of the society pass away. Joshua P. Blanchard died at the age of eighty-six, October, 1868, immediately preceding Lord's first appointment. Blanchard was a co-worker with Worcester and Channing, following Worcester as corresponding secretary of the Massachusetts Peace Society. He was a director of the American Peace Society, 1831-43, recording secretary, 1840-41, treasurer, 1841-47, vice president 1847-50, and 1856-57, and member of the executive committee, 1838-50. As a radical on the subject of peace, he joined the New England Non-Resistance Society in 1838; and as one of the organizers of the Universal Peace Society in 1866, he tried to cause a fusion of the two organizations. Nevertheless he had retained his connection with the American Peace Society and had written two of its tracts and many articles that appeared in the Advocate of Peace.

Rev. Joseph Addison Copp, D. D., since 1851 pastor of the Broadway Congregational Church, Chelsea, from 1861 to 1869 a director and from 1860 to his death a member of the executive committee, and at the time of his death chairman of that committee, died suddenly Nov. 7, 1869, at the age of sixty-five. His successor as chairman of the committee, Baron Stow, D. D., a Baptist clergyman in Boston from 1832, director from 1839 to 1847 and from 1859 to 1869, vice president from 1854, and a member of the

---

[1] A copy of the memorial is printed in the Advocate of Peace, February, 1872, p. 153.

executive committee from 1841 to 1844, and 1859 to his death, died Dec. 27, 1869, at the age of sixty-eight.

William C. Brown, register of the Probate Court of Suffolk County, embracing the city of Boston for fifteen years, and previously editor of Zion's Herald and the Mother's Magazine, recording secretary and director of the society from 1847, member of the executive committee from 1846, and recently appointed treasurer, died Dec. 9, 1870, at the age of sixty-nine.

John Tappan, one of the founders of the Massachusetts Peace Society and an officer of the American Peace Society from its organization in 1828—director 1828-39 and vice president after 1839—died March 25, 1871, nearly ninety years of age. He was treasurer and president of the American Tract Society for forty years, and at the time of his death was the oldest corporate member of the American Board of Commissioners for Foreign Missions.

Thomas C. Upham, a graduate of Dartmouth and Andover Theological Seminary, Professor of Philosophy at Bowdoin College from 1824 to 1867, author of several philosophical books and many magazine articles, director of the society from 1835 to 1843 and vice president from 1843 until his death, died April 2, 1872, seventy years of age. His attention was called to the subject of peace by William Ladd. Reference has already been made to his essay on a Congress of Nations, written in 1837. His Manual of Peace, which appeared in 1835, was reprinted several times, and at the time of his death it was considered the best general book upon the subject.

In addition, John Field, who had served as treasurer, director, and member of the executive committee of the society from 1847, felt called upon to resign his office in 1870.

The change in the officials between 1868 and 1873 was so nearly complete as to make the society practically a new organization. Of the twenty-nine vice presidents elected in 1873, but five had been in office in 1868; of the twenty-seven directors elected in 1873, but ten had been in office in 1868; of the fifteen members of the executive committee elected in 1873, but one had been in office in 1868. Moreover the president, secretaries, and treasurer had been changed. Howard Malcolm, D. D., LL. D., president of the society from 1861-72, was followed by Hon. Edward S. Tobey, 1873-90. William C. Brown was transferred from recording secretary to treasurer, 1870.

Dying in 1871, he was followed by David Patten, 1871-78. Following Brown as recording secretary, Nachob Broughton, Jr., served for a year, when Rev. Howard C. Dunham began his ten year service in 1872. At the annual meeting in May, 1871, women were elected to office in the American Peace Society for the first time. Mrs. Beckwith and Mrs. Julia Ward Howe were elected members of the executive committee, precursors of many other eminent women. The office of the society had been moved to 23 Chauncey Street in 1864, to the Congregational library, 40 Winter Street, in 1867, and to the building of the Wesleyan Association, 36 Bromfield Street, in July, 1870, following the death of Beckwith.

Immediately following our Civil War, several peace societies were organized in Europe. Three were formed in France in 1867 as a protest against the warlike attitude of France and Prussia over the Luxemburg question. The idea of peace societies in France was revived by Frédéric Passy who, when a student at Nice, became enthusiastic over the *Ligue Universelle du Bien Public* formed in 1859 by Edmund Potonié who had been at the congresses in Paris and Frankfort in 1849 and 1850. This society had headquarters in Antwerp with branches in several cities in Europe, and had among other objects the propagation of peace ideas. Passy was born in Paris, May 20, 1822. He became auditor of the Council of State, 1848-49, editor of *Journal des Economistes* in 1854, and successively professor in Paris, member of the Chamber of Deputies, member of the Departmental Council for Public Instruction, a writer, and a member of the Legion of Honor. Passy formed *La Ligue Internationale de la Paix* in Paris, in May, 1867, which in 1872 became *La Société française des Amis de la Paix*, and in 1889 *La Société française de l'Arbitrage entre Nations*. Its membership included such men as Michel Chevalier and Dufour of France, Visschers of Brussels, Garnier, editor of the Journal des Economistes, Dr. Varrentrapp of Frankfort, and Charles Sumner, men who had been connected with the earlier peace congresses.

Another organization, fraternal in character, *L'Union de la Paix*, was founded at Havre by N. F. Santallier, whose aim was to prepare an international code through a committee of jurisconsults belonging to all nations. It had branches in several towns in France, Germany, Switzerland, Italy and the French colonies.

A third was established by Charles Lemonnier at Geneva, where a convention, presided over by Gen. Garibaldi, met September 9-12, 1867, and adopted the name of *La Ligue internationale de Paix et Liberté*. Their object was to secure peace by substituting democratic for monarchical government, to form the United States of Europe as suggested by Victor Hugo in 1849, and to do so by molding public opinion by speeches, by meetings, by substituting a militia for a standing army, by separating church from state, and by solving social questions. Branch societies of the league were formed in various countries, and within a few months it had over twenty thousand members. Congresses were held every year presided over by prominent persons,—Victor Hugo was its honorary president at Lausanne, in 1869. Their objects were so contrary to those of the English and American peace societies as to prevent any affiliation of the two groups. However, after the league in 1872 adopted arbitration as a means of securing its object, the relations between the two groups became more friendly.

Peace societies were started in Holland in 1870 and in Belgium in 1871. The London society tried to preach peace ideas to workingmen who had received the franchise in England by the act of 1867, but they would not read the tracts handed them or attend the peace meetings of the society. In 1870, on the outbreak of the war between France and Germany, William Randal Cremer organized the Workingmen's Peace Association to insist upon a policy of neutrality on the part of Great Britain in the continental war. This society took the place of the international Workingmen's Association formed in London in September, 1864, to establish a system of international communication between workingmen of various countries and render war less frequent, a society that had passed under the control of the socialists as the International, and had forgotten the object for which it was formed.

In 1880, Hodgkin Pratt and Lewis Appleton, withdrew from the London Peace Society, and Aug. 16, formed the International Arbitration and Peace Association to get relief from armaments. Branches were formed in every country of the world. Among the adherents of this society in the United States were P. E. Aldrich, Prof. W. F. Allen, George T. Angell, Prof. Lewis H. Atwater, David Dudley Field, Merrill E. Gates, Prof. Albert Harkness, Thomas Wentworth Higginson, Alfred H. Love, B. C. Northrup, and David A. Wells, names known to the American Peace Society.

Chapter XVI

AN INTERNATIONAL CODE

June 17, 1871, immediately following the election of Miles as corresponding secretary of the society May 29, 1871, came the ratification of the Treaty of Washington, which had been concluded between Great Britain and the United States, May 8, and which had provided for the settlement of several misunderstandings between the two nations by arbitration at Geneva. This was hailed by the society as a most important step in the direction of the substitution of arbitration for war. A peace jubilee was convened in the Boston Music Hall, Sept. 26th, the largest peace meeting until then ever held in America.

It brought Burritt again to the front. After the close of the peace congresses in 1853, he had turned his attention to the abolition of restrictions upon international correspondence in an effort to obtain a universal penny ocean postage, advocated by him first, Jan. 25, 1847. In 1855, he returned to America and advocated a scheme for a compensated emancipation of the slaves. In 1863, he returned to England and was consular agent for the United States at Birmingham, from 1865 to 1867, where his voice was often heard in the interest of peace. In 1870, he returned to his early home in New Britain. During the rest of his life he was vice president of the American Peace Society and a frequent contributor to the Advocate of Peace. He took an active interest in the Society's meetings, cooperated with the secretary, contributed his time, strength, counsel and eloquence, preaching peace and paying his own expenses wherever he went.

On Burritt's suggestion following the Music Hall meeting, Miles originated a series of similar meetings, about forty in all, which were held during the winter at various cities and towns in New England and south as far as Washington. Miles and Burritt managed these meetings and spoke at most of them. They were held in

126

prominent churches, and given a religious character without sectarianism or politics. They were opened with prayer and reading of the Scriptures, followed by addresses made by local pastors, mayors, members of the legislatures and of Congress. Local color was given to them by securing speakers well known in the localities where the meetings were held. Hon. Charles Theodore Russell presided at the meetings in Cambridge, President Stearns at Amherst, Senator Buckingham at Norwich, Conn., Gov. Jewell of Connecticut at Hartford, Ex President Woolsey of Yale at New Haven, Hon. Reverdy Johnson at Baltimore, Rev. Howard Crosby, Chancellor of New York University with William Cullen Bryant on the platform, at New York. The meeting in Washington was held in the First Congregational Church, presided over by H. D. Cooke, Governor of the District of Columbia. Addresses were made by Rev. J. E. Rankin, D. D., the pastor of the church, Maj. Gen. O. O. Howard and Hon. Felix R. Brunot, chairman of the Indian Commission. In the audience sat Vice President Colfax, Hon. Russell Gurney, British Commissioner on the Alabama claims, and several congressmen. Great interest was manifested in all the meetings, and the local press gave full reports of the proceedings.

The evening meeting in connection with the annual meeting of the society at Boston in 1872 was held June 16, the evening before the opening of the musical peace jubilee under the general direction of P. S. Gilmore, a member of the executive committee of the society. The hall was crowded. Music was furnished by the Handel and Haydn Society under the direction of Carl Zerrahn and Dr. Eben Tourjée, with B. J. Lang at the organ. Hon. G. Washington Warren, President of the Bunker Hill Monument Association, presided. Addresses were made by Hon. E. S. Tobey, Hon. G. B. Loring, Dr. Burns of London, Elihu Burritt and Dr. Miles.

During these years a series of suggestions had been made of a practical character. At the beginning of the Civil War, Francis Lieber had urged the calling of an international congress to settle certain points on international law expected to arise. At the close of the war he wrote an open letter, Sept. 17, 1865, to Hon. William H. Seward, Secretary of State, urging that the questions growing out of the war affecting the United States and Great Britain be submitted to arbitration, not by monarchs and their deputies, but before the law faculty of some foreign university, such as Berlin or Heidelberg or Leyden.[1]

At the anniversary of the London Peace Society in 1866 Burritt, while still consul at Birmingham, urged the holding of an international congress of eminent jurists to discuss practical points of international law and to arrange for progressive and simultaneous disarmament. A little later in the year, David Dudley Field, then the most famous international lawyer in America, read a paper before the meeting of the British Association for the Promotion of Social Science, at Manchester, England, on the necessity of preparing an international code, enumerating several needed improvements and suggesting the appointment of a committee to prepare the outline of such a code with the view of having a complete code formed and presented to the various governments for consideration in the hope that it might receive their sanction. The suggestion was well received. A committee of eleven distinguished jurists of different countries was appointed to codify the existing rules, omitting the bad and obsolete and suggesting modifications and improvements.

In 1872, Field, as a member of this committee, issued his Outlines of an International Code, a draft outline of the suggested code, which was radical in many respects. He suggested the abolition of standing armies, the resistance of all nations to a war started by any member, and the settlement of international troubles by means of a joint high commission appointed by the parties to the dispute, with an appeal to a high tribunal of arbitration composed of representatives from nations not parties to the dispute. At the meeting of the Social Science Association in London, Jan. 25, 1871, Leone Levi read a paper on international arbitration. A little later the council of the Workingmen's Peace Association outlined a plan for the establishment of a high court of nations.

In an article entitled "A Preliminary Congress of Jurisconsults and Publicists," in the Advocate of Peace, April, 1871, page 40, Burritt suggested the calling of an assembly of the first and ablest jurists in the world to meet in London, Amsterdam or the Hague to consider the question of peace and well-being of nations. At this meeting of living authorities on international law he thought that an international code could be framed which all nations would

---

[1] The letter is printed in Advocate of Peace, December, 1865, pp. 360-64. His views are given on pp. 364, 365.

accept as the highest legal authority that could be established, a code that would supply the organic law for the action of any future congress of nations that might be convened. At the annual meeting of the society, May 27, 1872, a resolution was passed in favor of "convening at the earliest practicable opportunity an international peace congress for the purpose of elaborating and commending to the government and people of christendom an international code, and taking measures for the formation of an international court with reference to securing among all Christian nations the establishment of a permanent system of international arbitration, and that this society to the extent of its ability will aid in the great undertaking."[1]

During the spring of 1872 Burritt and Miles developed a plan to form a solid basis for a general and permanent system of arbitration by having the principles of international law defined, digested and codified by an unofficial body of forty or fifty eminent jurists, statesmen and philanthropists, after meeting, comparing notes, discussing and elaborating, in the manner of the joint high commission, following the treaty of Washington; the code drawn up by them then to be presented to the nations for their consideration and acceptance. An international court could then be established to which could be referred differences between nations to be settled according to law.

Following the announcement of the Geneva award, Sept. 14, 1872, the time seemed ready to carry this plan into effect. Three days later it was laid before the executive committee of the society which approved it and voted it expedient for Miles to go to Europe and there secure from the peace leaders their views of calling an international peace congress along the lines suggested. A call for such a congress was prepared by Burritt and issued Oct. 10, 1872, signed by Theodore Dwight Woolsey, president of Yale College, Mark Hopkins, president of Williams College, Emory Washburn of Harvard College, Hon. Reverdy Johnson ex attorney general of the United States, David Dudley Field, Hon. William E. Dodge and Peter Cooper of New York, Elihu Burritt of New Britain, Howard Malcolm and Jay Cooke of Philadelphia, Hon. Edward S. Tobey of Boston, Hon. Amasa Walker of North Brookfield, Mass., John Greenleaf Whittier of Amesbury, Mass., Hon. Charles Theo-

---

[1] Printed in the Advocate of Peace, July, 1872, p. 196.

dore Russell of Cambridge, Mass., Rev. Henry Ward Beecher and sixteen others, many of whom were officers of the American Peace Society.[1]

Miles left New York for Europe, Jan. 8, 1873. He had expected to be accompanied by Burritt who, however, at the last moment was detained by an accident, and Miles had to go alone. He took with him letters from the society, from Hamilton Fish, secretary of state, and others. His object was to sound leading publicists, jurists, statesmen, and friends of peace in Europe as to the workability of his plan, the advisability of calling such an international congress and the possibility of putting it across. He visited England, France, Italy, Austria, Germany, and Belgium. He conferred with the representatives of the United States government in various cities of Europe: Gen. R. C. Schenck, minister at London; Hon. E. B. Washburne, minister at Paris; Hon. P. Marsh, minister at Rome; Hon. John Jay at Vienna; and George P. Bancroft, envoy extraordinary to Prussia at Berlin. He met many notable men of Europe. In London, he conversed with Gladstone, the prime minister; the lord mayor of London; E. C. Clark, Regius Professor of Civil Law, Cambridge; Prof. Leone Levi of King's College, London; Rt. Hon. Montague Bernard, one of the negotiators of the Treaty of Washington in 1871; at Paris, Frédéric Passy, professor at the Sorbonne; M. de Parein, member of the Institute of France, Drouyn de Lhuys, prime minister of France under Louis Napoleon, Charles Calvo, formerly minister of state, Viscount Itajuba, one of the arbitrators of the Geneva court and ambassador from Brazil to Paris; at Turin, Count Sclopis, president of the Geneva court of arbitration and a member of the Council of Turin; at Rome, L. S. Mancini, former minister of state and professor of law in the University of Rome, Augusto Pierrantoni, professor of constitutional and international law in the Royal University of Naples, Crispi, later prime minister of Italy, Dr. Levy, the representative of the Jews; at Berlin, Prof. Heffter and Dr. Vichor, professors in the University of Berlin, Baron Von Holtzendorff, professor of international law at Munich; at Brussels, Auguste Visschers, president of the peace congress held in Brussels in 1848, and governmental delegate in the International Congress of Geneva in 1864 and 1868. At Ghent, he was entertained by Dr. Rolin Jac-

[1] The call is printed in the *Advocate of Peace*, November, 1872, p. 228.

quemyns, editor of the International Law Review, one of the most eminent writers upon international law, who at that moment was writing an article advocating a very similar plan. Miles also met the peace society in London, the Society of Economists in Paris and groups of prominent men in Paris and Brussels. Everywhere he was enthusiastically received. There was but one opinion expressed in regard to the plan. Most of the above mentioned persons gave him written expressions of opinion.[1]

Miles returned home greatly encouraged. He felt that Europe was behind him in this movement and that the preliminaries must be undertaken by himself. He arranged a meeting of several prominent men: Theodore Dwight Woolsey, Mark Hopkins, Howard Crosby, Emory Washburn, Charles Sumner, David Dudley Field, William Beach Lawrence, Reverdy Johnson, Howard Malcolm, John Greenleaf Whittier, William Cullen Bryant, Elihu Burritt, William G. Hubbard, Daniel Hill, Alfred H. Love, Sidi H. Brown, G. Washington Warren, W. A. Buckingham, George H. Stuart, Joseph A. Dugdale, Edward S. Tobey, C. W. Goddard, Homer B. Sprague, J. V. L. Pruyn, David H. Hitchcock, Noah Porter, William A. Stearns, and others, many of them officers of the American Peace Society.

They met May 15, 1873, at the residence of David Dudley Field in Gramercy Park, where Miles gave a report of the progress made. After a discussion of the matter it was resolved that the principles were wise and the plan reasonable, that the times demanded a new international code in respect to arbitration, that for the formation of such a code a meeting should be called to consult upon the best method of preparing it, that at such meeting publicists from different nations should be present and that a committee of five, consisting of David Dudley Field, Theodore Dwight Woolsey, Emory Washburn, William Beach Lawrence, and James B. Miles, be appointed to act for this country in issuing invitations and making arrangements for such meeting.[2] This group was hereafter known as the International Code Committee of America. Eleven days later at its annual meeting, the American Peace Society voted

[1] Which with others are printed in the Advocate of Peace, August, 1873, pp. 57-64, and September, pp. 65-72.
[2] The resolutions are printed in Advocate of Peace, July, 1873, p. 51, and September, p. 69.

that international law should be revised "and reduced to a definite code for the acceptance of nations."[1] Miles as secretary of each group consulted both groups—the code committee and the peace society—throughout these labors.

The committee suggested that Brussels be the first place of meeting, with Visschers as chairman of the meeting, in memory of the conference of 1848. They sent a letter, June 30, 1873, enclosing a copy of the resolutions of May 15, to about fifty persons inviting each to meet other publicists of learning and experience to elaborate an international code as a basis for the adjustment of differences between nations. A second invitation was sent out from Brussels in September. Miles and Field were on the ground a month before the conference opened and aided Visschers in making the needed arrangements. Both were well received wherever they went. The Belgian minister of justice approved the plan and the burgomaster of Brussels, M. Anspach, placed the Hotel de Ville at their disposal.

The conference opened October 10, 1873, at noon, and lasted for four days with thirty-five persons in attendance, forming a most august body. The authorities were present at the opening meeting and tendered a banquet to the visitors. Visschers was president of the reception committee and was elected president of the congress, with Field honorary president. The vice presidents were Dr. Bluntschli, Professor of Law, Heidelberg; Com. Sr. Mancini, Professor of Law, Rome; Prof. Ch. Giraud, France, and Rt. Hon. Montague Bernard, Professor of Law, Oxford; E. de Lavaleye, Professor of Law, Belgium, was secretary with Miles honorary secretary, and Carlos Calvo, Jr., of Paris and Adolphe Prims of Brussels assistant secretaries. Among others present were M. Arntz, Professor of Law, Belgium; Sheldon Amos, Professor of Law, London; Ch. Faider, Attorney General, Belgium; A. Marcoartu, Member cortes, Spain; Frédéric Passy, Paris; Aug. Pierrantoni, Professor of Law, Naples; Henry Richard, M. P., London; Ch. Rogier, Minister of State, Belgium; Rolin Jacquemyns, Ghent; Dr. J. P. Thompson, U. S. A., Sir Travers Twiss, Q. C., Great Britain; Hon. Auguste Visschers, Brussels. Letters were received from Count Sclopis, Drouyn de Lhuys, Prof. Holtzendorff,

---

[1] The resolutions are printed in the Advocate of Peace, July, 1873, p. 49.

Prof. Heffter, Vernon Harcourt, Levy, President Woolsey, Leone Levi, and others.

The program provided for a discussion of principles of the codification of international law, and the best way to prepare and publish the code, the principles of international arbitration, institution of courts of arbitration, course to be pursued, and the means of assuring the execution of the sentences and decisions of arbitrators. Miles told of the origin and progress of the movement. The body resolved that the establishment of a congress to consider the importance of an international code and arbitration was desirable. It appointed a committee to prepare projects to be submitted to a future conference and appointed a committee to report on the practicability of framing a code of international law and arbitration. It voted to regard arbitration as a means essentially just and reasonable. It constituted itself a permanent body under the title "The Association for the Reform and Codification of the Law of Nations," with a council consisting of the honorary president, president, four vice presidents and three secretaries. It recommended the organization of local committees in each country to hold frequent meetings, prepare and discuss elaborate papers on international subjects to be presented and discussed at the annual meeting, report their proceedings to the international body and nominate persons to be elected members. Such branches were organized in Paris, Oct. 6; in Rome, Dec. 26; and in the United States following a big reception to Miles on his return to Boston, Jan. 30, 1874.

It had been decided to hold the second meeting at Geneva, the arrangements for which were left in the hands of Visschers. His sudden death, June 3, 1874, disarranged matters so that it seemed best to the code committee, at a meeting June 28, 1874, for Miles to go to Europe as soon as possible and make the necessary preparations for the meeting which had been scheduled for August. Accordingly Miles left New York Aug. 1, followed by Field who was determined to aid in the reform of international law. Miles arrived in London, Aug. 13, called a meeting of those interested in the conference, prepared a program and issued the invitations in English, German and French. Miles and Field then proceeded to Paris and Geneva, arriving at the latter city Sept. 1.

The session opened Monday, Sept. 7, in the Hotel de Ville where the Geneva arbitration proceedings had been conducted, presided over by Miles who read the annual report. Letters were read from Victor Hugo, Count Sclopis, John Bright, Sir John Lubbock, Professors Seeley and Levi, M. Drouyn de Lhuys, and others. Speeches were made by Kawase, Minister Plenipotentiary from Japan to Italy, Passy, Mancini, and Pierrantoni. Papers were read by Miles, Prof. E. A. Lawrence, President F. A. P. Barnard of Columbia University, President Woolsey of Yale, Prof. Emory Washburn, Prof. Sheldon Amos, Henry Richard, Arturo Marcoartu, J. D. Daly of Geneva, T. Webster, Q. C., and others. Some of these papers were discussed. Others were referred to committees, who later reported on them. The draft outline of an international code was referred to the council of the association for examination and report at the next meeting. At a public demonstration addresses were made by Field, Richard, Kawase, Miles, Passy, Von Holtzendorff, Marcoartu, and Père Hyacinthe.

The organization was completed by the adoption of a carefully prepared constitution, having as officers an honorary president, president, vice president, treasurer, a council of twelve, and a secretary. Count Sclopis was elected honorary president, Field, president, Miles, secretary, Charles Francis Adams and Hon. Reverdy Johnson vice presidents from the United States. Those from other countries were friends of peace. On the council were Woolsey, Washburn and Thompson from the United States. Provision was made for annual meetings of the association to be composed of publicists, jurists, statesmen, economists, and philanthropists, elected by the council. The establishment of an international tribunal or court was left to the future.

The third meeting was held at the Hague, Sept. 1-6, 1875, with eleven present from America. The Dutch government displayed unbounded hospitality to the association. The sessions were held in the hall of the second chamber of the States General. The Minister of Justice gave them a reception, as did the queen in the royal palace. Field presided at the meetings. Sir Travers Twiss, Q. C., and Prof. Berchardt of Denmark acted as vice presidents. Dr. Miles read the annual report. Papers were read by Miles on an international tribunal, Richard on international arbitration, Bluntschli on disarmament and Birkbeck on non intervention. The committee appointed to report on the international code drafted by

Field, prepared a code affecting bills of exchange and considered international copyrights, patents and coinage. Resolutions were passed by the association recommending the adoption of resolutions by states favoring international arbitration. A copy of these resolutions accompanied by a letter written by the association was sent to the rulers of the various nations of the world in September, 1875. In addition Miles sent a letter to the principal secretary of state for foreign affairs of each government.[1]

[1] A copy of the resolution and of each letter are printed in the Advocate of Peace, November, 1875, p. 68.

Chapter XVII

A PERIOD OF INDEBTEDNESS

THE series of meetings during the winter of 1871-72 and the four trips to Europe taken by Miles in the interest of the international law society had cost the peace society considerable money.[1] It had been hoped that with the increase of public interest in peace matters following the making of the Treaty of Washington the contributions to the society would increase. But a series of unlooked for events happened. In November of 1872 occurred the great fire in Boston. While the office of the society was not in its path many of its stereotyped plates were with a printer whose office was destroyed by the fire, thus interfering with the distribution of tracts and rendering it necessary to raise money to replace the lost plates. As a result of the fire the society in March, 1873, moved its office from the Methodist building on Bromfield Street to the recently purchased Congregational House at the corner of Beacon and Somerset Streets.

Then came the financial panic in October, 1873, just after the successful formation of the international law society, and lack of funds and the inability to collect any caused the society reluctantly to urge Miles to return from Europe as soon as possible instead of working for a time in Europe as had been planned.

At the annual meeting in May, 1871, the indebtedness of the society was reported to be $1792.81; in 1872, $1084.14; April 28, 1873, $3139.81; May, 1873, $4300; and the treasurer was directed to borrow $4500 and pay the debt. Still it increased to $5050.71, May 27, 1874, and to $6000, Dec. 13, 1875.

At the time of Miles' first departure to Europe the society had appointed two general agents: Rev. B. A. Chase to cover New England and Canada, and Rev. L. H. Pillsbury at Manhattan, Kansas, as a general western agent, following the resignation of

[1] Miles' first trip cost the society $895.75; Advocate of Peace, July, 1873, p. 50.

Rev. Amasa Lord of Chicago. Incidentally it may be noted that Lord so far recovered his health as to be able to work and write for the society during the year 1874 and succeeding years until his death in Elgin, Illinois, in 1878. The system of agencies started by him was felt to be a failure and was given up.

To pay the indebtedness of the society and to raise money for current expenses, Rev. D. C. Haynes, of Lewiston, Maine, but eight miles from Minot, Capt. Ladd's home, who had been very successful in raising funds for benevolent societies, was appointed financial secretary of the society, May 13, 1873, at a salary of two hundred dollars a month, and the society issued an appeal for help. Together Haynes and Miles held numerous public meetings which were largely attended. During Miles' absence in Europe, Haynes continued the meetings, speaking before large audiences in Montreal, Toronto, Buffalo, Niagara Falls, Rochester, Norwich, Oxford, and Fulton, N. Y.,, aided by the pastors of the churches in the cities named. Miles, after his return from Europe, addressed conferences, public meetings and ministerial associations in Boston, Albany, New York, Philadelphia, Washington, and at Dartmouth College, and in three months raised two thousand dollars for the society. But the financial crisis rendered the collection of money difficult, and May 25, 1874, at the end of the year, Haynes resigned, leaving Miles alone to finance the society.

The sudden death of Miles, Nov. 13, 1875, after a two day illness, was a severe blow to the society. Rev. H. C. Dunham, who had been office agent for five years and recording secretary for three, assumed the work of the corresponding secretary until the next annual meeting, May 29, 1876, when the society elected as corresponding secretary Rev. Charles Howard Malcolm, D. D., of Newport, son of the Rev. Howard Malcolm, D. D., president emeritus of the society. He had been educated at Brown and Edinburgh Universities and Princeton Thelogical Seminary and had been pastor of the Second Baptist Church of Providence for twenty years. He accepted the election Sept. 20, 1876, and held the office for nearly four years, resigning at the annual meeting in 1880.

Malcolm's administration was quiet. He spent much of his time in the office, conducting an extensive correspondence. He planned to establish in every country a national society similar to the American Peace Society, and actually succeeded in forming one in

Sweden. He suggested to the English societies the formation of a world's peace society in order to give cohesion and unity to the work, and carried on an extensive correspondence in regard to this International League of Peace Societies, as he called it. He introduced resolutions in behalf of peace into several ecclesiastical conventions and secured their passage. He wrote many articles on peace which were published in the journals and newspapers. He published two new tracts and held peace meetings in Portland, Providence, Worcester, Philadelphia and other places. He was a cultured gentleman, but not able to raise funds during the years of financial depression. In the winter of 1877-78, he endeavored to raise ten thousand dollars by getting one hundred persons to join the society as honorary members on payment of one hundred dollars each. He opened a subscription list and appealed to five hundred friends of peace for aid. Two thousand appeals were made to Sunday schools. Much personal solicitation was made, but with slight results. Then he turned to borrowing money and settling with claimants at fifty cents on the dollar. After severing his relations with the society he also compromised in regard to the amount of back pay due himself. His salary, originally fixed at three thousand dollars a year, was at the annual meeting in 1878 reduced to one hundred dollars a month, much of which was never paid. Due to impaired health he withdrew from the society at its annual meeting in 1880, but continued ever after to be its most loyal friend, though not active in peace work. He joined the Episcopal Church, was for fourteen years secretary of its Church Building Fund Commission and for three years professor in St. Stephen's College, New York state, dying at Newport, Aug. 19, 1899, sixty-seven years of age.

Dunham again took charge of the work, first as acting corresponding secretary and from Nov. 8, 1881, to May, 1884, enjoying the full title. The debt left by Miles, toward seven thousand dollars, continued with the society. The financial panic which had spread over the entire country in 1873 did not finally subside until 1880. During these years it was with the greatest difficulty that the society was able to raise money enough to pay its very meager expenses. The rental of the office was four hundred dollars a year. Dunham, as office agent, recording secretary, editor, as well as corresponding secretary, received a salary of fourteen dollars a week.

By practising rigid economy and saving the salary of a corresponding secretary and doing all the work of the society himself, Dunham managed to pay current bills and the debt. At the annual meeting of the society in 1884, he announced that all debts had been paid. The Advocate of Peace had continued through these years, bi-monthly in 1877 and 1878, four times a year at irregular intervals in 1879, 1882, and 1883, three times in 1881 and 1884, and but twice in 1880. It was circulated as before among colleges, theological schools, Young Men's Christian Associations, pastors and others.

The close relation between the society and the American Code Committee came to an end with the death of Miles. The committee chose as his successor on this committee A. P. Sprague of Troy, N. Y., who had never had any connection with the society whatever, but whose interest in the subject was due to the fact that he had won the prize offered in the spring of 1873 by Arturo Marcoartu for the best essay on the Possibility of Establishing a Representative European Assembly. Malcolm attended a meeting of this code committee on the grounds of the Centennial Exposition, Philadelphia, in the Judge's Pavilion, Sept. 28, 1876, while the fourth meeting of the congress was being held in Bremen. He was also present at the next conference of the congress at Antwerp, Aug. 30 to Sept. 4, 1877, where was passed a resolution introduced by him appointing a committee to request governments to introduce into international treaties a clause agreeing to arbitrate their differences, instead of resorting to arms.[1] At the next meeting at Frankfort-on-the Main held in the summer of 1878, the society was represented by Philip C. Garrett, a vice president living in Philadelphia. Then all official connection with the organization ceased for two decades. The organization is still in existence, its name since 1895 being the International Law Association. It is composed of leading international authorities in Europe and America—three hundred or more—holding meetings generally every year in various cities for the discussion of suggested improvements in International Law.

The evening meetings of the American Peace Society held in connection with the annual meetings continued intermittently after the breaking out of the Civil War. In 1862, the meeting was held at the Central Church, Howard Malcolm, speaker; in 1863, at the same

[1] The resolution is printed in the Advocate of Peace, January-February, 1878, p. 5.

place, Amasa Walker, speaker; in 1867, at the Rowe Street Baptist Church, Rev. A. P. Peabody, speaker; in 1869, in the School Street Church, Rev. A. A. Miner, speaker. At subsequent meetings there were several speakers. Such meetings after 1872 were held on Sunday evening; in 1870, at the Bromfield Street M. E. Church; in 1872 and 1873, at the Music Hall; in 1874, at the South Congregational Church; and in 1878, at Park Street Church.

During the two decades following the Civil War several persons of note affiliated with the society. Among the vice presidents were John Greenleaf Whittier, Hon. Robert C. Winthrop, Hon. Felix R. Brunot, Hon. Reverdy Johnson, President Theodore Dwight Woolsey, Prof. Emory Washburn, Gov. William Claflin, President Mark Hopkins, President W. R. Stearns, Hon. William E. Dodge, Dr. Edward Everett Hale, Hon. Henry L. Pierce, Hon. William B. Washburn, Gov. Alexander H. Rice, Peter Cooper, President Paul E. Chadbourne, President Julius H. Seelye, and Wendell Phillips. Among the directors were Phillips Brooks, Jay Cooke, Hon. Alpheus Hardy, and Joseph Cook. At the annual meeting of the society May 26, 1883, Grant and Gladstone were elected honorary members and in 1886, David Dudley Field.

During these years the society also lost several of its leaders. Charles Sumner, born Jan. 6, 1811, senator from Massachusetts from 1851 until his death, director of the society, 1837 to 1853, and vice president thereafter, and advisor of the society, a contributor, its representative in congress, died March 11, 1874. Shortly after the Civil War he wrote "I had expected to make it my life work to oppose war, but I found myself confronted with slavery, and slavery is war, except that in this case the weaker party is beaten in detail." His feeling on the subject of peace was shown by his gift of one thousand dollars to Harvard College in trust, the income to be devoted to annual prizes for the best dissertations on universal peace and the methods by which war may be permanently suspended, by students of any department of the university, hoping thereby to attract the attention of students to the practicability of organizing peace among nations. The fund has accumulated until July 1, 1926, it amounted to $8502.80 with an annual income of $443.30. The college has offered a prize of one hundred dollars from this fund each year since 1885.

Hon. Amasa Walker, vice president of the society continuously from 1839, who had attended the peace conferences of 1843 and 1849, and had been ever ready to help the society and whose name has been mentioned in this account several times, died during the year 1875-76, as did Hon. Reverdy Johnson, who had become vice president in 1872. Hon. Emory Washburn died Mar. 18, 1876. He was born Feb. 14, 1800 in Leicester, Mass., was a graduate of Williams College and the Harvard Law School, had been a member of the legislature several times, governor of Massachusetts, a professor of law in the Harvard Law School for twenty years, and vice president of the society from 1872 to 1876.

A series of deaths occurred during the year 1878-79. Elihu Burritt died in March leaving a portion of his estate to the society. Rev. David Patten, D. D., treasurer, 1871 to 1878, died also. Rev. Howard Malcolm, D. D., LL. D., vice president from 1843 to 1861, and president 1861 to 1878 was a third. His interest in the peace movement dated from the time when as pastor of the Federal Street Baptist Church in Boston he had been made a life member of the society by a subscription from the members of the church following an address in that church by Capt. Ladd. Others were Isaac P. Hazard , a director from 1876 to 1879, and Myron Phelps of Illinois, a director from 1870 to 1879.

In the year 1882-83 occurred the death of Peter Cooper, the philanthropist, a vice president from 1875; William E. Dodge, vice president from 1873; Samuel Willetts, a director from 1872; Israel Washburn, a vice president from 1877; J. M. Manning, a director from 1875; and George Washington Warren, member of the executive committee from 1872. Dorus Clarke associated with Ladd and vice president from 1872, died Mar. 9, 1884, at the age of 87.

The receipts and expenditures of the society from 1861 to 1879 appear in the following table. These items for the years 1880 to 1887 do not appear in the records.

For the year ending May	Receipts	Expenditures	Balance on hand
1861	$ 2,546.51	$ 2,557.38	$ 197.41
1862	1,960.20	2,136.80	20.81
1863	2,083.41	2,092.93	11.29
1864	2.447.15	2,841.07	382.63
1865	3,060.04	2,978.88	81.16

1866	3,139.23	3,116.96	103.43
1867	3,268.08	3,087.24	284.27
1868	3,184.69	3,047.33	137.26
1869	3,173.93	3,258.99	52.30
1870	10,548.50	9,536.23	1,063.46
1871	9,665.60	11,069.06	—1,792.91
1872	12,102.36	12,102.36	—1,084.14
1873	10,322.38	10,322.38	—4,300.00
1874	10,928.22	10,928.22	—5,050.71[1]
1875	—.—	—.—	338.89
1876	2,637.06	2,315.41	660.54
1877	—.—	—.—	—.—
1878	2,856.00	2,559.00	296.79
1879	1,525.76	1,372.20	489.35

These figures are taken from the reports.   The writer does not attempt to harmonize them.

[1] $6000 in debt.

Chapter XVIII

THE PERMANENT PEACE FUND

If it had not been for the peace fund, Dunham's work of reducing the indebtedness of the society would have been much more difficult than it was. The establishment of this fund was not entirely accidental. The leaders in the society on examining the history of the movement saw that the work in the past had been performed by a select few. Noah Worcester, William Ladd, and George Beckwith, none men of great wealth, had in turn from their own small means, kept the movement alive. At the death of Ladd many had expected the movement to come to an end, but it had been kept going by the exertions of Beckwith, who had served practically without pay and had made himself responsible for current expenses until the failure of his health, Oct. 22, 1855, when he had been compelled to relinquish his labors for a time. The inability of the society to get any one to take charge of the work, without making such pledges for support as the society had no means of giving, seemed for a time to require a partial suspension of its operations.

To avoid any such precarious contingency arising in the future and to secure the steady perpetual attention of the public mind to the movement, the executive committee at the suggestion of Beckwith, Oct. 1, 1856, and the society at its annual meeting in 1857, voted to raise a permanent fund of $30,000, the income to be used to support a secretary, who should devote his whole time to the cause of peace, the publication of the Advocate of Peace, and the maintenance of an office—such secretaryship, periodical, and office to be perpetual. Beckwith pledged five thousand dollars of this amount, one half of what he was then understood to be worth, provided the remainder were raised within five years from Jan. 1, 1857, no subscription to be binding unless at least twenty thousand dollars should be subscribed within that time. Furthermore, Beckwith undertook to raise the whole amount.

To start the fund the society voted to apply to it all legacies and

income from investments and funds received that were not needed
for immediate use. In 1857, it was announced that five thousand
dollars had been pledged by one person, two thousand dollars by
another, one thousand dollars each from two persons, and five hundred dollars each from several more. In 1858, it was announced
that towards fifteen thousand dollars had been subscribed, or
promised toward the fund. But the times were unpropitious, and
here the matter rested for three years.

The financial troubles following the panic of 1857 and the increasing discussion of the slavery question rendered it difficult to
obtain many pledges. Dec. 30, 1861, at a meeting of the executive
committee, it was reported that $20,650 had been pledged, thus
securing the success of the fund. The subscribers and the amounts
of their subscriptions were as follows: George C. Beckwith, Boston,
$5,000; Anthony Boynton, New York City, $2,000; William F.
Mott, New York City, $300; Joseph E. Worcester, Cambridge,
Mass., $1,000; Howard Malcolm, Philadelphia, $1,000; Thomas
C. Upham, Kennebunkport, Maine, $500; Timothy Higgins, South-
ington, Conn., $500; Alvan Underwood, Woodstock, Conn., $100;
Ephraim Spaulding, Townsend, Mass., $50; Simeon N. Perry, Wal-
pole, N. H., $200; and George W. Thompson, Stratham, N. H.,
$10,000.

At a meeting of the committee, Feb. 10, 1862, at the request of
several subscribers to the fund, it was voted to add to the fund all
the existing investments of the society—amounting to $4700—and
to increase the amount to $30,000 as soon as possible; that the
fund should be held by a board of trustees consisting of five persons
to be called the Trustees of the Permanent Fund, with power to fill
vacancies in their number; that the first board of trustees should
be elected by the subscribers to the fund with the consent of the
executive committee; that no one should act as trustee unless in
good standing in some Christian church; that one trustee should
be a Baptist and one a Congregationalist since nine-tenths of the
fund had been subscribed by members of those two denominations;
that the trustees should appropriate from their income to the American Peace Society on condition that it have in its service a secretary or "equivalent actuary who shall devote his whole time to the
cause of peace," publish a periodical of at least twenty-four octavo
pages quarterly, and maintain an office as the center of operations,

all three—secretary, periodical and office—to be perpetual; that if the trustees of the fund should at any time think that the society had failed to observe these conditions for more than two years or had forfeited their confidence, they might spend the income in other ways as they deemed best for the cause of peace or appropriate it to some foreign or home missionary society or to the American Bible Society as seemed best; that no action of the trustees should be valid if taken without the concurrence of a majority of their number; that vacancies in the board should be filled before the transaction of any business; that the trustees should serve without pay and should keep a fair account of all funds and investments, with the income therefrom; and that they should meet semi-annually for the transaction of business and make an annual report to the American Peace Society. Beckwith was authorized to collect the subscriptions in money or in promissory notes as seemed best.

May 5, 1862, the executive committee concurred in the selection of the trustees by the subscribers to the fund: James W. Converse, Joseph W. Parker, Lewis T. Stoddard, William C. Brown, and George C. Beckwith, all except the first named intimately connected with the management of the society. In 1871, following the death of Beckwith, the trustees were: Rev. Horace H. Leavitt, North Andover, Mass., James W. Converse, A. I. Benyon, and Thomas H. Russell, Boston, and Rev. George R. Leavitt, D. D., Cambridge and later Cleveland. Later William F. Warren, President of Boston University, was substituted for A. I. Benyon. Thomas H. Russell, the treasurer of the American Peace Society from 1893 to 1910, was treasurer of the fund from the early days. He was succeeded by Arthur H. Russell who died Feb. 22, 1923, and who in turn was followed by his nephew, Thomas H. Russell.

At the same time that the trustees were first elected, the executive committee voted that all investments held by the treasurer be transferred to the trustees of the fund. These consisted of several items. One was $1000 which had been received March 18, 1856, from John Brewster of Shirleysburg, Pa., on condition that he be paid fifty dollars a year for his life. Another was a legacy of $1000 which had been received from Thomas W. Ward, and by the executive committee invested May 4, 1858.

At a somewhat later date, July 6, 1865, the amount received from the Ladd bequest was added to the fund. As has been stated,

Ladd had left the bulk of his property to trustees to pay the income to his widow for life and then the principal to the American Peace Society. Through the courtesy of his nephew, S. E. Coues, then president of the society, four hundred dollars of the legacy was given them in 1845 and forty-seven hundred dollars the following year, which sum was used in liquidating indebtedness. The widow died in 1856, but certain relatives of Ladd contested the will. Though the supreme court of Maine, in 1859, decided the will to be valid, it was not until Sept. 1, 1864, that the property in Maine was finally received by the society, and by vote of the executive committee, July 6, 1865, transferred to the permanent fund. The property in New Hampshire continued in litigation, and whether or not any of it was ever received by the society does not appear from the records. In all, the society realized less than $10,000 from Ladd's bequest. At the request of the contributors to the permanent peace fund the trustees became incorporated in Massachusetts in 1862.

At the meeting of the executive committee, Jan. 23, 1866, it was reported that the fund had reached the nominal amount of $30,254. Beckwith felt that it would all be eventually received, though much of it was not to be paid until the death of the donors. One thousand dollars of it was in unproductive real estate. Twenty-two hundred dollars was in stock, on which the dividends were to be paid to Mrs. Lydia B. Merrill for life.

By the will of Beckwith, his property was to go to the fund on the death of his widow, which occurred April 5, 1881. An inventory of his estate taken in 1876, shows real estate in Boston on Beach, Albany, Pine, and Merrimack streets assessed at $73,100 on which stood mortgages aggregating $20,000. An income of $5900 had been received during the year, from which however, $2400 had been paid to Mrs. Beckwith, $2200 for insurance, repairs, interest on mortgages and other items, leaving but $1300 as the net income. By 1884, the value of the Beckwith gift was considered to be $50,000. The value of the fund outside the Beckwith gift was in 1876 stated to be $14,800. In 1888, the total value of the fund was estimated to be $67,000. In 1872, the society transferred to the fund a piece of land in Chelsea, conveyed to it by Henry K. Coburn in 1863. In 1891, Rev. G. W. Thompson of Stratham, N. H., the largest donor to the original fund, and a director of the society from 1867, left the fund $4289.09. The fund then was considered valued at $80,000. It has since slowly grown. Some of the property has been sold and the money invested in better paying securities, while other property has increased in value, and additional gifts now and then have helped to swell the total.

The yearly net profit has been given by the trustees of the fund to the society. This amount has varied greatly year by year. Thus in 1866, the amount was $1077.88; in 1873, $380; in 1874, $1700; in 1890, $2992.20; in 1891, $3839.96; in 1918, $3852.29; in 1919, $2978.77; in 1923, $6663.63; and in 1927, $7206.95. May 20, 1878, the society borrowed $2200 from the fund; May 26, 1880, $1000; of which amounts $1200 was still due in 1883.

The report of the treasurer of the society for the year ending May, 1858, was the first to mention any income from investments. Until then legacies had invariably been used to liquidate indebtedness or to expand the work of the society. But in 1858, after subscription to the permanent fund had been made, the interest on investments was given as $82.50; in 1862, $90; and then as already stated, all investments were transferred to the permanent fund. In 1893, the society bought a one thousand dollar bond issued by the C., B. & Q. RR., for $1045.25. The number of securities held by the society has steadily increased until in 1927, they were valued at $15,000.

Chapter XIX

A CHANGE IN THE TIDE

The need of a corresponding secretary had been evident for some time. At the annual meeting of the society in 1883, when it was seen that the society would soon be out of debt, it was voted to hire such an official as soon as a satisfactory man could be found. That man appeared to be Rev. Rowland Bailey Howard, who was born at Leeds, Maine, Oct. 17, 1837, a brother of Maj. Gen. O. O. Howard, a graduate of Bowdoin College, the Albany Law School, and Bangor Theological Seminary, ordained to the ministry in 1860, with service in the Civil War. He had preached in several towns in Maine, at Princeton, Ill., East Orange, N. J., and at Rockport, Mass., where he had been settled for the preceding four and a half years. He had been editor of the Advance for seven years and was a "skilful platform speaker." The executive committee offered him the position Mar. 24, 1884, at a salary of twenty-five hundred dollars a year. He accepted the position, Mar. 29, and began work June 1, after his election had been ratified by the society at its annual meeting in May.

Howard preached his first peace sermon at Rockport, April 3, 1884, after offering his resignation to the church. His congregation replied by a contribution of $30.75, and by making him a life member of the society.

Dunham was continued as office assistant until July 31, 1885, when due to impaired vision he resigned. In recognition of his fourteen years of faithfulness, members of the society presented him with a purse of two hundred dollars. His place as office agent and recording secretary was taken by Rev. Daniel Richards, a pastor of the Methodist Episcopal church.

When Howard entered upon the duties of his office the society was out of debt save for a loan of twelve hundred dollars that had been made two years before. But collections were slow. Howard collected some money by personal solicitation. His requests

148

for congregational collection in churches where he spoke were generally declined, and the few taken were not large in amount. The society wanted to enlarge the list of its publications and send Howard to the sessions of the various national ecclesiastical bodies and secure from them the appointment of committees of co-operation. He also wished to present the work in educational institutions more generally and arouse public sentiment by correspondence. But he was hampered by lack of funds. Feb. 10, 1887, the executive committee voted to attempt to raise twenty-five hundred dollars to carry on the work,—the money to be raised by the secretary. During the year 1887 the society received four thousand dollars from the Lindley Murray fund in New York City, the Obadiah Brown fund in Providence, the Rhode Island Peace Society, and the Permanent Peace Fund. This made it possible for Howard to do some of the work planned.

Howard's aim was to enlighten and influence public opinion. He renovated and revamped the journal issued by the society. Its name was changed to the American Advocate of Peace and Arbitration. It appeared bi-monthly with an occasional monthly issue. Its size was increased to thirty-two pages. It became a journal of the peace movement, containing a summary of events bearing on the peace work with discussion of current topics of interest in foreign lands and at home, news notes, editorials, and longer articles which were freely contributed, for the society was without means to pay for them. The price of the magazine for a time was reduced to fifty cents a year. As before, it was sent out very freely. It was the practice of Howard to send copies of it to congregations about to be addressed by him. Toward the end of each year the magazine was advertised in other papers.

Carefully prepared and printed paragraphs and items enunciating the principles of the society and relating interesting peace facts were sent for insertion to fifty leading newspapers during the year 1888-89. Howard is referred to primarily as an orator. He spoke with dignity and eloquence, in a charming and discriminating manner. His views were clear, his manner gentle, his mind refined, and his character lofty. He spent much time speaking. Scarcely a Sunday passed without his occupying some pulpit, and week days he spoke from every platform open to him. There was scarcely a church, city, town, or hamlet in New England in which his voice was not heard. He spoke at educational gatherings of all kinds, at colleges, schools, and theological seminaries, at clubs, societies, and conventions, at state and national meetings, churches, Sunday schools, and at prayer meetings of all denominations.

Through his efforts many of these organizations passed resolutions in favor of the movement: The General Assembly of the Presbyterian Church at Minneapolis, May 29, 1886, and again at Omaha in 1887; the Triennial Congregational Council at Chicago, Oct. 13, 1886; the Episcopal Church Triennial Convention at Chicago, 1886; and the Massachusetts Universalist Convention in September, 1886. The Presbyterian Assembly approved the work and appointed a standing committee on peace.

In the fall of 1884, Howard took a trip west. In February, 1886, he spoke at a series of meetings held in New York City, Washington, Richmond, Petersburg, and Philadelphia; in May, 1887, at Gettysburg and New York City; in October of the same year, at the meeting of the American Missionary Association at Portland; in July, 1888, at the Christian Endeavor Convention in Chicago; in March, 1889, at the Congregational Club in New York City; in April, 1890, in Washington; in August, at the Congregational Conference in Maine; in October, at the annual meeting of the American Board of Commissioners of Foreign Missions at Minneapolis, speaking at many cities on his way home; in June, 1891, at the International Missionary Association convention.

Howard frequently attended the annual meetings of the near by peace societies, notably those in Providence, and carried on communication with the societies further away, and with those in Europe. A close connection with other societies was formed. Both Howard and Tobey, in 1885, became vice presidents of the Universal Peace Union with headquarters in Philadelphia, the society formed in 1867 by the extreme radical wing of peace men. Howard nearly every summer attended the meetings of that society in Mystic, Conn., and when present always appeared on their platform as a speaker. With their permission and sanction he, June 23, 1886, organized the Pennsylvania auxiliary of the American Peace Society at Germantown, Philadelphia, with several of the officers of the Universal Peace Union as members and its membership confined to Christian believers. It later became an independent organization under the name of the Christian Arbitration and Peace Society.

Following the suggestion of Don Arturo de Marcoartu, who addressed the American Peace Society, April 13, 1885, that steps be taken to secure a closer affiliation of the peace societies of the world, the society at its annual meeting, May 25, approved his suggestion and voted to open correspondence with others for "mutual fellowship and cooperation." Sept. 14, 1886, it approved a project prepared by Leone Levi for a council and high court of international arbitration forwarded to the society by the London Peace Society. In the winter of 1886-87, the society addressed the peace societies of Europe, urging them to memorialize their respective governments to attempt arbitration when negotiations failed to secure peace. Feb. 10, 1887, the executive committee adopted an address which it issued to twenty-two peace societies in Europe and to many societies and co-workers in the United States, asking sympathy with the movement, urging each society to memorialize its government in the interest of arbitration, protesting against the warlike attitude of nations, and asking them to unite in a protest against the same.[1] In 1890, it sent an appeal for government endorsement of the universal peace congress to one hundred papers and to every member of the next federal congress.

April 15, 1885, the society asked the committee having in care the preparation of the International Sunday School lessons to insert in the series one lesson relating especially to peace. May 23, 1887, the executive committee voted to send some peace documents to China to be translated and distributed throughout the nation. During the year 1888-89 the society published six new tracts and a Sunday School concert exercise and bought several publications of other societies for sale at cost. Most of its old tracts and publications were out of print. In this and succeeding years an appeal was made for a publication fund, the income to be used in issuing books and tracts, providing peace literature, increasing the library, and circulating the society's periodicals free. Philip C. Garrett of Philadelphia offered through the society a prize of ten dollars for the best essay on arbitration as a preventative of war, to be written by a member of the Junior class at Bowdoin College. At the same time Mrs. Hannah J.

---

[1] The letter is printed on the last page of the supplement of the American Advocate of Peace, March-April, 1887.

Bailey offered two prizes to students in the Maine Wesleyan Seminary at Kent's Hill, for the best essay upon some subject connected with peace.

June 1, 1890, the anniversary meeting of the society was held in Park Street Church, Sunday evening, for the first time since 1878. Addresses were made by Mrs. Laura Ormiston Chant of England and Mrs. Julia Ward Howe. At the same time, the society elected five women to its board of directors: Mrs. Julia Ward Howe, and Kate Gannett Wells of Boston; Mrs. Hannah J. Bailey, Winthrop, Maine; Hannah W. Blackburn, Zanesville, Ohio, and Ida Whipple Benham, Mystic, Conn. Hon. Josiah Quincy's oration on the Coming Peace, delivered July 4, 1891, at the Boston Theater, was characterized as the best address on the subject of peace and war by a person not a member of a peace society since Sumner's address on the True Grandeur of Nations, July 4, 1845. A copy of it was sent to every member of Congress and to the reading rooms, libraries, and newspapers of the country.

During these years few resolutions or petitions were made by the society. In the summer of 1885, resolutions were sent to Gladstone and to the Russian government congratulating each on its wise statesmanship in averting war with the other over the Afghan question.[1] Following the suggestion of England to submit to arbitration the questions of difference with regard to the jurisdiction in Behring Sea, the society sent a memorial to President Harrison, September 15, 1890, urging the acceptance of the offer provided the British government would consent to submit the whole question as to what rights Russia possessed in that sea, and what she conveyed to the United States.[2]

The erection of a monument to Beckwith and his wife in the family lot at Mt. Auburn cemetery was voted by the executive committee, Nov. 16, 1885. It was completed Sept. 4, 1886, at an expense of seven hundred dollars. One hundred and ten dollars more were given the cemetery for permanent care of the lot. The monument was prepared by McGrath Brothers of Quincy, a plain granite cenotaph containing this inscription: "George Cone Beckwith, D. D., 1801-1870. For 33 years secretary of the American

---

[1] The former resolution is printed in the American Advocate of Peace, July-August, 1885, p. 84; the latter in ibid., September-October, 1885, p. 112. The reply from A. Tswolsky, chargé d'affaires, thanking the society for its kind sentiments is printed in ibid., March-April, 1886, p. 27.

[2] Printed in American Advocate of Peace, October-November, 1890, p. 163.

Peace Society.   Martha Washington Leavitt, His Wife, 1812-1881.   Dr. Beckwith consecrated eminent ability and unremitting toil to establish peace on earth.   His wife fully shared his faith and work.   They bequeathed nearly their entire estate to the cause they loved.   Blessed peacemakers!   Children of God."

Howard died Jan. 25, 1892, after a short illness occasioned by overwork and a general breaking down.   A surgical operation was performed, Dec. 16, while attending the Peace Congress in Rome.   He lingered for a time at the American Hospital and died there.   His body was later brought to America and buried in the town of his birth, Leeds Center, Maine, June 7th.   The society bore all expenses connected with the funeral amounting to fourteen hundred dollars.   Mrs. Howard was invited to exercise oversight of the office until a successor was secured.   Succeeding chapters tell of the labors of Howard.

Chapter XX

INTERNATIONAL AMERICAN CONFERENCE

Aside from the attempt of Bolivar to get a meeting of representatives from the various American republics in 1826, the question of American union attracted no attention until 1879, when the English and American Peace societies communicated with President Hayes and suggested the appointment of a commission to visit other American governments and propose a treaty for systematic resort to arbitration in case of a difficulty and the establishment of two courts—one appellate and the other to follow precedents—as in the Alabama case. A bill to carry out this suggestion was introduced into the House of Representatives by Representative Williams of Wisconsin, but nothing further was done with it.

In 1881, at the suggestion of James G. Blaine, then secretary of state, Garfield concurred in the issuance of an invitation to all American governments to send two commissioners to a congress to be held in Washington, Nov. 22, 1882, to agree on a basis of arbitration to remove the possibility of war in the western hemisphere. The invitation was well received and accepted by most of the nations. After the death of Garfield, Arthur renewed the invitation; but in April, 1882, he indefinitely postponed the conference because Congress, fearing the plan to unite America might offend the powers of Europe and because some of the South American states were at the time at war, had failed to take action in the matter and to provide for the expenses incident to the convention. Whereupon Senator Hoar of Massachusetts, Dec. 20, 1882, introduced a resolution in the Senate, authorizing the President to negotiate with all civilized nations willing to establish an international system of arbitration. A similar resolution was introduced into the House by Congressman McCord. Both resolutions were referred to their respective committees on foreign relations, and there died.

At the next session of Congress, 1883-84, several bills were introduced to promote the calling of a convention of American republics in the interest of commerce and peace. One of these, introduced by Congressman Evans of Pennsylvania, Mar. 3, 1884, favoring the calling of an international convention on arbitration in Washington,[1] appealed to the executive committee of the society so strongly that Feb. 2, 1885, they voted to memorialize the legislatures of the various states and Congress in its favor. Such a memorial was drawn up and presented to the Massachusetts legislature.[2] Copies were sent to Maine, Illinois and Colorado, requesting the approval by the legislatures of those states of the bill in Congress. Howard, Dunham and A. E. Winship appeared before the Massachusetts Committee on Federal Relations, Mar. 25, 1885, and urged the adoption of the memorial, but it was rejected by the legislature. In Colorado it met the same fate. The Maine legislature, however, adopted it unanimously. In the fall of the year, an attempt was made to bring the memorial before the legislatures of other states. Howard at the suggestion of the executive committee prepared an address to the clergy requesting them to preach on peace Thanksgiving Day, and asked Cleveland to give prominent endorsement of arbitration in his annual message to Congress.

In 1886, on the reference to the Committee on Foreign Relations of a bill[3] introduced into Congress by Senator Wilson of Iowa in favor of international arbitration, it seemed well for Howard to go to Washington in the interest of arbitration legislation. He left Boston, Jan. 22, stopping in Poughkeepsie, New York City, and Baltimore, where he made addresses, reaching Washington, Jan. 25th. Here he spent two weeks, urging the passage of measures to provide for a court of arbitration to judge all disputes arising in the three Americas. Through Dr. Robert McMurdy, secretary of the Arbitration League in Washington, he met several congressmen. He found the idea endorsed by many, including Senators Hoar, Wilson, Voorhees, and Logan, and Representatives Rice, McKinley, and Worthington. He talked with President Cleveland, Secretary of the Treasury Manning, and Secretary of War Endicott. Feb. 7, he preached in Richmond, called on the governor and members of the legislature of Virginia,

[1] Printed in the Advocate of Peace, June, 1884, p. 19; and March, 1885, p. 60.
[2] Printed in the American Advocate of Peace, March, 1885, p. 60.
[3] Printed in ibid., January-February, 1886, p. 4.

and visited Petersburg. On his way home he stopped in Philadelphia, Feb. 21. There he found that Love, president of the Universal Peace Union, to which Howard had recently been elected a vice president, had arranged four peace meetings at which Howard spoke.

The trip of Howard did not seem to have been entirely in vain, for the committees of both houses of Congress reported bills favorable to the request of the petitioners. The House bill authorized the president to invite the governments to the south of the United States to be represented in an international conference to discuss plans for settling disagreements by arbitration and to improve existing commercial relations. The Senate bill in addition provided for an international court and code. The latter was passed by the Senate, but Congress adjourned before the House considered either bill.

The society, however, was in earnest over the matter. Petitions were addressed to the Massachusetts legislature the next winter, asking for a memorial to Congress in favor of a convention of the American states to promote peace and arbitration. Tobey and Howard appeared before the joint committee on Federal Relations of the Massachusetts legislature, Mar. 2, 1887, in support of several petitions for such a memorial to Congress, urging the legislature to give its moral support to the movement. But due to the nearness of the adjournment of Congress, the committee voted to refer the memorial to the favorable consideration of the next legislature.

At the next session of Congress an enlarged bill was introduced into the House by J. B. McCreary of Kentucky, a Democrat, and in the Senate by Senator Frye of Maine, a Republican, authorizing the President to arrange a conference between the states in the Americas to discuss measures to preserve the peace and promote their prosperity and to adopt a plan to arbitrate disputes between the countries. The bill was referred to the Committee on Foreign Relations, which Feb. 9, 1888, reported it favorably. It was immediately passed and became a law May 24, 1888. It contained an appropriation of one hundred thousand dollars to carry the plan into effect.

The conference was planned to be held in April, 1889, but it was postponed to October 2nd. Invitations were sent out by the State Department to the various governments July 13, 1888. It will thus be seen that the object in calling the conference was purely commercial. Trade was uppermost in the minds of the projectors, and naturally the ten commissioners appointed by the President to represent the United States at the conference were all business men. Only one—Andrew Carnegie—had ever been identified with the arbitration movement. But the call for the conference contained one article (vii) that related to arbitration, and the friends of peace determined to see that that article was not ignored by the convention.

The conference met in Washington, October 2, 1889, and adjourned April 19, 1890. Secretary Blaine acted as chairman. Committees were appointed at the outset to consider the various items mentioned in the call. The conference had barely opened when it received a memorial from the American Peace Society calling attention to Article VII and earnestly urging consideration of it. Later a letter was sent the conference by Tobey, Miner, and Howard, Mar. 2, 1890, again calling attention to the need of some definite recommendation of a system of American International arbitration, urging that a serious attempt be made to avert further wars in America by recommending a general system of arbitral treaties and courts, and adding that they had forwarded to Congress the names of many thousand petitioners for the conference on the ground that it would promote international concord by commercial and friendly intercourse and secure perpetual peace on this continent by presenting some practical scheme of arbitration as a substitute for war.

Howard went to Washington to urge the passage of the Sherman arbitration resolution of Jan. 15, 1890, by the House of Representatives, after its passage by the Senate Feb. 14, 1890, and to get some action on arbitration by the conference. The Sherman resolution passed the House, April 3rd. Five days later the Committee on General Welfare of the conference made its report recommending the negotiation of a general treaty by the American republics to settle all disputes that might arise between the nations,—compulsory except when a nation's independence was at stake. April 18, the conference adopted three reports, recommended a definite plan of arbitration for the settlement of differences between American nations, recommended the adoption of a similar plan by the nations of Europe and declared that the right of conquest could not be recognized by the American nations.

April 28th, a form of treaty was drawn up and signed by eleven
of the American countries pursuant to the proposals.

The treaty provided that the notifications were to be exchanged
in the City of Washington on or before May 1, 1891, and that
any other nation could accept the treaty and become a party
thereto by signing a copy of it and depositing it with the United
States. Sept. 3, 1890, the President transmitted to Congress the
recommendations of the International American Conference, touching arbitration, and suggested the ratification of the treaties contemplated. However, this government, like all the others, failed
to take any action in the matter. The treaties, therefore, expired
by limitation without action. A form of extension was submitted
to the eleven original signers, Oct. 22, 1891, and favorable replies
were received from seven; but nothing was done.

The conference decided to establish in Washington a Latin
American library composed of contributions from the various
nations—books, maps, documents, relating to the history and
civilization of America—and requested the United States govern-
bent to provide a suitable building for the purpose of housing
them. Blaine recommended that Congress appropriate $250,000
for such a purpose, the building to contain an assembly room to
be used as a place of meeting. This was the origin of the International Bureau of American Republics, now known as the Pan
American Union, maintained by annual contributions, and controlled by a governing board of the diplomatic representatives in
Washington with the secretary of state of the United States for
many years ex-officio chairman.

Chapter XXI

THE ENGLISH DEPUTATION

After the close of our Civil War a trend toward arbitration was manifest in this country as well as in England. Charles Sumner introduced two resolutions into the Senate, May 31, 1872, and Dec. 1, 1873, recommending the adoption of arbitration as a method for the determination of international differences. They were ordered printed.[1] In December, 1873, the society sent copies of a petition broadcast throughout the country for signatures, requesting the President and Congress to use all endeavors to obtain an express stipulation between nations not to resort to war "till peaceful arbitration had been tried and never without a full year's previous notice."[2] In the spring these petitions with two thousand names were gathered by the society and sent to Congress which with similar petitions from citizens of Iowa, West Virginia and New Jersey were presented by Senator Morrill of Vermont. Both sets were referred to the Senate Committee on Foreign Relations before whom Amasa Walker appeared with an argument in their behalf.[3]

At the same time Secretary Miles visited Washington, interviewed the President, Secretary of State, and many members of Congress, all of whom commended his plan for the codification of international law as a basis for a permanent system of arbitration. As a result Senator Hamlin, chairman of the Senate Committee on Foreign Relations, presented a report, June 9, 1874, with a resolution favoring international arbitration, which the Senate adopted a few days later. The House of Representatives, on the motion of Stewart L. Woodford, June 17, 1874, unanimously and without debate passed a motion suggesting that the President endeavor to insert arbitration clauses in all future treaties.

[1] The resolutions are printed in the Advocate of Peace, July, 1872, pp. 199, 200, and January, 1874, pp. 5, 6, and February, 1904, p. 31.
[2] Printed in ibid., December, 1873, p. 89.
[3] The argument is printed in ibid., June, 1874, pp. 41, 42.

Doubtless this action of Congress was hastened by the passage July 8, 1873, of Hon. Henry Richard's motion in the House of Commons, requesting the government to communicate with foreign powers for the purpose of establishing arbitration as a permanent method of settling differences between nations—adopted by a majority of ten votes—and by the passage of a similar resolution—introduced by Mancini—by the Italian Chamber of Deputies, Nov. 24, 1873.[1] Similar resolutions on the motion of Jonas Jonassen, were passed by the Second Chamber of the Diet of Sweden, Mar. 24, 1874, by the Second House of the States General of Holland, Nov. 27, 1874, on motion of M. Van Eck, and by the Belgian Chamber of Deputies and Senate, on motion of M. A. Couvreur, Jan. 19, 1875. There the matter lay for several years, each nation waiting for the other to make the next move.

A series of petitions was sent to Congress by Rev. L. R. Eastman, who for thirty-five years had been a member of the society, serving on the executive committee from 1865 to 1871, and who was responsible for securing the services of Miles as secretary. In January, 1873, he sent a petition to Congress which was presented to that body by Senator Wilson, later vice president of the United States, requesting the appointment of a joint high commission by the nations to codify international law and to arrange for the settlement of difficulties without war and for the gradual disarmament of nations. In 1874 and 1875, he prepared similar petitions which were presented to the Senate by Senator Boutwell, and in December, 1875, another which was presented by Rufus S. Frost to the House.[2]

The next move was made May 29 and 30, 1882, when a convention was held in Washington, called by the National Arbitration League of the United States, formed the year before, to discuss the question of arbitration. Of the various peace societies invited, fifteen, including the American Peace Society, were represented by about twenty-five delegates. The convention was called to order by Gov. Frederick P. Stanton of Kansas. E. S. Tobey, president of the American Peace Society, acted as chairman. Addresses were delivered by President Hobbs of Earlham College, Indiana, Gov. Stanton, Belva Lockwood of the Universal Peace Union, and Judge Warren, of the American Peace Society. The

---

[1] All these resolutions are printed in the Advocate of Peace, July, 1874, p. 49.
[2] Printed in ibid., January, 1876, third page of cover.

convention passed a resolution inviting the nations of the world to establish a congress of nations to settle international questions which cannot be settled diplomatically, and requested England and the United States to invite the governments to a conference to prepare a definite plan for organizing the congress.[1]

In 1881, Richard, in conversation with several American correspondents, suggested that circumstances appeared opportune for an effort to obtain an arbitration treaty between Great Britain and the United States. At the meeting of the Association for the Reform and Codification of International Law at Cologne, August 16-18, 1881, Field suggested that nations make treaties binding the contracting powers in reference to one another to the use of arbitration. Then Walter Hazell, treasurer of the London Peace Society, when on a visit to the United States two years later, found a strong feeling existing in favor of international arbitration. Several members of Congress expressed to him a desire to have an arbitration agreement made between the two countries. The council of the International Association in England espoused the idea, but did nothing for a time. When they learned that several bills proposing arbitration had been introduced into Congress at the session opening December 1, 1886, the council renewed its operations and drafted a memorial. Then came the fisheries dispute, followed by another suspension of activities.

In the spring of the year 1887, just after the appearance of his book "Triumphant Democracy," which had attracted a great deal of attention both in England and the United States, Andrew Carnegie visited England. Feeling that there was but little hope of securing the adoption of a treaty between the two countries through ordinary diplomatic channels, Hon. Thomas Burt, M. P., Hon. William Randal Cremer, M. P., respectively chairman and secretary of the Workingmen's Peace Association, Hodgson Pratt, president of the International Arbitration and Peace Association, and several others met Carnegie, June 16, 1887, and discussed with him the best way to obtain a treaty of arbitration between the two countries. Carnegie advised the preparation of a memorial immediately and its presentation to the Congress of the United States.

Cremer was enthusiastic. He had been elected to Parliament in 1885 on the workingmen's ticket at fifty-seven years of age, and was impatient to accomplish something. He had been a labor

[1] The resolutions are printed in the Advocate of Peace, July, 1882, p. 25.

leader for thirty years and had found by experience in labor troubles that arbitration had settled many labor difficulties without leaving a smart in its train. He felt that arbitration in international affairs would bring about equally good results. He went among the members of the House of Commons and in three days obtained eighty-two names to a memorial to the president of the United States in favor of a permanent Anglo-American treaty of arbitration. Eventually he obtained two hundred thirty-four names to the address, of whom forty-four were Liberal Unionists, one hundred seventy-five Gladstone Unionists, and thirteen conservatives. Thirty-seven members of the House of Lords expressed their approval, as did Rev. C. H. Spurgeon, Cardinal Manning, Rev. Newman Hall, and the Congregational Union. The address was written on a sheet of paper six feet long, with decorated borders at the head, forming an allegorical design representing a union of the two countries. It read as follows:

ADDRESS

To the President and Congress of the United States of America:

The undersigned members of the British Parliament learn with the utmost satisfaction that various proposals have been introduced into Congress, urging the government of the United States to take the necessary steps for concluding with the government of Great Britain a treaty which shall stipulate that any differences or disputes arising between the two governments which can not be adjusted by diplomatic agency shall be referred to arbitration. Should such a proposal happily emanate from the Congress of the United States our best influence shall be used to ensure its acceptance by the government of Great Britain. The conclusion of such a treaty would be a splendid example to those nations who are wasting their resources in war-provoking institutions, and might induce other governments to join the peaceful compact.[1]

This address Cremer planned to have brought to the United States by a delegation from Parliament. He asked the American Peace Society to cooperate with him while in the United States, whereupon the executive committee, Aug. 29, 1887, appointed a committee of five to meet the delegation and sent Cremer a letter promising to cooperate with him in Washington, inviting the delegates bearing the address to visit Boston, and agreeing to procure petitions to Congress in favor of an Anglo-American arbitration treaty, and to hold public meetings here to arouse interest in the subject if desired.

William Jones, the secretary of the London Peace Society, fol-

---

[1] The address with the names of the signers is printed in the *Advocate of Peace*, November, 1887, pp. 156, 157.

lowing the recent resignation of Richard, came here as a delegate to the general peace congress of Friends to be held in Richmond, Ind., Sept. 28th. He reached New York, Sept. 13th, and acted as a vanguard to the delegation. He went to Washington, met Cleveland Sept. 23rd, presented to him letters from Hon. John Bright, M. P., John Greenleaf Whittier, and George W. Childs, proprietor of the Philadelphia Public Ledger, and told him of the strong desire of friends of peace on both sides of the Atlantic to secure an arbitration treaty between Great Britain and the United States. Cleveland received him cordially and asked in regard to the memorial to be presented to him.

Carnegie sailed for New York, Oct. 9, 1887, to arrange the meeting with the President, and the deputation soon followed him. The deputation consisted of one member of the House of Lords, ten members of the House of Commons, and three representatives of the British Trades Union Congress comprising seven hundred thousand workers. Lord Kinnaird represented the House of Lords. The members of the House of Commons were: Sir Lyon Playfair, Sir George Campbell, Sir John Swinburne, Halley Stewart, Benjamin Pickard, William Randal Cremer, Caleb Wright, Andrew Provand, Octavius V. Morgan, and Munro Ferguson, all of them Gladstone Liberals. The labor deputation consisted of Charles Freck of London, John Inglis of Glasgow, and John Wilson of Durham.

Immediately on their arrival in New York they went to Washington. With Andrew Carnegie, William Jones, secretary of the London society, Howard, secretary of the American Peace Society, John B. Wood, secretary of the Philadelphia auxiliary, Philip C. Garrett of Philadelphia, and Rev. Charles H. Eaton, D. D., of New York City, the deputation was received by the President, Oct. 31, 1887, at three in the afternoon. Carnegie addressed the President and introduced the speakers. Sir Lyon Playfair as the head of the delegation spoke for the signers of the address. Cremer, as secretary, spoke for the Workingmen's Peace Association. John Wilson, president of the Trades Union Congress, read the resolutions adopted by that body. Cleveland replied sympathetically and with great cordiality. Then Carnegie presented each one to the President.

Some of the delegates were obliged to return home immediately. The rest as guests of Carnegie visited Pittsburgh and went over his mills and farm, returning to Philadelphia Nov. 4th. Three days later they were given a reception in Philadelphia, planned by the Universal Peace Union. The governor and citizens were present. In the evening a banquet was given by the Union League Club, Gov. Beaver presiding. There a resolution was adopted to request the President to incorporate in his next message to Congress a suggestion for arbitration. The governor appointed a committee of five headed by John Wanamaker to present the resolution to the President. The committee found it inconvenient to meet the President, but they sent him their suggestions in writing, Nov. 28, 1887, asking him to consider the resolution and the strong sentiment shown in its favor.[1]

From Philadelphia the delegates went to Boston where they were the guests of the American Peace Society, making the Hotel Vendome their headquarters. They were received by the governor at the State House, visited Fanueil Hall, the Old South Church, Bunker Hill, Harvard, Mt. Auburn, and other points of interest. A banquet was given them by the Commercial Club at the Vendome, Nov. 10th, where addresses were made by Mayor O'Brien, Ex Gov. Rice, Ex. Gov. Long, Senator Hoar, Gen. Francis A. Walker, Rev. Minot J. Savage, Andrew Carnegie, Oliver Wendell Holmes, President Tobey, Secretary Howard, and others, besides representatives of the delegates.

On the 12th a mass meeting under the auspices of the American Peace Society was held in the Tremont Temple, presided over by President Tobey. Speeches were made by Lieut. Gov. Brackett, Joseph Cook, Alexander McKenzie, Tobey, Howard, and several of the delegates. Letters were read from Whittier, Edward Everett Hale, Henry Cabot Lodge, and others. A committee consisting of Gov. Ames, Ex Gov. Rice, Charles Theodore Russell, H. O. Houghton, Edwin D. Mead, Dr. Alonzo A. Miner, and Secretary Howard was appointed to draft a proper memorial to Congress in favor of international arbitration. The memorial as drafted, an approval of the British memorial, urged the conclusion of a treaty of arbitration between Great Britain and the United States, and expressed a hope that the President would recommend to Congress an approval of a treaty of arbitration. It was signed by many prominent men living in Boston and vicinity, including Gov. Ames, Ex Gov. Rice, Henry B. Peirce, secretary of the commonwealth,

[1] The resolution is printed in the Advocate of Peace, January, 1888, p. 12.

Leverett Saltonstall, collector of customs, Mayor O'Brien of Boston, Ex Mayor Russell of Cambridge, President Eliot of Harvard College, President Seelye of Amherst College, Bishop Paddock (P. E.) of Massachusetts, Bishop Foster (M. E.) of Massachusetts, Prof. Andrew P. Peabody of Harvard, Dr. Edward Everett Hale, Dr. Phillips Brooks, Dr. A. A. Miner, Dr. David Gregg, Dr. A. H. Quint, Rev. S. Hopkins Emery, Taunton, Joseph Cook, lecturer, Rev. J. W. Olmstead, editor Watchman, Rev. B. K. Peirce, editor Zion's Herald, Edwin D. Mead, author, Rev. A. E. Winship, editor Journal of Education, Thomas Gaffield, of the Boston Board of Associated Charities, W. H. Baldwin, president dent Y. M. C. Union, Boston, H. O. Houghton, J. E. Farwell, printer, Dr. David H. Ela, Newton Talbot, president Massachusetts Charitable Mechanics Association, President Tobey and Secretary Howard.

Edwin D. Mead, as secretary of the committee, took the petition to Washington, Jan. 20, 1888, and presented it to the president "with rare delicacy and tact," at a meeting arranged by Hon. John D. Long.[1] Senator Hoar introduced it into the Senate, January 24, 1888, and caused its reference to the Committee on Foreign Relations.

Several of the deputation attended the annual dinner at the Chamber of Commerce in New York City, Nov. 15th. A great meeting was held Nov. 27th presided over by Mayor Hewitt, who with David Dudley Field, Andrew Carnegie, Dorman B. Eaton, Morris K. Jessup, and Charles A. Peabody, were appointed a committee to petition Congress to adopt a resolution requesting the President to propose to Great Britain the making of a treaty of arbitration.[2] This petition was presented to the House by August Belmont of New York City, Jan. 10, 1888, and heard by the Committee on Foreign Relations, February 16th.

These memorials from Pennsylvania, Massachusetts, and New York, with one from Rhode Island, were the only state papers of the kind presented to Congress at this time. The Quakers presented a memorial in favor of the treaty, Jan. 30, 1888, and appeared before the Committee on Foreign Relations which agreed to present a joint resolution to Congress requesting the President to negotiate

[1] The memorial is printed in the Advocate of Peace, January-February, 1886, p. 6.
[2] Printed in ibid., June, 1888, pp. 8-11.

a treaty with Great Britain.   But the opposition over the fishery treaty, the antipathy of the Irish, and the sensitiveness of politicians preceding a presidential election prevented any action by the committee.

William Jones while in America made many addresses in educational institutions, spoke in Chicago, Cincinnati, Baltimore, Philadelphia, Nashville, and at Boston Nov. 30, 1887, under the direction of the American Peace Society.   At Nashville, in November, he spoke at the national meeting of the W. C. T. U. so effectively that a department of peace was established, which, under the direction of Mrs. Hannah J. Bailey of Maine, was for years a power in the peace movement.

Chapter XXII

UNIVERSAL PEACE CONGRESSES

IT HAD been the intention at London in 1851, to hold another peace convention the next year; but the trouble following the assumption of the title of emperor by Louis Napoleon in 1852 kept the London Peace Society busy trying to prevent an outbreak of war in England. The Crimean War, the Austrian War in Italy, the Civil War in the United States, the war in Mexico, the Seven Weeks War, the Luxemburg question, the Franco-Prussian War, the Russo-Turkish War, and the various Balkan uprisings together with the rapid increase of armaments in European countries, and the continual succession of misunderstandings between nations kept the peace societies busy with matters at home.

Suggestions looking toward the calling of an international congress were made by the English societies in 1865 and 1872, and by the American Peace Society in 1883 and 1886. A few so-called international meetings were held. In September, 1875, an international meeting of French and English societies was called in Paris by Cremer. Sept. 26, 1878, the French societies held another in the Tuileries and resolved to form the International Congress of Peace Societies to include the leading societies throughout the world. On the formation of the International Arbitration and Peace Association in 1880, Pratt attempted to federate all peace societies with it and to hold international congresses. Such were held in Paris in 1881, in Brussels in 1882, in Berne in 1884. The International League of Peace and Liberty with headquarters at Geneva, held a congress every year in the various cities of Switzerland. But these congresses were international in name only. No peace congress generally recognized as international in character was held again until 1889. In that year the French government held an exposition at Paris, commemorating the establishment of the First French republic in 1789, and intended to show the advance made in industry during the century. In connection with it were held 169 congresses of various kinds.

Believing that one of these congresses should be a world's peace congress, Charles Lemonnier, president of the International League of Peace and Liberty, gathered at his home in Geneva, Nov. 11, 1888, representatives of eight peace societies. With Hodgson Pratt presiding they formed themselves into a committee on organization, adding to their number several publicists and deputies of France. They prepared a program including such subjects as international arbitration, neutralization of rivers, canals, territories and nations, the adoption of the principle of federation, the creation of courts of arbitration, the means for promoting university lectures on arbitration, the reform of international law, the basis of an international code, and the consideration of practical means whereby law may gradually be substituted for force, and sent it with a letter to the French Minister of Commerce and Industry, Nov. 15th, requesting that a universal peace congress be held at the exposition as a sequel to that of 1878.

Feb. 28, 1889, the Minister of Commerce and Industry and the general commissioner of the exposition approved the suggestion and appointed a committee of twenty-five in charge of the congress. The latter appointed Passy as president and Morin as secretary. The committee sent letters to friends of peace in all countries asking their cooperation. One hundred societies responded to the invitation and many individuals sent in letters of adhesion. The congress was held June 23-27, 1889, with three hundred and ten delegates representing one hundred societies in seven countries and three hundred individual adherents. The principal peace leaders of Europe were there. The congress was declared a success, and it was voted to hold another at London the next year, when it was decided to continue them indefinitely.

In all, twenty-four peace congresses of the second series have been held, as follows: 1st, Paris, June 23-27, 1889; 2nd, London, July 14-19, 1890; 3rd, Rome, Nov. 11-16, 1891; 4th, Berne, Aug. 22-27, 1892; 5th, Chicago, Aug. 14-19, 1893; 6th, Antwerp, Aug. 29 to Sept. 1, 1894; 7th, Buda-Pesth, Sept. 17-22, 1896; 8th, Hamburg, Aug. 12-16, 1897; 9th, Paris, Sept. 30 to Oct. 5, 1900; 10th, Glasgow, Sept. 10-13, 1901; 11th, Monaco, Apr. 2-6, 1902; 12th, Rouen, Sept. 22-25, 1903; 13th, Boston, Oct. 3-7, 1904; 14th, Lucerne, Sept. 19-24, 1905; 15th, Milan, Sept. 15-22, 1906; 16th,

Munich, Sept. 9-14, 1907; 17th, London, July 27—Aug. 1, 1908; 18th, Stockholm, Aug. 1-5, 1910; 19th, Geneva, Sept. 23-28, 1912; 20th, Hague, Aug. 18-23, 1913; 21st, Luxemburg, Aug. 10-13, 1921; 22nd, London, July 25-29, 1922; 23rd, Berlin, Oct. 2-8, 1924; 24th, Paris, 1926.

Two, which will be treated in a later chapter, have been held in the United States, the rest in Europe. The latter have been conducted along similar lines, and often attended by four to five hundred delegates and adherents representing all the leading peace societies in Europe. Occasionally delegates have come from Africa, Asia and South America. The American Peace Society has kept in touch with them and with the exception of the eleventh has been represented at them. Seven Americans were at the first congress; eleven at the second; from four to six at the next ten: fifty at the fourteenth, fifteenth, and seventeenth; twenty-one at the sixteenth; twenty-nine at the nineteenth, forty at the twentieth, two at the twenty-first, and twelve at the twenty-third. Most of them represented the American Peace Society. Some of the delegates attended several congresses; Dr. Trueblood missed but one. Dr. Call began attending with the twentieth. Other American societies have sent delegates: the Universal Peace Union, the Christian Arbitration and Peace Society of Philadelphia; the Women's Christian Temperance Union; the National Arbitration Association of Washington; in 1902, the National Council of Women sent delegates; in 1905, the Massachusetts State Board of Trade, the New York Board of Trade, the Cincinnati Peace Society, and the New York Friends.

The congresses have generally been held in cities on invitation of the local peace societies. Frequently the meetings have been held in buildings of historic interest: at Paris in 1889, in the Palace of the Trocadero, and in the maire of the XVIth Arrondisement, Place Saint Sulpice; at London, in 1890, in Westminster Town Hall, adjacent to the Houses of Parliament and Westminster Abbey; at Rome, in 1891, in the Capitol; at Berne, in 1892, in the Swiss Parliament Hall; at Antwerp, in 1894, in the Royal Athenaeum; at Buda-Pesth, in 1896, at the Council Chamber of the Municipal Palace; at Paris, in 1900, in the hall of the Palais des Congrès, in the Department of Social Economy in the exhibition grounds; at Glasgow, in 1901, in the Berkeley Hall, St. Andrew's Hall; at Monaco, in 1902, in the hall of the Oceanographic Museum; at

Rouen, in 1903, in the council chamber of the City Hall; at Lucerne, in 1905, in the Kursaal; at Milan, in 1906, in the Villa Reale, one of the king's palaces; at Munich, in 1907, in the concert hall of the Hotel of the Four Seasons; at London, in 1908, in Caxton Hall; at Stockholm, in 1910, in the Palace of the Nobility; at Geneva, in 1912, in the University of Geneva; at the Hague, in 1913, in the Hall of the Knights, where the second Hague conference was held; at Berlin, in 1924, in the Reichstag.

There is no set system of procedure followed by the congresses. However, in general, congresses have been composed of delegates appointed by peace, arbitration, labor, cooperative, religious, and such other societies and organizations as are sufficiently interested in the subject of peace to elect them, and also individuals, adherents so called, not members of any society sending delegates, but interested in the subject.

The presidents of the congresses have always been prominent men, generally of the nation where the congress is held. Assisting the president are several vice-presidents, representing the various countries sending delegates to the congress. The United States has been represented on this board by Howard, Trueblood, Paine or Edwin D. Mead. The president, vice presidents, secretaries, and honorary officials form a bureau or executive committee or steering committee and attend to the details of management, though the first few congresses chose or appointed the bureau.

Congresses are opened by a speech by the president, followed by an address of welcome by some prominent person,—mayor, member of the city council, prime minister or other member of the cabinet —with, until 1906, responses by one delegate from each country represented, telling the progress of the peace movement since the last meeting. That report from the United States was generally given by the secretary of the American Peace Society. Since 1906 the response has been given by one person for all. Then letters and telegrams are read from persons unable to be present and messages have been sent to them and others. The official language used at the congresses is French, English and German, and sometimes Italian.

The congress divides itself into sections or committees, having to do with arbitration, current questions, international law, propaganda, disarmament, labor, education, and organization, each discussing in an informal manner subjects relating to its section or referred to it by the congress. Sections usually meet in the morning or afternoon, leaving the other parts of the day for general meetings, receptions, public functions, entertainment, or excursions. In the later conferences, the first two or three days have been given over to section work. Members sit with the section considering questions most interesting to them. The work of the sections consists in preparing material for the general meeting, presented in the form of resolutions. Here is where the discussions are the warmest, where the moderates and extremists clash and where the opposing opinions are smoothed into statements acceptable to all. When ready, a section reports its resolutions to the general meeting.

General meetings of the whole convention are held at stated intervals where all the sections meet together and examine the work of the others. The chairman of each section in introducing a resolution delivers an address explaining the matter and favoring the resolution as suggested. Minority reports are common and occasionally adopted. A resolution is often discussed at length, amendments offered, and finally the resolution passed or defeated, referred back to the section, postponed to the next year, or referred to a special committee for further study and examination. The questions discussed at the meetings vary somewhat from year to year; though each congress shows but little novelty over the preceding. The congresses in the English speaking countries have been conducted more along the lines with which people in those countries are acquainted with less section work and more addresses, often with two or three meetings held in different parts of the city at the same time.

The resolutions adopted relate to many subjects and vary yearly according to the circumstances, recommending among others the insertion of arbitration clauses in treaties, the establishment of a permanent international tribunal, the adoption of a conventional language, the abolition of military instruction in schools, the unification of weights and measures, disarmament, neutrality of straits and isthmuses, removal of customs barriers, war loans, duelling, federation of societies, propaganda, and the relation of war to women and children, labor, education, the press, Christianity and cooperation. Beginning with the new century, more attention has been paid to actualities, and resolutions have been passed in regard to individual wars and questions, such as the Transvaal,

Armenia, Egypt, Morocco, Congo, Macedonia, Venezuela, Scandinavian neutrality, and the Hague conventions. On Sundays, before, during or after the congress, religious services are generally held in Protestant churches or chapels, conducted frequently by the American delegates, and a prayer meeting, fifteen to thirty minutes in length, is held each morning during the congress. Since the war, additional questions have been discussed, such as the League of Nations, economic restoration of Europe, control of foreign affairs, protection of minorities in a state, and the release of political prisoners.

Generally the congresses have devoted their time to discussion. Occasionally papers have been read before the congress, generally written or translated into French, as the language known to the larger number of the delegates. The American delegation has always expressed itself freely in the section meetings and frequently in the general meetings. At London, in 1891, Secretary Howard read a paper entitled "The New Sympathy of the Nations," and Rev. Dr. Alonzo A. Miner of Boston, read one on limiting conscription to persons of property. At Glasgow in 1901, Secretary Trueblood was chairman of the International Law committee and presided at one of the meetings, and Edwin Mead spoke at one of the meetings in Paisley town hall. At Lucerne, in 1905, Edwin Ginn read a paper on creating a propaganda fund. At London, in 1908, Mr. and Mrs. Mead spoke. At Stockholm, in 1910, Mrs. Fannie Fern Andrews and Miss Anna B. Eckstein read papers. The congresses have generally drawn up an appeal to the nations, following the practise of the earlier series.

The congresses generally end with a banquet, and frequently there are receptions by the officials of the country where the congress is held. Thus the municipal authorities gave a reception to the congress at Paris in 1889, London in 1890, Antwerp in 1894, Buda-Pesth in 1896, Glasgow in 1901, Rome in 1903, Lucerne in 1905, Milan in 1906, Munich in 1907, and at Geneva in 1912. President Carnot at Paris in 1889, invited the delegates to a garden party at the palace of the Elysee; Yves Guyot, minister of public works, invited them to a reception at the palace of the ministry; Whitelaw Reid, American minister in Paris, entertained the American delegates. At Antwerp, in 1894, the king received a delegation from the congress. Then at London, in 1908, the king and queen gave a reception to a deputation in Buckingham Palace, the congress visited Windsor Castle and the prime minister presided at the banquet. At Stockholm, in 1910, a garden party was held at the king's palace. Excursions were taken and places of interest visited in the various cities. These social gatherings have enabled the members to get better acquainted with one another.

The motive power back of the congresses has been the Bureau International de la Paix, or Peace Bureau as it is commonly designated in this country. Its organization was urged at the congress held in Rome in 1891, by Pratt, president of the International Arbitration and Peace Association, Bajer of Denmark, and Ducommun, secretary of the International League of Peace and Liberty in Geneva. A committee of five was appointed at that congress to consider the matter. This committee reported a complete organization at the congress held at Berne the next year. The bureau organized Sept. 22, 1893, at Berne, with the American Peace Society a charter member, as the executive committee had voted to adhere to it Feb. 19, 1891, and the board of directors, Nov. 7, 1892.

The bureau consists of a board of directors; at first fifteen, later increased to nineteen, then to twenty-six, and in 1907 to thirty-five. The directors are elected by the congress. The directors in turn elect a council at first of five, later three, who with the president and secretary manage the affairs of the bureau. The secretary of the American Peace Society has been a member of the board of directors since 1893. Mrs. Belva A. Lockwood was a member from the same year to her death. In 1906, on the occasion of the last increase in membership, Edwin D. Mead, a vice president of the American Peace Society, and Prof. Samuel T. Dutton, secretary of the Peace Society of New York, and later a director of the American Peace Society, were elected to represent the United States, thus giving the United States four representatives at that time. Fredrik Bajer was president from 1893 to 1906, and Senator Henri Martin of Belgium since that time. Elie Ducommun, the vice president of the International League of Peace and Liberty at Geneva, was secretary from 1893 until his death, Dec. 6, 1906, followed by Dr. Charles Albert Gobat, a member of the Swiss national parliament from then until his death, March 16, 1914, and by H. Golay since.

Berne was made the headquarters of the bureau and later Geneva where it now is. The bureau has ordinarily met twice a year, once during the winter and once preceding, during, or following the congress, or in the late summer in years when no congress is held. The President and Secretary have been the principal executive officers and the mainstays of the bureau.

The bureau was incorporated under the laws of Switzerland immediately upon its organization. Its object has been to represent the peace societies when they were not in session, to bind them more closely together, to be a clearing house for the movement, and to act as a bureau of information. It has made a report to each congress telling of its actions during the year and narrating the progress of the peace movement. It executes the decisions of the congresses. Every year it has sent copies of the resolutions of the congress to all peace societies and frequently to foreign departments of the various governments. It has gathered a library, prepared peace material, and carried on an extensive correspondence relative to the peace movement. It has decided where the various congresses are to be held, made a preliminary appointment of the committee in charge, prepared a provisional form of the program, and published the official proceedings of the various European congresses. Its actions have always been subject to review and approval of the congresses. It began the issue of a small semi-monthly paper called *Correspondance Autographié du Bureau International de la Paix*, Dec. 12, 1892, which Oct. 25, 1895, became *Bureau International Permanent de la Paix Correspondance Bimensuelle*. On receiving a subvention from the Carnegie Foundation, Jan. 1, 1912, the magazine was enlarged and issued in three languages, French, German, and English, the title of the English edition being the *Peace Movement*. Since August, 1914, only the French edition has been printed.

The expense of running the bureau has never been large. Secretary Ducommun served without pay. The expenses of the bureau for the first year were 1192 francs; for 1904, 9000 francs. At first, its expenses were met from private subscription. The American Peace Society sent it one hundred dollars the first year. It started a permanent endowment fund in 1894. In that year the Swiss federal council voted it 1000 francs for its support. Denmark, Norway and Sweden later voted it 700 francs each. In 1910-11, eighteen governments gave it 9000 francs. In that same year, Dec. 10, 1910, it received the Nobel prize of forty thousand dollars.

The bureau also started a fund under the direction of the Rouen congress in 1903 and the Boston congress in 1904 to be used for propaganda purposes. The fund was incorporated under Swiss laws as *Caisse Internationale de Propaganda Pacifiste*, with Henri Morel, director of the International Bureau of Literary Property, Dr. Ludwig Stein, a professor, and Ducommun as trustees. The capital consisted of funds heretofore received and managed by the bureau. In 1906, the fund amounted to 16,812.10 francs; in 1911, 14,098.80 francs.

Chapter XXIII

THE INTER-PARLIAMENTARY UNION

THE arbitration treaty which Cremer had hoped to get as a result of the visit of the British parliamentary delegation to Washington was not obtained. He felt somewhat discouraged therefore. Recalling the statements made to him by several Americans, that an international arbitration treaty with France would be acceptable to America, as well as one with England, and learning that a memorial was being prepared to be presented to the French government requesting it to try to get an arbitration treaty with the United States, he wrote to Passy requesting a conference with him as the recognized leader of the peace movement in France.

Passy's reply caused Cremer to go to Paris July 19, 1888. From Passy he learned that Goblet, the French minister of foreign affairs, was desirous of obtaining information in regard to the object and results of the British delegation to America. On the suggestion of Goblet a meeting was arranged July 25th where were present Goblet, Cremer, Passy, Guyot, Faure, Gailland, and others, eleven in all. For an hour and a half, Cremer explained the object of the British memorial, its reception, the feeling produced in America, its very general cordial reception, and told of the apparent desire by many to have an international arbitration treaty with France. At a subsequent meeting, Cremer suggested a conference between members of the French and British parliaments who were friendly to the cause. Such a conference the meeting directed Cremer and Passy to call, if possible in the fall.

Oct. 31st they got together forty members of the French and English parliaments at the Grand Hotel, Paris. One hundred others announced their sympathy with the meeting. Passy was elected president, and Cremer and Sir George Campbell vice presidents. They discussed the question of arbitration treaties, resolved to hold a conference in Paris the following year, and to invite to it representatives from other parliaments interested in

176

the question of obtaining perpetual peace by promoting treaties of arbitration. Passy acted as secretary of the French members, and Cremer of the British.

In April, invitations were sent by the joint committee to the state department of each country, explaining the object of the meeting and urging the attendance of members of parliament, interested in the question of arbitration, at the "Inter-Parliamentary Conference for International Arbitration." The American Peace Society, believing that the venture was a good one, sent a circular to all members of Congress, May 4, 1889, calling their attention to the conference to be held in Paris and urging them to see that America was adequately represented on that occasion.[1]

And thus the first unofficial meeting of representatives from various parliaments met at Paris, June 29 and 30, 1889, immediately following the first meeting of the Universal Peace Congress. It was not a delegated body. No one was sent. Any member of the highest legislative body in his country was admitted to discuss questions more of a legislative and judicial character than those discussed at the peace congress. The aim was to enable the delegates to carry the peace sentiment there created back to the governing authorities at home, and to resist the war policies then stalking through the lands.

Ninety-six members of parliaments, of whom eighty-five were from France and England, met in the Salle des Fetes in the Hotel Continental at Paris and there, presided over by Jules Simon, formerly prime minister of France, were welcomed most cordially. They voted to meet again the next year in London, following the meeting of the peace congress. They also voted that membership in the organization should be extended to include such former members of parliament as had been members of any conference while a member of parliament. In 1912, the size of the body was further increased by admitting representatives from dependent states having foreign departments. The meetings have continued to the present time. In all, twenty-four conferences have been held, as follows: 1st, Paris, June 29, 30, 1889; 2nd, London, July 22, 23, 1890; 3rd, Rome, Nov. 3-8, 1891; 4th, Berne, Aug. 29-31, 1892; 5th, Hague, Sept. 4-6, 1894; 6th, Brussels, Aug. 13-15, 1895; 7th, Buda-Pesth, Sept. 22-24, 1896; 8th, Brussels, Aug.

[1] Printed in American Advocate of Peace and Arbitration, June, 1889, p. 84.

6-11, 1897; 9th, Christiania, Aug. 2-4, 1899; 10th, Paris, July 31 to Aug. 2, 1900; 11th, Vienna, Sept. 7-9, 1903; 12th, St. Louis, Sept. 12-14, 1904; 13th, Brussels, Aug. 28-31, 1905; 14th, London, July 23-25, 1906; 15th, Berlin, Sept. 17-19, 1908; 16th, Brussels, Aug. 29 to Sept. 2, 1910; 17th, Geneva, Sept. 18-20, 1911; 18th, the Hague, Sept. 3-5, 1913; 19th, Stockholm, Aug. 17-19, 1921; 20th, Vienna, Aug. 28-30, 1922; 21st, Copenhagen, Aug. 13-18, 1923; 22nd, Berne and Geneva, Aug. 22-28, 1924; 23rd Washington and Ottawa, Oct. 1-6, 1925; 24th, Paris, Aug. 25-30, 1927.

It will be noted that the first four conferences were held immediately following the meeting of the peace congresses. In fact, it was intended at first, to have each supplement the other and to have some subjects considered by both organizations; but it was soon found that they had but little in common, and the interests of each could be better subserved by having them meet separately.

The meetings have been conferences. The bodies have been divided into three or four committees where resolutions have been prepared on matters laid before them by the committee on program and submitted to the full gathering for final adoption or rejection. The number of resolutions adopted by a conference has generally been small. The object of the organization as stated by it in 1892, was to discuss principles that conflict between states and submit them to an arbitration tribunal for final settlement and to discuss other international questions of general interest connected with the idea of arbitration. In 1912, the object was said to be to obtain united action on the part of members of all parliaments through the recognition of the principle that disputes between nations should be settled by arbitration or by other friendly or judicial means and to study other questions of international law and of problems pertaining to the development of peace relations between nations. In 1922, the object was stated to be to study all questions of an international character suitable for settlement by parliamentary action.

Since arbitration was the original cause of its existence, the conference has spent most of its time studying that subject. At its first conference six resolutions were passed urging governments to conclude treaties agreeing to submit to arbitration the settlement of all differences arising between them, and that, until such time as permanent treaties are made, a special arbitration clause should be inserted in all special treaties of commerce. In 1889 and 1890 they discussed the conclusion of treaties and how to get all nations to submit disputes to arbitration. In 1891, 1892, and 1893, they discussed the initiation of permanent arbitration tribunals. In 1894, a committee of six was appointed to submit a draft for the organization of a permanent court of arbitration. In 1895, the report of the Committee was discussed and accepted and submitted to all governments by Chevalier Descamps, a professor of international law at Louvain and a member of the Belgian senate. Descamps represented Belgium at the Hague conference in 1899 The convention adopted by the Hague conference "for the pacific settlement of international disputes" was based on this draft. In 1905 and 1906, they studied a model arbitration treaty.

Among the many resolutions passed were several, approving the attempts made to secure the passage of resolutions requesting the president to open up negotiations with other powers for the purpose of concluding treaties of arbitration, calling for a congress of the powers to consider the methods of arbitration, recommending a permanent congress of nations, against war loans, approving the formation of the international labor office, disarmament, mandates, and against obligatory military service. An address to the press was sent to the journals of Europe in 1895.

With two exceptions the meetings since the third have been held in government buildings and to a certain extent under government patronage, inasmuch as the meetings have generally been opened by cabinet officials or the president of one of the houses of parliament. As a rule non-members are not allowed to sit with the conference. An exception to this rule was made in the case of William Jennings Bryan by the conference in London in 1906. He had recently given a fourth of July address before the American Peace Society, in which he had urged the adoption of international arbitration. Though not strictly a member of the conference, because not a member when he had been in Congress, he was invited to sit with it and to speak.

If there is little speechmaking in the official gatherings, there is plenty of it at the unofficial meetings, for the government entertains the delegates; while receptions, teas, and banquets occur in almost endless succession, at every one of which members are called upon to speak. In fact, entertainment and sight seeing have generally occupied much of their time, thus enabling the lawgivers of each country to become acquainted with the views and surroundings of other nations at first hand. Even the rulers of the countries are interested in the conferences. Since 1899, they have extended great courtesies to the conference. In 1921, the king of Sweden, and, in 1923, the king and queen of Denmark gave state receptions to the delegates. In 1925, the President of the United States, after the passage of an act by Congress, sent an invitation to the Union to meet in Washington, and when the delegates arrived he received them at the White House.

Probably a good idea of the amount and character of the entertainment given can be obtained from reading an account of that given in this country on the occasion of the meeting in Washington, Oct. 1-6, 1925, with a closing session in Ottawa, October 12th. The United States Congress voted $50,000 to meet the expenses of the meeting and the entertainment of the visitors. The headquarters of the American group were opened at the Hotel Pennsylvania, New York City, Saturday, September 26th, at ten o'clock in the morning, where the delegates registered on their arrival. The mayor's reception committee met at quarantine the incoming steamers bearing members and conveyed them from the pier to the hotel, while the War Department transferred their baggage. Sept. 28th the Mayor's committee conveyed them from the hotel to the city hall, where they met the Mayor, then to luncheon at the Astor Hotel given by the League of Nations Non-Partisan Association. Sept. 29th, the delegates were taken on a sight seeing tour around the harbor, followed by a dinner to the officers of the Union and the heads of each delegation held at the Harvard Club by the Council on Foreign Relations. Sept. 30th, they took a special train to Philadelphia, where they were met by the Mayor's committee, received by the Mayor, and shown around Philadelphia. Following luncheon they were taken to Chester and visited Swarthmore College, leaving Chester at evening on the Pennsylvania Railroad, with dinner on the train at the expense of the company. On arrival at Washington at 9:30, they found a delegation of congressmen with the marine corps, the navy band and the commissioners of the District of Columbia, who took them to the Mayflower Hotel, where they remained as the guests of the American group while in Washington. They registered at the Capitol for the first session of the conference which was held in the hall of the House of Representatives. At noon, luncheon was served at the Mayflower to the ladies. At 7:00 p. m., a reception was given at the Shoreham by the League of Pen Women. At 9:00 p. m., a reception was given by Mrs. J. B. Henderson. Oct. 2nd, they met at the Pan American building in the morning. In the afternoon they were received by the President at the White House with a reception following at the Red Cross headquarters. Oct. 3rd, in the afternoon a garden party was held at Twin Oaks. Oct. 4th, tea was served by Mrs. Thomas F. Walsh. Oct. 5th, luncheon was served by the Chamber of Commerce and tea for the ladies by the National University Woman's Club. Oct 6th, they went to Mt. Vernon and had dinner in the evening at the Mayflower with the Secretary of State presiding. Oct. 7th, at four o'clock in the afternoon, they left for New York via the Baltimore & Ohio Railroad, with dinner on the train at the expense of the company. The Carnegie Endowment for International Peace took care of them while they remained in New York. The next day they were taken through the city, with a banquet in the evening. Oct. 9th, they visited the Stock Exchange, the Museum of Natural History and the Metropolitan Museum. Oct. 10th, they went to Niagara Falls, which they saw illuminated in the evening. Oct. 11th, after luncheon, they were turned over to the Canadian group, which took them to Hamilton, Toronto, Ottawa, Montreal, and Quebec, where the former round of drives, sight seeing, receptions and banquets was repeated.

The attendance has varied according to circumstances and the city where the conference has been held. At Rome, in 1891, there were two hundred present; at Paris, in 1900, six hundred and fifty; at Berlin in 1908, eight hundred; at Stockholm, in 1921, one hundred and twenty; at Washington, in 1925, three hundred and thirty-five. In addition, members are generally accompanied by wives, daughters, or other members of their families.

The programs of the first three conferences were prepared by local committees. At the second meeting at London in 1890, Bajer of Denmark moved the formation of an international bureau with a secretariat to represent the conference between sessions. His plan was to bring forward a similar motion at the next peace congress and have a combined bureau created to act for both the peace congress and the inter-parliamentary conference. But when the matter was brought before the congress it adopted a bureau of its own. So at Berne, in 1892, the conference created a bureau with Albert Gobat, a member of the Swiss council, as director, secretary and agent. He held the office until July 1, 1909, when he withdrew to give his undivided attention to the International Peace Bureau at Berne, of which he had been acting as director since the death of Elie Ducommun in 1906. He kept in communication with the various groups, advised them, prepared for the meetings, advertised their results, brought the attention of the public to the work of the conference, sent copies of the resolutions to the various governments and issued appeals to public opinion.

At the Hague in 1894, a constitution prepared by the bureau was adopted by the conference, giving it the name of Inter-Parliamentary Union. The bureau or central office was to be composed of one member, two after 1899, from each parliament in which it had a branch. The members in each parliament were to form local committees or groups with their own constitutions, rules, and offices. In 1908, a reorganization took place. A paid secretariat was established. Heretofore, a chairman had been designated for each session. Hereafter the conference took a permanent chairman. Auguste Beernaert, the Belgian minister of state and later prime minister and president of the lower chamber, was the first permanent chairman. At his death in 1912, he was followed by Lord Weardale, who had attended all the conferences and was the chief promoter of the reorganization of 1908. The chairman with four others elected, one each year, by the conference and belonging to different groups, form the executive committee directly controlling the bureau which in 1909 was transferred from Berne to Brussels. The management of the bureau was placed in the hands of a secretary general nominated by the council. Above the executive committee and secretary general and overseeing them is the council composed of two members elected by each group, and controlling the finances, fixing the estimates of expenses and passing on the resolutions to be submitted to the conference for consideration. By changes made in 1921, each group now elects two delegates to the council, and five more if the group has fifty members, and one for each additional ten up to one hundred.

The procedure of the conference was also changed. Formerly the subjects to be discussed at the conference were not submitted until a day or two before the meeting. Since 1912, it has been the practice to prepare the program and circulate it some time before the conference is to be held. The aim is to make the discussions constructive.

From July 1, 1893, to Dec. 1, 1897, Gobat published *La Conférence Interparlementaire Revue Mensuelle,* a monthly paper giving an account of the work of the bureau. From 1896 to 1908, the minutes of a conference were published by the group responsible for the organization of the meeting. Since 1910, the bureau has prepared the minutes and printed them in a uniform manner. An annual was issued from 1911 to 1914. Since 1921, the bureau has issued *Bulletin Interparlementaire Organ Oficial du Bureau de l'Union Inter-parlementaire,* with an English edition since 1926.

These changes cost money. Passy had paid the expenses of the preliminary meeting in 1888. The International Arbitration League of which Cremer was secretary paid the expenses of the first regular conference in 1889. The various countries where the conferences were held had since 1899 granted money for the entertainment of their guests, and Norway had granted them money to pay their running expenses. Lord Weardale was largely responsible for the changes in 1908. He secured promises guaranteeing a subvention for five years or until it could be shown whether or not the governments would support the Union. He persuaded the British Parliament to appropriate £300 a year for the support of the Union after 1908. In 1910, Bartholdt got a bill through Congress appropriating $2500 a year for the support of the Union, increased to $4000 in 1923, and to $6000 in 1925. Most if not all the countries now grant governmental help in the support of the bureau. In 1914 its income was $12,000 to $14,000 a year; in 1921, $14,000.

When Gobat ceased to act as director, Christian L. Lange, the first secretary of the Nobel Prize Committee in Norway, became director of the Union and moved its headquarters from Berne to Brussels, from where it was moved to Norway in 1914. During the war the activities of the Union were suspended. Merely an organization was maintained. Subventions from the governments practically ceased. The groups in the neutral countries kept up their organization and kept in touch with the central bureau in order that when the end of the war came the Union might be ready for work. The council of the Union met for the first time after the war, Oct. 7 and 8, 1919, and called a conference of the Union at Stockholm in 1921, where they discussed their relation with the League of Nations and voted to continue the Union. June 25, 1921, the headquarters of the Union were moved to Geneva.

Although the Inter-parliamentary Union had its germ in the desire to obtain an international arbitration treaty with the United States, there was but one American present at the Paris meeting, in 1889, Justin R. Whiting, a member of Congress from Michigan. Whiting was well treated by the conference, was elected one of four vice presidents, and presided over one of the sessions. The absence of Americans from succeeding conferences was so noticeable that at Buda-Pest in 1896, the conference formally regretted the absence of members from the United States and invited them to be represented at future conferences. In 1897, the invitation was presented to the House of Representatives by Speaker Reed, with the result that Samuel J. Barrows, member of Congress from Boston, went to the next meeting at Brussels in 1897. He was warmly welcomed, was made a member of the business committee, and delivered an address on the subject of arbitration. He went also to the succeeding meetings at Christiania in 1899 and Paris in 1900. Richard Bartholdt from Missouri was at the meeting at Christiania in 1899 and Vienna, in 1903. In 1899, the year that both were present at the conference, they were chosen members of the council.

With the exposition at St. Louis in mind, Bartholdt at Vienna in 1903, invited the conference to meet at St. Louis the following year. After some hesitation, the invitation was accepted. Bartholdt on his return to the United States organized a group of forty-three members, of whom twelve were registered at the St. Louis conference. There has been no conference since where the United States were not represented. Twenty went to Brussels in 1905; eight to London in 1906; eight to Berlin in 1908; sixteen to Brussels in 1910; four to Geneva in 1912; seven to the Hague in 1913; eight to Stockholm in 1921; nine to Vienna in 1922; twelve to Copenhagen in 1923; nine to Berne in 1924; forty-three to Washington in 1925; and twenty-four to Paris in 1927.

Bartholdt was elected president of the American group in 1904, a position he held until 1915, when he retired from Congress. James L. Slayden of Texas, who had been at Brussels in 1905, was elected his successor. When he left Congress in 1919, he was followed by

Senator William B. McKinley of Illinois. On the death of Senator McKinley, in December, 1926, Representative Theodore E. Burton of Cleveland, who had been at the St. Louis conference in 1904, was elected president. It is worthy of note in this connection that all four presidents of the American group had been members of the Inter-Parliamentary Union for many years and that all of them have held office in the American Peace Society, three of them having been its president. Another close bond between the American group and the American Peace Society is that Dr. Arthur Deerin Call, the secretary of the society, has, since Feb. 24, 1920, served the American group as its executive secretary. For his work as Director of the Washington Conference in 1925, Call received thanks and congratulations from all the Groups, from France the cross of the Legion of Honor.

Chapter XXIV

AT THE END OF THE CENTURY

At about the time of Howard's death, in 1892, there was a complete change of officers of the American Peace Society. Thomas H. Russell became treasurer in 1893; D. C. Heath was auditor, 1890 to 1896, followed by William E. Sheldon from 1896 to 1900. Hon. Edward S. Tobey, president of the society since 1873, resigned in 1891. The executive committee showed their appreciation of his work by making him a life director of the society, Mar. 25, 1892. In his place was elected Hon. Robert Treat Paine, a descendant of the person with the same name who signed the declaration of independence. He graduated from Harvard College in 1855 at the head of his class. He originated the Wells Memorial of Boston, the workingmen's loan association, and the workingmen's building association to provide homes and rational amusements for workingmen, and to loan them money at low rates of interest. He was a lawyer, a member of the Trinity Club, a member of the legislature, and president of the Boston Board of Associated Charities.

At a meeting of the directors of the society, Feb. 8, 1892, a committee of five was appointed to submit names for a corresponding secretary. Benjamin Franklin Trueblood had graduated from Earlham College, Richmond, Indiana, in 1869. In 1887 he received the degree of LL. D. from Iowa Wesleyan University, and in 1890, from Iowa State University. He had been president of Wilmington College, Ohio, for five years, and of Penn College, Iowa, for twelve years. He spoke French fluently and Italian and German well. During the year 1890-91, he had been in Europe representing the Christian Arbitration Society of Philadelphia and had delivered twenty lectures in France. In 1891, he had attended the peace congress at London. Chosen secretary of the society, he began his labors in 1892. Both men, Paine and Trueblood, president and secretary, in the prime of life, travelled together in their work for nearly two decades.

Trueblood made no radical changes in the society. At the annual meeting in 1891, the constitution was amended slightly for the first time since 1839. In Article VII, the word "finances" was substituted for "bills." In Article VIII, the auditor was added to the executive committee as ex-officio member. At the annual meeting in 1892, several amendments were made to the constitution. In Article IV, "and every donor of five dollars" was omitted. In Article V, "and fifty dollars a life member," was omitted. Article VII was entirely rewritten as follows: The officers of the society shall be a president, vice presidents, a secretary, a treasurer, an auditor, and a board of directors consisting of not less than twenty members of the society, including the president, secretary, and treasurer, who shall be ex-officio members of the board. All officers shall hold their offices until their successors are appointed; and the board of directors shall have power to fill vacancies in any office of the society. There shall be an executive committee of seven, consisting of the president, secretary, and five directors to be chosen by the board which committee shall, subject to the board of directors, have the entire control of the executive and financial affairs of the society. Meetings of the board of directors or of the executive committee may be called by the president, secretary, or two members of such body. The society or the board of directors may invite persons of well-known legal ability to act as honorary council.

In 1893, further amendments were made as follows: Article IV was changed to read: "Every annual subscriber of two dollars shall be a member of this society." Article V was changed to read: "The payment of twenty dollars at one time shall constitute any person a life member." In Article VI, "the two highest officers," was changed to "the officers and delegates."

Oct. 17, 1892, the executive committee appointed Rev. W. G. Hubbard of Columbus, Ohio, to be soliciting agent, to obtain conference with representatives of other peace societies, and to appoint a committee on organization. A few pamphlets were added nearly every year to the list of those already in circulation, and peace literature of all kinds was kept by the society for sale or distribution. The executive committee continued to meet to look out for finances and the directors to look out for the work of the society. The Advocate of Peace underwent but little change. It became a monthly magazine in June, 1892, and has remained such ever since.

Dr. Trueblood was editor of the paper and attended to the work in the office.

The correspondence of the society demanded more of his time and left the secretary but little time for outside speaking. However, he spoke whenever an opportunity presented itself, mainly in New England, though he made speeches occasionally at a distance from home. Dec. 7, 1892, he addressed the National Reform Association at Philadelphia. In December, 1894, he spoke at a memorial service of the Christian and Arbitration Society of Philadelphia. In August, 1895, he addressed the meeting at Mystic, Conn., and at Ocean Grove, N. J. Oct. 8, 1896, he spoke at the Women's Christian Temperance Union convention at Brooklyn; and April 6, 1897, before the Meadville (Pa.) Theological Seminary. In February, 1900, he gave twenty-three lectures in Kentucky, Tennessee, Georgia, and South Carolina, under the auspices of the Alkahest Lecture Lyceum of Atlanta, Ga., the subjects being the Hague Conference, militarism, federation of the world, and the like, following it up the next winter by a similar course in Georgia, Alabama, Mississippi, and North Carolina. He attended the peace congresses in Europe. In 1897, he was elected a corresponding member of the Central Committee of the International Association of Journalists, organized at Paris for the promotion of industrial peace.

At the annual meeting of the society, in 1893, it offered three prizes of one hundred dollars, fifty dollars, and twenty-five dollars each for essays written by members of the senior and junior classes in the academic department of colleges and universities in the United States on some subject connected with peace propaganda. In December, the executive committee, in informing the presidents of the colleges of the offer, announced the subject as the Economic Waste of War, the essays to be from two thousand to thirty-five hundred words in length, typewritten, and to become the property of the society. Each writer was to send his essay to the president of his college who was to send to the executive committee the best one written in his college. The executive committee was to take into consideration in awarding the prizes the force of the argument and the general character of the composition. Essays were to be received until July 15, 1894. They were received from eight colleges. In December, the examining committee, consisting of Dr. Alfred C. Garrett of Harvard University, G. W. Stearns of

Middleboro, and Dr. Trueblood, awarded the prize of one hundred dollars to Henry Salent of the University of the City of New York, fifty dollars to B. F. Arnold, of Iowa College, and of twenty-five dollars to Arthur K. Kuhn of the College of the City of New York.[1]

The annual business meetings of the society were held in Pilgrim Hall from 1886 to 1898, when they were changed to one of the smaller halls in the Tremont Temple. During the last decade of the century three evening meetings were held in connection with the annual meetings; in 1892, at the First Baptist Church, with Robert Treat Paine and Secretary Trueblood as speakers; in 1895, at the Y. M. C. A. hall, with Edward Atkinson, Dr. Reuen Thomas, George S. Hale, and Samuel B. Capen as speakers; and in 1896, in the Huntington Hall, with Lyman Abbott, Edward Everett Hale and Gen. Francis A. Walker as speakers. In May, 1892, the office of the society was moved from number 1 to number 3 Somerset Street.

During the last two decades of the nineteenth century a number of prominent officials of the society died: In 1887, Mark Hopkins, vice president from 1872; in 1889, Jacob Sleeper, vice president from 1873; in 1892, John Greenleaf Whittier, vice president from 1870; in 1893, Bishop Phillips Brooks, vice president from 1888; and Dr. Andrew P. Peabody, a director in 1835, a vice president from 1843; in 1894, Bishop Matthew Simpson, (M. E.), vice president from 1876; in 1895, Dr. Alonzo A. Miner, member of the executive committee from 1886; and Senator Robert C. Winthrop, vice president from 1871; in 1896, George F. Magoun, vice president from 1876; in 1897, Gen. Francis A. Walker, vice president from 1892; in 1898, Dr. J. H. Allen, director from 1892; Frances E. Willard, vice president from 1894; and Rev. Luther H. Angier, director, 1862 to 1892, and vice president thereafter; and in 1900, William E. Sheldon, member of the executive committee from 1888; and Bartholdt Schlesinger, director since 1893. Dr. Peabody had served the society for fifty-two years. Whittier left $500 to the society.

During the same time several men and women of note assumed office in the society. Among the directors were Rev. J. Graham Brooks, and D. C. Heath. Among the vice presidents were: Wendell

[1] These essays are printed in the Advocate of Peace, February, 1895, pp. 30-35.

Phillips, Bishop Henry W. Warren, Hon. Frederick A. Douglass, David Dudley Field, Hon. Thomas N. Hart, William Wetmore Story, Senator Sherman, Bishop Lawrence, Mrs. Mary A. Livermore, Dr. Lyman Abbott, Dr. Merrill E. Gates, Jane Addams, and Edwin D. Mead. Among those who held both offices at various times were: Hon. H. O. Houghton, Dr. Edward Everett Hale, Everett O. Fisk, Rev. Joseph Cook, Rev. A. E. Winship, Rev. Reuen Thomas, and Mrs. Julia Ward Howe.

The report of the treasurer from 1888 to the end of the century shows the following:

For the year ending May 1	Receipts	Expenditures	Balance on hand
1888	$5256.04	$5166.72	$ 89.32
1889	5063.84	4420.18	437.88
1890	4428.02	4772.00	93.90
1891	9560.30	7323.30	2350.45
1892	6335.90	7679.04	1007.31
1893	7030.00	6819.57	176.49
1894	6645.90	6408.61	413.78
1895	5989.10	5838.45	150.65
1896	5346.85	5419.19	78.31
1897	6518.47	6287.41	309.37
1898	5636.69	5834.14	111.92
1899	5498.59	5250.17	360.34
1900	5127.43	5410.10	77.67

In 1893, the society invested $1045.25, and in 1895, borrowed $500, which debt is reported in subsequent years as follows: 1896, $578.95; 1897, $1270.60; 1898, $1177.13; 1899, $1400; and 1900, $1349.22.

The Venezuela question for a time disturbed the society. Dec. 23, 1895, six days after Cleveland had sent a strong message to Congress relative to the Venezuela boundary dispute, the directors of the society adopted a lengthy resolution opposing a war between the United States and Great Britain, referring to threats of war as "worse than stupendous blunder," objecting to the extension of the Monroe doctrine to cover boundary disputes, approving intervention "by honorable diplomatic appeal and protest, including urgent request for arbitration."[1] The resolution was sent to the press. Telegrams were sent to the Marquis of Salisbury,

[1] Printed in the Advocate of Peace, January, 1896, pp. 10, 11.

urging arbitration, and to Senators Sherman and Allison, urging delay.

Churches, educational institutions, reform associations, chambers of commerce, literary clubs, societies of various kinds, passed strong resolutions in favor of peace. Public meetings were held in several large cities by prominent and influential citizens. Washington's birthday was observed very generally throughout the country in the interest of the movement, culminating in the national conference at Washington, April 23, 1896, attended by four hundred delegates from forty-six states and territories.

In Great Britain there was great activity also. A series of meetings and conferences was held in London and other cities. Organizations of all kinds passed resolutions in favor of peace. A big demonstration was held in London, March 3rd, presided over by William T. Stead, with letters read from A. J. Balfour, Rt. Hon. Henry Asquith, James Bryce, Hall Caine, and others. And quiet was restored. Nov. 23, 1896, on the settlement of the question, the directors of the American Peace Society conveyed an expression of profound gratification to the President that an agreement had been reached by which the Venezuela boundary was to be referred to arbitration.

The work of the societies began to change. In the past they worked to get people to listen to them and governments to adopt peace methods in dealing with one another. They had now succeeded in gaining some attention. No longer was it necessary to create a peace atmosphere. Inertia had been overcome. The most vehement protests against war were now made by persons having no connection with the peace societies. Everybody believed in peace. They differed only in the method of procuring it. In latter days the work of the American Peace Society has been to keep the train on the track, to furnish the new drivers with the proper fuel, to criticise those who in their eagerness wander too far from the orthodox views of peace and to curb the hyperradical peace element, to separate the practical from the impractical. Peace societies, to be sure, continued to hold meetings and to issue literature; and they ceased to be laughed at as mere theorists. In narrating the further history of the American Peace Society, mention will necessarily be made more frequently of many elements at work outside the society.

Chapter XXV

THE CHICAGO PEACE CONGRESS

The American Peace Society was soon interested in the Columbian Exposition. Before it had been decided when or where the exposition was to be held, a committee, consisting of Secretary Howard, William E. Sheldon, C. B. Smith, Dr. A. A. Miner, and C. T. Durham, wrote a letter in 1889 to Chauncey M. Depew as chairman of the New York general committee on the world's exposition for 1892, urging the desirability of holding a world's peace congress in connection with the exposition and calling attention to the great success of the peace congress held at Paris earlier in the year.[1] Again the executive committee, Dec. 23, 1890, instructed the above committee to take decisive measures toward calling the congress as soon as the place of exhibition had been determined.

After the place of the exposition had been decided upon and the exposition authorities had been definitely organized, they appointed a world's congress auxiliary to the World's Columbian Exposition, which with Charles C. Bonney as chairman, Thomas B. Bryan as vice president, Benjamin Butterworth as secretary, and Lyman J. Gage as treasurer, was to arrange a series of congresses to be held during the exposition. Among the congresses suggested was one to consider the substitution of arbitration for war, known later as the Arbitration and Peace Congress. This seemed an excellent opportunity to Trueblood to bring the series of peace congresses to this country; and at his invitation the fourth peace congress at Berne in 1892 voted to hold its fifth congress at Chicago, leaving its management in the hands of the American peace societies.

[1] The letter is printed in the American Advocate of Peace, September-October, 1889, p. 120.

192

Representatives of the leading American peace societies—the American Peace Society, Universal Peace Union, Christian Arbitration and Peace Society, Peace Association of Friends in America, National Association for the Promotion of Arbitration, Human Freedom League, and the Pennsylvania Peace Society—held a conference in Philadelphia, Dec. 15, 1892, to make arrangements for the congress. The interests of the American Peace Society were looked after by Trueblood, Paine, Baily, and S. L. Hartman of Lancaster, Pa. The nature and purpose of the congress were discussed, committees on arrangements, program, and exhibit were appointed, on each of which Trueblood was a member.

To the committee on exhibit was assigned 495 square feet of space in the Manufacturers and Liberal Arts building, where were placed the arbitration rules of several chambers of commerce, Senator Sherman's resolution on arbitration, charts showing the cost of war, the history of our public debt, size of armies, portraits of prominent peace men, list of peace publications, peace flags, and copies of the publications of the American Peace Society. At the end of the exposition, its exhibit received an award from the exposition authorities.

The committee on arrangements decided that it would not be advisable to hold a separate congress independent of the general one sponsored by the auxiliary. Thus the fifth annual peace congress was held at Chicago under the direction of the American peace societies as the International Arbitration and Peace Congress under the direction of the World's Congress Auxiliary of the Columbian Exposition. The auxiliary provided room free in the Permanent Memorial Art Palace on the Lake front and paid the greater part of the expenses. The societies provided the program and paid all incidental expenses amounting to $652.44. Of this amount the American Peace Society paid $122.50, the Universal Peace Union, $50, and the Rhode Island Peace Society, $80. Jonathan W. Plummer, a business man in Chicago, acted as treasurer.

The arrangements for the congress were made jointly with the auxiliary, the name of C. C. Bonney appearing as chairman. Trueblood was made a member of the auxiliary and chairman of the committee on Program and Correspondence. The congress was well advertised. The committee invited all peace societies and institutions interested in the cause of peace to send delegates

to the congress. The auxiliary also sent invitations through the
State Department to other governments, requesting them to be
represented. The International Bureau at Berne likewise sent
invitations to all peace societies, asking them to be represented
at Chicago. The program was prepared jointly by the committee
of the peace societies and the committee on arbitration and peace
of the World's Congress Auxiliary, of which Trueblood was a
member and Thomas B. Bryan chairman.

The congress opened Aug. 14, 1893, and lasted for five days,
having two sessions daily. It was distinctively American. Only
the English language was used in discussions. Of the three hundred delegates in attendance only twenty came from abroad. Most
of the leading American peace workers were present, including
many who were familiar with the working of former peace congresses. The morning sessions were opened with prayer. At former congresses the Christian members had held private prayer
meetings before the opening of sessions, but here most of the peace
workers were Christians and took the prayer as a matter of
course.

Josiah Quincy, Assistant Secretary of State, acted as president,
Trueblood as secretary, with vice presidents from the various
countries of Europe. Bonney gave the address of welcome, which
was replied to by delegates from the various foreign countries.
Letters of regret were read from many of the peace leaders of
Europe. The program consisted mainly of the reading of papers
carefully prepared beforehand on the subject of peace societies,
international law, Pan American Congress, economic aspects of
war, women and war, fraternal unions of peoples, labor and capital, the religious principles of the peace movement, and an international tribunal of arbitration. The leading peace societies in
the United States were well represented on the program. For the
American Peace Society, Trueblood read the History and Work
of the Peace Societies in America, Edward Everett Hale spoke
on the organization of a court, William E. Curtis on the Pan
American Congress. Mrs. Belva Lockwood, Amanda Deyo, and
Love represented the Universal Peace Union.

One afternoon was given over to the Ecclesiastical Peace conference which had been organized in New York in 1891. One
session was given over to the discussion of the plan for an international court of arbitration, prepared by William Allen Butler,

Dorman B. Eaton, and Cephas Brainerd, at the suggestion of the directors of the American Peace Society, who Jan. 9, 1893, had asked the honorary counsel of the society to prepare a draft of a constitution for a high court of arbitration, with a paper supporting, explaining and answering all possible objections. The plan was enthusiastically received and a committee appointed to urge speedy action in reference to a permanent treaty of arbitration between the United States and England.[1] A committee consisting of Love, representing the Universal Peace Union, Darby, representing the London Peace Society, and Trueblood, representing the American Peace Society, was appointed to name a committee of jurists and publicists to study and formulate a plan for the organization of an international tribunal of arbitration and do what might be possible to induce the civilized nations to set up such a tribunal. A committee of eleven was appointed to interview President Cleveland to encourage early action in commencing negotiations on the arbitration treaty between the United States and England.

There was less discussion at this congress than was customary at the congresses in Europe, thus rendering the meetings less lively. The auxiliary had ruled that no resolutions should be voted in any of the congresses. So the resolutions were presented by a committee that had drafted them before the meeting took place, inserting only such statements as they were sure would meet with unanimous approval. The draft, therefore, was accepted without formal voting.

The congress ended with a religious service on Sunday, the sermon being preached by Rev. Dr. Philip S. Moxom, of Springfield, Mass., a vice president of the American Peace Society. The press gave excellent and sympathetic reports of the proceedings, and much peace literature was distributed at the meetings.

A memorial prepared by William E. Blackstone of Oak Park, one of the honorary commissioners of the exposition, asking that governments agree by mutual treaties to submit to settlement by arbitration all international questions and disputes that fail to be satisfactorily settled by diplomacy, and signed by seventy-nine commissioners of the exposition appointed by the various governments, thirty-six directors of the exposition, officers of the lady managers, the officers of the World's Congress Auxiliary, com-

---

[1] The plan is given in the Advocate of Peace, October, 1893, pp. 237, 238.

missioners from forty countries, and many prominent theologians, educators, social economists, editors, statesmen, and merchants, including Cardinal Gibbons, Joseph Cook, Dwight L. Moody, President Harrison, Gen. Sherman, Cornelius Vanderbilt, George M. Pullman, Jay Gould, John D. Rockefeller, and J. Seligman, was adopted by the congress and delivered to Secretary of State Gresham at Washington. He consented to send the appeal to all foreign governments and to urge the holding of an international conference to consider the plan. The memorial was entitled "The World's Columbian Exposition Memorial for International Arbitration."

Chapter XXVI

THE ANGLO-AMERICAN ARBITRATION TREATY

At the session of Congress opening in December, 1887, James F. Wilson, of Iowa, introduced a bill into the Senate, December 12th, authorizing the president to negotiate with other governments for the creation of a tribunal for international arbitration.[1] Somewhat later, April 9, 1888, Senator Allison of Iowa introduced a bill to establish a permanent bond of arbitration between the United States, Great Britain and France.[2] June 14, 1888, Senator Sherman of Ohio reported a concurrent resolution from the Committee on Foreign Relations, of which he was chairman, providing that the president be requested to invite from time to time negotiations with any government with which the United States have diplomatic relations to refer to arbitration differences arising between the two governments which can not be adjusted by diplomacy. The resolution passed the Senate unanimously, but was not considered by the House. At the opening of the next session of Congress in December, 1888, the executive committee of the society sent a petition to Congress, urging the enactment of Sherman's concurrent resolution, followed by others the following February. But nothing was done, for the short session of Congress required that attention be paid to other matters.

In the summer of 1889, Senator Sherman, in Paris, learned that the French were desirous of making an arbitration treaty with the United States; that in December, 1887, a petition prepared by Passy and adopted by four societies and 111 deputies in the French chamber had been presented to the French minister of foreign affairs requesting that the government negotiate a treaty of arbitration with the United States; that May 30, 1888, a similar petition signed by 120 persons had been presented to

[1] Printed in American Advocate of Peace, October-November, 1888, pp. 120, 121.
[2] Printed in American Advocate of Peace, November, 1888, p. 121.

Secretary Goblet, and that June 14, 1888, a similar resolution had been passed on the motion of Passy and favorably reported. Aug. 17, 1889, Ambassador Reid sent to Secretary Blaine the resolutions of the peace congress that had just been held in Paris, recommending that an arbitration treaty be made between France and the United States. President Harrison, who in his inaugural address, Mar. 4, 1889, had spoken approvingly of arbitration, sent these papers to the Senate, by whom they were referred to the Committee on Foreign Relations.

Jan. 15, 1890, Sherman again reported the concurrent resolution of 1888, which was in the identical terms with the resolution offered in the House of Representatives, June 17, 1874, by Representative Woodford and passed. The Senate unanimously passed this resolution, Feb. 14, 1890, and sent it to the House. Immediately Secretary Howard went to Washington to render any assistance he could in securing its passage. The House soon took up the resolution and passed it April 4, 1890.[1] Five days later, the committee on arbitration nominated by the Pan American Congress reported to that body recommending identically the resolution just passed by Congress; and this resolution after acceptance by the Pan American body was sent to Harrison for adoption Sept. 3rd following.

During the summer to help matters along petitions were circulated in France and England in favor of a treaty of arbitration between those countries. The American Peace Society sent memorials to the president of each house of Congress and to the secretary of state requesting that in connection with the Columbian Exposition the government invite to an international conference of governments all those with whom it had diplomatic relations to mature a plan to introduce arbitration clauses into treaties, to recommend an international code and some project for a high court of nations.[2] A copy was sent to the peace departments of the Women's Christian Temperance Union in twenty-three states and to some one in each of the 332 congressional districts, with the request that the recipient have it signed by as many prominent persons in his district as possible and sent to the members of Congress from that district before Dec. 1,

[1] Printed in American Advocate of Peace, June-July, 1890, p. 107; February, 1904, p. 32.
[2] Printed in ibid., August-September, 1891, p. 143.

1891. A bill in accordance with the request was introduced into Congress, Jan. 25, 1892, and passed by the House. But, as the act creating the World's Fair contained a clause giving power to the auxiliary to call such a meeting, further consideration of the matter was rendered unnecessary.

In October, 1891, Blaine sent a circular letter to the various European governments enclosing a copy of the arbitration treaty adopted by the Pan American congress, and invited them to enter into a similar treaty with the United States. In a letter to Lord Salisbury, prime minister of England, he said he hoped "that the important objects now sought to be obtained may favorably impress this upon Her Majesty's Government." Most of the countries acknowledged receipt of the letter, but only one, Switzerland, expressed herself as willing to enter into such an agreement. Switzerland, it might be said in passing, as far back as 1883, had proposed to the United States to enter into an arbitration agreement for thirty years, and submit all differences between the two governments to a tribunal of three persons. The Storthing of Norway also, June 16, 1892, approved an address to the king in favor of concluding treaties to establish permanent courts of arbitration, and Nov. 21, approved a resolution introduced by Bajer, Oct. 19, 1892, proposing that Denmark vote adhesion to the principle of permanent treaties of arbitration and reply favorably to the invitation of the United States.

But no nation seemed to want to take the initiative. So Senator Sherman, June 23, 1892, introduced a bill in the Senate, authorizing the president to appoint a commission to visit other governments to initiate negotiations for an arbitration treaty.[1] Cremer also became nervous because nothing was done. He, therefore, presented to the House of Commons a resolution accompanied by 1348 petitions signed by two million persons, expressing sympathy with the action of Congress in favor of international arbitration and hoping the British government would cooperate with the United States upon the basis of the resolution. Carnegie and the American ambassador were present in the House when the discussion took place and when the final vote was taken without a division, June 16, 1893. The resolution, which was considered to be a reply to Blaine's request of 1890, was communicated by Lord Roseberry, Secretary of State for Foreign Affairs, through the British ambas-

[1] Printed in the Advocate of Peace, September, 1892, p. 141.

sador to Gresham, Secretary of State. The president alluded to it in his message to Congress in December, 1893, and laid it before that body a few days later.

And still neither side moved. In the spring of 1894, Sherman again introduced a bill in the Senate to establish an international court of arbitration.[1] June 19, 1894, Trueblood went to Washington and saw Senator Allison, who introduced a resolution into Congress requesting the president to negotiate an arbitration treaty between the United States and Great Britain for twenty-five years. John F. Lacey of Iowa introduced a similar bill into the House of Representatives June 2nd. Both resolutions were sent to their respective committees on foreign relations. The House committee referred it to a sub committee, with William Everett chairman, which reported it to the full committee favorably. But while the committee was considering it the Bluefields incident occurred and the bill was shelved.

In December following, President Paine, Secretary Trueblood, and William E. Sheldon went to Washington in the interest of the treaty and interviewed members of Congress and the secretary of state in regard to the possibility of making an arbitration treaty between the two nations. Their efforts were in vain. The senators said that the State Department was sufficiently authorized under a former resolution. But the State Department was occupied with other matters and unable to consider an arbitration treaty at this time.

So Cremer prepared another memorial which was signed by 354 members of the House of Commons representing all shades of political opinion, favoring a permanent arbitration treaty between the United States and Great Britain, and suggesting that Congress follow the resolution of Great Britain made June 16, 1893, and invite her to join in framing an arbitration treaty that would bind the two nations together.[2] In January of the following year, he brought this memorial to the United States. He had several talks on the subject with Secretary Gresham and found him friendly, even enthusiastic, indeed securing for him an interview with President Cleveland. Cremer interviewed members of both houses of Congress, both committees on foreign relations, and sent a copy of the memorial to every member of both houses. The press com-

[1] Printed in the Advocate of Peace, May, 1894, p. 111.
[2] Printed in Advocate of Peace, February, 1895, p. 36.

mented on it favorably. Jan. 14, Senator Sherman made a report from the Committee on Foreign Relations, with a bill similar to the one introduced the year before to enable the President to carry into execution the resolution of April 4, 1890. Coombs of New York introduced a similar bill in the House, which was sent to the Committee on Foreign Affairs. But the short session of Congress again prevented any consideration of the question, and the complexion of the Senate was changed as a result of the election.

During the following summer, July 8, 1895, the French Chamber of Deputies passed a resolution introduced by Claude Barodet asking the government to enter into negotiation with the United States for a permanent treaty of arbitration.[1] This was considered as the French reply to Blaine's letter of 1891. But no attention was paid to it.

In the following spring, April 22, 1896, the American Conference on International Arbitration was held in Washington, called by 300 men from thirty-seven states, many until then not in touch with the peace societies, thus showing how the peace idea had spread. Among them were Erastus Blakeslee, C. W. Dabney, William Everett, D. C. Gilman, J. A. Kasson, J. B. Thayer, Francis Wayland, S. B. Capen, W. F. Crafts, Dan Smiley, George T. Angell. Gardiner G. Hubbard was chairman of the committee on arrangements. Hon. J. W. Foster called the meeting to order. Senator George F. Edmunds presided. Among the vice presidents were Charles Dudley Warner, Cyrus H. McCormick, Gov. Morrill of Kansas, Gov. Rich of Michigan, Charles A. Pillsbury, Abram S. Hewitt, Dr. Josiah Strong and John Joy Edson. W. R. Thompson acted as secretary. Addresses were made by Carl Schurz, Edward Atkinson, J. Randolph of Virginia, President Merrill E. Gates of Amherst College, President Eliot of Harvard University, President Patton of Princeton University, President Angell of the University of Michigan, Prof. John Bassett Moore of Columbia University, Bishop Keane, president of the Catholic University of America, and Gen. O. O. Howard. Letters were read from Chief Justice Fuller of the United States Supreme Court, Andrew Carnegie and Gov. Buckner of Kentucky. Among others who were present and served on committees were Andrew D. White, Robert Treat Paine, George S. Hale, Edward Everett Hale, Lyman J. Gage, Charles Francis Adams, Simeon E.

---

[1] Printed in ibid., September, 1895, p. 201.

Baldwin, William Howard Taft, Philip S. Moxom, Edwin D. Mead, and Hodgson Pratt of London. Most of these men were new at the peace business. The conference resolved in favor of an arbitration treaty, "providing for the widest practicable application," and prepared a memorial to the Senate in one hundred pages, containing the statements of many prominent Americans in favor of arbitration. Six days before, the Bar Association of the State of New York adopted a recommendation in favor of an international court of arbitration.

Both governments seemed friendly to the cause. Sir Julian Pauncefote, ambassador from Great Britain to the United States, was friendly. Secretary of State Gresham was friendly. So in the spring of 1895, Secretary Gresham and Ambassador Pauncefote began work on a treaty of international arbitration. The death of Gresham, May 28, 1896, caused a cessation in negotiations, which were resumed however by Richard Olney, the new secretary of state. The Olney-Pauncefote treaty was signed for five years, Jan. 11, 1897. It was sent to the Senate where it was referred to the Committee on Foreign Relations. Feb. 1st, the committee reported the treaty amended beyond recognition. The Senate did not seem to take the matter seriously. It discussed it and finally, May 5th, rejected it by a vote of fifty-five to thirty-one, lacking four votes of a two-thirds majority. The causes of the rejection seem to have been two: A dislike for England, a feeling that she was not sincere in making the treaty but wished to tie our hands for some foul unknown purpose; and a dislike for Cleveland by many of his party. Of the thirty-one who voted against the treaty, twenty-five were silver men, who in addition to their distrust for England disliked the gold policy of Cleveland and Olney. Furthermore, there were no active well known peace leaders in Congress to press its importance.[1] During these stirring days, the American Peace Society sent petitions to the president and Senate.[2]

---

[1] The text of the treaty is printed in the Advocate of Peace, February, 1897, pp. 37-39.

[2] Ibid., February, 1897, p. 40.

Chapter XXVII

THE WAR WITH SPAIN

THEN we drifted into the war with Spain. President McKinley
was opposed to the war, and for some time he succesfully restrained
those most insistent upon it. In spite of Spain's willingness to grant
America's every demand, the destruction of the Maine increased the
heat of the war men and thrust our nation into the war. The
society was not in sympathy with the procedure of Spain in Cuba.
March 28, 1898, the directors sent a message to McKinley expressing satisfaction with his policy in dealing with Spain in regard to
Cuba, deploring the distress and suffering of the Cubans and
approving the efforts of the federal government to end those fright-
ful conditions.

The war was short. Congress passed an act, April 25, 1898,
declaring that a state of war with Spain existed. The peace protocol
was issued August 12th. Just before the declaration was made, the
society expressed itself as follows, in an article entitled "The
Struggle for Peace," in the Advocate of Peace, April, 1898, p. 81:
"The efforts of the violent men in Congress who are bent on war at
all hazards, who have gone mad at the very wisdom of the president's message on the Maine disaster ought signally to fail. No
greater national madness could be conceived of than a declaration
of war with Spain after those months of patient negotiation, contrary to the president's wishes and at the very moment when his
policy seems about to be crowned with victory. In such a case, we
would deserve the just judgment of Almighty God and the contempt
of all the civilized world for the weakness and childish loss of self-
control. If war follows, then * * * * we shall have substituted for
inhumanities which we do not approve others awful to contemplate
of possibly much greater proportions and duration which will have
been brought on by our own voluntary act. * * * * We shall have
taken a step leading straight to a policy of meddlesomeness. * * * *
We shall have deliberately thrown away our unique and com-

manding position among the nations as the leaders of the world in the paths of international friendship, goodwill and peace. We shall have become an object to hatred and distrust."

Immediately after the war began the society expressed itself as sorry that we had gone into the war, that nothing could give us greater pain and shame than that America blinded and misled by an unrighteous zeal for righteousness should fall from her unique position, lose the respect and confidence of other nations and forfeit her leadership of the world toward genuine international friendship and peace.

As the war progressed the society expressed itself thus in the May number of the Advocate of Peace, p. 101, under the title "A Fearful Responsibility:" "It seemed reasonable to believe that the United States would never have another war, but would hold and strengthen its proud position as the leader of the nations towards a civilization relying for its strength on right and good will and not on the soulless methods of brute force. We make no effort therefore to conceal our intense disappointment and deep sense of humiliation at what seems to us an irretrievable mistake on the part of those to whose lot it fell to control the nation's destinies at this supreme hour."

"We do not see any ground for changing the position heretofore taken in these columns. * * * * We yield to nobody in sympathy for the suffering Cubans nor in abhorrence at the past oppression and the recent inhumanities practiced by the Spanish colonial officials. * * * * We have said from the beginning, that Cuba ought to be free. If her people desire independence, that though as yet little fitted for self-government the people of the island would never learn to govern themselves except by actually practising self-government. But no end, however noble or desirable, justifies the use for its attainment of a means which is essentially inhuman and iniquitous."

"We have not believed that our government would be justified, even from its own point of view as to war, in stepping off its own territory and attempting by violence, disastrous results of which are sure to follow, to right the wrongs of those neighbors about whose real character and responsibility for their own sufferings there is so much uncertainty."

"The course on which Congress had forced the too pliant administration to enter seems to us still in the highest degree culpable, because another way was open to attaining the same end, a way on which the administration was far along toward success. Of the several reasons urged for going to war there is only one that has even a show of respectability,—the motive of humanity. * * * * With this generous sentiment of the administration, of some members of Congress, and of a large portion of the people, we have the deepest sympathy."

In the June number of the Advocate of Peace, p. 125, is the following under the head of "Conscience and Patriotism": "Patriotism is a grand and noble thing when rightly understood. But no man is a patriot in any worthy sense who throws down his judgment and his conscience and goes with his country to do what he is solemnly convinced is iniquitous. No such unconscientious service can ever promote the welfare of the nation. Men who thus belie their own moral nature can never be depended upon to help lift the national life and conduct to higher level. To proceed as those men have proceeded is to proceed on the theory that the government is infallible and that its behests are always to be obeyed and its policies followed, that it is above conscience and God. * * * * If patriotism means not only love of one's country and desire and earnest effort to promote its welfare and to keep it in the paths or righteousness and truth, but also absolute and unquestioning obedience of all its governmental demands and subservience to all its policies, then patriotism becomes one of the deadliest and most ruinous of tyrannies."

"What the country needs above all else is a patriotism full of conscience and always guided by an enlightened conscience. Patriotism without conscience will ruin any land."

After the close of the war the society said briefly under the title of "The Return of Peace," in the Advocate of Peace, August-September, 1898, p. 173: "The war is over. In common with others, we shall sincerely rejoice over whatever means real freedom and promise of improvement shall come to the population which the war has severed from the control of Spain."

The Treaty of Paris was signed Dec. 10, 1898. It handed the Philippines to the United States, their destiny to be settled later. Grave doubts were awakened in the minds of the society as to the policy adopted by the administration in dealing with the Philippines. While the treaty was under consideration the society sent a resolution to the government, Nov. 28, 1898, through Senator Hoar, stating that the sovereignty of the United States ought not to be extended over any foreign territory without its free consent, and the Philippines ought not to be annexed to the United States, but allowed to set up a government of their own. President Paine made a special visit to Secretary Hay to urge the reopening of negotiations, but without result.

The war that was continued with the Philippines before the insurrection finally came to an end, met with the disapproval of the society. Occasional remarks and resolutions were made in regard to the spirit of imperialism that was spreading over the United States.

A meeting to protest against the subjugation policy toward the Philippines was held in Tremont Temple, April 4, 1899. Great enthusiasm was shown at the meeting. An appeal to the people of the United States was sent out in the middle of March signed by twenty-nine prominent persons, including Samuel Gompers, President David Starr Jordan, Charles Francis Adams, Carl Schurz, Edward Atkinson, Dr. Theodore L. Cuyler, Andrew Carnegie, and Thomas Wentworth Higginson. They urged a cessation of hostilities in the Philippines, help to the inhabitants to organize a government of their own, and the recognition of their independence.

In 1901, President Paine called upon McKinley and urged him to end the war in the Philippines. The society sent a petition to Congress, Feb. 4, 1902, requesting Congress to adopt a resolution declaring it the purpose of this government to grant the Filipinos political independence as soon as feasible.[1]

[1] Printed in the Advocate of Peace, March, 1902, p. 48.

Chapter XXVIII

THE HAGUE CONFERENCE OF 1899

August 24, 1898, Nicholas II, Czar of Russia, through his Minister for Foreign Affairs, Count Mouravieff, handed to the representatives of the European powers residing in St. Petersburg, a rescript suggesting a conference of European powers to consider the question of peace and a reduction of armaments.[1] So unexpected was this note that it fell like a thunderbolt on the governments receiving it and produced a profound impression upon them. Many motives for the issuance of this note were offered. But the reason seems to have been the same as that put forth by the American Peace Society for years, a belief that an excessive amount of armaments tended toward insecurity instead of peace, and that progressive development of armaments cause no nation to be relatively better prepared than before.

According to the story, the czar while considering the question of an increase in armaments had his attention called to the report of an unofficial visitor at the meeting of the Interparliamentary Union at Buda-Pesth in 1896 where that body declared for an international court of arbitration. The czar wondered whether an international conference on the subject would lead to any results, and, thereupon, issued the rescript.

The note was not received at first with any degree of sympathy by the nations, for the suggestion was thought to be visionary and utopian. Nevertheless all the governments except France replied approvingly, though several with reservations.

January 11, 1899, the czar issued a second circular, defining more precisely the several subjects to be considered at the conference, suggesting an interchange of ideas to prepare the way for the diplomatic discussions, and recommending eight points to be considered of which one related to the processes of good offices, mediation

[1] Translated in the Advocate of Peace, August-September, 1898, p. 191.

and voluntary arbitration. This was followed April 6, 1898, by a formal invitation to meet at the Hague, issued by the Netherlands government to each nation with diplomatic representation at the Dutch Capital.

The American Peace Society showed its interest in the suggestion by passing two resolutions Sept. 26, 1898, one sent to the Czar through the Russian ambassador in Washington, expressing approval of the issuance of the rescript and gratitude that the czar had taken the step, and the other to President McKinley, expressing the hope that he would instruct the American delegates to the conference to bring before it the subject of a general arbitration treaty.

To promote public interest in the conference a committee of three appointed by the directors of the society held a series of meetings Monday noons in Tremont Temple, with prominent persons as speakers: Edward Everett Hale, March 6, Samuel Gompers, March 20, Lyman Abbott, March 27, George C. Lorimer, April 3, and Julia Ward Howe, Mary A. Livermore, Lucia Ames Mead, and Alice Freeman Palmer, April 10. A meeting was also held at Worcester, addressed by Mrs. Mead and Secretary Trueblood.

The Hague conference opened May 18, 1899, at 2 P. M., in the Orange Hall, an octagonal chamber in the palace of the Queen of Holland. There were present ninety-six delegates from twenty-six nations: twenty in Europe; China, Japan, Persia and Siam in Asia, and the United States and Mexico in America. The number of delegates sent by a country varied. Thus Russia sent eight, the United States six, Great Britain five, and minor states only one each. In addition there were thirty-two secretaries and attachés and several military and naval delegates. All of them were men of ability and high standing. Thirty had been ambassadors and ministers plenipotentiary to foreign countries, several had been members of cabinets, two were university presidents and seven were members of parliament. It would have been difficult to bring together a more superior body of statesmen, diplomats, jurists, and scholars. The American delegates were Andrew D. White, ambassador to Germany; Seth Low, president of Columbia University; Stanford Newell, minister to Holland; Capt. A. T. Mahan, naval expert; William Crozier, military expert, and Frederick W. Holls, a New York lawyer, who acted as secretary of the group.

M. de Beaufort, the Dutch Minister of Foreign Affairs, was made honorary president of the conference, and M. de Staal, the Russian ambassador to Great Britain, presided over the conference. After the opening exercises the conference separated into three sectional committees;—armament, presided over by Auguste Beernaert of Belgium; laws and customs of war, presided over by Prof. de Martens of Russia; and arbitration and mediation, presided over by Leon Bourgeois of France. Each section was divided into two subdivisions, and the work of the conference was done in those divisions.

In addition to the accredited delegates at the conference were many not accredited:—newspaper men, representatives of the peace societies in various countries, and others interested in the proceedings, whose advice at times seems to have been sought by the accredited delegates. Among these was Secretary Trueblood, who was at the Hague during the first four weeks of the session. He was treated with great respect by the members of the conference and the officials of the Dutch government. He kept in touch with the proceedings, saw and conversed with the delegates, furnished them with information relative to the peace movement, studied the spirit and workings of the conference, observed the characteristics of the different delegations, talked with newspaper correspondents, and cooperated with the other peace workers in quiet effort to make the deliberations as fruitful as possible.

The conference gathered with a great deal of skepticism and uncertainty. Several looked upon it as a diplomatic picnic where they were to have a fine time, pass a few resolutions in favor of peace and then go home. Many of the delegates knew nothing of peace ideas or of peace work. Few expected any thing tangible to result from the conference. But after they had heard a few addresses and became acquainted with the movement, there arose a determination on the part of many delegates to accomplish something practical. The committees worked with a will. Diplomacy as it was formerly known was cast to the winds. Perfect freedom and frankness of expression were shown. The spirit of friendliness and cooperation was strong. Differences often harmonized at the dinner table made it possible for something tangible to be accomplished.

Each committee sat behind closed doors and gave out daily meager reports of what was done. This has been suggested as the reason why the conference was so successful, for there were no galleries, no visitors, no spectators, no reports, no applause, no appeal to the passions. The committee on armaments found too great opposition to allow anything to be done, and therefore contented itself by resolving that it was desirable to find relief from the heavy military burdens resting upon the people. The committee on the laws of war drafted a convention giving a body of improved rules for the conduct of "civilized warfare."

But the greatest work of the conference was the convention for the pacific settlement of international controversies. This matter had been carefully studied of late. At the Chicago peace congress in 1893, a plan for an international court of arbitration had been introduced. At Brussels, in 1895, the Interparliamentary Union had discussed a well digested plan for a permanent tribunal of arbitration, prepared by a committee appointed the year before. The New York State Bar Association had also studied the question, and had referred the report of its committee, April 16, 1896, to the president of the United States. The American Bar Association had thrown its influence in its favor. A national conference on international arbitration had been held in Washington in 1896. The Anglo-American treaty of arbitration had been considered in 1897.

Secretary Hay took the scheme of the New York Bar Association as a basis and introduced into it the best of the arbitration treaties that had been made. After consulting with members of the United States Senate and judges of the Supreme Court and others, he formulated a plan for an international tribunal which the president sent to the Hague conference, where it became known as the American proposition. Lord Pauncefote suggested a permanent court of arbitration, taking the draft of the Interparliamentary Union as a basis for consideration, together with plans introduced by delegates from France, Italy, Belgium and Russia.

As adopted, the scheme provided for a voluntary permanent court of arbitration to be located at the Hague, with secretary, archivist, and assistants. The central office was to be called the International Bureau, under the direction of the foreign ministers resident at the Hague as a permanent council of administration under the presidency of the Dutch minister of foreign affairs. The court was to consist of a panel comprising a board of four jurists appointed for six years by each nation cooperating. Nations having differences of a judicial character or over the interpretation of treaties were each to select one, two, or three members of the board according to agreement to adjudicate their case, those so selected to choose one of their members chairman. The judges were to receive no salary, but an honorarium when sitting. A scheme of special mediation by neutral powers was also agreed upon, as well as international commissions of inquiry to investigate facts in controversies.

The conference closed July 29, after being in session two months and eleven days. At the closing session the conference adopted three conventions: one for the peaceful adjustment of international disputes, one concerning the laws and customs of warfare on land, and one for the adaptation to maritime warfare of the principles of the Geneva convention of August 22, 1864. There were also three declarations, forbidding the use of dum-dum bullets, throwing projectiles or explosives from balloons, using projectiles whose aim is to emit asphyxiating gases. There were *voeux, a voeu* being a cross between a wish and a hope, relating to rights and duties of neutrals, the nature of guns, limitation of armed forces, private property in naval war, and the bombardment of ports.

The Hague conference is of great importance in the history of the peace movement. In the first place it was the first diplomatic gathering called to discuss guaranties of peace without reference to any particular war. Also it was the inspiration of many international congresses since, called to deal with questions of international peace. It showed that it was possible for nations to get together to consider questions relating to peace; that such questions were practical as well as ideal. The court of nations so long sought for by the American Peace Society was now actually established. The conference itself had acted as a quasi-legislative body, thus paving the way for the calling of subsequent similar conferences. Moreover, the machinery had been worked out by persons outside the peace movement, and from this time on it was no longer necessary to prove the value of international peace to the nations, for peace ideas were accepted by statesmen as a part of their creed.

It was generally felt that the court set up was of little value and that no powerful nation would invoke its services. Yet no government felt inclined to reject it, and one by one all except China and Turkey ratified it. The convention provided that when nine nations ratified it the court should begin to function. Accordingly Sept. 5, 1901, by which time a sufficient number of countries had

ratified the action of their delegates, the ministers at the Hague met
and organized the Permanent International Court of Arbitration.
President Roosevelt appointed as the American members of the
court ex President Harrison, Judge George Gray of the Circuit
Court of the United States, Melville W. Fuller, chief justice of the
United States Supreme Court, and John W. Griggs, attorney
general of the United States, and on the death of President Harrison, Oscar S. Straus, minister to Turkey.

Even then it was thought by many that no case would be referred
to the court; indeed for nearly a year it was ignored. Then President Roosevelt suggested to the government of Mexico that it would
redound to the credit of the two governments to be the first to submit a case to the Hague Court for determination, and suggested
that the irreconcilable disagreement between the two governments
over the so-called Pious Fund, which had been pending ever since
the cession of California to the United States, be referred to the
court. A protocol for the submission of the case was signed by the
two governments, May 22, 1902. The names of the arbitrators
were drawn, July 21, 1902. The court met Sept. 1, and decided the
case October 14. The case was of relatively small importance in
itself; but it showed that the court could function, and in the eyes
of many that was its salvation. The court has continued to function. By 1923, it had settled eighteen cases that had been referred
to it.

The court was at first located in a dwelling house plainly
furnished. In 1903, Andrew Carnegie offered to give $250,000 to
the court for the creation of an international law library. April
22, of the same year, he wrote a letter to Baron Gevers, the Netherland minister at Washington, offering $1,500,000 with which to
erect a temple of peace for the court of arbitration, the work to be
done under the direction of the Dutch government. Three days later
the offer was accepted.

A sixteen acre site on which had stood an old palace, for which
the government paid $300,000, was selected, on the left hand side of
the beautiful avenue leading from the Hague to Scheveningen, near
the old boundary of the Hague. The temple was erected under the
direction of a committee of five, of whom four were named by Queen
Wilhelmina and one by the council of the Permanent Court. The
corner stone, a block of Bavarian granite, was laid by Nélidow,

president of the second Hague conference, July 30, 1907. The temple, an imposing architectural ornament, 260 feet square, a combination of Dutch and Flemish architecture, was dedicated August 28, 1913.

Acting on the suggestion of the Hague conference of 1907, that each government contribute materials for the peace palace, there have been contributed to it gates, doors, windows, candelabra, a fountain, a clock, vases, a monument, tapestries, a bust of King Edward of England, of Mr. Carnegie, a portrait of President Taft, and other gifts. The gift of the United States consisted of a marble group costing $20,000, placed at the foot of the Grand stairway, and symbolizing peace.

Chapter XXIX

THE PAN AMERICAN UNION

ASIDE from the creation of the Bureau of American Republics which was to last for ten years and the establishment of better feelings between the republics in America, the International American Conference which had met at Washington in 1890 had produced few results. The arbitration treaty that had been so carefully drawn at that time lapsed, through the absence of any one to bring the attention of the governments to it.

In December, 1899, toward the expiration of the ten year period, President McKinley, in his annual message to Congress, called attention to the expediency of inviting the American republics to a second conference to consider the advisability of continuing the bureau, questions of better trade relations, health, quarantine, and other problems of interest to them all. Secretary Hay, early in the year 1900, addressed a letter to the diplomatic representatives of the republics in Washington in regard to the matter, suggesting later that the conference be held in Mexico, which was agreed to by the parties interested.

Accordingly, President Diaz through the Mexican minister of foreign affairs invited the American republics to meet for this purpose in Mexico. All accepted the invitation and appeared at the time designated. The Bureau of American Republics acted as a committee of arrangements and prepared a program covering the subjects of international arbitration and the establishment of an international court of claims, the two leading subjects considered and lost at the meeting of 1889-90.

The conference was held in the National Palace of the City of Mexico, opening Oct. 22, 1901, and adjourning Jan. 31, 1902. It was called to order by the Mexican minister of foreign affairs, who, with the American secretary of state, were elected honorary presidents. Don Genaso Raigosa, Mexican member of the permanent tribunal of arbitration at the Hague, presided over the deliberations.

Nineteen committees were appointed. As a result of their deliberations, twenty resolutions were passed and good feeling between the republics generated. The Bureau of American Republics was continued and broadened. Provision was made for holding future international American conferences at intervals of five years. Though the question of international arbitration for a time threatened to disrupt the conference, a way out of the difficulty was finally found. The Hague convention on arbitration was adopted, with a provision allowing such states as wished to adopt a system of obligatory arbitration covering all questions not affecting national honor or independence. The United States and Mexico were requested to negotiate with the Hague powers to secure admission of the American republics into the fold.

The third conference of the American republics was held in the pavilion of St. Louis, Rio de Janeiro, Brazil, July 21 to Aug. 26, 1906, at the close of the five year period. The council of administration prepared the program. The delegates received free telegraph, telephone, and mail service, with translators, stenographers, and clerks at their call, thus expediting the work of the sessions. The Brazilian minister of foreign affairs and the American secretary of state were elected honorary presidents and Joaquim Nabuco, the Brazilian ambassador to the United States, president of the conference.

The conference was divided into committees where all the work was done. The committees made unanimous reports to the conference, which were immediately adopted. As suggested by the American Peace Society[1] the Bureau of the American Republics was reorganized on a permanent and enlarged basis, directed to define the topics to be placed upon the program at the next conference, and to secure the ratification of resolutions and recommendations passed by the conference. The principle of arbitration was adhered to. Hon. William I. Buchanan of Buffalo, formerly minister to Argentina and later an officer of the American Peace Society, served on the committee on arbitration as he had also done at the previous conference in Mexico. The codification of international law and various commercial subjects were discussed.

[1] In letter to President Roosevelt, printed in the Advocate of Peace, May, 1906, p. 107.

The fourth conference took place in Buenos Aires, July 12 to August 30, 1910, with the Argentine minister of foreign affairs and the American secretary of state as honorary presidents. C. J. Bernejo of Argentina served as president. The conference discussed commercial matters entirely. The name of the International Bureau of the American Republics was changed to the Pan American Union. The control passed to a governing board composed of the diplomatic representatives in Washington, acting under the direction of the American secretary of state as chairman, and devoted to the development and conservation of peace, friendship, and commerce between them all.

The fifth conference was planned to meet in September, 1914, at Santiago, Chile, and a program was prepared for its consideration; but due to the outbreak of the war it was not held until March 25 to May 3, 1923. At this conference, as at the fourth, commercial matters occupied the major attention of the delegates. A treaty, however, was approved to prevent conflicts between any of the nations, by providing for an impartial commission of inquiry to investigate the facts involved in any controversy, which was later accepted by the various governments interested.[1] The Pan American Union was also reorganized so that the chairman of the board should in the future be elected and a state not having a diplomatic representative in Washington may appoint a member of the governing board. The fact of special interest here, however, is that the American governments here accepted the principle of international arbitration, for which the American Peace Society has consistently stood and striven for so long.

Andrew Carnegie was a delegate to the first Pan American conference in 1889-90; and his interest in the movement continued unabated, as he believed it to be an instrumentality to bring about international peace. After it became evident, following the third conference in 1906, that the bureau would undoubtedly be permanent, and as a home for it was being sought, Carnegie came forward with an offer of $750,000 for a building if the United States would furnish a site therefor and the various governments would agree to support it in the future. The offer was accepted, and a marble palace erected near the State, War and Navy buildings in Washing-

---

[1] The text of the treaty is printed in the Advocate of Peace, April, 1924, pp. 244-247.

ton, at a cost of $1,000,000, the additional cost being defrayed by the republics interested. It was dedicated April 26, 1910.

In 1908, Carnegie gave $100,000 for a building for the Central American court of justice which had been established for a period of ten years by treaty between the several Central American republics, Dec. 20, 1907. It was located at Cartago, Costa Rica. Following its destruction by an earthquake in 1910, Carnegie erected another, at the same cost, in San José.

Within a year following the organization of the Court it was able to avert a general Central American war; but, due to the frailties of human nature, it expired at the end of the ten years.

Chapter XXX

THE BOSTON PEACE CONFERENCE

THE holding of the Louisiana Purchase Exposition in St. Louis in 1904 led the American peace leaders to consider the advisability of holding the peace congress that year in the United States, as had been done in Chicago, eleven years before. Accordingly at the Rome congress in 1903, the American delegates urged their claims for holding the next peace congress in America and presented a petition signed by fifty prominent Americans requesting that the thirteenth peace congress be held in the United States.

The names of the petitioners were as follows: Hon. A. D. White, Hon. George F. Edmunds, Hon. John W. Foster, Andrew Carnegie, Alfred K. Smiley, Hon. William I. Buchanan, Pres. Jacob G. Schurman, Pres. Daniel Coit Gilman, Clinton Rogers Woodruff, Joshua L. Bailey, William Dean Howells, Edwin Burritt Smith, Hon. George F. Seward, Rev. Jenkin Lloyd Jones, Prof. Bliss Perry, Rev. Philip S. Moxom, Pres. L. Clark Seelye, Alfred H. Love, Thomas Wentworth Higginson, Hon. Samuel W. McCall, Edwin D. Mead, Robert Treat Paine, Benjamin F. Trueblood, Edwin Ginn, Rev. Edward Everett Hale, Mrs. May Wright Sewall, Mrs. Hannah J. Bailey, Mrs. Julia Ward Howe, Mrs. Mary A. Livermore, Jane Addams, Pres. M. Cary Thomas, Bishop William Lawrence, Bishop Henry W. Warren, Edward Atkinson, Samuel B. Capen, Edward H. Clement, Philip C. Garrett, Moorfield Storey, Walter S. Logan, Rev. Charles F. Dole, Felix Adler, Rev. Charles E. Jefferson, Prof. John B. Clark, Hon. George S. Boutwell, George T. Angell, Augustine Jones, L. H. Pillsbury, Judge William L. Putman, Hon. Oscar S. Straus, Judge George Gray, Cleveland H. Dodge, Grace H. Dodge. A long list of notable persons many of them officers of the American Peace Society. After listening to the request and hearing the names, the congress voted to hold the next meeting in America.

The American Peace Society which was responsible for this vote requested Edwin D. Mead to arrange a meeting with the peace leaders of the country where preliminary plans for the congress were to be made. Representatives of the peace societies therefore met in Washington Jan. 13, 1904, with Hon. George F. Seward as chairman. Secretary Trueblood explained the purpose of the meeting and stated that it would require ten thousand dollars to finance the congress on the scale desired, and that half of the amount had been pledged by Andrew Carnegie, and a thousand dollars by others. An executive committee of twelve, including Mead, Trueblood, Seward, Edwin Burritt Smith, Prof. Graham Taylor, Mrs. Hannah J. Bailey, Mrs. May Wright Sewall, Walter S. Logan, Hon. William N. Ashman, Dr. Henry Richard Thomas, Mrs. Charles Russell Lowell, and Philip C. Garrett, was appointed to determine the time and place of the congress, with full power to make all arrangements necessary. Other committees were appointed to raise the necessary funds and to prepare the program. The fifty who had joined in the petition extended to the congress at Rome were made a general committee on the congress.

The executive committee met Feb. 13, elected Mead chairman, and Trueblood secretary of the committee, and decided to hold the congress in Boston the first week in October, with Robert Treat Paine, president, A. D. White, Hon. George F. Edmunds, Andrew Carnegie, Edward Everett Hale, David Starr Jordan, Edwin Ginn, and Alfred K. Smiley vice presidents, all but one officers of the American Peace Society or closely affiliated with it. The business men of Boston took an interest in the congress. On invitation of Mayor Collins, two hundred and fifty of them met, April 22, to consider how the interest of the congress might be promoted by the city, and appointed a committee of five to cooperate with the committee on organization to make all necessary local preparations.

Efforts were made to obtain a representative congress and to obtain as large a delegation from Europe as possible. The International Peace Bureau at Berne sent notices of the congress to all peace societies in Europe, advising them of the meeting and urging the presence of as large a delegation as possible.

The congress was held in Tremont Temple, October 3 to 7, 1904, the building in which Burritt gave his first peace address in 1841 and Sumner his address on the True Grandeur of Nations in 1845. Representatives were present from nearly 200 organizations including fifty-five peace societies and arbitration organizations, forty-five church and ministerial associations, eighteen philanthropic and benevolent societies; thirty-four women's clubs, fifteen labor organizations, four chambers of commerce, four boards of trade, and one teachers' association. One thousand delegates were present. One hundred delegates representing fifty-seven organizations were present from sixteen foreign countries. Robert Treat Paine acted as president of the congress and B. F. Trueblood as its secretary. A. K. Smiley represented the United States on the board of vice presidents. Letters and telegrams were received from Andrew Carnegie in Scotland, the Nobel committee in Norway, Cardinal Gibbons, and others, including one from Melbourne, Australia. The subjects discussed were the economic causes of war, reduction of military burdens, arbitration, and our Pacific allies.

The Sunday before the opening of the congress was observed as preparation day. Peace services were held in the various churches of the city. In the evening a free musical service was held in Symphony Hall by the Handel and Haydn Society assisted by an orchestra. The great peace hymns were sung on that occasion.

The official welcome to the visitors was given by Hon. George R. Jones, president of the Massachusetts Senate, representing the governor, and by Mayor Patrick A. Collins, on behalf of the city. The morning sessions were devoted to business, considering the questions of the day, international law, and propaganda, closing with resolutions and an appeal to the nations. The afternoons were devoted to sight seeing. The evenings were devoted to addresses at the Tremont Temple, Park Street Church, and other buildings where the auditoriums were filled. Among the speakers were Hon. John Hay, the Secretary of State, Rev. Francis E. Clark, Mrs. Lucia Ames Mead, Mrs. Julia Ward Howe, Mrs. Mary A. Livermore, Mrs. Belva Lockwood, Samuel Gompers, Oscar S. Straus, Prof. A. P. Peabody, Hon. Samuel W. McCall, Gen. Nelson A. Miles, Rev. Charles E. Jefferson, Pres. G. Stanley Hall, Rev. Paul Revere Frothingham, and Perrin, Cremer, Pete Curran, Darby, La Fointaine, and Quidde from Europe. A reception was given by Gov. Bates at the state house and by the mayor at the public library. A pilgrimage was taken to Mount Auburn Cementery where wreaths were laid on the graves of Noah Worcester, William E. Channing, Longfellow, Holmes, Lowell, Sumner, and Phillips Brooks. The German societies of Boston gave a reception to the delegates from

Germany. Daily concerts were given in the South Congregational Church. The congress closed with a banquet. The congress was pronounced by many as one of the best in the series.

Following the congress, forty supplementary meetings were held in Worcester, Springfield, Northampton, New Bedford, Providence, New Britain, New York, Philadelphia, Pittsburgh, Cincinnati, Guelph, Toronto, Portland, Maine, and other cities, ending with a meeting in Music Hall, Boston, at which addresses were made by the foreign delegates and local citizens.

Chapter XXXI

THE MOHONK LAKE CONFERENCES

Nestled peacefully in the Catskill Mountains in Ulster County, New York, about one hundred miles from the city of New York in a spot of unsurpassed loveliness and on the top of the mountain, lies Mohonk Lake, by the side of which in an area of four thousand acres is the Mountain House, kept for many years by Albert K. Smiley. Since the death of Albert K., Dec. 2, 1912, his brother Daniel has managed the business. Albert had been appointed a member of the United States Board of Indian Commissioners, in 1879. Due to his desire to obtain just and humane treatment for the Indians, he held yearly conferences at his hotel in regard to them.

About 1894, the question of international arbitration and peace began to assume a larger importance, and Smiley conceived the idea of starting a series of conferences on international arbitration similar to those he had held relative to Indian questions. In 1895, June 5 to 8, he held the first annual meeting of the Lake Mohonk conference on international arbitration. This conference was followed by others, one each year for twenty-one years, the last being held May 19-21, 1915, when they were interrupted by the war. Each conference was held for three days, late in May or early in June, signalizing the opening of the hotel for the summer.

The object of the Mohonk conferences was to awaken, concentrate, direct, and utilize the peace sentiment of the country in favor of international arbitration, arbitration treaties, and an international court, and to devise practical ways of settling international disputes. This was done by inviting thoughtful, serious, and intelligent persons with strong convictions on the subjects to discuss the present status of the question and to examine plans and suggestions made in its interest, with the intention of doing some constructive and helpful work. These people came from various walks in life, statesmen, diplomats, judges, jurists, college presidents and professors, ministers, literary men, editors, mayors, and business men. In 1904, there were present two members of the Hague conferences, ten judges, several members of Congress, fifteen college presidents, forty business men, and several foreigners. Every year a large proportion of the guests belonged to the American Peace Society.

The members of the conference were guests of the Smileys and present at the conference on the personal invitation of the hosts. Their numbers varied from year to year. At the first conference there were fifty-six; at the second one hundred and twenty-five; increasing to three hundred in 1904, at which figure the number remained, as that was the capacity of the hotel. During the three days, mornings and evenings were devoted to discussion, while the afternoons were devoted to recreation,—boating, riding, mountain climbing, sports, games, reading, and social intercourse.

For the first few years, Mr. Smiley directed the conference. In this he was aided by Secretary Trueblood who was responsible for the inauguration of the plan and for carrying out the details. In December, 1901, William C. Dennis, a graduate of Earlham College and with degrees of A. M., and LL. B., from Harvard University, was appointed permanent secretary of the conference. He advertised it and carried on a continuous propaganda among business organizations, colleges, and universities, correspondents, and interested persons in favor of international arbitration.

The meeting was always opened by Smiley, who welcomed his guests, gave an outline of the program of the conference, and nominated a chairman of the meeting. A secretary and business committee were also selected, and Trueblood was always a member of the latter. Trueblood was present at every conference with but one or two exceptions, and each year gave an account of the progress made by arbitration since the preceding meeting.

The subject selected for consideration was chosen before the meeting, and topics were given to persons deemed best able to speak understandingly upon them. Besides general treatment of arbitration, the conference considered the proposals brought before the Hague conference and the results, the permanent court of international arbitration, the American Peace Society and other organizations formed to aid in producing peace. After the reading of the papers the subject was thrown open for general discussion. Marked differences of opinion were brought out. Subjects warmly discussed at one conference were placed on the program in succeeding years and discussed until differences in views had faded away.

The chairmen of the meetings were always men of prominence: John B. Garrett, Hon. George F. Edmunds, Col. George E. Waring, Judge J. H. J. Stinnes, Hon. John W. Foster, Hon. George Gray, President Nicholas Murray Butler, Prof. John Bassett Moore, William Howard Taft, and James Brown Scott. The list of speakers at the conferences included the names of many men well known in the peace movement and mentioned in this history of the American Peace Society or contained in the list of its officers, as George D. Boardman, Merrill E. Gates, Edward Everett Hale, Robert Treat Paine, Hon. George S. Hale, William G. Hubbard, Mrs. Hannah J. Bailey, Lyman Abbott, Dr. William A. Mowry, Prof. J. B. Clark, Dr. Reuen Thomas, Cephas Brainerd, Edwin D. Mead, Mrs. Lucia Ames Mead, Alfred H. Love, Dr Philip S. Moxam, Samuel B. Capen, President W. H. P. Faunce, Edward Atkinson, Joseph Cook, Dr. Scott F. Hershey, Dr. Charles E. Jefferson, Dr. James L. Tryon, Hon. Theodore Marburg, Dr. Frederick Lynch, Hon. Charlemagne Tower, Prof. C. C. Hyde, Arthur D. Call, Mary E. Woolley, William Jennings Bryan, and Prof. George Kirchwey. Others who attended the conferences and have attained prominence were: Rev. B. Fay Mills, Gen. O. O. Howard, Rev. Theodore L. Cuyler, President L. Clark Seelye, Chancellor MacCracken, Prof. Seligman, Amos R. Wells, Hon. F. W. Holls, Ainsworth R. Spofford, Hon. W. L. McKenzie King, B. B. Gobart, C. L. Lange, Dr. Charles P. Neill, Dr. P. P. Claxton, Dean Charles R. Brown, Gen. Wood, Felix Adler, Prof. E. A. Steiner, and Prof. Eugene Wambaugh. A report of the conference was printed each year.

Resolutions were passed at the close of each conference and a platform drawn up. In 1895, the conference sent a copy of its declaration to the governor of each state, with the request that he lay it before the legislature.

In the last few years the conference administered two prizes for essays on the subject of arbitration: one the Chester D. Pugsley prize of $100 beginning 1908, for the best essay written by a male undergraduate of any college in the United States or Canada; and two, the Mrs. Elmer Black prizes of $200 and $100 respectively beginning 1910, for the best essay written by a woman student in any college of the United States.

Chapter XXXII

THE HAGUE CONFERENCE, 1907

THE Interparliamentary Union at its meeting in St. Louis passed a resolution Sept. 13, 1904, introduced by Hon. Theodore E. Burton, of Ohio,[1] framed by the Hon. Richard Bartholdt of Missouri, requesting the president of the United States to invite all nations to send representatives to an international conference to deliberate on the questions postponed from the conference at the Hague in 1899: the arrest and reduction of armaments, the negotiation of arbitration between the states, and the establishment of an international congress to meet at stated periods to discuss questions of international interest. At the close of the conference a delegation consisting of Bartholdt, president of the union, Gobat, secretary of the union, with Cremer and others, went to Washington and presented the resolution to President Roosevelt, who answering them said, that he would invite the governments at an early day.

October 21, 1904, Secretary of State Hay sent a letter[2] to the representatives of the United States accredited to the governments signatories to the acts of the Hague conference of 1899, directing them to bring the matter to the attention of the foreign department of the governments and ascertain to what extent the governments were disposed to act in the matter, formulating the program in a way to separate public international law from the individual governments. The replies received were very cordial, as contrasted with the coolness shown in 1899. The government of the Netherlands offered to have the conference held at the Hague as before. However, in view of the war then existing between Russia and Japan, Secretary Hay sent a second note[3] to the powers Dec. 16, 1904, suggesting that the conference be deferred until the war was over, in order that it might include all nations. He also sug-

---

[1] The resolution is printed in the Advocate of Peace, October, 1904, p. 190.
[2] The letter is printed in ibid., November, 1904, pp. 205, 206.
[3] The note is printed in ibid., January, 1905, p. 10.

gested that the arrangements for the conference and the preparation of the program be made through the bureau of the administration council of the Hague court, that is, the thirty or more foreign ministers at the Hague.

Later, Roosevelt very graciously stepped aside and allowed Russia at the end of the war to take the initiative in the matter. Accordingly in the fall of the year after the signing of the Treaty of Portsmouth, Oct. 14, 1905, the czar issued a manifesto[1] officially announcing the holding of the conference. Frederick de Martens visited the various European capitals discussing the questions to be placed upon the program and the date for the conference.

April 7, 1906, the czar formally issued an invitation[2] to the nations that had been represented at the Hague conference in 1899, together with the Central and South American states, requesting them to be represented at the conference at the Hague. Among other subjects suggested for discussion were the rights of neutrals at sea, codification of international law, arrest of armaments, neutralization of trade routes of the ocean, an obligatory arbitration treaty, and the establishment of an international assembly.

During the two years elapsing between the request to Roosevelt to call the conference and its gathering together, peace societies, public officials, and individuals studied the subjects for the program and obtained the public reaction thereon. So that when the delegates came together, June 15, 1907, they had many definite ideas of what should be done. The delegates appointed by President Roosevelt to represent the United States were Joseph H. Choate, ex ambassador to Great Britain, Horace Porter, ex ambassador to France, Judge Uriah M. Rose of Little Rock, ex president of the American Bar Association, David Jayne Hill, ex Assistant Secretary of State, Gen. George B. Davis, Judge Advocate General of the United States army, William I. Buchanan, Admiral Charles S. Sperry, ex-president of the Naval War College; James Brown Scott and Charles Henry Butler, technical delegates. A. J. Nélidow, the head of the Russian delegation and ambassador to France, was made president, and William H. de Beaufort, the head of the Dutch delegation, vice president. Nélidow appointed the officers.

As in 1899, the conference was divided into four committees sit-

---

[1] The manifesto is printed in Advocate of Peace, November, 1905, p. 223.
[2] The invitation is printed in ibid., May, 1906, pp. 108, 109.

ting daily behind closed doors.   The presidents of the committees directed the conference.   Proposals of all kinds were introduced: to regulate war, to form international courts, to call future conferences, to make the Hague conference a permanent body reassembling at stated periods and becoming a permanent council, and to improve international law and the methods of its administration. Every proposition was argued out in committee.   Members kept in close communication with their home governments from whom they received daily instructions, thus rendering progress very slow. When a committee had agreed upon a question it was reported to the full session for action.   The question of disarmament though loudly called for was not discussed for it was evident from the outset that nothing could be done with it.

It was expected that a general treaty of obligatory arbitration would be signed for a fixed period of time, to cover certain questions in controversy, as had been urged by the Interparliamentary Union and the Mohonk conference.   A memorial in its favor signed by two million people was presented to the conference by Miss Anna B. Eckstein, a vice president of the American Peace Society.   The Portuguese delegation submitted to the arbitration committee a model treaty of arbitration prepared by Bartholdt and adopted by the Interparliamentary Union at its meeting in London in 1906.[1] Though delegates from thirty-five countries were in favor of such a treaty it was not considered because of the opposition of the German delegates, who objected to any general treaty of this character, though not opposed to such treaties being made with a few of the larger powers.

The American delegation urged the formation of a high court of international justice.   In this they were supported by the British and the German delegates and a plan was introduced, supported by all three countries, but failed because of the inability to decide upon some satisfactory method of appointing the judges.   Another suggestion which was favorably received by a few was that a congress be formed with the Hague conference acting as the upper house and the Interparliamentary Union acting as a lower.

As in 1899, the leading peace men of the world were present. Robert Treat Paine represented the American Peace Society and

[1] The draft of a general treaty of arbitration by Bartholdt is printed in the Advocate of Peace, October, 1905, pp. 206-208.

Richard Bartholdt the Interparliamentary Union group, talking with delegates and endeavoring to make the conference successful.

Thirteen conventions were finally drawn up: nine of law and four of practice. An international prize court was provided for. The convention of the first Hague conference under which the arbitration court had been set up was enlarged from 61 to 97 articles and reissued as a new document. The procedure of the court was improved. A party feeling itself aggrieved was permitted to declare its wish to have the controversy settled by the Hague court, and then to use moral suasion to bring the other party to consent to an arbitration. The conference also voted to have periodical meetings in the future, the next one to be in about seven years, the governments to appoint special commissions two years in advance of the meeting to study and prepare a program for it.

The outstanding fact of this conference, as of the conference of 1899, is the fact of the conference itself. Both conferences were the fulfillment of one-half of William Ladd's creative life. The Permanent Court of International Arbitration came close to fulfilling the other half.

Chapter XXXIII

THE ARBITRATION TREATIES

No sooner was it known that the arbitration treaty drawn up between Great Britain and the United States in 1896 had been defeated than it was announced that McKinley was preparing to revise the treaty drawn so as to avoid the features that had brought about its defeat in the Senate. Nov. 18, 1897, a deputation from the Mohonk conference, consisting of ex Senator George F. Edmunds, president of the Mohonk conference that year, Samuel B. Capen, chairman of the executive committee, and Robert Treat Paine, Philip C. Garrett, and Secretary Trueblood, members of the executive committee, all but one officers of the American Peace Society, went to Washington to try to secure attention to the subject of arbitration in the president's forthcoming message to Congress and an early revival of a project of an Anglo-American arbitration treaty. They interviewed President McKinley, who seemed interested in the matter, Secretary of State Sherman, who gave the impression that he would treat the question as a most pressing international problem, and Sir Julian Pauncefote, whose interest in the matter seemed unabated. The next year, Sept. 26, 1898, the directors of the American Peace Society resolved that the time was opportune to revive efforts to secure a treaty between the two countries, and requested President McKinley to reopen negotiations for such a treaty at the earliest practical moment.

At the same time Cremer was at work in England. He prepared a memorial to Congress signed by 7432 officers of the Congregational, Baptist, Wesleyan, and Presbyterian churches. Failing to get a delegate to bring the memorial to the United States, he went himself to Washington for the third time in November, 1897, and tried to interest the churches in the matter. In the spring of 1899 he prepared an address in support of the Hague conference, had it endorsed by 641 representatives of workingmen and sent it by a British workingman to every county in England. In 1900 President Paine interviewed several authorities in Washington upon the subject. But too many other questions that seemed more pressing prevented McKinley from considering an arbitration treaty with Great Britain.

Through the efforts of Dr. Thomas Barclay, formerly president of the British Chamber of Commerce in Paris, an arbitration treaty was signed between Great Britain and France, Oct. 14, 1903, followed by others in identical terms until by the end of the year 1904, twenty-eight such treaties had been made, and by May, 1906, forty-four. These treaties were generally for a period of five years and called for a submission to the Hague court of all disputes arising between the two signatory nations that could not be otherwise settled, excepting alone questions of independence, honor, and vital interests of the country.

The signing of this treaty between Great Britain and France caused the question of a treaty between Great Britain and the United States again to be revived. Dr. Barclay went to the United States with the Mosely Education Commission and urged the necessity of immediately negotiating a treaty of obligatory arbitration between the United States and Great Britain. He found President Roosevelt and Secretary Hay very friendly to the proposition but unwilling to make any move at that time, fearing the opposition in the Senate to be strong enough to prevent the approval of a treaty of this character.

Another group was at work also. The executive committee appointed at the close of the American Conference on International Arbitration in Washington in 1896, with the expectation of calling another conference soon, but for a variety of reasons had remained dormant, now revived. They met in New York City, Nov. 19, 1903, shortly before the meeting held in the Boston Chamber of Commerce, and decided to call a second conference in Washington, Jan. 12, 1904, in order to impress upon Congress and the press the desirability of obtaining an arbitration treaty with Britain. This meeting was held in the Assembly Hall of the New Willard Hotel, at ten o'clock in the morning with about two hundred persons present. The chairman of the conference was Hon. John W. Foster, a few of the other members of the committee being Thomas Nelson Page, Charles J. Bell, Admiral George Dewey, John Joy Edson, Carl Schurz, President Daniel Coit Gilman, Hon. Martin A. Knapp, J. B. Larner,

H. B. F. Macfarland, Wayne MacVeagh, Gen. Nelson A. Miles, Dr. Charles W. Needham, C. S. Noyes, S. W. Woodward, Henry L. West, Rev. S. H. Greene, Rev. Teunis S. Hamlin, and Bishop Satterlee. No member of the cabinet or of Congress was invited. Besides Robert Treat Paine, Samuel B. Capen, Edwin Ginn, E. D. Mead, Philip C. Garrett, Joshua L. Bailey, Andrew Carnegie, Hon. Jackson H. Ralston, Edward Everett Hale, Merrill E. Gates, and Secretary Trueblood, members of the American Peace Society, there were present Dr. Barclay, Judge George Gray of Delaware, Hon. Oscar S. Straus, Hon. J. M. Dickinson, Cardinal Gibbons, President David Starr Jordan, Samuel Gompers, Gov. Durbin of Indiana, Hon. Frank W. Seward, Hon. Hannis Taylor, Hon. Samuel R. Thayer of Minneapolis, Hon. George F. Seward of New York, Hon. Stuyvesant Fish, and Horace White. Hon. John W. Foster acted as chairman and Thomas Nelson Page and Clinton Rogers Woodruff as secretaries. The mere mention of these names shows how far the peace movement had spread at the opening of the present century.

Letters of approval of the plan were read from the mayors of New York, Chicago, Detroit, and Boston. Resolutions were passed recommending that the government endeavor to enter into an arbitration treaty with Great Britain. In the afternoon a public meeting was held in the Lafayette Theater with music furnished by the Marine Band, and addresses by Edward Everett Hale, Andrew Carnegie, Gen. Miles, Cardinal Gibbons, and ex Secretary Foster. In the evening a reception was given by Secretary Foster.

The next morning a committee of sixteen with Hon. Henry St. George Tucker of Virginia as spokesman called on President Roosevelt and presented the resolutions to him. He received them cordially, expressed himself as in accord with them and promised to devote careful consideration to the subject and take all possible action thereon. The committee called upon Secretary Hay, who expressed himself as in accord with them. A large committee with Gov. Durbin as spokesman likewise presented the resolutions to the Senate committee on Foreign Relations.

Following the Washington arbitration conference was the formation of the American branch of the Interparliamentary Union by Richard Bartholdt, June 13, 1904, and the invitation by President Roosevelt to the Interparliamentary Union to meet in America later in the year, with the appropriation of $50,000 by Congress for the entertainment of the delegates. At the same time the Anglo-American League in London petitioned the British government to make an obligatory arbitration treaty with the United States. Several of the European governments informed the state department of their willingness to conclude such treaties. Still Roosevelt hesitated. Then, in the presidential campaign of 1904, the Prohibition and Republican parties declared in favor of international arbitration and the Democratic party in favor of a reduction of armaments.

Then between Nov. 1, 1904 and Jan. 20, 1905, President Roosevelt through Secretary Hay made treaties with thirteen different nations having representatives at Washington: France, Switzerland, Germany, Portugal, Great Britain, Norway, Denmark, Netherlands, Italy, Sweden, Mexico, Japan, and Austria, all similar to one another and based on the Anglo-French treaty of 1903, agreeing for five years to send to the Hague court all international controversies of a judicial nature and all treaties for interpretation that could not be settled by diplomatic action, provided they did not affect the vital interests, the independence or the honor of the state, or the interests of third parties, also that in each case a special agreement should be concluded defining clearly the matter in dispute and the scope and power of the arbitration. In December, Roosevelt sent the French treaty to the Senate.

Immediately meetings were held to urge the prompt ratification of the treaty by the Senate. One was held at Carnegie Hall, New York, Dec. 16, where Mayor McClellan presided and speeches were made by Judge Gray, Oscar S. Straus, Archbishop Ireland, and letters were read from ex President Cleveland, Carl Schurz, John Mitchell, Gen. Miles, and Andrew Carnegie. Another held at Chicago, Jan. 31, 1905, was addressed by Judge J. J. Kohlsaat, Hon. J. M. Dickinson, Franklin MacVeagh, Gen. O. O. Howard, and Robert T. Lincoln, and letters read from William Jennings Bryan, and others. The newspapers, business and religious organizations, and boards of trade, state and local, approved them. Cremer prepared a memorial signed by representatives of British industrial and provident organizations with a membership of nearly thirteen million persons as an expression of opinion from workingmen in favor of the pacific settlement of international disputes and sent a copy to each member of the United States Senate, Jan. 24, 1905.

The Committee on Foreign Relations reported the treaty

changing the word "agreement" to "treaty," so as to give the Senate power to pass on each case submitted instead of giving that power to the President; in other words, making it impossible for the President to submit any case to arbitration, except by a special treaty approved by the Senate. The treaty with amendments was ratified by the Senate, Feb. 11, 1905. Roosevelt, however, considered the treaty valueless as amended, for it meant that every case of arbitration would have to be presented to the Senate for consideration. Nevertheless it placed the Senate on record as in favor of international arbitration, for which the American Peace Society had striven for years.

Following the failure of the second Hague conference to agree upon a general treaty of obligatory arbitration, the treaties of Roosevelt were changed to include the Senate amendments and thus modified to make a special agreement to submit to the Hague court for arbitration certain classes of controversy that might arise, the French treaty was sent to the Senate by Secretary Root and ratified, Feb. 19, 1908. This was followed by similar treaties with twenty-two other countries, each for a period of five years, which on their expiration shortly before the war were continued by Secretary Bryan for a second period of five years.

Taft early became interested in the question of international arbitration. At a meeting of the American Society for the Judicial Settlement of International Disputes, Dec. 17, 1910, he expressed himself clearly upon the subject in terms which were announced by Sir Edward Grey in the House of Commons to be acceptable to Great Britain and an example to the world. As a result, Secretary Knox and Ambassador Bryce drew up an unlimited treaty to refer to the Hague court all difficulties arising between the two countries including all questions of honor and most of those relating to vital interests, which was signed Aug. 3, 1911, and the next day sent to the Senate, which immediately referred it to the Committee of Foreign Affairs. A similar treaty was signed with France.

Nicholas Murray Butler, President of Columbia University, called the peace workers of the country to New York to confer in regard to the plan of action to be taken. This conference created a Citizens' National Committee, composed of prominent men known to be supporters of international arbitration. Different lines of work were assigned by the committee to various organizations. Trueblood with the department directors of the American Peace Society and the leaders of its branch societies organized great public meetings in various sections of the country and secured influential speakers for them. At Washington, they held a meeting in the Pan American building, Dec. 8, 1911, addressed by President Taft and others. Trueblood also prepared a special edition of the Advocate of Peace containing the most important things that had been written and said on the subject and sent out one hundred thousand copies of it in December, 1911.

Prof. Richard of Columbia University worked with the Germans to remove any misunderstandings they might have in regard to the matter. Resolutions in favor of the treaty were passed at mass meetings held in Buffalo, New York City, Philadelphia, and Atlanta, by churches, clubs, chambers of commerce, and other meetings of various kinds. The American Peace and Arbitration League caused thirty thousand sermons to be preached Nov. 26, in favor of the treaties. The New York Peace Society sent letters to every church in the United States, one hundred and fifty thousand in number, relative to the treaties. The Federal Council of the Churches of Christ in America created a commission on Peace and Arbitration, with Frederick Lynch of New York as secretary, communicated with all churches and secured the preaching of sermons and the passage of resolutions in their favor. The churches put themselves on record as favoring unlimited arbitration of all international disputes. So did the religious papers and many of the dailies. The subject was discussed in the colleges. Committees distributed tons of literature in their favor. Petitions and letters poured into the Senate.

But to no purpose. The committee reported the treaties to the Senate, striking out the last paragraph of article III permitting a joint high commission of inquiry to state whether a question was justiciable, and changing "shall" to "may" in the first paragraph of the same article.[1] That is, the Senate was unwilling to allow any one except itself to decide whether a matter should be arbitrated. It was unwilling to surrender any of what it considered to be its prerogatives. Taft insisted that the treaty should be accepted as negotiated, and so it was lost.

Secretary Bryan entered the cabinet, March 4, 1913, well known to the world as a pacifist, and Wilson was known to be in sympathy

---

[1] The text of the treaty with Great Britain is printed in the Advocate of Peace, September, 1916, pp. 196-198.

with furthering the peace of the world.   April 23, Bryan appeared before the Senate Committee on Foreign Relations and laid before it a project which had been approved by Wilson.   He said it was one that he had had in mind since he attended the meeting of the four-teenth Interparliamentary Union at London, in 1906, and had more recently been suggested in his paper the Commoner, Feb. 17 and 24, 1905, and if it met with their approval he would propose it to the powers of the world.   His plan was to have an investigation and report by a committee of inquiry before a declaration of war; the investigation to be automatic but not to look towards arbitration or to restrict the future freedom of action.   The expectation was that by securing an investigation, opportunity would be given to both sides to cool off and become willing to submit to arbitration later.   After hearing Bryan's suggestion the committee promised favorable consideration of a treaty drawn according to such plan.

The next day Wilson communicated with the diplomats in Washington and found a majority willing to make a treaty agreeing after diplomacy had failed, to submit all questions for investigation and report to an international commission and not to declare war or begin hostilities till the investigation had been made and report submitted.   The first of this series of treaties was signed with Salvador, Aug. 7, 1913.   Other treaties followed, varying from one another only in details.

July 15, 1914, Bryan went before the Senate Committee on Foreign Relations and outlined to them the treaties that had been made.   July 24, Wilson referred to the Senate twenty-one treaties as follows: Salvador, Guatemala, Panama, Honduras, Nicaragua, Netherlands, Bolivia, Persia, Portugal, Costa Rica, Switzerland, the Dominican Republic, Venezuela, Denmark, Italy, Norway, Peru, Uruguay, Brazil, Argentine Republic and Chili.   The Senate immediately referred them to the Committee on Foreign Relations. The committee reported them favorably, with a slight change in the treaties with Persia and the Central American states.   No action was taken upon the treaties with three states, but the rest were ratified.   Similar treaties were signed with Paraguay, Great Britain, France, Spain, China, Russia, Ecuador, Greece, and Sweden, the last three on October 13, 1914.

Thus the efforts of the American Peace Society to obtain satisfactory arbitration treaties with foreign nations, taken up by men in public office, had finally succeeded.   Thirty-three such treaties were eventually signed. The preamble of each contained this identical phraseology: "Desirous to strengthen the bonds of amity that bind them together and also to advance the cause of general peace." These treaties supplemented the Roosevelt treaties, but did not abrogate them.

Chapter XXXIV

THE AMERICAN PEACE CONGRESSES

THE first national peace congress was held at Toulouse, France, October 16-19, 1902. England and Italy started national peace congresses in 1904; Germany in 1908, and Belgium in 1913. Many of these congresses were held yearly, a few biennially. They closed in 1914 with the outbreak of the war.

Following the European example, national congresses started in the United States in 1907 and were held biennially until 1915, when they ceased because of the war. The first one was held in New York City, upon the initiative of the American Peace Society aided by the newly formed New York Peace Society. This latter society had been organized on the initiative of Prof. Ernst Richard of Columbia University at the Broadway Tabernacle, Jan. 23, 1906, by a group of forty persons among whom were Hon. Samuel J. Barrows, Cephas Brainerd, Prof. John B. Clark, Cleveland H. Dodge, Dr. Charles E. Jefferson, Chancellor MacCracken of New York University, and Josiah Strong. Dr. Jefferson presided at the meeting. Oscar S. Straus was elected president. Prof. Samuel T. Dutton of the Teachers College at Columbia University was elected secretary. At the first annual meeting in February, 1907, Andrew Carnegie was elected president, a position that he held until his death, August 12, 1919. The American Peace Society sent it a telegram of greeting on the eve of its organization.

It was on the eve of the meeting of the second conference at the Hague, when Trueblood and Mead thought it expedient to hold a national peace congress in New York to voice the sentiment of the nation in regard to what should be done at the conference. In accordance with a vote of the directors Oct. 23, 1906, they called a meeting at the City Club in New York, Dec. 10th, where were present representatives from the leading peace societies in the country. Robert Treat Paine acted as chairman and Prof. Dutton as secretary. Secretary Trueblood explained the purpose of the meeting.

After discussion it was voted to hold a congress to arouse and concentrate American public sentiment in support of the proposition put forth by the Interparliamentary Union and other peace organizations. They appointed an executive committee of fifteen among whom were Prof. Dutton as chairman, Robert E. Ely as secretary, and Trueblood, Mead, Profs. Kirchwey and Richard, Dr. Frederick Lynch, Hayne Davis, Dr. Jenkin Lloyd Jones of Chicago, and H. C. Phillips, the secretary of the Mohonk Lake conferences, as members. The executive committee was directed to create a general advisory committee of one hundred to cooperate with them in promoting the success of the congress. It met Jan. 7, 1907, and appointed several committees, among others, program, finance, local arrangements, publicity, and workingmen. For three months meetings were held Sunday evenings to increase the enthusiasm of the hearers. The New York Peace Society gave a dinner at the Yale Club to the editors of the city, Feb. 7. One hundred and twenty persons were present and addresses were made by Secretary Trueblood, Lyman Abbott, Dr. Jefferson, Prof. John Bassett Moore, and others.

The congress was held in Carnegie Hall, April 14 to 17, 1907. Invitations had been sent to thirty thousand commercial bodies, labor unions, farmers' granges, churches, religious organizations, peace societies, ethical, reform and philanthropic societies, colleges, universities, and educational institutions, learned societies, women's organizations and patriotic societies, governors, mayors, and members of Congress and of legislatures, requesting each to send two delegates to the congress. Twelve hundred and fifty-three delegates appeared from thirty-nine states and territories.

April 14, peace sermons were delivered in every town in the country containing five thousand inhabitants. Services were held in the churches of the city of New York in the morning. A great musical consecration service by the Oratorio Society of New York with a full orchestra was held in the evening with Bishop Potter presiding and Archbishop Farley and Rabbi Hirsch among the speakers. The opening meeting of the congress was held in Carnegie Hall. Andrew Carnegie was president of the congress. Among the vice presidents were Andrew D. White, Seth Low, Richard Bartholdt, A. K. Smiley, Robert Treat Paine, Alton B. Parker, Samuel Gompers, John Mitchell, Mayor McClellan, Gov. Hughes, Justice Brewer, William Jennings Bryan, Oscar S. Straus, and all the members of Roosevelt's cabinet except Secretary Root. Addresses of welcome were made by Mayor McClellan, Gov. Hughes, Secretary Root and a letter read from President Roosevelt. In the evening addresses were made by Viscount Bryce, Sir Robert Cranston, Sir Robert S. Ball, William T. Stead, Baron d'Estournelles de Constant, Baron Descamps of Belgium, Hugo Munsterberg, Oscar S. Straus, Dr. Ernst Richard, and others.

The meetings during the next two days were in sections. Jane Addams, Mrs. Helen M. Henrotin, Mary E. Woolley, Mrs. Lucia A. Mead, Mrs. May Wright Sewall, and Miss Anna Garlin Spencer spoke to the women. Presidents Butler, Eliot, Wilson, James, Drinker, and J. H. Finley, and Professors J. B. Moore, Kirchwey, Richard, and Clark spoke to college students who also listened to music by college glee clubs. Bryan, Bartholdt, Burton, Justice Brewer, and John Sharp Williams spoke on the legislative and judicial aspects of the peace movement. Ex Governor Batchelder of New Hampshire spoke to the business men at the Astor House, W. H. Maxwell, superintendent of the New York schools, Dr. Nathan C. Schaeffer, state superintendent of public instruction in Pennsylvania, and Rabbi Wise spoke to the young people at Carnegie Hall. Hon. Joseph I. Buchanan, William Stead, Terence V. Powderly, Dr. Algernon S. Crapsey, James J. Murphy and Samuel Gompers addressed the labor men at Cooper Union Hall, Bartholdt, Bryan, Chancellor MacCracken, Samuel J. Barrows, Seth Low, Judge Gray, John W. Foster, Kuno Francke, Archbishop Ireland, Edward Everett Hale, addressed the women workers. There was a reception at the City Club, a banquet where the cross of the Legion of Honor was conferred upon Andrew Carnegie by Baron d'Estournelles, and a dinner given by Carnegie to the foreign guests.

Trueblood was chairman of the committee on resolutions. As passed, the resolutions urged the Hague conference to form a more permanent and comprehensive international union, to become permanent with periodic meetings, to draft a general treaty of arbitration, to reduce armaments and to revise the laws of war.[1] They thanked Roosevelt for calling the second conference and voted to send a copy of the resolutions to him, to Secretary Root, and to each delegate to the conference.

The congress was felt to have been very successful. Great enthu-

[1] The resolutions are printed in the Advocate of Peace, May, 1907, pp. 102-103.

siasm had been shown at the meetings. The attendance far exceeded all expectations. Carnegie Hall containing five thousand seats an.l Cooper Union with three thousand were filled and overflow meetings were held in the Broadway Tabernacle, Calvary Baptist Church and the Majestic theatre. The leading peace men in the country had attended, ten United States senators, nineteen congressmen, four judges of the United States Supreme Court, twelve state chief justices, nine governors, two members of the Hague court, sixty New York editors, twenty-seven multi-millionaires, thirty labor leaders, ten mayors, eighteen college presidents, forty bishops, twenty state superintendents of public instruction, and twenty-six noted men. Aside from the speakers from abroad already mentioned were John Rhys, pro vice chancellor of Oxford University, Rev. E. S. Robert, vice chancellor of the University of Cambridge, Col. Sir Robert Cranston, ex lord provost of Edinburgh, and Maarten Maartens of Holland.

The Chicago delegates at the New York congress requested that the second congress be held in Chicago. Accordingly, in November, 1908, the American Peace Society sent Field Secretary Charles E. Beals to Chicago, where he interviewed the leading peace workers in regard to holding the peace congress there as suggested. He called a meeting at the City Club, Dec. 16, 1908, where it was decided to hold the congress. They appointed an executive committee, and committees on organization, program, finance, and reception. Royal L. Melendy was appointed executive secretary. Peace and arbitration societies, church organizations, boards of trade, chambers of commerce, universities, colleges, educational associations, industrial organizations, women's societies, governors, mayors, business men's organizations, labor and socialist bodies were invited to send delegates. The Chicago Association of Commerce agreed to finance the undertaking which cost in the vicinity of twelve thousand dollars. Several local meetings were held in Chicago and vicinity to arouse interest in the congress.

The congress was held in Orchestra Hall, May 3-5, 1909, and was similar in character to the congress held in New York. Six hundred delegates were present mainly from the middle west. President Taft was elected honorary president and Secretary of War J. M. Dickinson, president. Robert Treat Paine presided. Among the vice presidents were Jane Addams, E. A. Alderman, J. B. Angell, John Barrett, Richard Bartholdt, Justice Brewer, William J.

Bryan, T. E. Burton, Andrew Carnegie, Gov. Deneen, J. W. Foster, Edwin Ginn, Sam. Gompers, Edward Everett Hale, Rabbi Hirsch, Charles E. Jefferson, David Starr Jordan, Philander C. Knox, von Lengerke Meyer, Robert Treat Paine, Horace Porter, Secretary Root, James Brown Scott, A. K. Smiley, Oscar S. Straus, Booker T. Washington, and Attorney General Wickersham.

Meetings in the various churches were held on the Sunday preceding the opening of the congress. The labor and socialist organizations had a meeting of their own in Music Hall, addressed by Samuel Gompers and Prof. Graham Taylor. The business men had a meeting presided over by Hon. George E. Roberts, and the women were addressed by Mrs. Henrotin, Mrs. Mead, and Jane Addams.

Among the speakers at the congress were Bob Burdette, Dr. Jenkin Lloyd Jones, Rabbi Hirsch, Jacob Schurman, Gov. Deneen, Edwin D. Mead, Robert Treat Paine, Secretary Trueblood, Paul S. Reinsch, David Starr Jordan, Prof. Graham Taylor, H. M. Higinbotham, James Brown Scott, Edwin Ginn, Richard Bartholdt, Hamilton Holt, Ambassador von Bernstorff, and Wu Ting-Fang. Letters were read from President Taft and others.

Besides those already mentioned there were present Presidents Nollen of Lake Forest University, Scovel of Wooster University and Brooks of Baylor University, Dean Rogers of Cincinnati University, Profs. F. S. Blair, W. I. Hull, and C. C. Hyde, Prof. Hirst from Norway, Hon. James B. Moore of the Supreme Court of Michigan, Hon. William I. Buchanan, Tryon, Root, Lochner, Miss Eckstein, Mrs. Fannie Fern Andrews, Viscount Bryce, and Matsubara, the Japanese consul at Chicago.

Resolutions introduced by a Committee which included Trueblood and Mead, were adopted[1] favoring the arbitration of all international disputes, the ending of rivalry in armaments, the completion of the work begun by the Hague, and approving the arbitration treaties already concluded. The congress closed with a banquet addressed by Gen. Fred Dent Grant. As an aftermath came a gift of $25,000 to Northwestern University by the Swedish consul in Chicago to be used in promoting international peace and interdenominational harmony.

The third national congress was held in Baltimore at McCoy Hall, Johns Hopkins University, May 3-5, 1911. On the call of

[1] Printed in the Advocate of Peace, June, 1909, p. 127.

Hon. Theodore Marburg, president of the Maryland branch of the American Peace Society, a meeting of representatives of the various peace organizations met Feb. 14, 1911, to make the necessary plans for the congress. At this conference Turnstall Smith was appointed the organizing secretary of the congress. Like its predecessors it was considered very successful. It was the first peace gathering of any kind ever opened by the head of a nation.

Hamilton Holt acted as president. Among the vice presidents were Lyman Abbott, E. A. Alderman, W. J. Bryan, T. E. Burton, N. M. Butler, Simeon E. Baldwin, Richard Bartholdt, Alexander Graham Bell, James Bryce, Andrew Carnegie, C. W. Eliot, J. W. Foster, Myron T. Herrick, P. C. Knox, Seth Low, Theodore Marburg, Hamilton W. Mabie, Franklin MacVeagh, Thomas Nelson Page, Ira Remsen, Secretary Root, Jacob Schurman, I. N. Seligman, Hoke Smith, A. K. Smiley, Jacob H. Schiff, Secretary Trueblood, C. R. Van Hise, Attorney General Wickersham, and William A. White. The number of prominent speakers at the meetings was unusually large. In addition to the president of the United States there were Cardinal Gibbons, Andrew Carnegie, ex Secretary of State Foster, Senator Burton, Congressmen Bartholdt and Slayden, Presidents Remsen, Thwing, Warfield, Brooks, and Sharpless, Dean Henry Wade Rogers, Professors Dutton and Hull, Champ Clark, Secretary Trueblood, James Brown Scott, John Barrett, Lyman Abbott, Leo S. Rowe, E. D. Mead, A. D. Call, A. K. Smiley, Edwin Ginn, P. P. Claxton, the Mayor of Baltimore, the Bishop of Maryland, Baron d'Estournelles, and Senator La Fontaine of Belgium. The meeting closed with a banquet presided over by Champ Clark, the speaker of the House of Representatives.

The congress voted to become a permanent organization known as the American Peace Congress, managed by a permanent executive committee consisting of representatives from all peace societies in the country. The executive committee appointed at the Baltimore congress voted, in the fall of 1912, to leave the inauguration of the next congress to the American Peace Society. After some correspondence and a visit to St. Louis by Arthur D. Call, the Executive Director of the society, the society decided to hold the fourth congress in St. Louis, and placed it under the direction of the Business Men's League of that city. Prof. Manley O. Hudson, of the University of Missouri, later professor in Harvard University, was appointed chairman of the program committee. An organization secretary was hired and a general committee of distinguished men placed in charge.

As before, all peace societies and organizations interested in the peace movement were invited to send delegates to the congress. The governors of eight states appointed delegates. The Navy League sent delegates and six of the Latin American countries were represented.

The congress was held May 1-3, 1913. Pres. Wilson was elected honorary president and Congressman Bartholdt acted as president. Among the vice presidents were Champ Clark, Senator Burton, Andrew Carnegie, and W. J. Bryan. On the Sunday preceding the congress peace sermons were preached in the pulpits of the city. April 29, an oratorical contest was held under the direction of the Intercollegiate Peace Association. April 30, peace exercises were held in the high schools and colleges of the state, solemn high mass was said at the college church of St. Louis University, and the Jefferson Memorial costing half a million dollars was dedicated and presented to the city.

Addresses were given by Thomas E. Green, Senator Burton, Andrew Carnegie, E. D. Mead, Vice President Fairbanks, James Brown Scott, P. P. Claxton, Presidents Thwing, Mitchell, Jordan, and Myers, Dr. Jenkin Lloyd Jones, John Barrett, Profs. William I. Hull and Paul S. Reinsch, Arthur D. Call, Charles E. Beals, Booker T. Washington, Shailer Mathews, and James L. Tryon.

The last congress in the series was held in San Francisco, October 10-13, 1915, during the Panama-Pacific Exposition. It had been planned to hold it in Washington, but on the suggestion of several persons in California, the American Peace Society aided by the Church Peace Union decided for San Francisco. The general direction of the congress was placed in the hands of Robert C. Root, the representative of the society on the Pacific coast.

David Starr Jordan acted as its president. Robert C. Root was secretary and Capt. Robert Dollar, treasurer. Invitations were issued to the various peace organizations, and delegates were present from the League to Enforce Peace, American Peace Centenary Committee, state and national governments and organizations of the diverse character represented at previous congresses. The subjects discussed were the world court and league of peace. Among the speakers were Mrs. Mead, S. L. Gulick and Senator La Fontaine of Belgium. The congress recommended calling a conference of neutral nations and approved the program of the League to Enforce Peace. Nov. 12, President Jordan, as directed, laid the resolutions before President Wilson, and copies were sent to members of Congress, the cabinet, and governors of the various states.

Chapter XXXV

STATE PEACE CONGRESSES

In ADDITION to the national congresses, mention should be made of three congresses of a more local character in which the American Peace Society was interested. S. P. Brooks, president of Baylor University, Waco, Texas, and a vice president of the American Peace Society, was so impressed with the first American congress which he attended in New York, that on his return home he called a congress at Waco, Nov. 19-21, 1907, to develop a peace sentiment among the people of the southwest and to advance world civilization in that region which had never been cultivated by the peace societies. The principal subjects discussed were national armaments, the permanent international court, peace propaganda, and arbitration. The congress was addressed by the grand master of the Grand Mason's Lodge of Texas, the president of the Business Men's Club of San Antonio, the district attorney, congressmen, editors, clergymen, and by Secretary Trueblood, who went there for that purpose. As a result of the congress, a Texas State Peace Society was formed.

The second state peace congress was held in Philadelphia, May 16-19, 1908. It was inspired by the leading spirits of the American group of the Interparliamentary Union, who desired a series of state congresses to be held to form public sentiment in favor of the expected third Hague conference. The plan was to arrange a series of meetings representing the cause of peace along lines of popular appeal addressed by able men. Nine hundred delegates were present from various churches, civic societies, labor unions, women's clubs, religious associations, granges, and ethical, social and commercial associations.

President Roosevelt was elected honorary president of the congress. Gov. Stuart and Congressman Moon acted as presiding officers. Among the speakers were Justice Brewer, Senator Cullom, William Jennings Bryan, Richard Bartholdt, Mayor Guthin of Pittsburgh, Provost C. C. Harrison, President Sharpless, Edward Everett Hale, Hon. J. W. Foster, Andrew Carnegie, Mr. and Mrs.

Mead, James Brown Scott, Mrs. May Wright Sewall, Dr. Nathan C. Schaeffer, Secretary Trueblood, Charles E. Beals, Hon. Jackson H. Ralston, Wayne MacVeagh, T. E. Burton, and John Barrett.

The conference was divided into small groups,—women, lawyers, business men, and educational men—closing with a banquet. The platform called for the ratification of the Hague convention, the establishment of an international prize court, the establishment of an international court of arbitral justice as soon as three states should agree upon a method of selecting the judges, and a limitation of armaments.

As early as 1903, a movement was started to erect a memorial to Elihu Burritt in New Britain on the occasion of the one hundredth anniversary of his birth, Dec. 10, 1910. A public meeting held at the Lyceum, Feb. 23, 1904, with addresses by Edwin D. Mead and others, resulted in the appointment of a committee to raise funds for the memorial. This developed later into the Burritt Memorial Association, with $12,000 raised by the end of the year 1907.

Later, on the suggestion of Secretary Trueblood it was decided to hold a peace congress at Hartford in connection with the celebration of the one hundredth anniversary of the birth of Burritt at New Britain and to invite business, municipal, civic, literary, patriotic, legal, educational, religious, philanthropic, charitable, labor and farm organizations of various kinds throughout New England to send delegates to it.

The congress was placed under the joint direction of the American Peace Society and the Connecticut Peace Society, which had been organized May 31, 1906. Arthur Deerin Call, president of the society from its organization and District Superintendent of Schools at Hartford, was made chairman of the executive committee and program committee with Dean Henry Wade Rogers of the Yale Law School as president, Rev. Rodney W. Roundy of Hartford as executive secretary, and the governors of the New England states as vice presidents. This was the first peace congress organized for all New England. The meetings were held May 7-10, 1910, in the Center Church House of the Center Congregational Church at Hartford, with an afternoon and evening spent at New Britain, some ten miles distant.

Sunday morning peace was mentioned in the pulpits of the city. At a mass meeting in the afternoon addresses were made by Charles J. Donahue, president of the Connecticut Federation of Labor,

Charles E. Beals, field secretary of the American Peace Society, John B. Lennon, treasurer of the American Federation of Labor, and others. A general peace meeting was held in the evening in Parsons Theatre. Dean Henry Wade Rogers of the Yale Law School acted as president of the Congress. Bishop Brewster, Dr. Jacobus of the Hartford Theological Seminary and others presided at various meetings. Lieut. Gov. Brooks and Mayor Edward L. Smith welcomed the guests. Letters were read from President Taft, W. J. Bryan, Secretary Knox, Gov. Draper of Massachusetts, Secretary of War Dickinson, ex Vice President Fairbanks, and Samuel Gompers. Addresses were made by Mr. and Mrs. E. D. Mead, President Thomas of Middlebury College, Mrs. Fannie Fern Andrews, Mrs. May Wright Sewall, Rev. O. P. Gifford, Edwin Ginn, Hon. J. W. Foster, and others.

At New Britain an address was given by Secretary Trueblood and a stereoption lecture on the Federation of the World by Hamilton Holt Sunday evening. The exercises Tuesday were very attractive. The whole city celebrated the one hundredth anniversary of the birth of Burritt. The stores were closed. The city was decorated with flags and bunting. The guests were taken from Hartford to New Britain in automobiles. Secretary Trueblood spoke at a religious and musical service in the High School. The program had been arranged by a committee of seventy. The success of the meeting was due largely to Rev. Herbert A. Jump, pastor of the First Congregational Church. A printed sketch of the life of Burritt was given to everybody. Mrs. Annie S. Churchill as secretary of the Burritt Memorial Committee had raised the fund for the memorial.

A civic procession, led by the mayor and the common council, went with bands, floats, and three thousand school children bearing flags from the center of the city to the cemetery where wreaths and flags were placed on the grave of Burritt. An oration was given at the grave by James Brown Scott. Principal White of the State Normal School presided. A reception followed with supper in the church. In the evening a mass meeting was held at the Lyceum with an overflow meeting in the church. The mayor welcomed the people. Rabbi Wise and ex Gov. Utter of Rhode Island made addresses. Music was furnished by a jubilee chorus. It was felt that the memory of Elihu Burritt, the sage of New Britain, still lived in the hearts of his countrymen.

Chapter XXXVI

LAST DAYS IN BOSTON

As HAS been seen in the last few chapters, much was crowded into the history of the society during these years. A change in the range of vision of the society had come with the opening of the twentieth century. The war with Spain broadened the outlook, the Hague conference extended the views, and participation in the meetings of the Interparliamentary Union had widened the interests of men and women throughout the country. The provincialism of the United States had come to an end. The work of the society was likewise becoming extended. For years the society had acted as a seer and a prophet, engaged in creating sentiment against war. It had urged churches, colleges, politicians, and statesmen to act. It had organized meetings, circulated tracts, pleaded to be heard, and shown the way. Now a big peace meeting at the Hague, conducted by politicians and statesmen, had been successfully handled, almost ignoring the peace societies. It had passed through the scoffing and doubting period. The arguments, pleas and petitions of the society had been heard. Some seed had fallen upon fertile soil. An international court had been established and put into successful operation. The vigils of the peace leaders had not been in vain. So it became necessary to conduct the society on a larger and different scale.

More and larger public meetings were held, developing into the peace congresses already described. Jan. 16, 1901, it held two meetings at Lorimer Hall, Tremont Temple, one at noon and the other in the evening, end of the century meetings where the transformation of public sentiment in regard to arbitration was recounted. Speeches were made by Secretary Trueblood, President Paine, Edward Everett Hale, Edward Atkinson, John Willis Baer, Mary A. Livermore and others. April 15, 1903, the society and the Committee on International Relations of the Twentieth Century Club jointly held a public meeting in the interest of international

248

arbitration and peace at Tremont Temple, addressed by Hon. William I. Buchanan of Buffalo, a delegate to the Pan American conference, Edwin D. Mead, and Edward Everett Hale. Following a vote of the directors June 29, 1906, forming a committee for peace propaganda among workingmen, with Edwin D. Mead as chairman, a joint meeting of the society was held with the Central Labor Union at the Parker Memorial, Dec. 11, 1906. A. M. Huddell presided. W. A. Appleton of the Lace Workers Union, Nottingham, England, spoke and there were brief remarks by President Paine and Secretary Trueblood.

A plan suggesting a world legislature with power to enact laws to be observed by the nations had been laid before the Massachusetts legislature in 1902. Trueblood studied the plan carefully and from it developed an advisory congress, which the society laid before the legislature requesting it to pass a resolution inviting Congress to authorize the president to propose to the governments of the world the establishment of a regular international congress to meet at stated periods—five or seven years—to deliberate upon such questions as concerned the nations jointly and to make recommendations thereon to the governments, thus not encroaching at all upon the sovereignty of the individual states.

A memorial[1] to this effect dated January 1, 1903, was presented by Honorable Robert Thomas in the lower house of the legislature, January 16, and referred to the Joint Committee on Federal Relations, Senator Henry R. Skinner, chairman. A hearing was given on this memorial February 11, and also on another in regard to a world legislature which had been presented to the legislature by Raymond L. Bridgman, later a director of the society, two years before and referred to the next legislature, and then introduced as a new memorial bearing 700 signatures. The committee reported a resolution covering both memorials February 18,[2] which was approved by the House the next day and by the Senate Feb. 25, and a copy sent to the senior senator and senior congressman from the state requesting them to present it to the United States Congress at its next session.

Copies of the memorial with the resolution of the Massachusetts legislature were sent by the society to the governors of the states and the mayors of all the important cities of the United States and

[1] Printed in the Advocate of Peace, February, 1903, pp. 23-25.
[2] Printed in the Advocate of Peace, March, 1903, p. 37.

to public men in Europe and America. The petition of the society and the resolution of the Massachusetts legislature were presented to Congress Nov. 1, 1903, and by it referred to the Committee on Foreign Affairs. Jan. 14, 1904, the House committee gave members of the board and friends of the society a hearing. In March, it was referred by the Senate committee to a subcommittee consisting of William P. Frye, president of the Senate, Charles W. Fairbanks of Indiana, and John T. Morgan of Alabama for consideration, and there remained.

January 21, 1907, another petition signed by Robert Treat Paine, John L. Bates, Edwin D. Mead, Samuel B. Capen, Charles F. Dole, Raymond L. Bridgman, Charles S. Hamlin, William E. Huntington, Elwyn G. Preston, Edwin Ginn, and James P. Munroe, was presented to the Massachusetts legislature asking that body to urge the president and secretary of state to try to get from the coming Hague conference favorable action on the five recommendations of the Interparliamentary Union in behalf of a regular international parliament, an obligatory arbitration treaty, limitation of national armaments, a commission to report on contested issues between nations before hostilities are brought, and immunity of private property at sea in time of war. It was referred to the committee on Federal Relations which had hearings Jan. 30, at which Paine, Trueblood, Dole and Bridgman appeared and were heard. The committee unanimously voted favorably on the petition and added to it a resolution of the Massachusetts Board of Trade that the trade routes of the ocean be neutralized. The report was adopted by the House, February 18, and by the Senate, Feb. 21.[1]

The practise of observing a Sunday in December as peace day, which started almost with the founding of the society, seems to have fallen into disuse during the Civil War. In 1883, efforts were made to revive the custom, and in 1889 the society sent circulars and letters to the press in regard to it. At the peace congress in London in 1890 it was voted to recommend that Christian ministers devote one Sunday, preferably the third Sunday in December, to a consideration of the subject of peace. In 1892, the society sent a letter to one hundred and twenty religious journals calling the attention of pastors to the observance of peace day. Many of the journals published the letter and several made editorial comment in regard to it. Every year thereafter until the breaking out of the World

---

[1] Printed in the Advocate of Peace, April, 1907, p. 80.

War the society urged upon the ministry the advisability of observing the third Sunday of December as peace day and preaching a peace sermon in connection with it. The peace department of the Women's Christian Temperance Union gave special attention to the matter and cooperated in spreading information in regard to it, but with varying success. The day was better observed in England and by some of the Protestant churches in France than in America.

On the continent, however, February 22 was more generally observed as peace day. As early as 1896, Felix Moscheles, the chairman of the Arbitration and Peace Association in London, suggested that all peace societies on that day pass a peace resolution in identical terms, affirming the principles held in common by the societies. Moscheles prepared the resolutions which varied year by year. The International Peace Bureau at Berne sent them to the various societies and the societies on that day passed them in public meeting.

Another day observed as peace day was May 18, the day on which the first Hague conference had opened its session. The American Peace Society noticed the day in 1901 and held its annual meetings on that day in 1902, 1903, 1904. The International Council of Women suggested its observance in 1901, and Mrs. May Wright Sewall persuaded several organizations in the United States to observe it.

At the suggestion of Mrs. Mead, Secretary Trueblood, April 11, 1905, approached George H. Martin, secretary of the Massachusetts Board of Education, who issued a letter to local superintendents of schools recommending the observance of May 18 as peace day. The state commissioner of Common Schools of Ohio took up the matter and after conference with Trueblood published a program to be observed upon that day. The superintendent of schools in the state of New York fell into line. At the Mohonk conference that same year it was suggested that colleges and schools be urged to observe that day. Also the Fourteenth International Peace Congress at Lucerne urged its general observance.

In 1906, and again in 1907, Trueblood sent circulars to the state superintendents of schools asking their cooperation in bringing about the observance of the day by the schools and published a program suitable for the occasion. In 1908, he sent a letter to all state superintendents and to superintendents of schools in cities containing 25,000 inhabitants, calling attention to the fact that

May 18 was observed by schools in six states as peace day and urging their cooperation in securing its general observance throughout the country. In 1909 similar letters were sent to superintendents in cities of 10,000 inhabitants, and in 1910, to those of 5000 inhabitants.

In 1906, the Kansas Superintendent of Public Instruction designated May 18 as peace day to be observed by the schools. The Department of Superintendance, National Education Association, resolved in favor of such observance. Arthur Deerin Call, as president of the Connecticut Peace Society and as president of the Board of Principals of Hartford, and with the approval of the governor of the state, the state board of education, and the Common School Superintendents' Association, on May 11, 1907, sent a letter to the school boards and teachers of the state urging them to observe May 18 as peace day.

The work was then taken up by the American School Peace League, organized in 1908, and carried on independent of the American Peace Society. In 1912, its secretary, Mrs. Fannie Fern Andrews, a member of the executive committee of the American Peace Society from 1908 to 1911, prepared a bulletin containing a program with supplementary material which Hon. P. P. Claxton, United States Commissioner of Education, issued as a federal bulletin, fifty thousand copies being printed, with a second edition issued the next year. By 1914, half of the state superintendents and all those in the large cities recommended the observance of May 18 as peace day. In 1910, on motion of Moscheles, the International Peace Bureau at Berne recommended the observance of May 18 as peace day, and two years later that day had entirely superseded Feb. 22 on the continent as peace day.

Incidentally the society at its annual meeting May 18, 1904, passed the following resolution: "Resolved, That our government be urged to seize the first opportunity to offer mediation to the belligerents according to the Hague convention, with a view to bringing about an end of the war between Russia and Japan." A copy of this resolution was sent to President Roosevelt, Jan. 9, 1905. It was followed up by a letter from President Paine and Secretary Trueblood to Secretary Hay, Jan. 24, 1905, asking whether under the Hague treaty after the surrender of Port Arthur, he could not offer the good offices of the United States. June 8, 1905, Roosevelt wrote to Japan and Russia suggesting opening negotiations to end the war, which led to the signing of the Treaty of Portsmouth later in the year.

Likewise, when in 1908, 1909, and 1910, proposals were made to increase the size of the American navy, the society sent remonstrances to Congress. Through their efforts a remonstrance was sent to Congress signed by six hundred ministers and religious leaders of Boston and twenty other cities, in March, 1910.

At the annual meeting, May 18, 1905, the constitution underwent a slight revision, by amending sections 2, 3, 4, 5, and 8. In section 2, the statement that "all war is contrary to the spirit of the gospel" was changed to read "war is contrary to the spirit of Christianity and of all true religion and morality," and "Christianity" later in the section was changed to "this spirit." In section 3, membership in the society formerly open to "persons of every Christian denomination" now becomes open to "all persons." Section 4 formerly reading "Every annual member of the society shall pay a yearly contribution of $2" became "every annual subscriber of $2 shall be a member of this society." By section 5, the amount of contribution necessary to constitute a person a life member was reduced from twenty-five dollars to twenty. Sections 4 and 5 were combined into one section. In section 8, the number of directors stated formerly to be not "less" than twenty became not "more" than twenty.

In 1908, a new constitution was drawn up modifying somewhat the articles in the constitution of 1837 relating to branch societies, which with a few changes had been in force until then. Articles I, II, and III were unchanged. Articles VIII and IX on the annual meeting and amendments were the same as articles IX and X of the old constitution with slight changes in phraseology. Article IV was changed to read as follows: "Every annual member of the society shall pay a yearly contribution of one dollar; the payment of five dollars a year shall constitute one a sustaining member; the payment of twenty-five dollars at one time shall constitute any person a life member." Article V provided for branch societies, members of which were to be members of the American Peace Society, and one half the membership fee of one dollar was to go to the parent society in return for the Advocate of Peace. Article VI provided that presidents of the branch societies were to be vice presidents of the parent society. Article VII related to officers. It was the same as the amendment made in 1892 except that the number of the board of directors was to be more than twenty.

At the St. Louis Exposition in 1904, the society took a unit of space in the Department of Social Economy with a case 3½ feet high and 2½ feet wide containing card statements of the cost and waste of war, the attainments of arbitration, and pictures, prepared by a committee of which Mrs. Lucia Ames Mead was chairman. The exhibit was then moved to the Lewis and Clark Exposition at Portland, Oregon, under the care of the Massachusetts Sociology Section, and received a gold medal by the committees at each exposition.

The close relationship with the Universal Peace Union continued. Paine, Trueblood, Hezekiah Butterworth, and Scott F. Hershey, officers of the American Peace Society, were also vice presidents of the Universal Peace Union, and all of them with Edwin Ginn, Edwin D. Mead, Richard Bartholdt, Homer B. Sprague, and James L. Tryon, frequently spoke at their meetings and anniversaries.

Secretary Trueblood was elected a member of the International Law Association, the one founded by Secretary Miles in 1873, at its annual meeting in Buffalo in 1899, its first meeting held in the United States, and was placed on a special committee to study in detail and report the next year on the convention adopted by the Hague conference. He met with the committee Nov. 9, 1899, in New York City, which passed a resolution approving the Hague arbitration and mediation convention as a practical working scheme and urged the United States Senate to ratify it. He spoke and read a paper on a Regular International Advisory Congress at the meeting of the association held in Antwerp in 1903, and was at the meeting in Christiania in 1905, and Berlin in 1906. At Christiania he was elected a member of the executive council, a position he held for several years.

Trueblood lectured as opportunity presented. He spoke at the congress of religions at Buffalo in June, 1901, at several colleges in Iowa and the University of Minnesota in February, 1902, in Chicago, Indianapolis, and Richmond, Ind., in February, 1904, and at the state normal school in Oswego, N. Y., in October, 1907. He lectured before churches, ministers' meetings, clubs, conventions, Y. M. C. A's, conferences, educational institutions, and business organizations, in various cities, all in addition to the many activities described in this and preceding chapters. In the latter days at Boston other members of the society aided him,—Paine, Mr. and Mrs.

Mead, Miss Anna B. Eckstein, Mrs. Fannie Fern Andrews, Homer B. Sprague, Charles F. Dole, R. L. Bridgeman, James L. Tryon, and many others. In 1906 a board of lecturers was organized. In 1908, 125 lectures were delivered by the members of this board, and that number increased in succeeding years.

Following the holding of the second Hague conference interest in the question of peace extended rapidly throughout the country. Rev. James L. Tryon of Attleboro was appointed assistant secretary of the society Feb. 1, 1907, at $2000 a year, to establish and manage a press bureau, voted by the directors May 22, 1906. He sent peace articles to two hundred weekly journals during his first year and sent many letters and circulars to various religious bodies. He aided the secretary in handling the correspondence and delivered many addresses. The office of the society, located at 31 Beacon Street, Room 32, after September, 1901, continued to be a bureau of information open to all inquirers.

The annual business meeting between 1901 and 1910 was held at two o'clock in the afternoon at the office of the society. In the evening following the annual meeting May 18, 1903, one hundred members and friends of the society sat down at a dinner in the rooms of the Twentieth Century Club in commemoration of the seventy-fifth anniversary of the society. The custom was continued yearly until 1909. At these banquets addresses were made by such persons as President Paine, Secretary Trueblood, Richard Bartholdt, Samuel J. Barrows, President Mary E. Woolley, Bishop Hamilton, ex Secretary J. W. Foster, Moorfield Storey, Rev. Charles F. Dole, Mrs. Lucia Ames Mead, Mrs. Anna Garlin Spencer, ex Gov. John L. Bates, George H. Martin, secretary of the Massachusetts Board of Education, Charles E. Adams, president of the state board of trade, Elwyn G. Preston, secretary of the Boston Chamber of Commerce, Rev. Walter Walsh of Dundee, Scotland, and Bliss Perry, editor of the Atlantic Monthly, and later professor in Harvard University.

On the suggestion of Mrs. Mead the society also adopted social activities for a time. A social and tea was given by the president and directors of the American Peace Society to one hundred and fifty members and friends at the Twentieth Century Club, 3 Joy Street, Feb. 27, 1906, from 4 to 6 P. M. Remarks were made by the president, secretary, Mr. and Mrs. Mead, and Rev. Edward Cummings. The occasion was so enjoyable that during the next season a social committee was appointed which during the year held six receptions at the same place with addresses by Mr. and Mrs. Mead, Homer B. Sprague, Dean Irwin of Radcliffe, and the president and secretary of the society. Several parlor meetings under the direction of Mrs. Fannie Fern Andrews were held at the homes of different members of the society and friends in Boston and vicinity with remarks by C. F. Dole, Anna B. Eckstein, Homer B. Sprague, Bliss Perry, and Secretary Trueblood, and annual receptions at the rooms of the Twentieth Century Club by the president and directors with refreshments.

The Advocate of Peace continued to be sent as in former years to colleges, universities, Y. M. C. A's, libraries, ministers, members of the society and certain others selected for various reasons. The number of copies printed monthly slowly increased to 5500 in 1908, 6000 in 1909, and 7000 in 1910. The Angel of Peace, the paper for children which had been issued since 1883 came to an end with the number for December, 1905, due to insufficient patronage. The literature continued practically unchanged. A few pamphlets were added to the list and several old ones were revised. Eight thousand copies of the proceedings of the Boston congress of 1904 were printed and twelve thousand copies of a Primer of the Peace Movement in 1905. In 1906, the society published 209,700 copies of pamphlets on "Limited Armaments" in the French Senate and distributed them among members of Congress and of the state legislature; also 5000 copies of the Report of the Committee to investigate the Teaching of History in Schools in Reference to War and Peace. A general stock of peace literature was kept on hand for sale and free distribution.

The need for funds continued. The rentable value of the houses held by the Permanent Peace Fund shrunk at the time of the Spanish war, thus causing requests for money to be frequently made by the society. At the annual meeting in 1901, Trueblood called attention to the need of a building to be owned by the society and used for permanent quarters. In 1905, the need for such a building became more apparent and an attempt was made to raise $100,000 with which to build an adequate home. In 1906, the society put into the building fund two bonds of the Chicago, Burlington & Quincy RR., valued at $2,000, which it had bought in 1901, and $2,500 given by James Callanan. The building fund increased until by 1912 it was valued at $12,435, and in 1913, at $14,684.25.

The receipts and expenditures of the society from 1901 to 1911, with the balance on hand at the end of each year were as follows:

	Receipts	Expenditures	Balance on hand
1901	$ 5031.72	$ 4872.88	$ 236.51
1902	5256.44	5454.10	38.85
1903	9016.06	6132.00	2922.91
1904	5055.54	5730.00	2248.45
1905	6342.34	6462.43	2128.36
1906	7840.16	5996.20	1634.32
1907	13744.70	8897.54	8819.48
1908	15097.38	11015.47	8000.70
1909	15665.41	16722.95	1057.54 [1]
1910	17160.98	17130.41	30.57
1911	19595.36	18324.38	--.--

[1] Deficit

During these years several persons of prominence accepted office in the society: Jane Addams, vice president, since 1900; Edwin Ginn, director, 1901-03; vice president 1903-14; Bliss Perry, director, 1905-16; Booker T. Washington, vice president, 1905-16; Hon. Richard Bartholdt, vice president, 1906-11; Alice Stone Blackwell, director, 1904-06, vice president 1906-13; President David Starr Jordan, vice president since 1906; Hon. T. E. Burton, vice president, 1907-11, president, 1911-16, 1924 to date; Prof. John Bassett Moore, vice president, 1907-19; President Mary E. Woolley, vice president 1907-1925; Andrew Carnegie, vice president, 1908-17; Hon. J. W. Foster, vice president 1908-18; Hon. James Brown Scott, vice president since 1908; and Hon. E. E. Brown, vice president 1909-21.

Robert Treat Paine, president of the society from 1891, died Aug. 11, 1910. He had been in poor health for a year. He was a member of Trinity Church and a philanthropist. He was president of the associated charities in Boston for thirty years. He was at the first Mohonk conference and at nearly all its subsequent meetings. He presided over one of the peace meetings at Chicago in 1893 and at the first session of the Chicago congress of 1909. He was president of the Boston congress in 1904. He visited the State Department and the President several times in the interest of arbitration and it was largely due to his suggestion and representation that the negotiation for the arbitration treaty was opened by Secretary Gresham in 1896. He was at the Hague conference in 1907 and signed the circular letter that initiated the proposition for the first national peace congress in New York in 1907. For several years he gave the society annually $1,000 and supported it in every way possible.

Among other prominent officers of the society claimed by death during this period were Joseph Cook, June 24, 1901, vice president from 1891; C. C. Bonney, in 1904, vice president from 1891; Hezekiah Butterworth in 1905, director, 1894-99, vice president from 1899; Edward Atkinson in 1906, vice president from 1897; Edward Everett Hale, June 9, 1909, vice president from 1893; Hon. William I. Buchanan, Oct. 6, 1909, vice president from 1904; and Julia Ward Howe, Oct. 17, 1910, director from 1889. Dr. Hale was 87 years old at the time of his death, and Mrs. Howe, 92.

Chapter XXXVII

THE RISE OF PEACE FOUNDATIONS

In HIS autobiography, chapter 21, page 283, Andrew Carnegie states that he became interested in the peace societies on one of his early visits to Great Britain and attended a meeting of one of the societies there. The name of the society is not mentioned, but there is a statement in Concord, July, 1885, p. 139, the organ of the International Arbitration and Peace Society of which Hogsdon Pratt was secretary, that Carnegie was present at the meeting of the society, July 22, 1885, addressed them, and paid a deficit of £574. He subscribed $100 to the international arbitration fund in 1886. In 1887, he advised Cremer and others to send the English deputation to the President of the United States, and on their arrival in Washington presented them to President Cleveland. From that time he said that the desire for the abolition of war grew with him. He was greatly pleased with the action of the Hague conference in 1899. At the suggestion of Hon. F. W. Holls and Hon. Andrew D. White, Carnegie offered $1,500,000 to the Dutch government with which to build a temple of peace. Later he gave $750,000 for the building of the Pan American building in Washington and $100,000 for the Central American court at Cartago and again at San José.

His address on the occasion of his reelection as rector of the University of St. Andrews, Oct. 17, 1905, was a League of Peace. In 1907, he became president of the New York Peace Society to which he gave five thousand dollars a year. He had given millions of dollars to found libraries and had established a fund of $5,000,000 for the benefit of heroes in peace, besides giving money for research and education. He was vice president of the American Peace Society, from 1908 to 1917. He also contributed to the leading peace organizations,—the American Peace Society, the American International Conciliation Association, the Intercollegiate Peace Association, School Peace League, besides societies of a similar character in Europe. He also contributed heavily to the peace congresses at Boston, in 1904, New York in 1907, Chicago in 1909 and Hartford in 1910. It was reported in 1910 that he was contributing $50,000 a year to various peace organizations and enterprises.

Dec. 14, 1910, Carnegie announced at a meeting in the building of the Carnegie Institution in Washington that he had established a $10,000,000 fund to be used in hastening the abolition of war and to promote the establishment of a lasting peace. This sum in first mortgage bonds of the United States Steel Corporation to the value of $11,500,000 was given to twenty-seven trustees almost all of them well known in the peace movement: Senator Elihu Root, ex secretary of state; Dr. Nicholas Murray Butler, president of Columbia University; Dr. Henry S. Pritchett, president of the Carnegie Foundation for the Advancement of Teaching; Joseph H. Choate, ex ambassador to Great Britain; Albert K. Smiley, Lake Mohonk; Charles William Eliot, ex president of Harvard University; James Brown Scott, ex solicitor of the Department of State; John W. Foster, ex secretary of state; Andrew J. Montague, ex governor of the state of Virginia; William M. Howard, member of Congress from Georgia; Judge Thomas Burke, Seattle, Wash.; James L. Slayden, member of Congress from Texas; Andrew D. White, ex ambassador to Germany; Robert S. Brookings, St. Louis; Samuel Mather, steel manufacturer, Cleveland; J. C. Schmidlapp, Cincinnati; Arthur William Foster, regent of the University of California; R. A. Franks, banker, Hoboken, N. J.; Charlemagne Tower, ex ambassador to Germany and Russia; Oscar S. Straus, ambassador to Turkey; Austin G. Fox, New York City; John S. Cadwalader, New York City; John Sharp Williams, Senator from Mississippi; C. L. Taylor, of the Carnegie Hero Fund Commission; George W. Perkins, New York City; Robert S. Woodward, president, and Cleveland H. Dodge, secretary, Carnegie Institute. Among those present at the meeting was Secretary Trueblood with whom Carnegie had discussed his plans two or three weeks before.

The deed of trust conveying the property, which was witnessed by his wife and daughter,[1] stated, that the trustees were to use the income from the money to hasten the abolition of war, "the foulest blot upon our civilization," that they could sell or reinvest the funds, but should form a corporation to whom the fund was to be conveyed, that they could fill vacancies in or add to their number, pay their president a salary, and reimburse themselves for their

---

[1] Printed in the Advocate of Peace, January, 1911, pp. 7, 8.

expenses. Continuing, the deed recites: "I leave them the widest discretion as to the means and policy they shall from time to time adopt, only promising that the one end they shall keep increasingly in view until it is attained, is the speedy abolition of international war between so called civilized nations. When civilized nations enter into such treaties as named or war is discarded as disgraceful to civilized man as personal war (dueling) and man selling and buying (slavery) have been discarded within the wider boundaries of our English speaking race, the trustees shall then please consider what is the next most degrading evil or evils whose banishment—or what new elevating element or elements if introduced or fostered or both combined— would most advance the progress, elevation, and happiness of man, and so from century to century without end, my trustees of each age shall determine how they can best aid man in the upward march to higher and higher stages of development unceasingly, for now we know that as a law of his being man was created with the desire and capacity for improvement to which, perchance, there may be no limit short of perfection even here in this life upon earth."

The trustees of the Carnegie Peace Fund organized March 9, 1911, as the Carnegie Endowment for International Peace with Elihu Root, president, Joseph H. Choate, vice president, James Brown Scott, secretary, and Walter M. Gilbert, treasurer. The executive committee consisted of Root, Scott, Butler, Foster, Montague, Pritchett, and Tower. The purposes of the trustees were stated to be to employ expert services to collect information on ways and means tending to prevent war, to investigate the causes of war, to study the history of what the peace cause has actually accomplished, to promote the development of international law, and assist in molding public oponion to a point where the people will refuse to go to war. They stated that they would use governmental agencies for collecting information, and the important peace organizations in so far as they were useful. They also stated that the contributions of Carnegie to the various peace organizations would be continued for the year when it would be decided what agencies would be helped in the future.

The trustees organized the undertaking as an institution for research and public education in three divisions: (a) a division of International Law, under the direction of James Brown Scott, solicitor for the Department of State, member of the Institute of

International Law, editor of the American Journal of International Law, technical delegate to the second Hague conference, to promote a progressive development of international law and teach that intercourse between nations should be based upon a correct and definite idea of international justice so that nations shall settle international disputes according to law; (b) a division of Economics and History under the direction of John Bates Clark of Columbia University, to educate public opinion and formulate conclusions for the guidance of governmental polity, to study the causes and effect of war; and (c) a division of Intercourse and Education, under the direction of Nicholas Murray Butler, president of Columbia University, to educate public opinion, promote international friendship, diffuse information, establish better understanding, cultivate friendly feeling, increase the knowledge and understanding of one another, promote peaceable methods of settling disputes, and assist established organized agencies necessary or useful in the accomplishment thereof.

As suggested, investigations have been carried on. Conferences have been held and agents have been sent to foreign countries and even around the world. Their reports, books on arbitration and peace and international law, and collections of statements, views, and treaties have been published. A library has been collected, a bureau of translation formed, a book exchange has been organized. The Institute of International Law, established in 1874, was appointed its official adviser. A European bureau was opened in Paris. The endowment bought the property at numbers 2 and 4 Jackson Place, opposite the White House, and has since been located there. During the war many of its activities rested, but it has since been at work gathering and disseminating information, extending its three departments, adapting to the new times the purposes of its founder.

The Department of Intercourse and Education secured correspondents in the various capitals of the world. It also distributed money among the various societies and journals published in France, Germany, Belgium, and America. Correspondence bimensuelle, the organ of the Universal Peace Congresses, heretofore published in French only, was given a subvention from January, 1913, to the outbreak of the war in July, 1914, sufficient to permit it to be issued with editions in German and English also, and the number of copies to be increased to 20,000 monthly.

Among the American societies benefited were the American Peace Society, the New York Peace Society, and the World Court League. From 1913 to 1916, the endowment gave the American Peace Society $31,000 a year, much of which went to the branches; from 1916 to 1920, $20,000; from 1920 to 1923, $15,000; and from 1923 to 1927, $7,500, when the subventions ceased altogether.

The principal foreign societies to which subventions were made was the Association for International Conciliation founded by Baron d'Estournelles de Constant shortly after the first Hague conference in 1899. Its object was to stimulate home activity under the safeguard of good foreign relations, to educate the public, especially the heads of educational institutions, correct false reports, promote foreign trips and international visits. Its Paris office was the agency used by the Division of Intercourse and Education for special propaganda. It had branches in England, Germany, Japan, and the United States. The American branch was started in 1909, with Nicholas Murray Butler as president, Andrew Carnegie honorary president, and Lyman Abbott and Seth Low members of the executive committee. The publications of the association in 1913 had a circulation of 80,000 copies in the United States. Its work was merged into that of the Carnegie Endowment, July 1, 1924.

The World Peace Foundation dates back to January, 1903, when Edwin Ginn, who had become interested in the peace movement as a result of attending the Mohonk conferences in 1897 and later years, and was a director or vice president of the American Peace Society from 1901 until his death Jan. 21, 1914, announced that he would issue cheap editions of the great peace books at cost price and urged their use in schools. Edwin D. Mead, the editor of the New England Magazine and a vice president or director of the American Peace Society from 1900 to 1917, was engaged as editor of the series.

Ginn gave $1,000 toward the expenses of the peace congress in Boston, in 1904, and increased his gifts for peace purposes until, in 1909, he was giving $10,000 a year culminating, Dec. 15, 1909, in the opening of the International School of Peace. This became a corporation, with officers and directors and a bureau of education to modify the course of study in the schools, to eliminate literature and history tending to inculcate unduly the military spirit. Mr. Ginn announced his intention to endow such a school.

Early in 1911, the name was changed to the World Peace Foundation. Ginn gave it $50,000 a year and provided in his will an endowment of $1,000,000. Among the trustees of the foundation were Edwin Ginn, A. Lawrence Lowell, president of Harvard University; W. H. P. Faunce, president of Brown University; Joseph Swain, president of Swarthmore College; Samuel T. Dutton, professor in Columbia University; Sarah L. Arnold, dean of Simmons College; Rev. Edward Cummings; and Hon. Samuel W. McCall. The board of directors consisted of David Starr Jordan, Edwin D. Mead, Hamilton Holt, James Brown Scott, Rev. Charles R. Brown, and John B. Mott.

They organized lecturers for work in colleges and schools. In 1911, they circulated 300,000 pamphlets, sent David Starr Jordan to Japan and Mead to England and Germany to promote closer cooperation between the peace leaders. They cooperated with the American Peace Society and other peace organizations in working for the arbitration treaties in 1911 and 1912. In 1912, Louis P. Lochner became secretary of the college work located at Boston. Mead became the managing director. George W. Nasmyth had charge of the work with students. Denys P. Myers was engaged in publicity work. Mrs. Anna S. Duryea worked with the women's organizations. Evidence that the foundation worked with the American Peace Society, is seen in the fact, that in 1912, nine of the trustees of the former were directors or vice presidents of the latter.

The American School Peace League, not exactly a foundation, was an outgrowth of the national peace congress at New York in 1907. On the offer of Carnegie to give it $1,000 a year for ten years, it was organized the following year with James H. Van Sickle, superintendent of the schools of Providence, as president, and Mrs. Fannie Fern Andrews of Boston, a member of the executive committee of the American Peace Society, 1908-1911, as secretary and a director later, the object being to promote through the schools and educational publications international justice and fraternity. Branches were organized in the various states. The secretary spent her time in travel and speaking to teachers on subjects relating to peace. Up to the time of the war it was supported mainly by the World Peace Foundation, and Mrs. J. Malcolm Forbes of Boston, also a vice president of the American Peace Society.

Another foundation deserves mention in this chapter. Feb. 10, 1914, Carnegie gave $2,000,000 in 5 per cent bonds of the United States Steel Corporation to twenty-nine representatives of different religious denominations to hold as trustees of a Church Peace Union to promote the cause of universal peace, the plan to be worked out by an executive committee. Among the trustees were Charles E. Jefferson, chairman, Francis E. Clark, W. H. P. Faunce, Cardinal Gibbons, Hamilton Holt, William I. Hull, Jenkin Lloyd Jones, Bishop Lawrence, Frederick Lynch, Shailer Matthews, Edwin D. Mead, Robert E. Speer, Judge Henry Wade Rogers. Lynch, who had been secretary of the commission on Arbitration and Peace of the Federal Council of the Churches of Christ in America, became secretary of the board. The work of this foundation, confined to the churches, has extended to various sections of the world, through a wide literature and many conferences.

Chapter XXXVIII

TO WASHINGTON

With the rapid spread of peace sentiment and the increase in the number of peace societies, the directors at a meeting January 28, 1908, considered the question of the advisability of securing a national charter to enable the society to hold its annual business meetings in connection with branch societies or national or local peace congresses held outside the state of Massachusetts and thus to increase the knowledge of its character and work. At the annual meeting of the society in May, 1908, at the time of the adoption of the new constitution, a special committee consisting of Frederick Brooks, Frederick Cunningham, Augustine Jones, Dr. William A. Mowry, J. Robert Raymond, and Secretary Trueblood was appointed to examine into the matter.

This committee reported at a special meeting of the society held December 14, 1909, that it could get a charter from Congress with a provision authorizing it to hold meetings anywhere in the United States, but that it would have to maintain an office in the District of Columbia; also that it could get a special act from the Massachusetts legislature authorizing it to hold meetings in any state or territory of the United States and at the same time retain its present charter. The committee therefore recommended applying to the Massachusetts legislature for a special act covering the matter desired. This was done, and Feb. 1, 1910, the governor of the state signed an act reading as follows:[1] "The American Peace Society is hereby authorized to hold its meetings in any state or territory of the United States, in the District of Columbia, or elsewhere."

Then the question arose whether a national society around which the peace workers of the country centered should not be at the capital of the nation, which would give it a national standing and prestige, enable it more easily to spread its work over the United

[1] Printed in the Advocate of Peace, March, 1910, p. 54.

States and have a closer contact with its friends in Congress and the Department of State. In fact, Trueblood raised this question at the special meeting of the society held Dec. 14, 1909. After considering the question, since there was nothing in the charter of the society requiring it to be located in Massachusetts and since the recently obtained legislation permitted it to hold its annual meeting at any point outside the state, the directors voted, Feb. 27, 1911, to move to Washington as soon as practicable. May 15, the executive committee held its monthly meeting in the Colorado Building, Washington, which has ever since remained the headquarters of the society. There the annual meeting was held in May, and the number of directors increased from twenty to twenty-five.

The need of reorganizing the peace societies of America had been evident for some time. At the Mohonk conference in 1909, a committee of ten had been appointed to consider the matter of a more perfect organization and consolidation of the peace societies of the United States in order to bring them into more harmonious cooperation and to secure greater unity and efficiency. The committee consisted of Elihu Root, Andrew Carnegie, A. K. Smiley, Secretary Trueblood, President E. D. Warfield of Lafayette College, Lyman Abbott, E. D. Mead, Dean George W. Kirchwey, Dr. James Brown Scott, and President Nicholas Murray Butler, nearly all connected with the American Peace Society.

With the removal of the society to Washington and its adoption by the Carnegie Endowment as the agent of its general propaganda work of the Department of Intercourse and Education, in December, 1911, on condition that it reorganize itself, a committee of five with Dr. Kirchwey as chairman was appointed at a special meeting of the society, held Dec. 8, 1911, at the New Willard Hotel, to revise its constitution so as to federate the local societies of the country and have them coordinated with and directed by the American Peace Society as the center of peace activities, and thus make the society a federal representative organization, and prevent duplication and overlapping of the work.

As a result of their deliberations and with the approval of the Carnegie Endowment and the New York Peace Society, a new constitution—the fourth in the history of the society—was presented at its annual meeting, May 10, 1912, and adopted. It was a much

longer constitution than that of 1908, which it superseded. An out·
line of it is as follows :[1]

1.   The name—American Peace Society—was retained.

2.   The purpose of the Society was stated to be "to promote
permanent international peace, to educate and organize public
opinion in opposition to war as a means of settling international
difficulties, and to promote in every proper way the general use of
conciliation, judicial methods, and other peaceful means of avoiding
and adjusting such difficulties."

3.   Membership in the society to consist of "persons, societies,
and organizations in the United States interested in promoting the
cause of international peace," who pay a fee of one dollar annually,
and enroll as members of a branch society or of the American Peace
Society at large. "All members of constituent societies are members of the American Peace Society in full standing and have the
right to participate in all meetings of the same."

4.   Autonomous societies are local and affiliate with the American Peace Society and cooperate with other groups. The Advocate
of Peace is sent to such members on payment of fifty cents each.

5.   The society is managed by a board of directors at large
elected at the annual meeting of the society and representative
directors chosen by the society, one for the first one hundred members of the society and one for each additional five hundred members. Peace societies not constituent may elect a director. The
board determines the eligibility of societies and fills vacancies in
its own membership. It maintains a central clearing house and
bureau of information for the branch societies.

6.   The society at its annual meeting elects a president, vice
presidents, secretary, executive director, treasurer and auditor.

7.   The board of directors chooses five of its members who with
the president, secretary, executive director, and treasurer form an
executive committee to administer the affairs of the society.

8.   The society is divided into two departments: organization
and propaganda, under the direction of the executive director; and

[1] Printed in the Advocate of Peace, June, 1912, pp. 137, 138.

publications, under the direction of the secretary. The executive director is to bring into close cooperation the peace forces of the United States, organize new societies, increase the membership of those in existence, advise with peace workers, organize and strengthen public sentiment, and make an annual report to the society. The secretary is to edit the publications of the society and distribute them, advise with the peace leaders as to the best form of publishing propaganda and preventing duplication and unnecessary expense, and make an annual report to the society.

9. The annual meeting is to be held in May when reports from the secretary, executive director, and treasurer are to be made.

10. "The object of this society shall never be changed, but the constitution may in other respects be amended at the annual meeting of the society by a two thirds vote on the recommendation of the board of directors or a majority of the constituent societies."

At the annual meeting May 7, 1915, a clause was added to article 5, paragraph 3, permitting a society to send to a meeting of the directors a substitute for a director who might not be able to attend.

Later it seemed advisable again to revise the constitution. At the annual meeting May 13, 1916, a new constitution, prepared by Dr. Kirchwey, James Brown Scott, and Hon. Jackson H. Ralston, was adopted, the fifth in the history of the society, and similar in many respects to its predecessor with few changes. Article 3 provided for six classes of members, all expect the last to belong to the branch societies and none to be members at large of the society; annual members, $1 per year, sustaining members $5 per year, contributory $25, life $100, institutional $25, honorary members elected by two third of the directors. Article 4 divided the field into departments consisting of groups of states. Each state was to be divided into divisions, and each division into sections. The former state societies were therefore to be known as divisions, and the branch societies as sections. By article 5, the board of directors was to consist of the president, secretary and treasurer ex officio, and others elected by divisions or states. Each division to choose one director and an additional one for every two hundred and fifty members with the right to appoint a substitute in case of the inability of a regular director to attend a meeting. The directors were allowed to give other organizations representation on the board. Article 6 omitted the executive director from the list of officers. By article 7, the executive committee was to consist of the president, secretary, treasurer, six directors and six others chosen by the board of directors. The constitution abolished voting by members in the annual meeting. The entire management of the society has since been vested in the board of directors meeting annually, whose wishes are carried out by an executive committee elected by the board from its own membership and meeting monthly.

These changes in the constitution were designed to secure greater interest in the affairs of the American Peace Society by the members of the branches and make the board of directors representative of the entire peace movement of the country. At the annual meeting in 1912, nine branches were represented by fifteen delegates and the constituent branches elected thirteen members of the board of directors. During the year all the various divisions and sections of the society ratified the new constitution except Massachusetts, New York, Pennsylvania, and Cincinnati. Under the constitution of 1912 honorary vice presidents superseded the former vice presidents, and the number of vice presidents was reduced to three or four.

In line with the clause in the constitution allowing the directors to invite other peace societies to elect representatives on the board of directors, the society at its annual meeting in 1912 invited the Carnegie Endowment, the Mohonk Arbitration conference, the World Peace Foundation, the Society for the Judicial Settlement of International Disputes, the American Association for International Conciliation, the American Society of International Law, and the American School Peace League to elect such directors; in 1914, the Church Peace Union; in 1915, the Federal Council of Churches of Christ in America, and the World's Court League, and in 1917, the Commission on International Justice and Good Will.

Leaving Assistant Secretary Tryon in Boston in charge of the New England division rendered necessary the employment of a new assistant in Washington upon whom the title of executive director was conferred according to the provision of article 8 of the constitution of 1912 already mentioned. The man selected to fill the position was Arthur Deerin Call. He was born in Fabius, N. Y., in

September, 1869, was a graduate of Brown University, district superintendent of schools in Hartford, co-author of the Metcalf and Call readers, and author of other texts.   He had heard True- blood speak in December, 1900, at one of the Saturday luncheons of the Twentieth Century Club in Boston and six years later became president of the New Connecticut Peace Society at the time of its formation.   He was in charge of the New England Peace Congress at Hartford and New Britain in 1910, "a man of good presence and an excellent public speaker," according to Secretary Trueblood. He had been a director of the American Peace Society for four years.   After repeated invitations, Call abandoned his career as an educator, gave up his Hartford life, and assumed the duties of his office September 1, 1912, having general charge of the work of organization and propaganda, and relieving Secretary Trueblood of many details, doing much lecturing away from home.   In 1916, he had two public debates with Col. Robert M. Thompson of the Navy League, with the result that Col. Thompson proposed a working arrangement for cooperation of the two societies.

Secretary Trueblood now attended primarily to the office work. June 7, 1913, he had a cerebral hemorrhage which caused aphasia. He was given a leave of absence for six months and slowly improved; but resigned Dec. 11, 1914, formally withdrawing from his office in May, 1915, with the title of honorary secretary.   He removed to his former home in Newton Highlands, Mass., on a retiring allowance of $600 a year.   He had another attack, Oct. 5, 1916, and died three weeks later, universally beloved by his associates and friends.   He had been a worthy successor to Ladd and Beckwith.   For twenty- two years he had guided the society, having during the most of that time a sympathetic supporter in President Paine.   As a friend, he was quiet, approachable, affable, simple but effective in his speech. As has been said, he was a linguist, speaking French, Italian, and German easily, and therefore a valued representative at the Euro- pean peace congresses, which he missed but twice.   He was a large man, an indefatigable worker, and a member of many learned socie- ties.   It was through his influence that the society moved from Boston to Washington.

The following resolution, drawn by Call, was passed by the executive committee at a special meeting, Nov. 10, 1916: "The Executive Committee of the American Peace Society record with

profound sorrow the death of Dr. Benjamin E. Trueblood, who
served this society as its general secretary for twenty-three years.
His death, which occurred Oct. 26, at his home, Newton Highlands,
Massachusetts, brought to its close a life rich with service and of
large importance to the cause of international peace. We of the
committee express our sympathy to Mrs. Trueblood and her two
daughters and wish them to know that we as best we can, purpose
to keep alive in the work of the American Peace Society the com-
manding spirit of this great and good man who has gone from us."

J. W. Hammond of Minnesota proposed that a bronze tablet be
secured by the society in memory of Dr. Trueblood and offered to
contribute a small sum for such a memorial. The executive committee voted April 6, 1917, that the advisability of raising a Trueblood fund instead of the testimonial be brought before the meeting
of the board of directors in May. In July active efforts were begun
to secure $250,000 as a memorial to Dr. Trueblood, the income to
go to the work of the American Peace Society.

Trueblood's mantle naturally fell upon Executive Director
Call, who was elected secretary and editor December 11, 1915. Since
July, 1915, the Advocate of Peace has had assistant editors.   Fred
B. Foulk served in that capacity from July to October, 1915; Dr.
John Mez, from October, 1915, to February, 1916; Malcolm W.
Davis, February 25, 1916, to May 26, 1916, when Clarke F. Hunn
took the position. This office is now filled by Leo Pasvolsky.

Following the death of President Paine, Hon. Theodore E.
Burton of Cleveland, was elected president, Feb. 27, 1911. He was
a graduate of Oberlin College, 1872, a member of Congress from
1889, and of the Senate from 1909. He joined the Interparliamentary Union on the organization of the American group by Bartholdt
in 1904, and, in Congress, had consistently opposed extravagant
demands for navy appropriations. On the expiration of his term in
the Senate he resigned the presidency of the society, Dec. 11, 1915;
but remained with the society as vice president. Dr. George W.
Kirchwey, Dean of the Columbia Law School and an active leader
in the New York Peace Society, was elected to succeed him,
assuming the duties of the office, Jan. 1, 1917, devoting his whole
time to the society at a salary of $6,000 a year. The following
May he was succeeded by Hon. James L. Slayden, member of Congress from San Antonio, Texas, since 1897, president of the Amer-

ican group of the Interparliamentary Union, member of the executive committee of the American Association for International Conciliation, and a trustee of the Carnegie Endowment for International Peace. Francis B. Sears who had served as treasurer of the society during the last year of its residence in Boston, was succeeded by George W. White, President of the National Metropolitan Bank of Washington.

The society continued its system of lecturers. In 1911, it had 27 lecturers on its rolls who devoted time to the organization without pay except for expenses; in 1912, it had 30 lecturers. During the year 1913, 116 lecturers gave 954 lectures; in 1914, 1500 lectures were given; in 1915, 2000; in 1917, 1000. Pressure was brought to bear upon Congress sufficient to cause the repeal of the Panama Canal exemption clause. When the Baroness v. Suttner, the leader of the peace movement in Austria and the recipient of the Nobel peace prize in 1905, was in this country on the invitation of the Federation of Women's Clubs to address them at their convention in San Francisco, in June, 1912, she slowly returned to the Atlantic coast, stopping and speaking to 120 audiences in sixteen states, at Chautauquas, colleges, churches, labor unions, and suffrage organizations. She assisted in the formation of the Missouri and Wisconsin state peace societies, branches of the American Peace Society, and was invited to innumerable teas and social functions.

The Advocate of Peace was greatly strengthened by the removal of the society to Washington. For the year ending May, 1911, the number of copies issued monthly was 7500, an increase of 500 over the preceding year; in 1912, 9000; in 1913, 10,000; in 1914 and 1915, 11,000; in 1917, 10,000. In 1916, the number of pages was increased from 24 to 32. Copies were sent to members of the branch societies and the members of the New York Peace Society who were furnished the paper at half price, to members of Congress, the cabinet and the federal judiciary. In March, 1913, an extra edition of 10,000 copies was struck off for the use of the Maryland Peace Society. Free copies were sent to the Y M C A's, colleges, theological schools, and other organizations as in former years. A book "Peace through Justice" and fifty new pamphlets were issued and many old ones revised soon after the removal to Washington. A librarian spent part of the year 1916 in cataloguing the library.

Following the passage of the act of Massachusetts permitting the society to hold its annual meeting outside the state, the society held its annual business meeting in 1910 at the Centre Church house, Hartford, Conn.; in 1911, at McCoy Hall, Johns Hopkins University, Baltimore; and in 1912, at the Odeon, St. Louis. In 1913, 1914, 1915, and 1916, the meeting was held at Hotel Raleigh, in Washington; in 1917 and 1918 at the office of the society. These meetings have been held at various hours in the afternoon: 2:00, 2:30, 3:00, 4:00, or 4:30 o'clock. In the evening following the business meeting addresses were given by ex Secretary John W. Foster at Hartford, in 1910; by William J. Bryan, Richard Bartholdt, and Walter L. Hensley at the Hotel Raleigh in 1914. At St. Louis in 1913, the address was given by President S. C. Mitchell of South Carolina.

Among the more prominent persons who accepted office in the society during these years were Mrs. Lucia Ames Mead, director or vice president, 1899 to 1911; Dean Charles R. Brown, vice president, 1911-27; Hon. Jackson H. Ralston, vice president or member of the executive committee, 1911 to date; William Knowles Cooper, director or member of the executive committee, 1912-22; Hon. James L. Slayden, director, president or vice president, 1913-24; Robert S. Brookings, director, 1913-17; William Howard Taft, vice president, 1913-20; William Jennings Bryan, vice president, 1913-24; Hon. Samuel W. McCall, member of the executive committee or vice president, 1918-24; Ernest Fox Nichols, vice president, 1912-14; Dean Henry Wade Rogers, vice president, 1910-27; ex Vice President C. W. Fairbanks, vice president, 1914-18.

At the same time death claimed a few: Hon. John W. Hoyt, died May 23, 1912, governor of Wyoming, president of the University of Wyoming, speaker at the Chicago meeting in 1893, and vice president of the society from 1894; Bishop Henry W. Warren, died 1912, vice president from 1885; Albert K. Smiley, died 1912, vice president from 1907; Samuel B. Capen, president of the American Board of Commissioners of Foreign Missions, a trustee of the World Peace Foundation, died Jan. 29, 1914, vice president or director of the society from 1896; Edwin Ginn, died Jan. 21, 1914, a vice president or director since 1901; Samuel T. Dutton died 1919, a director since 1911; William A. Mowry, died May 22, 1916, a director, member of the executive committee, or vice president from 1886; and John Watson Foster, secretary of state under President Harrison, minister to Mexico, Russia, and Spain, died Nov. 15, 1917, a vice president of the society from 1908.

A shortness of funds continued to be referred to. With the grant of money by the Carnegie Endowment came a falling off in contributions from others. In 1915, the finances were such that the amounts granted to the branches had to be reduced. The receipts and expenditures of the society from 1912 to 1918, with the balance on hand at the end of each year were as follows:

	Receipts	Expenditures	Balance on hand
1912	$31,878.66	$25,156.07	$8,025.14
1913	46,700.71	45,503.75	9,222.70
1914	39,632.53	43,002.43	5,852.20
1915	43,664.56	44,105.93	5,410.83
1916	40,125.61	40,324.00	5,212.43
1917	35,652.92	36,147.03	4,718.32
1918	27,645.22	32,306.95	56.59

Chapter XXXIX

EXPANSION OF THE SOCIETY

WITH the growth of interest in the question of peace and arbitration came an increase in the amount of work of the society. As before stated James L. Tryon, Ph. D., became assistant secretary of the society in 1906. His work at first was mainly in the office, speaking away from home as opportunity presented. The expansion of the peace sentiment to the West was evidenced by the holding of the peace congress in Texas and the organization of peace societies in that district; and by the offer of Carnegie, Feb. 1, 1908, following a banquet to Paine, Trueblood and Mead, tendered them by the New York Peace Society in honor of their success in initiating the peace congress in New York, to give the American Peace Society $5000 a year for four years in addition to the $1000 he was then giving them. The directors of the society decided to enlarge the scope of their work and appoint two field secretaries to devote their attention to cultivating the field generally. March 13, 1908, Rev. Charles E. Beals, recently pastor of the Prospect Street Congregational Church, Cambridge, well educated, energetic, and enthusiastic, was appointed field agent of the society at $2500 a year. His work began April 15th, with headquarters in Boston. His work was to visit and address important conventions and meetings, industrial, educational and religious, organize branch societies and interest people wherever possible in the cause of peace. March 24, Robert C. Root of Huntington Beach., Cal., with a salary of $1000 a year, was placed in charge of a newly created Pacific Coast Agency with headquarters in Los Angeles. A supply of literature was deposited with him to be sold or given away according to circumstances.

In February, 1912, after the removal of the society to Washington, and as a part of its reorganization, the country was divided into five departments, over each of which the society placed a director and in which it was planned to have in each state a state

276

society, with local branches or sections. Assistant Secretary Tryon was placed in charge of the New England department created Mar. 28, 1911, at $2500 a year. Field Agent Beals, who in May, 1910, had moved to Chicago, was placed in charge of the Central West department. Root at $1600 a year in Los Angeles was placed in charge of the Pacific Coast department, as the successor of the Pacific Coast agency. Dr. Samuel T. Dutton, professor in the Teachers College at Columbia University, was made director of the New York-New Jersey department, at $1000 a year, with headquarters in New York City, created Dec. 29, 1911. Dr. J. J. Hall of Fayetteville, N. C., was made director of the South Atlantic States department with headquarters at Atlanta, Mar. 23, 1912, at $2,000 a year. After the resignation of Director Beals, Feb. 27, 1914, the Central West department was placed under the charge of Louis P. Lochner, from May 1, 1914, to April 1, 1916; and Harold G. Townsend, April 1, 1916, to April 30, 1918.

Each director gave all his time to the work of the society. The duties of each were similar: to visit the various states in his district where work was needed, to present the cause on every possible occasion at meetings of every character,—religious, educational, industrial, commercial, national, state or local; to organize and hold meetings and conferences, to supply pulpits, to exhibit and distribute peace literature, to organize branch societies, to solicit members, subscriptions, and contributions for the cause, to write letters to the papers, to prepare programs, and to promote the work of the society in every way possible. During the year ending May, 1909, they doubled the membership of the society. Tryon and Beals attended and took part in the Mohonk Lake meetings, and Tryon attended congresses in Europe. In 1908, Tryon was in Washington in connection with the peace treaties then under discussion, and in 1912, sent to Congress a petition signed by eight thousand persons in favor of the peace treaties. May 4 and 5, 1914, he conducted a state peace convention in Massachusetts. Dr. Hall held state conventions in North Carolina in 1913, 1914, and 1915. Dr. Joynes, superintendent of public instruction, presided at the first one with the governor as honorary president, and speeches were made by William Jennings Bryan, A. D. Call, and others.

During these years several societies were founded as auxiliaries of the American Peace Society. By 1908, there were seven such branches. At the annual meeting that year a new constitution was adopted, of which article 5 read as follows: Branch societies shall be formed on the following basis. The members of the branch societies shall be members of the American Peace Society. The membership fee in the branch societies shall be paid to the American Peace Society in return for which the Advocate of Peace shall be furnished to the members of the branch societies. Article 6 provided that "the presidents of the state branch societies shall be ex officiis vice presidents of the American Peace Society." Auxiliaries then began to be formed rapidly. In 1910, their number was 10; 1911, 15; 1912, 24; 1913, 27 societies and 5 sections, with 4532 members; 1914, 31 societies and 13 sections; 1915, 34 societies and 21 sections with 7875 members; 1916, 48 societies with 7849 members; and in 1917, 55 societies with 7296 members. The branch societies did vigorous work. They circulated literature, held meetings and lectures, and worked for the arbitration treaties.

The first auxiliary formed was the Chicago Peace Society which was organized Nov. 17, 1902, at the Palmer House, with Rev. Hiram W. Thomas, D. D., as president. On his leaving Chicago the activities of the society came to an end. In February, 1910, as a result of the national peace congress at Chicago held the preceding year, the society was reorganized through the efforts of Jane Addams, Rabbi Hirsch, Rev. Jenkins Lloyd Jones, Robert L. Melendy, and Charles E. Beals, who had been the organizers of the congress. The society started with a fund of $160, collected for the Chicago congress and not used. In May, 1910, on the removal of the office of field secretary from Boston to Chicago, Beals continued the work as field agent of the American Peace Society and as secretary of the Chicago Peace Society, the latter organizing to finance both offices. Hon. George E. Roberts was elected president the first year and after his appointment as Director of the Mint, he was followed by Leroy A. Goddard, president of the State Bank of Chicago.

The society was very active. It had an office in the Chicago Stock Exchange building, circulated peace literature, gave a dinner to Baron d'Estournelles de Constant and William J. Bryan, April 29, 1911. In 1911, each member wrote a letter to the Senate urging that body to ratify the arbitration treaties then before them and held several mass meetings at the time in the interest of the treaties where addresses were made by ex Vice President Fairbanks, Jane Addams, Rabbi Hirsch, Col. Watterson, Prof. C. C.

Hyde and others.   A banquet was given in honor of the Baroness von Suttner, Oct. 29, 1912, on the occasion of her visit to Chicago.

In 1913, the society repaired the lot of William Ladd in the Proprietors cemetery in Portsmouth and reset the curbing around it.   In connection with it was held a commemoration of William Ladd at Portsmouth, N. H., May 18, 1913.   Special peace services were held in the morning.   In the afternoon a service was held at the grave, consisting of prayer, peace hymns sung by children, and an address by Beals.   In the evening there was a union meeting in the North Church with addresses by Beals and the secretaries of the Maine, Massachusetts, and Rhode Island peace societies, and Dr. Hall of Atlanta who cooperated with the Chicago society in making the occasion a success.

The Chicago society became incorporated Oct. 9, 1913.   In 1911, it had a membership of 600.   At its annual meeting in 1914, addresses were made by Norman Angell, E. D. Mead, and Prof. Manley O. Hudson.   In 1915, the peace work of the Chicago churches was placed under its direction as a department with Secretary Beals in charge.

Another active local society was the Massachusetts Peace Society, reorganized April 27, 1911, on the departure of the American Peace Society to Washington, by Rev. S. C. Bushnell, Dr. William A. Mowry, and Mrs. J. Malcolm Forbes, directors of the American Peace Society.   Samuel B. Capen was elected president, James L. Tryon, secretary, President Lowell of Harvard University and Bishop Lawrence of Boston were among the vice presidents.   The society held monthly meetings with addresses by prominent men. It raised $4,000 in 1910 and had a series of Sunday afternoon talks in Tremont Temple during the year 1914-15.   In 1916, it bought a stereopticon, and Secretary Tryon gave illustrated lectures on peace in many cities and towns of New England.

Among other branch societies organized were the Utah State Peace Society organized in May, 1908, at Salt Lake City, with ex Governor John C. Cutler as president; the Pennsylvania Arbitration and Peace Society organized Dec. 23, 1908, as a result of the state congress held in Philadelphia earlier in the year, with Prof. William I. Hull as secretary; the Cleveland Peace Society, organized in 1909, with President C. F. Thwing as president; the Maryland Peace Society, organized Feb. 1, 1910, with Theodore Marburg as president, and Cardinal Gibbons, President Ira Remsen, and Gov. Crothers among the vice presidents; the Oregon Peace Society, organized January 6, 1911, with Judge John B. Cleland as president, and the governor of the state and the mayor of Portland among the members; the New Hampshire Peace Society, organized February 1, 1912, with Ernest Fox Nichols, president of Dartmouth College, as president; the Nebraska Peace Society, organized Feb. 5, 1912, with Prof. George E. Howard as president and William J. Bryan as honorary president; the Missouri State Peace Society, organized Sept. 24, 1912, with Dr. R. H. Jesse as president, and Prof. Manly O. Hudson, secretary, and Richard Bartholdt as vice president; the Wisconsin State Peace Society, organized Oct. 12, 1912, with Hon. John B. Winslow, chief justice of the supreme court, as president; the Washington (D. C.) Peace Society, organized in 1912 with Hon. Willet M. Hays as president and Justice Siddons as vice president; and the Minnesota Peace Society, organized Jan. 13, 1914, with President Cyrus Northrop as president and the governor of the state as honorary president.

Several other societies, organized independently, later became auxiliaries or branches of the American Peace Society, as the Connecticut Peace Society, with Arthur Deerin Call as president, organized 1906, which became an auxiliary in 1907; and the New York German-American Peace Society organized by Dr. Ernst Richard, professor in Columbia University, in 1902, for the purpose of helping to get the arbitration treaties approved by the Senate, which became an auxiliary of the American Peace Society in 1912.

Probably the Peace Society of the City of New York was the most prominent of the societies in this group. It was organized Feb. 23, 1906, through the efforts of Dr. Richard. Hon. Oscar S. Straus was president the first year, and Andrew Carnegie thereafter. Prof. Dutton was secretary. William H. Short was executive secretary after 1909. Dr. Charles E. Jefferson presided at the first meeting and became chairman of the executive committee. Frederick Lynch was chairman of the committee on meetings and Hamilton Holt on publicity.

The society grew rapidly. At the end of its first year it had a membership of 592. It cooperated with the American Peace Society in holding the congress in New York City in 1907. Beginning

July, 1909, it furnished the Advocate of Peace with a page of items each month and sent copies of the magazine to each member of its society. May 3, 1910, it became incorporated as the New York Peace Society. In 1909 it held a peace musical festival in Carnegie Hall. Feb. 26, 1909, it gave a peace dinner to Secretary Root in recognition of his services in the interest of peace, following a reception to the three Scandinavian ministers, Feb. 15th. During the years 1910-11, it sent out nearly a million pieces of literature, had forty speakers on its list, and arranged 459 meetings. It brought Count Albert Apponyi here, who delivered eighteen lectures under its direction. In 1911-12, it held a series of mass meetings in the interest of the arbitration treaties. In 1913, 227 addresses were given under its direction and $17,660 were spent. From May, 1912 to May 13, 1916, it was a branch of the American Peace Society; but on the latter date it united with the League to Enforce Peace.

May 26, 1912, the Rhode Island Peace Society voted to become a branch of the American Peace Society. This was the now oldest peace society in America, having been organized March 20, 1817. It was the only New England society that did not affiliate with the American Peace Society on the formation of the latter in 1828. It was composed of Quakers and for much of its life had but one meeting a year. Moses Brown, one of its members, left it $1,000 in bank stock, the income from which was devoted to spreading the gospel of peace. In 1870 and again in 1877, the society voted fifty dollars to the American Peace Society; in 1875, eighty dollars; and in 1906, two hundred dollars. April 3, 1914, it was reorganized as the Rhode Island and Providence Plantations Peace Society with a constitution drawn up by Dr. Tryon.

Besides the state societies, there were several societies organized for special purposes, which during these years united with the American Peace Society as branches or auxiliaries. The oldest of these was the Intercollegiate Peace Association, a movement that started in 1905 when an oratorical contest among the colleges of the Friends and the Mennonites was held at Goshen College, Indiana. In the same year at the Mohonk Lake conference a committee was appointed to promote international arbitration among the colleges. On the invitation of this committee representatives of thirty colleges met at Earlham College, Richmond, Indiana, in 1906, and debated the question of international arbitration. Hon. William Dudley Foulk welcomed them to the city; and addresses were made by Trueblood, Mead, and Prof. Richard of Columbia University. Carnegie offered a prize of $1,000 for the best oration given in the colleges of the middle West.

Jan. 1, 1908, the debating work was organized by the appointment of George Fulk of Cerro Gordo, Ill., as field secretary, who gave his services free. Groups of debaters were organized in the various colleges of the association, and at the annual meeting at the De Pauw University in 1908 it was decided to extend the society to cover all colleges in the country. Jan. 28, 1908, it became a branch of the American Peace Society. In 1910, it was reported that 225 students in sixty colleges had participated in oratorical contests and $1,500 had been offered them in prizes. In 1912, prizes aggregating $2,500 were offered in eighty colleges.

The Cosmopolitan Club was the outgrowth of a club formed by eighteen foreign students in the University of Wisconsin, March 13, 1903. It, with seven others of a similar character—consisting of foreign students studying in American universities in the middle western states—formed the Association of Cosmopolitan Clubs at Madison University, Dec. 28, 1907. At its next meeting at Ann Arbor, in December, 1908, it became an auxiliary of the American Peace Society. At its third meeting at Cornell, in December, 1909, Secretary Trueblood, Andrew D. White, and Edwin D. Mead were present and addressed the association. In 1909 also, it united with the Corda Fratres, an international federation of students, comprising 15,000 students connected with sixty-three universities of Europe, founded in 1897, as a result of the efforts of the international peace congresses held in Europe in 1892, the name of the new organization being Fédération internationale des Etudiants Corda Fratres. Louis P. Lochner, a Wisconsin graduate, became its general secretary in 1912 and visited the colleges of the country in the interest of the association. George W. Nasmyth, of Cornell, became its president in 1909, and toured the universities of Europe in its interest. In September, 1913, the eighth congress of the society was held at Cornell with 208 delegates from thirty countries present. Secretary Trueblood, President Wilson, P. P. Claxton, A. D. White, John Barrett, E. D. Mead, Samuel T. Dutton, and Hamilton Holt served on the committee. Upon their visit to Washington, the American Peace Society took sixty-six of the students on a trip to Mt. Vernon where they placed a wreath on the tomb of Washington.

The war put an end to the activities of the societies organized for special purposes. Dr. Dutton resigned as director of the New York-New Jersey department in June, 1917. Because of the war the work of the New England department, the Pacific Coast department, and the South Atlantic States department was discontinued, June 28, 1918, and the salaries of the directors the following September. Tryon became professor of international law at the University of Maine, later in Massachusetts Institute of Technology; and Root, professor of Economics at Occidental College, Los Angeles.

Chapter XL

THE WORLD WAR

ON THE outbreak of the war in Europe, the American Peace Society jointly with the American Association for International Conciliation, the Church Peace Union, the German American Peace Society, the New York Peace Society, and the World Peace Foundation, drafted a memorial to President Wilson thanking him for tendering the nations at war the good offices of the United States and proffering mediation. It was presented to Secretary Bryan, Aug. 19, 1914, by a deputation including Hamilton Holt, Ernst Richard, and George E. Roberts. They urged settling the controversy in a way to prevent war in the future. Later in the year the society signed a manifesto against the war, prepared by the International Peace Bureau at Berne.

The position of the society in regard to the war, with its reasons therefor, is shown in the following extracts from the Advocate of Peace. In an article entitled "Can Ye not Discern the Signs of the Times?" (October, 1914, p. 197) the society expressed its views of the cause of the war as follows: "Some of us had realized for years that the catastrophe could not long be avoided. All the great powers of Europe were nervously increasing their armies, perfecting their fortifications, drilling their troops, enlarging their bursting war budgets, adding battleship to battleship, indeed doing everything possible, on land and sea and air, to make it absolutely certain that a great conflict was near. The wonder was not that the war broke out this summer upon Europe, but that it did not begin years before. Whoever may or may not have fired the first gun or have caused it to be fired, the real cause of the conflict was the piled-up armaments and war materials of Europe which had been accumulating for forty years, and the suspicions, jealousies, falsehoods, and ambitions which attended and vitalized them."

"No delusion was ever greater than that implements of war, however multiplied or destructive they may be, are guaranties of peace and safety. This is the supreme lesson of the world war now devouring Europe and mocking civilization."

In the number for January, 1917, p. 2, is an article entitled "Another Year," which contains the following: "The last two and a half years, horrible beyond description, have affected our work and our workers. We have been assailed by pro-Germans and by pro-Allies. We have had heaped upon us more than usual the familiar opprobrious epithets. But our vision is not dimmed, our program is not changed, our hopes are not daunted."

"* * * Today, as ever, we hold that war as a means of settling international disputes represents a barbaric, an unnatural, and a dying civilization. We hold that the program for overcoming war is deducible to two simple formulas; first, that we must set up effective instruments or organs for the establishment of international justice; second, we must will to use these instruments or organs rather than the instruments and organs of war."

On the eve of the United States entering the war the society stated its position as follows, (April, 1917, pp. 99, 100): "We are opposed to war as a means of settling international disputes. We recognize, however, that we are living in an ungoverned world. Our aims and purposes are to make of our world a governed world. The problems involved in the realization of this program are international problems, and can be solved only by international cooperative effort. No one nation is capable alone of deciding the issues or accomplishing the result. Believing as we always have in adequate defense for this nation so long as nations are unorganized as now, yet justice, arbitration, peace between states cannot, we believe, be coerced. But the decision whether the United States shall or shall not enter this war is a decision to be made by the United States government. The American Peace Society cannot decide this question."

"At the meeting of the executive committee of this society, March 9, the following was unanimously voted: 'We, the members of the executive committee of the American Peace Society, recognize with deep appreciation the efforts of President Wilson to avoid war and at the same time to protect the honor of the nation and the rights and lives of our citizens. We wish to assure him of our hearty support in his determination to secure recognition of the claims of justice and humanity.'

"From this vote it will appear that the American Peace Society leaves the question whether we shall or shall not enter this war to the government of the United States. In our loyalty to the principles of humanity we are not unmindful of our loyalty to the land which makes our work for international justice possible. But we shall continue to hold before the eyes of men the hideous and collective unnaturalness of all war methods, and the wisdom of the ways of international cooperative order."

*   *   *

"If we are asked, Is the United States going to enter this war? our reply is, 'We hope not. There ought to be a better and more hopeful way. * * * In our sad condition of international anarchy there is a plain duty for every American citizen and that is to abide by the decision of the American government'."

After the declaration of war, three articles appeared in the Advocate of Peace, May 1917, pp. 132-34, bearing upon the subject. From the first, entitled "A Governed World," the following extract is taken. "The American Peace Society is not an obstructionist organization. Its opposition to war as a means of settling international disputes, clear and inveterate as it is familiar, takes the direction of a governed world as a substitute for war. While in the present instance it agrees that a German victory would be a calamity for the world—indeed, that this country should do everything in its power to make such a victory impossible—it purposes to waste no ammunition on a local situation beyond its control. * * * Peace with justice is indeed the goal of civilization. To attain that end is impossible without international organization, plus a will to use it. Unfortunately such international organization does not as yet sufficiently exist. It is true that we have made some progress toward such a condition, and we believe that the futile imperialistic designs of aggressive nations, of one in particular, all ending in the present colossal devastation, will make the attainment of such a governed world more easily possible at the close of this war then ever before in history."

From the second entitled "Our duty to Germany," the following extracts are taken: "Our first duty to Germany is to convince her with all the power at our command, that we are launched upon this enterprise as a serious matter of business. We are at war. As a people we are in no frame of mind to blink this fact. There is no

The World War
287

disposition anywhere to embarrass our government with casuistries, personal oppositions, or even conscientious objections. We are a united nation. We have a duty to perform and we purpose to perform it. Because we consider this our duty to civilization, we conceive of it therefore as our duty to Germany."

* * *

"Germany must be led to see, and it is our duty to help her so to see, that this war is not a war of territory, of trade routes, or of commercial concerns, but of eternal principles. * * * The great aim is that war may be rendered impossible and that the calamity of 1914 may not happen to the world again. This is the moral basis of our entrance upon the war. * * * The only hope of civilization is that nations base themselves upon the moral forces of law and not upon the treacherous bases of brutal force."

In the third article entitled "The American Peace Society and the War," are the following statements: "Our government has declared a state of war to exist with Germany. If the government is at war with Germany, its citizens are at war, and, in turn, the American Peace Society, membered and supported by American citizens, finds itself an integral part of a belligerent nation. But how may an organization founded and maintained for the purpose of establishing international peace reconcile itself in the support of a nation that declares war? The answer is not difficult."

* * *

"The American Peace Society stands for international peace and justice. * * * It calls to its ranks those who believe in the principles set forth in its program for international order. It finds nothing unpatriotic in that program, nothing conflicting with the action of any American citizen in the present situation. Whether he enlists for active service or joins the ranks of conscientious objectors, he may still be a loyal and enthusiastic supporter of this society. What his personal prejudices are is entirely his own affair. We have said that the American Peace Society supports the government in this war. * * * But for the whole society and all of its members we may say this much at present: First, this society, individually and collectively, stands back of the president on the ground that in war the president speaks for the whole people; second, whatever specific duties it shall be called upon to perform, it holds still to its ancient ideal of a governed world and established peace through international organization; third, each of its members, holding that ideal, will work out in his own way his own responsibilities and duties in the service of his government. We believe that no true member of this society will withhold that service. We believe that the man who stays at home may well give as much in his way as the man who goes to the front or who enters in active military or naval service whatever sort may be required. We believe that if our members can conscientiously engage in active service they will do so; that if they cannot, they will lend their efforts in other directions behind the firing line. We believe that if there are those whose honest conviction prevents them from engaging in war even in a secondary capacity, they will yet do all in their power generously and selflessly to aid their country, if not to wage and win the war, at least to emerge from that war with clean hands and clear vision."

"In brief, then, the American Peace Society reiterates its pledge of loyalty to the government, and gives assurance on behalf of its members that it will support and not obstruct the actions of that government in the present situation so long as those actions represent the will of the majority. Furthermore, it feels itself justified in declaring that its members, each after his own fashion, will corroborate this declaration in free and generous service of every possible sort which they can render to their country."

In an article appearing in the August number, pp. 230-31, entitled "What We are Supporting," are these statements: "Before our government declared itself in a state of war we did everything within our power to advertise the principles of judicial settlement of international disputes. It is not a matter of theory, but a matter of fact, that the world has reached a situation where the judicial settlement of international disputes is for the time impracticable. After the government to which we owe allegiance declared itself in a state of war, the judicial settlement of the disputes between this country and Germany became not only impracticable, but unthinkable. That we sense this does not mean that our opposition to war is abated. Quite the contrary."

* * *

"We are opposed to war. We are opposed to any war. We are opposed to this war. Two great groups of nations are locked, and trying in the only way they know to bring it to a close. It so happens that we are thrown with that group to which belongs the

United States of America. We purpose to stand by our government in this terrific enterprise upon which it is launched. If this be an offense, we shall have to take the consequences."

"It is clearly within the realm of defensible duty that when our country is in danger we should rally to our country's support. Our country is in danger now. The inevitable conclusion, therefore, is, we must rally to the aid of our country now. To embarrass the United States at this time would be folly, if not treason. The abolition of war is an international job. * * * War is a universal disease. This particular war is but one type of that universal disease. Were we to stop this war today, it would not mean that the disease of war would be cured, or even ameliorated. A universal disease requires a universal remedy. Our sentimental oppositions to this war constitute no remedy for war. War is the direct outcome of human wrongs and injustice. Only as we are able to overcome wrongs and injustice shall we be able to overcome war."

In an article entitled "Win and End the War," in the number for December, 1917, pp. 320-21, are the following statements: "With the situation as it is, there can be no governed world of the kind that rational men would have. Judicial processes are at the time internationally impossible. The methods of peaceable settlement must wait, because there in the way of these things stands the Imperial German government. To go back now would be disastrous. The only way to the attainment of our aims is forward. Law, justice, common sense, the world peace we purpose to establish, all call now for a perfect unity of opinion and purpose, a call which should and must be heard by us all, whether we are members of this or that group or of no group at all. The clarion, unmistakable call to us all is, that we must now end this war by winning it."

Extracts from an article entitled "We are for Peace," in the number for February, 1918, p. 40, follow: "No one who has followed the course of this magazine can be in the least doubt about our attitude toward the military necessities of this war. We have accepted the verdict of America as expressed through our chosen representatives. We are quite convinced that this war cannot be ended, that there can be no end of war until after the collapse of the existing Imperial German government. This is a military necessity, the physical achievement of which is the specific task facing the war machine of the nations arrayed against the European cen-

tral powers. We are utterly out of sympathy with those who would
obstruct in any way the efficiency with which we are attacking this
job. Our moral judgment condemns those who do not support the
United States, and that unequivocally in the performance of the
physical task now set before us. The pan-German must be un-
horsed. The forces that systematically stimulated the war spirit
through the Pan-German League, the Defense Association, and
their like, through the years immediately preceding August, 1914,
are to be forever overcome by the combined physical strength of
democracies. * * *

"The Imperial German government has developed such an opposition to international justice and good-will that the Imperial
German government must be overcome if international good-will is
ever to prevail. The military and economic yoke of a successful
Germany would, we believe, be subversive of the peace we must have.
* * * In short, the Imperial German government blocks the progress
of the cherished ideals of constructive peace workers everywhere.
Germany's armies, ships, and air fleet must, under no circumstances,
be allowed to dominate Europe or nations elsewhere. John Hay's
assertion that 'war is not only the most ferocious, but also the
most futile of human follies' is as sound today as when it was ut-
tered, and that the Imperial German government must be made to
understand. "Liberty and justice will secure a genuine triumph"
when the Imperial German government shows a disposition to meet
the terms of "liberty and justice" set forth by the collective conscience of liberal democracy which the president of the United
States has so clearly voiced. The "bleeding, weeping, warring
world" will secure peace and justice only after the German people
throw over their faith in the effectiveness of brute force. It is because we are opposed to the principle that brute force should impose its will upon the world that we support the United States as
she goes forth to counteract that force and to demonstrate its
futility."

In the annual report of the secretary to the society at its annual
meeting, May 25, 1918, he used these words as reported in the
Advocate of Peace, June, 1918, p. 171: "Your secretary and editor
is of the opinion that the position taken by the society in its organ
is the only defensible position possible. Our country is at war. It
has been demonstrated beyond the shadow of a doubt that the

Imperial German government is ruthless in its adulation of force. It has entered this war saying officially that "necessity knows no law," and that "war is the noblest and highest expression of human activity." For a generation at least its creed has been the creed of kings, subscribing to the principle that the "state can do no wrong." Its philosophy and activities establish it as a menace to free peoples, our own not excepted. It has precipitated a conflict between the will to might and the will to right; between the rights of kings and the rights of peoples. The result is that democratic governments, deriving their just powers from the consent of the governed, are in danger of being stifled, beaten, and lost, America included. The issue, therefore, is clear; the war is a fact. We must advance or retreat. Our only way out is through. We believe that brute force is inferior to the force of ideas and ideals. We believe, therefore, that it is the duty of the United States to counteract the onslaughts of the Teuton hordes and to prove the futility of the German behavior once and forever."

"The American Peace Society stands for the cooperation of states in the name of a governed world. It believes in that marriage of liberty and justice, which shall beget a permanent peace. It believes, therefore, that the scales must be removed from the eyes of the Imperial German government; in short, that we must win this war."

This principle, like the preceding utterance, phrased by Call, became the voice of the Society. At its annual meeting, May 19, 1917, the society passed a resolution relative to the president in which it stated in part: "We heartily approve of his high stand in behalf of a governed world to the end that wars may ultimately cease; that national differences may be adjusted by reason rather than by force, and that the peace of justice may prevail."

Again at its annual meeting May 25, 1918, it reaffirmed its allegiance to the government and to the cause that the government was defending. It announced its belief that the highest present duty of the allies was to win and end the war. It offered its magazine, offices, and entire resources to the government to the end that out of the war might arise an ordering of nations under law and the establishment of peace, flowing from freedom and justice. On the cover of the magazine from July, 1918, through June, 1919, was the statement: "The clarion, the unmistakable call to us all is that we must now end this war by winning it."

Peace propaganda gave way to war effort. Call represented the society on the advisory committee of the Speaking Division of the Committee on Public Information. As a four minute man he spoke many times a week in Washington and vicinity. During the liberty loan campaign his services were at the disposal of the Liberty Loan Committee for the District of Columbia. He delivered many patriotic addresses in theaters and other public places, and spoke in behalf of the Red Cross Society. His pamphlet on "The War for Peace," issued by the Government's Committee on Public Information, was widely distributed.

The directors of the three departments of the society still organized during the war were helpful. Director Tryon of the New England Department attended the Maine War Conference at Portland, met legal advisory boards, and represented the society at the conference of the League to Enforce Peace. Director Root of the Pacific Coast Department was elected a director of the American Council of the World Alliance for International Friendship and executive secretary of the National Campaign on the Moral Aims of the War. Director Hall of the South Atlantic States Department represented the society in Armenian and Syrian Relief funds, the Red Cross and the Committee on the Moral Aims of the War.

The war of course produced a disquieting effect upon the peace movement. Many of the peace men turned to war activities. The directors of the departments found difficulty in retaining the interest of their members. The organizations of the state peace societies in many cases disintegrated. The section societies melted away. The Delaware society composed mainly of Quakers withdrew from the American Peace Society, as did the New York society. Some of the groups remained intact and others retained merely a skeleton organization. Many of the members of the state and local societies became direct members of the national society. For the year ending May, 1916, the number of such members was 958; May, 1917, 1099; and May, 1918, 1178.

Feeling that the excellent organization of the society for propaganda work perfected before the war was inadequate during the war, which seemed to require a more centralized government and direction, the work naturally concentrated upon the publication of the

Advocate of Peace. The executive committee, June 28, 1918, suspended its field work. The increased cost of printing caused the number of free copies of the Advocate of Peace to be reduced and delinquent subscribers to be dropped, so that the number of copies printed by May, 1918, had been reduced to six thousand. Clarke F. Hunn, the assistant editor of the magazine, served as office secretary also. Outside the American Peace Society, very little peace work was done.

Chapter XLI

THE LEAGUE OF NATIONS

THE League of Nations did not spring into existence suddenly. It was the result of long planning. Ladd had thought out a form of international organization, consisting of two branches: a legislative and a judicial, the executive being left to public opinion of the various countries entering into the agreement. Burritt spread the idea. At the first Hague conference, the judiciary was created; and at the second, provision was made for stated similar conferences in the future, thus creating the second branch. So the beginning of international legislative and judicial bodies was made. The advocates of the scheme however considered those to be but the beginning, and planned for a more stable judicial system and a surer legislative. Carnegie in his rectorship address at the University of St. Andrews, Oct. 17, 1905, urged the formation of a League of peace, as he did at the first national peace congress in New York in 1907. At the Brussels peace congress in 1905, a committee was appointed to consider the establishment of a permanent congress of nations. Their report recommended the establishment of a permanent congress of nations, the upper house to be the Hague conference, a body representing the national executives, and the lower to be the Inter-Parliamentary Union, representing the lawmakers.

The final act of the Hague conference in 1907 was a recommendation to the powers to call a third conference about 1915. In order that a program might be prepared a sufficient time in advance to insure its deliberation being conducted with the necessary authority and expedition, the conference recommended the selection of preparatory committees by the governments to collect the various proposals to be submitted to the committee, to ascertain what subjects were ripe for embodiment into international regulation, and to prepare a program which the governments should decide upon in sufficient time to enable it to be carefully examined by the countries interested, the committee also to propose a system of organization and procedure.

The American Peace Society lent its efforts to shape the meeting according to its views. In the spring of 1909, it sent to President Taft a memorial urging that preliminary steps be taken relative to calling the conference. July 28, 1909, Bartholdt introduced into Congress a concurrent resolution providing for the appointment of two committees, one to find a method of appointment of judges in the international court of arbitration to be established, and the other to consider the question of a limitation of armaments, the president to ask all the powers to create similar committees to make similar studies. As a starter, Prof. William I. Hull in the spring of 1912, proposed a program consisting of nine topics to be considered at the conference.

With the recommendation of the second Hague conference in mind, Secretary Knox suggested to President Taft, April 5, 1912, the appointment of a committee to consider the program wanted by the United States, in regard to a limitation of armaments. Taft appointed such an advisory committee, June 10, 1912, which made a report to the Department of State in December, 1913. Senator Root speaking for others wrote to Secretary Bryan, Dec. 10, 1913, urging the selection by the United States of its members of the international committee in order to show the interest of this government in the plan. As a result, President Wilson wrote Secretary Bryan Jan. 31, 1914, to instruct the diplomatic officers of the United States, accredited to the governments which took part in the second Hague conference, to propose to their governments that the duties of the international preparatory committee be committed to the Administrative Council of the Permanent Court of Arbitration at the Hague, which was composed of the diplomatic representatives of the powers accredited to the Hague, thus saving time and expense. Feb. 5, 1914, the American government announced that it had taken steps toward calling the third Hague conference to meet in the summer of 1915.

Accordingly, July 2, 1914, the Dutch government invited the nations represented at the Hague to choose delegates to serve on a committee to arrange the program for the next Hague conference. A meeting of this committee was called to meet in June, 1915. In the meantime Miss Anna B. Eckstein, head of the School of Languages in Boston, who had presented to the second Hague conference a petition signed by two million people requesting that body to sign a general arbitration treaty, spent three years in Europe getting signatures to a new petition of similar import.

Sept. 28, 1914, Hamilton Holt, editor of the Independent, printed an article in his paper, suggesting the formation of a federation of nations with a government founded on law and using force only as a police power against nations not willing to abandon aggression and enter the league, the federation to have an assembly meeting periodically to make general rules binding all. The plan was approved by Lord Bryce, Taft, Roosevelt, Carnegie, A. Lawrence Lowell, and others. Several organizations were formed to carry out the ideas here suggested. The New York Peace Society formed a World Federation Department to get the leading nations to form a federation of nations to maintain international peace or to form a league of peace with a supreme court to settle controversies between nations.

Earlier, before the war, Feb. 6, 1910, the American Society for the Judicial Settlement of International Disputes had been formed at Baltimore, with Joseph H. Choate as president, Charles W. Eliot, John Hays Hammond, and Judge Simeon E. Baldwin as vice presidents, and James Brown Scott as secretary, to create a permanent tribunal for the judicial settlement of international controversies. They held a conference at the New Willard Hotel and the Pan American building in Washington, Dec. 15-17, 1910, presided over by James Brown Scott, with Theodore Marburg as secretary. Among the speakers were ex Secretary of State John W. Foster, Senator Root, Joseph H. Choate, Stewart L. Woodford, Judge Simeon E. Baldwin, Andrew Carnegie, Edwin Ginn, Richard Bartholdt, ex Gov. Montague, Rear Admiral Stockton, Presidents Eliot, Jordan, Judson and Benjamin Ide Wheeler, Hon. Jackson H. Ralston, Commissioner H. B. F. Macfarland, Andrew D. White, the ambassadors from Mexico and France, ministers from the Netherlands and Chile, and Francis W. Hirst. It was at this meeting that President Taft spoke just before drafting the Taft treaties. At subsequent conferences, between 1911 and 1916, papers were read by J. G. Schurman, John Temple Graves, C. W. Dabney, Senator Knox, Attorney General Wickersham, Paul S. Reinsch, A. D. Call,

Secretary Lansing, Hannis Taylor, W. D. Foulk, Secretary Root and others.

The World Court Congress was held at Cleveland, May 12-14, 1915, to organize sentiment in favor of the international court of justice, spoken of at the Hague in 1907. It resulted in the formation of the World Court League at New York City, with John Hays Hammond as president, and Samuel T. Dutton, secretary. It advocated a world court to settle all justiciable questions. In 1919, it joined the New York Peace Society in supporting the League of Nations Union and sought union for the United States with the League of Nations.

Jan. 6, 1915, the New York Peace Society appointed a Plan of Action Committee which brought together thirty professors and students of International Law affairs, formulated principles to establish an effective league and reduced them to a plan signed by 120 persons who were constituted into a National Provisional Committee. It called a conference at Philadelphia, June 17, 1915, and under the presidency of Taft, organized the League to Enforce Peace, approving the use of force between nations when necessary. Among its vice presidents were Lyman Abbott, Alexander Graham Bell, Charles R. Brown, Francis E. Clark, J. H. Finley, W. D. Foulke, Cardinal Gibbons, Washington Gladden, Myron T. Herrick, John Mitchell, Alton B. Parker, Jacob H. Schiff, Andrew D. White, Victor L. Berger, Edward Bok, Isaac Sharpless, Daniel Smiley, and St. George Tucker. On the executive committee were Leo S. Rowe, Prof. John B. Clark, Oscar S. Straus, A. Lawrence Lowell, men whose names have been frequently mentioned in the peace movement. The only persons at the Philadelphia meeting who voted against the plans for a League to Enforce Peace were Kirchwey and Call.

July 12, 1915, the League was approved by the World Peace Foundation, and May 27, 1916, by President Wilson at a banquet of the League, when he said that the United States "is willing to become a partner in any feasible association of nations formed to realize these objects and make them secure against violation."[1] In a letter to the belligerents, Dec. 18, 1916, President Wilson endorsed a League of Nations. Jan. 22, 1917, before the United States entered into the war, he spoke of the League approvingly in

[1] As quoted in the Literary Digest, June 10, 1916, p. 1683.

an address to the Senate, and again in his inaugural address on the fourth of March following.

Wilson wanted the peace at the end of the war to be lasting, to create a force as a guarantee of the permanency of the settlement greater than the force of any state in the war. He wanted the balance of power to be superseded by a community of power. In several of the European countries many statesmen held similar views. So when in December, 1918, Wilson went to Paris with his not too carefully thought out plan, he found it possible to get the peace leaders to agree to it, Jan. 25, 1919, just one week after the peace conference had opened. Feb. 14, he reported to the conference the draft of a covenant creating a League of Nations. Though accepted by the other nations, June 28, it was finally rejected by the United States Senate after a bitter contest, Nov. 19, 1920. The United States made a separate treaty of peace with Germany, May 24, 1920.

The Covenant of the League was never endorsed by the American Peace Society. Immediately after the formation of the League to Enforce Peace, June 17, 1915, the society objected to it because of the international police to be used against recalcitrant members, believing that the use of force endangered the whole progress of peaceful settlement of international disputes. Nov. 26, 1915, the executive committee voted to continue supporting Ladd's program of a congress of nations and a court of nations. At the annual meeting, May 13, 1916, the society passed a resolution adopting the program of Ladd and opposing any policy not in harmony with it.

The position of the society in regard to the use of force was clearly shown by Call in an article entitled "Force and the League of Nations," which appeared in the Advocate of Peace, July, 1918, pp. 199, 200, a part of which reads as follows: "* * * this society believes in a league of nations. Not that we hold a brief for that particular name, because the society of nations by any other name would be to us just as sweet. We are concerned with the thing. Whatever the name the nations may be brought to agree upon will be generally acceptable and accepted whether that name be a league of nations, a federation, a confederation, an association, a consociation, or even a verband. We may note that the United States and the British empire are both leagues of nations. That about which we are concerned we repeat is not the name, but the thing."

" During 120 years the Supreme Court of the United States has handed down eighty-one decisions in cases between states and in no instance has it employed force to hale a state before it or to compel the observance of its decrees. * * * Surely the nations will find it easier to go about the business of getting up a governed world by establishing first some form of an international law-making body to be accompanied by some form of an international court of justice than by tying around the neck of the whole enterprise at the outset the millstone of physical force."

"If in this country from 1787 to the present all of the intelligence that has made our nation possible has opposed the principle of coercing states, it would seem the part of American sense to apply the same experience to the wider affairs of international government. Force we must have, but real force, the force which creates and directs physical force, the superior force, the super-force, the force of public opinion, without which physical force is always a menace. Preparedness to use physical force has brought civilization to the brink of ruin, and unless nations collectively succeed in developing this super-force greater than physical force, this ultimate sanction of all law, this "decent respect to the opinion of mankind," physical force will yet push civilization over the brink. If physical force were indeed the sanction of law, we human beings would now be living in holes of the ground, the constant prey of sabre toothed cats, and the playthings of Brobdingnagian beasts of land and sea."

In an editorial entitled "The Two Questions," in the Advocate of Peace, June, 1919, pp. 167, 168, are these words: "The League, as provided in articles XI and XV of the Covenant, if established, would have full power not only to pass upon questions as to their ultimate merits, but to decide the very question of its own jurisdiction. Instead of placing the ultimate decision of an issue, in the hands of a Parliament as in England, or in the hands of a court as in America, this Covenant of the League of Nations proposes to set up an international organization, a council of nine persons dominated by five, which council, and if not the council then the League, would have power over questions of prime importance affecting the United States, questions which may be in their nature, legislative, judicial, or executive. As recently pointed out by Mr. George Wharton Pepper, the plan is quite as if we in the United States were to put into the hands of the president and his cabinet full power to make, interpret and execute the laws of these United States."

In an article entitled "Compromise and Barter," in the issue for July, 1919, pp. 210, 211, is this paragraph: "Readers of this magazine, familiar with the course which this society follows, must be aware that we have never advocated as our program for the peace of the world a League of Nations. We have stood rather for progressive adjustment under the society of nations which already exists, a union which has functioned from time to time in the Hague conferences, in the establishment of a Universal Postal Union, indeed in resisting the onslaught in the great war. It has seemed to us easier, more logical, more promising, to develop institutions already tried and familiar, than to take up again the task of bringing a new Minerva out of a new head of a new Jove."

In an editorial entitled "Our Way out—A Conference of the Nations," in the issue for November, 1919, p. 307 is the following statement: "A League to Enforce Peace never has succeeded; we believe it never can. As we have frequently argued, it is a contradiction in terms, and it has in it from the outset the canker of failure. Laws can provide for the coercion of individuals, but there is but one way to coerce a state, and that is by war. Nations cannot be expected to set over themselves voluntarily the machinery of organized warfare, controlled by foreigners, and operative at any time against themselves. The League of Nations as proposed out of the Paris conference, a scheme which for all practical purposes has been defeated in the United States Senate, represents, we may believe, the last attempt on the part of the nations to set up such an organ, because it is now seen to be wrong in principle, contrary to the teachings of history, and dangerous to the peace of the world." While these were Call's views, the society has never repudiated them.

At the close of the war, Dec. 1, 1918, Secretary Call went to Paris, returning May 10, 1919. During this time he watched events and reported them as they occurred. He furnished the commissioners of the peace conference with memoranda of the society's attitude toward the League of Nations, and its conviction as to the right form of international relations in a pamphlet entitled "Suggestive Memoranda for the Honorable Commissioners to Negotiate Peace at Paris, Submitted by the American Peace Society of Washington, D. C." He also prepared another pamphlet "Thinking it Through in Paris," which was widely distributed in Paris.

Two articles in the Covenant of the League of Nations represented what the society had fought for in the past,—article XIII, where the members agreed to submit to arbitration any dispute that they failed to settle by diplomacy and not to resort to war against any member of the League that complied with any award rendered; and article XIV, where the council of the League was to formulate and submit to the members plans for the establishment of a permanent court of international justice. Because of these articles the society passed a resolution at its annual meeting in May, 1919, declaring "its unshaken faith in the ultimate victory of the modes of peace over the methods of war" and in view of the inclusion of articles XIII and XIV and "the ancient program of this society thus being provided for substantially in its entirety," it "respectfully called attention of the United States Senate and the people of our country to the beneficent promise of these provisions and we urge their earnest consideration in all discussions relating to a League of Nations."

In an article entitled "The Inevitable Repudiation," in the Advocate of Peace, November, 1920, p. 335, are these statements: "The Advocate of Peace is not especially concerned with Mr. Wilson's administration; but with his proposed Covenant of the League of Nations we are vitally concerned. It has been our attempt to examine and to explain this Covenant. We have found it to be wrong in principle, contrary to the teachings of history, and a menace to the peace of the world. * * * We heard Mr. Wilson confess in Paris that his league is a League to Enforce Peace. For us that was enough. * * * Again and again we have tried to show, throughout the war and since, that any league to enforce peace is and by its very nature must be a league for war.* * * The history of the American Peace Society is one long opposition to any league to enforce peace. For nearly a century it has repudiated the idea."

* * * The reason why the United States is not in the League of Nations is because we felt that organization to be an attempt to set up a government of men and not of laws. They planned to create an international organization of nine men dominated by five, and the five represent the great powers which could dictate foreign policies. The United States won't go in until that ends."

The American Peace Society has, therefore, opposed the military clauses of the Covenant of the League. It has viewed them as of the essence of a military alliance to which under its constitution the United States could not subscribe. The Society, has, however, welcomed heartily the various opportunities for cooperation offered by the League. With the exception of 1925, Call has attended each of the Assemblies at Geneva, from the beginning to and including 1927. President Burton and others of the Society's directorate, have also attended a number of the assemblies. The Society is greatly encouraged by the activities of the League of Nations. It views them, outside the military phases, as the climax to date of collective human effort in the interest of world peace.

Chapter XLII

INTERNATIONAL QUESTIONS

OF THE many international questions which arose after the signing of the Treaty of Versailles, only a few of those in which the society was interested need be mentioned in this connection.

The covenant of the League of Nations provided that the council should prepare a plan for a permanent court of international justice for submission to the members of the League of Nations. At its second meeting, Feb. 11, 1920, the council of the League of Nations invited ten eminent jurists to perfect plans for the establishment of a permanent court of international justice, one of the things for which the American Peace Society had pleaded from the outset. This advisory committee, which included Elihu Root with James Brown Scott as adviser, sat at the Hague from June 16 to July 24, and presented to the council the results of its labors. The council, Oct. 27, 1920, modified certain parts of the report and sent it to the assembly of the League of Nations which, after consideration, made further modifications and adopted it Dec. 13, 1920. It went into effect on its ratification by twenty-two states. These changes left the Court very nearly identical with the Court of 1907, but with the addition of a method for appointment of judges and a permanent panel.

By the terms of the draft the judges were to be eleven to fifteen in number with from four to six alternates, the latter to sit in the absence of the former. No one was to be appointed a judge unless eligible for appointment to the highest judicial position in his own country or an international lawyer of repute, and not more than two judges were to come from the same country. The judges were to be nominated by the members of the Permanent Court of Arbitration at the Hague from a list of four nominees of each nation represented in the arbitral court. The names of the nominees were to be sent to the secretary general of the League of Nations who was to submit them to the council and assembly separately; and those securing a majority vote of approval in each house were to be declared elected for a term of nine years with the privilege of a re-election. In case of a deadlock the two bodies were to appoint a committee of three each to decide, and in case of their inability to agree the vacancies were to be filled by those already elected. The court was to elect its own president and clerk, who were to reside permanently at the Hague.

The jurisdiction of the court was to cover justiciable disputes between nations, which diplomacy had failed to settle. Though the court is supported by the League of Nations, it is organized in such a way that it could continue to function independently of the league. It does not supersede the Permanent Court of Arbitration at the Hague, but supplements it. The judges were elected Sept. 14, 1921, at Geneva, and the court inaugurated at the Palace of Peace in the Hague. Though the United States is not a member of the league, Prof. John Bassett Moore was elected one of the judges of the court. It is a fact that Root and Scott are, and Moore has been, officially connected with the American Peace Society.

Dec. 16, 1920, three days after the adoption of the court by the League of Nations, President Harding suggested that we adhere to it, a suggestion that was not accepted because it was felt that such action on our part would be a stepping stone to entrance into the League of Nations which as a nation we had repudiated.

The advisory council in reporting its draft for a permanent court also recommended the opening of the Academy of International Law founded at the Hague in 1913, and which but for the war would have been opened in August, 1914. It was fully inaugurated July 14, 1923. The course consisted of two six week terms extending from July 16 to August 3, and from August 13 to September 1. Seventy-one courses were offered the first term and sixty-four the second, attended by 304 persons from twenty-nine countries during the first term, and 350 persons from thirty-one countries the second, and taught by twenty-eight specialists from fourteen countries. Seven of the lecturers and thirteen of the students came from the United States. Arthur D. Call was a member in attendance of the opening session of the Academy. The courses have been continued each successive summer.

The academy is supported by fees, from the income of a portion of the Nobel prize received by Dr. Asser in 1911, and by a subsidy from the Carnegie Endowment.

This advisory council also recommended the consideration of an early summoning of a new conference to carry on the work of the two earlier Hague conferences and the preparation of a draft plan for the business of the conference by the leading international law associations. Similar requests that a new Hague conference be called were made by the American Institute of International Law at its session at Havana, June 22, 1917, as did the American Peace Society May 27, 1921. The Interparliamentary Union made a similar recommendation in 1925. At the same time the Netherlands government asked Secretary of State Kellogg the position of the United States in regard to calling such a conference on codification of international law, and he replied, showing a willingness to co-operate. The League of Nations, however, denied this recommendation of its advisory council.

Congressman Tinkham of Massachusetts introduced a resolution into Congress in December, 1925, for the calling of a third conference at the Hague by the United States. April 5, 1926, he introduced a joint resolution requesting the president to propose to the nations of the world the calling of a third Hague conference and recommending the codification of international law.[1] This was referred to the Committee on Foreign Relations, which held hearings on the subject May 3, 4, 5, 21, and 22. Secretary Call, C. H. Butler, David Jayne Hill, James Brown Scott, Prof. W. I. Hull, and many others appeared before the committee and argued in favor of the passage of the resolution. The committee reported in its favor, July 3, 1926, but press of other business caused Congress to take no action in the matter.

The call for the arms conference by President Harding was a natural result of preceding events. The first Hague conference in 1899 was called to consider the question of a reduction of armaments. Nothing was done in regard to this except to express a hope that armaments might be reduced. At the second conference at the Hague in 1907, the United States pressed the subject of disarmament to no use. Hamilton Holt in an article in the Independent, April 22, 1909, suggested that the world was ready for practical efforts toward universal peace and that the United States was the

[1] Joint Resolution 221, 69th Congress, 1st Sess. Printed in the Advocate of Peace, May, 1926, p. 272.

one nation best fitted to lead in the movement and gain the cooperation of the other nations.

To carry out the idea the World Federation League was organized, and April 5, 1910, at its request, Congressman Bartholdt introduced a resolution into Congress authorizing the president to appoint a world federation committee of five to bring about world peace. This bill was endorsed by the New York Peace Society, the International School of Peace, the Mohonk Arbitration Conference, and the American Peace Society at its annual meeting at Hartford, May 11, 1910. Six days earlier, March 30, William S. Bennett of New York, had introduced a bill requesting the president to consider the expediency of calling an international conference for the purpose of considering the possibility of limiting armaments by international agreement. Both bills were referred to the Committee on Foreign Relations. A delegation went to Washington and appeared before the committee in behalf of the bill. The committee combined both bills and reported them favoably, and they were passed June 24, 1910, authorizing the president to appoint a commission of five "to consider the expediency of utilizing existing international agencies for the purpose of limiting the armaments of the world by international agreement and of constituting the combined navies of the world an international force for the preservation of universal peace."

The act was approved by the International Peace Congress, and the Interparliamentary Union which pledged its delegates to work for the creation of similar commissions in other countries. France, Holland, Sweden, Denmark and Norway appointed commissions to study the question, and several other nations intimated to President Taft their willingness to appoint commissions after he had appointed them for the United States. But he failed to appoint any because of his inability to find satisfactory men willing to serve. And then came the war.

In the bill making appropriations for the naval service, Aug. 29, 1916, was a clause authorizing the president to invite all the leading governments to send representatives to a "conference which shall be charged with the duty of formulating a plan for a court of arbitration or other tribunal to which disputed questions between nations shall be referred for adjudication and peaceful settlement and to consider the question of disarmament and submit their recommendations to their respective governments for approval." Under this nothing was done.

After the treaties of peace were made, attention was again turned to armaments. Senator Borah introduced a resolution authorizing the President to invite the governments of Great Britain and Japan to send representatives to a conference with a view to entering into an agreement to reduce naval expenditures for the next five years. This was followed by a bill granting $100,000 toward the expense of holding a conference with other nations relative to disarmament. After informally approaching Great Britain, France, Italy, and Japan, and finding them willing to engage in such a conference, they were invited to meet in Washington, Nov. 11, 1921, where "the question of naval armaments may naturally have the first place." China was invited to participate in the discussion of the Pacific and Far Eastern questions. Belgium, Portugal, and Holland were invited to sit in and listen.

Nov. 12, the day after the opening of the conference, the American Peace Society wrote to each member of the conference on the Limitation of Armament a letter and enclosed a pamphlet entitled "A Governed World, Three Documents," which it was hoped the recipients would read and find of some value. These documents had been accepted by the American Institute of International Law and the American Peace Society.

Upon request of the government the society ascertained the views of the members of the society regarding an association of nations, the use of submarines, and poison gas in time of war and reported them to the government.

The conference lasted until February 6, 1922. Hughes, Lodge, Root, and Underwood represented the United States in the conferences. The sessions were secret, except the first, which President Harding attended and to which he gave an address of welcome. The treaties drafted by the conference were soon ratified by the United States and the other interested Powers.

Chapter XLIII

REORGANIZATION

AFTER the war the society found itself bereft of its branches, and with but little peace sentiment of the old kind existing throughout the country. Under the circumstances it felt it unwise to take the initiative immediately toward holding an annual public meeting or organizing another peace congress. But it had to consider its method of development in the future. It doubted the wisdom of reviving the various state societies, though because of the interest shown by the New Hampshire Peace Society it granted it a subvention from time to time.

The war had rendered unworkable the constitution adopted by the society in 1916 because of the ending of its constituent branches. A committee consisting of George A. Finch, Jackson H. Ralston, and Thomas E. Green, was therefore appointed to draw up a new constitution which—the sixth—was adopted by the society at its annual meeting in May, 1922. It was longer than any of the preceding constitutions. Its main provisions are as follows:

I. The name remained unchanged the "American Peace Society."

II. The purpose of the society was stated a little more fully than before: "to promote permanent international peace through justice; and to advance in every proper way the general use of conciliation, arbitration, judicial methods, and other peaceful means of avoiding and adjusting differences among nations, to the end that right shall rule might in a governed world."

III. The society is to consist of three departments: Publications, Home Affairs, and Field Work.

IV. The management of the society is placed in the hands of a board of directors, comprising the president, secretary, treasurer, executive committee, and forty-eight other directors each representing one state "as far as practicable," each director to hold office until his successor is elected, vacancies in an office to be filled by the board of directors at the annual meeting in May or at any specially called meeting. Nominations to be made by members of the board of directors, in writing, fourteen days before an annual or called meeting. Names of nominees with vouchers are to be mailed to each member of the board of directors seven days before a meeting and no other nominations are to be considered except by the unanimous consent of the directors present. A director without an acceptable excuse who is absent from three successive annual meetings of the board ceases to be a director. No director is to receive any compensation for his service as director. The board of directors is to maintain a central clearing house and bureau of information for all persons and organizations in this or other countries engaged in promoting the cause of international peace and good will. Annual meetings are to be held in May with provisions for the calling of special meetings.

V. At the annual meeting in May, the directors are to elect a president, vice presidents, honorary vice presidents, secretary, editor, and treasurer. "The secretary may serve as editor of the society's magazine and other publications."

VI. An executive committee, consisting of the president, secretary, treasurer, and twelve others elected by the directors at the annual meeting, administer the affairs of the society and decide the salaries of the paid officials of the society. They are to meet monthly except through the summer.

VII. "The executive work of the society shall be organized under the charge of the president and secretary, who shall undertake to bring into close and active cooperation the peace forces of the United States, promote the organization of the society as herein provided, and advise with peace workers in this and other countries to the end that public sentiment favorable to the principles for which the society stands may be organized and strengthened. The president and secretary shall make annual reports of their work, which shall include the work of the executive committee and the board of directors." The president, secretary, editor, and treasurer, with their assistants perform the work ordinarily performed by such officers in other societies. Further, the president "shall, as far as possible, guide and develop the peace forces of the country in accordance with the principles of the American Peace Society, its constitution and by laws." The secretary keeps the minutes of meetings of the society, directors, and executive committee, thus superseding the recording secretary which the society had formerly had. He also "performs such other duties as are incident to his office or may be required of him by the president, the board of directors or the executive committee." Assistant secretaries are "appointed by the president of the American Peace Society on nomination by the secretary and approval of the executive committee." The society is to issue a periodical to be known as the Advocate of Peace.

VIII.   The headquarters of the society are to be in Washington.

IX.   Public meetings and conferences are to be held as fixed upon by the executive committee.

X.   The constitution provides for six classes of members: Annual, paying dues as fixed by the board of directors; sustaining, $5; contributing, $25; life, $100; institutions, $25; honorary, elected by the directors.

XI.   "The object of this society shall never be changed, but the constitution may in all other respects be amended at the annual meeting of the board of directors by a two thirds vote on the recommendation of the executive committee, provided that notice of the proposed amendment shall have been mailed to each member of the board of directors at least ten days prior to the meeting."

Since the war the society has had three presidents: Hon. James L. Slayden, of San Antonio, Texas, who served from 1917 to 1920; Hon. Andrew J. Montague, of Richmond, Virginia, a graduate of Richmond College and of the law school of the University of Virginia, formerly United States District Attorney and dean of the law school of Richmond College, president of the American Society for Judicial Settlement of International Disputes, a trustee of the Carnegie Institution and of the Carnegie Endowment for International Peace; and Hon. Theodore E. Burton, of Cleveland, Ohio, who began his second term of service in 1924. Since the adoption of the constitution of 1916, the control of the society has been in the hands of the board of directors, a representative body composed in part of persons each representing a state in the union. Not all the states are or have been represented. The intention is to have every state represented by the time of the celebration in May, 1928. The

Board has an annual meeting, taking the place of the annual meetings of the society held before 1917.

There has been an entire change in the personnel of the management of the society since its removal to Washington in 1911. President Burton was first elected president in 1911; Secretary Call executive director in 1912, though he had been a vice president in 1910; and Treasurer White in 1911. Of the present vice presidents, Hon. Jackson H. Ralston has served the longest, having been elected to that position in 1917. Of the members of the executive committee, two served before the war: Hon Jackson H. Ralston elected in 1911, and Rev. Jay T. Stocking, elected in 1916. Of the board of directors, Henry C. Morris of Chicago, has seen the longest service, having been first elected in 1917. Of the honorary vice presidents, President Charles F. Thwing, of Western Reserve University, was elected director in 1885 and vice president in 1888; Bishop William Lawrence of Massachusetts was elected vice president in 1894; Hon. James Brown Scott of the Carnegie Endowment, vice president in 1908, and President E. E. Brown, of New York University, in 1909; and all became honorary vice presidents in 1913.

Since the removal to Washington several new men of prominence have become officers of the society: Senator McKinley, Congressman Hensley, Hon. William Jennings Bryan, Hon. David Jayne Hill, and William Howard Taft have served as vice presidents. Among the Honorary vice presidents have been President William Lowe Bryan, President W. H. P. Faunce, Hon. Samuel W. McCall, Dr. Charles Cheney Hyde, Hon. Elihu Root, Senator Thomas Sterling, Bishop Darlington, and Vice President Fairbanks. Among the members of the executive committee have been Hon. P. P. Claxton, Dr. Jay T. Stocking, Prof. Arthur Ramsey, Hon. Frank W. Mondell, Dr. Charles Cheney Hyde, and Justice F. L. Siddons. Since the war the society has lost a few officers by death; in 1924, Hon. James L. Slayden, member of the executive committee, 1914-17, president, 1917-1920, vice president, 1920-24; in 1926, Senator William B. McKinley, vice president from 1924.

The annual meetings of the directors continued to be held during the daytime at the office of the society until 1923. In the evening banquets were held at Rauschers in 1920, 1921, and 1922, attended by upwards of one hundred persons, with speeches by prominent members of the society and others, among whom were Hon. P. P. Claxton, George Soule, Frederick Wile, Dr. Paul S. Reinsch, Hon.

Jackson H. Ralston, Hon. John Burke, and Dr. Thomas Green in 1920; Dr. J. Franklin Jameson, Hon. T. E. Burton, and Dr. James Brown Scott in 1921; and Rev. Jay T. Stocking, Dr. C. C. Hyde, Capt. Gordon Gordon-Smith, and Dr. Leo S. Rowe in 1922.

Since 1922, with one exception, the meetings have been held at the Cosmos Club, in connection with a luncheon, without speeches. In 1924, in the evening following the annual meeting, William Ernest Hocking, Alford Professor of Philosophy at Harvard University, gave an address at the First Congregational Church on "Emanuel Kant and the Foreign Policies of Nations," Dr. James Brown Scott presiding. In 1927, after a meeting at the office in the morning, the members repaired to the Cosmos Club for luncheon after which Brig. Gen. John McAuley Palmer gave an address on Armaments, War and Peace. The monthly meetings of the executive committee were held at the office of the society until the fall of 1923; since, at the Cosmos Club, at 12:30 until April 30, 1926, in connection with a luncheon, and at 6:30 since then in connection with dinner.

According to the reports of the treasurer, the receipts and expenditures of the society with the amount on hand at the end of the year since the war have been as follows:

Year ending May 1	Receipts	Expenditures	Amount on hand
1917	$35.652.92	$36,147.03	$4,718.32
1918	27,645.22	32,306.95	56.59
1919	27,635.15	21,284.06	6,407.68
1920	26,596.10	20,230.30	12,773.48
1921	18,826.91	29,288.49	2,311.90
1922	45,185.15	46,982.39	514.66
1923	48,465.34	48,757.78	222.22
1924	41,892.70	38,895.47	3,219.45
1925	25,673.29	27,860.98	1,031.76
1926	26,164.96	28,814.46	382.26
1927	32,626.81	32,317.93	691.14

In addition to these amounts, the endowment fund was reported as follows: 1917, $12,600; 1922, $27,100; 1915, $20,900; 1927, $9,000. The home expenses of the society have increased since the removal to Washington. The rental of the rooms in the Colorado

Building in 1911 was $780, and in 1925, with an additional room, $1683 a year.

Since the war the society has had three associate editors: George Perry Morris, assistant editor, a graduate of Rutgers College with twenty-five years service on the Mail and Express, New York, the Congregationalist, the Boston Herald, and the Christian Science Monitor, served from Nov. 15, 1918, to his death Jan. 21, 1921. He was succeeded by John W. Owens as associate editor until November, 1922, now Editor of the Baltimore Sun; and since by the present incumbent, Leo Pasvolsky, a graduate of the College of the City of New York and connected with the Institute of Economics.

Since the war Secretary Call has spoken occasionally in the interest of peace, as opportunity has offered. He is a member of the Cosmos Club, a member of the Sons of the American Revolution, and a trustee of the Mount Pleasant Congregational Church, of Washington. In 1923, he was elected chairman of the Committee on International Relations and Good Will of the Washington Federation of Churches. He is frequently to be seen at social gatherings, writes for the press, and is in evidence wherever it is possible to aid the cause of peace. He spoke in Pittsburgh, Pa., over the radio, April 29, 1926, on the True Voice of America in International Affairs. He received the degree of LL. D., from Howard University in 1926.

Secretary Call believes the work of the American Peace Society at present to lie in the direction of influencing public opinion, especially that of the thinking class. His aim is to make the Advocate of Peace an authority in international matters, to have it contain articles by prominent men on matters of public interest, to write editorials that will lead, by clarity of style and sound reasoning, public opinion to demand the rational settlement of international disputes. He has endeavored to develop it into an international monthly magazine with a wider and deeper influence. Most of its articles are carefully written by experts. The magazine, intensely patriotic with no squint of extremism, advertises the United States of America as an illustration of an attainable peace organization. It covers a wide range of topics, all bearing relation to the subject of international justice,—world problems in review, controversies between nations, race questions, international conferences, near and far Eastern questions, treaties, permanent court of international justice, the League of Nations, American influence in Europe, soviet-

ism, communism, militarism, international loans, procedure of legislative bodies bearing on arbitration and international movements,
speeches by prominent men, book reviews, and international notes.
It has abiding faith in the precepts of its founders. It holds for
principles of justice, for direct negotiation between nations, good
offices, mediation, commissions of inquiry, councils of conciliation,
arbitration, and judicial settlement.

The influence of the magazine is recognized by Congress. The
leading editorial in the issue of April, 1925, for example, was reprinted in the Congressional Record, on the motion of Senator Dill
of Washington, and Call's article on James Madison was reprinted
in the Congressional Record for April 14, 1926, at the request of
Senator Copeland of New York. In order that its magazine might
be more widely known and read, the society conducted a three year
campaign, advertising it in some of the better magazines of the
country. It goes to many libraries, colleges, and to government
officials.

Through the work of Mrs. Call, the library of the society, containing 3506 volumes and 234 bound volumes of magazines, has been
carefully classified and catalogued. The records and many old letters written by and to Ladd, Coues, Burritt, and other workers connected with the early history of the society are carefully kept in a
fireproof safe.

Because of the increased expense of carrying on the work of the
society, the feeling has grown strongly during the past years that
an endowment ought to be secured for the society as a part of its
centennial exercises. With this in view the executive committee engaged H. C. Phillips, a former secretary of the Mohonk Lake Conferences, to study the work of the society from a business point of
view, and January 15, 1927, secured Lacey C. Zapf as Business Man-
ager of the Society, to take charge of the membership and endowment
division of the work. Mr. Zapf is a graduate of DePauw and George
Washington Universities. He spent four years in special legal work
for the Department of Commerce and six years as secretary of the
International Chamber of Commerce. He has raised large sums of
money and has set out to secure an endowment for the American
Peace Society that will produce fifty thousand dollars a year.

Under the general direction of Secretary Call the Centennial
Celebration of the Society was held at Cleveland, Ohio, May 7 to 11,
1928. The celebration was international in scope. The Honorable

Theodore E. Burton, President of the Society, presided. President Coolidge acted as Honorary Chairman of the Conference Committee. Dr. James Brown Scott was Chairman of the Program Committee. Men of international reputation were present.

At the same time the State of Maine, with a Committee of arrangements composed of the presidents of the three colleges and the State University, the State Commissioner of Education, and others, prepared a celebration of the sesqui-centennial of the birth of Capt. Ladd, the founder of the society and long a resident of Maine. The Society accepted an invitation to be present at the exercises, and assisted in them.

Thus the society in its attempt to supersede the ancient custom of nations of settling international disputes by war has had its failures and its successes. Its method of spreading its hope in international justice, kindling enthusiasm in its behalf, persuading others to come to its point of view, securing local and later congressional cooperation, has not been profitless. It presses for a friendlier relation with the other American republics to the south of us, with Canada, and with the various governments over seas. It is inspired by the Hague Conference, by the League of Nations as an agency of cooperation, and by the promise of the Permanent Court of International Justice. With all of these movements the American Peace Society keeps in closest touch.

Philosophizing has been intentionally omitted from this account. No attempt has been made to praise unduly the achievements of the society. Its work is not completed. It has barely begun. A glance at our world today is sufficient to show the need of the continuance of its work. Surely in the lifetime of no one now living will the ideal condition of international relations be reached. It is reasonable to expect, however, that with the foundations already laid the chroniclers of the society during its second century will turn to the workers of the first and find there no little carefulness, persistence, ability and sincerity. One thing seems to stand out. It has been phrased by James Brown Scott, leading authority in the matter, who wrote under date of December 17, 1926, "The story of modern arbitration cannot be told without constant reference to the American Peace Society."

APPENDIX A

THE ADVOCATE OF PEACE

The Friend of Peace was published by Noah Worcester for the Massachusetts Peace Society, beginning in 1816 and ending in 1828, by which time fifty numbers and four appendices had appeared. The numbers appeared at irregular intervals, generally four each year. The first three volumes consisted of twelve numbers each, and volume four of fourteen numbers and four appendices. The first few numbers were printed at Philadelphia and the rest at Cambridge. The numbers of volumes I and II are paged separately, of volumes III and IV and the four appendices are paged continuously. Each number of the first two volumes contains forty pages, except numbers 5 and 11 of Vol. I, which contain thirty-six pages each, and number 12 of the same volume, which contains thirty-seven pages and an appendix of twenty-three pages. Number 4 of volume II contains an appendix of eight pages. Each number and appendix of volumes III and IV contains thirty-two pages each. The pages were of quarto size.

The Harbinger of Peace was started by Capt. Ladd, on the organization of the American Peace Society, the Friend of Peace coming to an end shortly after. It was a monthly magazine of twenty-four pages of duodecimo size. The first number appeared in May, 1828, and the last in April, 1831. The numbers for January and February, 1831, were issued as a double number. It was published wherever convenient for the editor.

The Calumet, published in New York, was the successor of the Harbinger of Peace. It appeared bi-monthly, each number carrying the names of two months. The first number was dated May and June, 1831; the last March and April, 1835. The first eighteen numbers were paged continuously as Vol. I; the last six likewise as Vol. II. A title page and index were prepared for Vol. I. The number of pages in an issue was generally 32, but the number for September and October, 1832, contained 28 pages, January and February, 1833, 36 pages, March and April, 1834, 40 pages, and March and April, 1835, 46 pages.

The American Advocate of Peace was published by Wm. Watson at Hartford, Conn., quarterly, the first number appearing June, 1834, and the last—number 11—in December, 1836, quarto size. The individual numbers were entitled Advocate of Peace, but the title page of Vol. I, and the covers were entitled American Advocate of Peace. An index was prepared to Vol. I. Volume I, consisting of eight numbers, June, 1834, to March, 1836, contained 386 pages. The individual numbers vary from 46 to 56 pages each. Each number of volume II contains 48 pages. Beginning with the number for June, 1835, the magazine was issued for the American Peace Society, but was not under its control, and was discontinued in December, 1836, on the death of Watson.

Beginning with June, 1837, the society, now in Boston, again published its own magazine under the title Advocate of Peace. The title has varied slightly with the years. During the year 1846, it was the Advocate of Peace and Universal Brotherhood, published in Worcester, Mass., returning to the old title, and Boston headquarters, at the end of the year. It became The Advocate of Peace, March-April, 1857, American Advocate of Peace and Arbitration, June, 1892, The Advocate of Peace, January, 1894, Advocate of Peace, January, 1901, The Advocate of Peace, January, 1914, Advocate of Peace, January, 1915. Since March, 1920, the cover has borne the name Advocate of Peace through Justice, though the old title has been retained on the title page and in the body of each number.

The frequency of publication has varied, being generally monthly or bi-monthly. From 1878 to 1884, it appeared irregularly. Since June, 1892, it has appeared monthly, generally omitting one month during the fall of the year.

The volume for 1846 appeared from Worcester, Mass. The numbers from January, 1871, through January, 1872, were issued from Boston and Chicago. Other numbers through May, 1911, appeared from Boston; subsequent numbers from Washington.

A volume since 1872 has generally coincided with the calendar year. Previous to that time a volume generally covered two years. Since 1842, volumes have generally begun with the January number. In the earlier years a volume generally consisted of twelve numbers, irrespective of their frequency of publication. Previous to 1869, the volumes were not numbered, though at the bottom of the first page of volumes III to XI, from June, 1839, to January, 1854, the number of the volume commencing with that issue was placed in small letters. The volume beginning January, 1869, is called New Series, that beginning with January, 1871, being designated as New Series, Vol. III, a system continued through N. S. Vol. XV, ending in June, 1884. The next number, August, 1884, is entitled Vol. 47, and since then the numbers for each year have been numbered consecutively. Since the removal of the society to Boston and the establishment of the Advocate of Peace in June, 1837, it would seem that "47th year," would have been a more appropriate term to use in 1884 than "Vol. 47," for previous to the starting of the new series in 1864, the numbers of the Advocate of Peace had been gathered into eighteen volumes. The pagination in a volume is continuous with a few exceptions as noted hereafter.

Beginning 1898, a title page has been issued each year. Previous to that time title pages were issued with Vol. XIV, 1862-63, and Vol. XV, 1864-65. Indexes began to be issued regularly with Vol. 57, for the year 1895. Previous to that time indexes had been issued as follows: Vols. I and II, on the last two pages of the number for May, 1839; Vol. III, on the last two pages of the number for April, 1841; Vol. IV, on the last two pages of the number for December, 1842; for 1858 and 1859 on the last two pages of the number for November and December, 1859; for 1862 and 1863, on the last three pages of the number for November-December, 1863; Vol. XV, 1864 and 1865, on the last three pages of the number for November-December, 1865; for 1866 and 1867, on the last three pages of the number for November-December, 1867.

Through 1868 the size of the page was duodecimo. January, 1869, through 1923, the size was octavo. Beginning January, 1924, the size has been 6¾x10 inches. Advertisements appeared on the cover of the magazine from June, 1871, through May, 1911. From August, 1884, through 1900, the covers were paged with the rest of the magazine. Previous to Vol. 47, the price of the magazine was one dollar per volume. Beginning with Vol. 47, the price became one dollar per year, increased January, 1920, to one dollar and a half a year, January, 1921, two dollars a year, and January, 1927, to three dollars.

APPENDIX B

OFFICERS

The list of officers of the Society and the members of the Board of Directors and the Executive Committee, including only those who have been elected at annual meetings of the Society or the Board of Directors, and omitting those elected by the Executive Committee to fill a vacancy, is as follows:

PRESIDENTS
Presidents were first elected in 1837

William Ladd, 1837-41.
Samuel E. Coues, 1841-Dec., 1846.
Theodore Frelinghuysen, Dec., 1846-47.
Anson G. Phelps, 1847-48.
William Jay, 1848-59.
Francis Wayland, 1859-61.
Howard Malcolm, 1861-73; Honorary President, 1874-78.

Edward S. Tobey, 1873-91.
Robert Treat Paine, 1891-1910.
Theodore E. Burton, 1911-16.
George W. Kirchwey, 1916-17.
James L. Slayden, 1917-20.
Andrew J. Montague, 1920-23.
Theodore E. Burton, 1924 to date.

SECRETARIES AND EDITORS

William Ladd, Secretary and Editor, 1828; Corresponding Secretary for Eastern District and Editor, 1829-30; Secretary for Foreign Correspondence and Editor, 1830-31; General Secretary and Editor, 1831-32; General Agent, 1832-41; Editor, 1832-33; 37-41.

Rev. Alexander G. Fraser, Corresponding Secretary for the Southwest District, 1829-30.

Prof. J. C. Rostan, Secretary for Foreign Correspondence, 1831-33.

D. E. Wheeler, Secretary for Domestic Correspondence, 1831-33.

R. M. Chipman, Corresponding Secretary and Editor, 1833-34.

Rev. George Bush, Corresponding Secretary and Editor, 1834-35.

Francis Fellowes, Editor, June 1835-37.

Rev. T. H. Gallaudet, Corresponding Secretary, 1835-37.

Rev. George Cone Beckwith, Corresponding Secretary, 1837-70; Editor, 1841-46; 47-70.

Elihu Burritt, Editor, 1846-47.

Rev. Amasa Lord, Corresponding Secretary and Assistant Treasurer pro tem, 1870-71; Western Secretary, 1871-72; Editor, 1870-71.

Rev. James B. Miles, Corresponding Secretary, Editor, and Assistant Treasurer, 1871-76.

Rev. D. C. Haynes, Financial Secretary, 1873-74.

Rev. Charles H. Malcolm, Corresponding Secretary and Editor, 1876-79.

Rev. H. C. Dunham, Acting Corresponding Secretary, 1880-82; Corresponding Secretary, 1882-84; Editor, 1880-84.

Rev. Rowland B. Howard, Corresponding Secretary and Editor, 1884-92.

Rev. Benjamin F. Trueblood, Corresponding Secretary, 1892-1908; Secretary, 1908-15; Honorary Secretary, 1915-17; Editor, 1892-1915.

Rev. Charles E. Beals, Field Secretary, 1908-12.
Rev. James L. Tryon, Assistant Secretary, 1908-12.
Arthur Deerin Call, Executive Director, 1913-15; Acting Secretary and Editor, 1915-16; Secretary and Editor, 1916 to date.

RECORDING SECRETARIES

Rev. Alexander G. Fraser, 1829-30.
Rev. L. D. Dewey, 1830-35.
Francis Fellowes, 1835-37.
Thomas Thompson, Jr., 1837-38.
Edward Noyes, 1839-40.
J. P. Blanchard, 1840-October, 1841.
Lewis T. Stoddard, October, 1841-42.
Thomas Drown, 1842-44.
James L. Baker, 1844-46.
William C. Brown, 1847-71.
Nachob Broughton, Jr., Jan. to July, 1871.
Rev. Howard C. Dunham, Rec. Sec., 1872-80; and Acting Cor. Sec., 1880-83; and Office Agent, 1884-86.
C. W. Dunham, 1883-84.
Rev. Daniel Richards, Rec. Sec., and Office Agent, 1886-90; Office Agent, 1890-92.

OFFICE SECRETARIES

Georgia B. Birdsall, 1893-99.
Frederick A. Smith, 1900-01.
Lyra D. Trueblood, 1901-03, 1906-07.
Edith Bertha Ordway, 1903-06.
Mabel H. Kingsbury, 1907-11.
Grace M. Mason, 1911-13.
Susan R. Cutts, 1913-16.
Joseph B. Schaaf, 1916-17.
Clarke F. Hunn, 1917-18.
Ruth E. Burr, 1919-21.
Virginia Miller, 1921-22.
W. I. Smalley, 1922-26; 27 to date.
Louise Anderson, 1926-   .

    The office secretaries acted as recording secretaries until 1917.
    The records since 1917 are signed by the Secretary of the society.
    Since 1913 the office secretaries have been assistant treasurers.

ASSISTANT EDITORS

Rev. L. M. Dewey, 1830-31.
J. P. Blanchard, 1856-57.
Fred B. Foulk, July to October, 1915.
Dr. John Mez, 1915-16.
Malcolm W. Davis, February to May, 1916.
Clarke F. Hunn, 1916-18.
George Perry Morris, 1918-21.
John W. Owens, 1921-22.

ASSOCIATE EDITORS

Leo Pasvolsky, 1922 to date.

AUDITORS

Auditors have been elected on a few occasions. In the earlier days the treasurer's accounts were accepted as presented or were perfunctorily examined by a committee appointed for the purpose before or after presentation. In later days the treasurer's books have been examined by boards of audit not connected with the society.

T. H. Russell, 1872-1873.
Francis B. Gilman, 1885-1890.
D. C. Heath, 1890-1896.
William E. Sheldon, 1896-1900.
Dr. William F. Jarvis, 1900-1912.
Edward White, 1912-1916.

MEMBERS EXECUTIVE COMMITTEE, DIRECTORS, VICE PRESIDENTS, HONORARY COUNCILLORS

From 1913 to 1916 there were two classes of directors,—representative directors and directors at large. Vice Presidents were first elected in 1839. Honorary Vice Presidents were first elected in 1913. Honorary Counsellors were elected between 1892 and 1912.

Benjamin Abbot, LL. D., Exeter, N. H. Director, 1829-35.
Jacob Abbott, Director, 1837-39. Graduate Bowdoin and Andover, Prof. Amherst, Author.
Rev. J. P. Abbott, D. D., Medford, Mass. Director, 1886-87.
Rev. Lyman Abbott, D. D., Brooklyn. Vice pres., 1896-1913; Hon. Vice pres., 1914-22.
E. O. Achorn, Boston. Director, 1888-89.
Jane Addams, Chicago. Vice pres., 1900-13; Hon. Vice pres., 1913-27.
Rev. S. C. Aiken, Cleveland. Director, 1837-44.
Hugh Aikman, N. Y. C. Ex Com., 1829-35; Director, 1829-35; Treasurer, 1830-34. Merchant.
Magnus W. Alexander, Lynn, Mass. Director, 1908-10.
Rev. J. H. Allen, D. D. Cambridge, Mass. Ex. Com., 1891-92; Director, 1892-98. Prof. Harvard. Editor Unitarian Review. Graduate Harvard.
Nathaniel T. Allen, West Newton, Mass. Vice pres., 1882-87; Director, 1887-89, 1892-1904; Ex. Com., 1889-92. Educator.
Willard S. Allen, Boston, Ex. Com., 1883-88.
Rev. William Allen, Brunswick, Me. Director, 1835-38. President Bowdoin.
William H. Allen, M. D., LL. D., Philadelphia. Vice pres., 1853-65.
William T. Allen, West Newton, Mass. Ex. Com., 1888-89.
Rev. Charles G. Ames, Boston. Director, 1896-1905; Vice pres., 1905-12.
Hon. Oliver Ames, Boston. Director, 1886-87; Vice pres., 1887-90. Governor Massachusetts.
Mrs. Fannie Fern Andrews, Boston. Ex. Com., 1908-11; Vice pres., 1911-13; Representative Director, 1913-16; Director, 1906-13. 1916-19.
John A. Andrews, Boston. Director, 1854-56.
George T. Angell, Boston. Vice pres., 1896-1909.
Rev. L. H. Angier, D. D., Rockport, Malden, Everett, Boston. Director, 1865-92; Ex. Com., 1870-74; Vice pres., 1892-98.
Hon. James Arnold, New Bedford, Mass. Vice President., 1848-53.
Edward Atkinson, Brookline. Vice pres., 1897-1906.
Samuel Austin, Providence. Director, 1893-96; Vice pres., 1896-97.
Origen Bacheler, N. Y. C. Director, 1835-37.
Mrs. Hannah J. Bailey, Winthrop Center, Me. Director, 1889-1906; Vice pres., 1905-13; Hon. Vice pres., 1913-24.
Joshua L. Baily, Philadelphia. Vice pres., 1895-1913; Hon. Vice pres., 1913-16.
Gov. Conrad Baker, Indianapolis. Vice pres., 1870-77.

James L. Baker, Boston. Recording Secretary, 1844-46; Ex. Com., 1844-47.
Joseph Baker, Boston. Director, 1844-46.
Rev. Smith Baker, D. D., Lowell, Mass., Minneapolis. Director, 1886-91; Vice pres., 1891-92.
Rev. Elihu W. Baldwin, N. Y. C., Crawfordsville, Ind. Director, 1829-38; Ex. Com., 1829-35.
William H. Baldwin, Boston. Vice pres., 1873-76; Director, 1888-93.
Jacob Bancroft, Boston. Director, 1849-66.
S. C. Bancroft, Peabody. Director, 1882-88.
John Barrett, Washington. Ex. Com., 1917-21.
C. C. Barry, Boston. Director, 1868-71.
Hon. Richard Bartholdt, Washington. Vice pres., 1906-11; Ex. Com., 1911-16; Director at Large, 1912-16; Director, 1911-12. M. C.
George A. Barton, Boston. Ex. Com., 1883-84.
Rev. William E. Barton, D. D., Boston, Oak Park, Ill. Director, 1898-99; Vice pres., 1899-1912.
Rev. Joshua Bates, D. D. Middlebury, Vt., Dudley, Mass. Vice pres., 1839-44.
Rev. Charles E. Beals, Stoughton, Mass. Field Secretary, 1908-12; Director Central Western Department, 1912-14; Hon. Vice pres., 1914-16.
Rev. George Cone Beckwith, Boston. Corresponding Secretary, 1837-70.
Mrs. George C. Beckwith, Boston, Ex. Com., 1871-72.
A. T. Bell, Atlantic City. Hon. Vice pres., 1920-21.
George Bemis, Ex. Com., 1841-42.
Ida Whipple Benham, Mystic, Conn. Director, 1890-92; Vice pres., 1892-1904.
George Benson, Brooklyn, Conn. Director, 1828-36.
M. M. Binford, Lynn, Mass. Director, 1886-87.
Mrs. George W. Bingham, Derry, N. H. Vice pres., 1899-1902.
Hannah W. Blackburn, Zanesville, Ohio. Director, 1889-91.
Alice Stone Blackwell, Dorchester, Mass. Director, 1904-06; Vice pres., 1906-13.
Rev. Amos Blanchard, Lowell, Mass. Director, 1836-44.
Joshua P. Blanchard, Boston. Recording Secretary, 1840-41; Treasurer and General Agt., 1841-43, 1844-47; Treasurer and Stationary Agt., 1843-44, Director, 1831-43; Ex. Com., 1837-47, 1849-50; Vice pres., 1847-50, 1856-57.
Prof. George Dana Boardman, D. D., Philadelphia. Director, 1886-92; Vice pres., 1892-1903.
Rev. George N. Boardman, Chicago, Pittsford, Vt. Director, 1871-88; Vice pres., 1886-1912.
Rev. S. W. Boardman, D. D., Middlebury, Vt., Stanhope, N. J., Marysville, Tenn. Director, 1866-70; Vice pres., 1886-93. President Marysville College.
John A. Bolles, Boston. Ex. Com., 1840-41.
George W. Bond, Boston. Ex. Com., 1841-42.
Rev. T. E. Bond, D. D., N. Y. C. Vice pres., 1846-47.
Hon. Charles C. Bonney, Chicago. Vice pres., 1891-1904.
George Herman Borst, Philadelphia. Representative Director, 1915-16.
Rev. George W. Bosworth, Boston. Director, 1853-55; Ex. Com., 1852-55.
Rev. Gilbert Bowles, Tokyo, Japan, Richmond, Ind. Vice pres., 1912-13; Hon. Vice pres., 1913-27.
Luman Boyden, Boston. Ex. Com., 1849-50.
Hon. J. Q. A. Brackett, Arlington, Mass. Vice pres., 1890-91. Governor Mass.
Cephas Brainerd, N. Y. C. Honorary Counsel, 1893-1911.
J. D. Bridge, Boston. Ex. Com., 1849-50.
Raymond L. Bridgman, Auburndale, Mass. Director, 1905-08.
William Brigham, Boston. Director, 1843-44.
Robert S. Brookings, St. Louis. Representative Director, 1913-16.
Rev. Charles Brooks, Boston, Medford, Mass. Director, 1847-71; Ex. Com., 1844-53, 1856-59; Vice pres., 1871-72.
Frederick Brooks, Boston. Director, 1902-11; Ex. Com., 1903-11.
Rev. J. Graham Brooks, Brockton, Mass. Director, 1889-90.
Phillips Brooks, D. D., Boston. Vice pres., 1888-93.

S. P. Brooks, Waco, Texas. Vice pres., 1908-13; Hon. Vice pres., 1913-16.
President Baylor University.
Nachob Broughton, Jr., Boston. Recording Secretary and Treasurer, Jan. to
July, 1871.
Dean Charles R. Brown, New Haven. Vice pres., 1911-13; Hon. Vice pres.,
1913-27.
Hon. Elmer Ellsworth Brown, Washington, N. Y. C. Vice pres., 1909-13; Hon.
Vice pres., 1913- . U. S. Commissioner of Education, President N. Y.
University.
Moses Brown, Providence. Director, 1828-36.
Nicholas I. Brown, Providence. Director, 1828-35. Founder Brown University.
Philip Marshall Brown, Princeton, N. J. Director, 1827-28.
Dr. S. W. Brown, Hartford, Conn. Director, 1835-37.
Rev. Sidi H. Brown, Columbia, S. C. Director, 1870-92; Vice pres., 1892-1901.
Dr. Sylvanus Brown, Boston. Director, 1836-37.
William C. Brown, Boston. Recording Secretary, 1847-70; Treasurer, 1870-71.
A. B. Browne, Washington. Director, 1911-12; Director at Large, 1912-15.
Hon. Felix R. Brunot, Pittsburgh. Vice pres., 1872-98.
Hon. Thomas B. Bryan, Chicago. Vice pres., 1891-1905.
Hon. William Jennings Bryan, Washington, Lincoln, Neb., Miami, Florida.
Vice pres., 1913-24.
Pres. William Lowe Bryan, Bloomington, Ind. Hon. Vice pres., 1914-24.
W. H. H. Bryant, Boston. Director, 1907-11; Ex. Com., 1908-11.
Hon. William I. Buchanan, Buffalo. Vice pres., 1904-09.
Judge Thomas Burke, Seattle, Wash. Hon. Vice pres., 1913-18.
George Burnham, Philadelphia. Representative Director, 1915-16; Director,
1916-17; Hon. Vice pres., 1919-27.
Rev. Everett Burr, D. D., Newton Center, Mass. Vice pres., 1900-07.
Elihu Burritt, New Britain, Conn. Ex. Com., 1845-47; Vice pres., 1869-79.
Hon. Theodore E. Burton, Cleveland. Vice pres., 1907-11, 1916-25; President
1911-16, 1924- ; M. C. U. S. S.
Rev. George Bush, D. D., Boston. Director, 1832-36; Corresponding Secretary,
1834-35.
Rev. S. C. Bushnell, Arlington, Mass. Ex. Com., 1890-92; Director, 1892-1912.
Hon. William A. Butler, N. Y. C. Honorary Counsel, 1892-1903; Vice pres.,
1892-1903.
Hezekiah Butterworth, Boston. Director, 1894-99; Vice pres., 1899-1906.
Hon. S. H. M. Byers, St. Gall, Switzerland. Vice Pres., 1893-94.
Arthur Deerin Call, Hartford, Conn., Washington. Vice pres., 1910-12; Repre-
sentative Director, 1912-13; Director at Large, 1913-16; Executive Director,
1913-16; Acting Secretary, 1915-16; Secretary and Editor, 1916 to date;
Director, 1910-12.
Bishop J. P. Campbell, Philadelphia. Director, 1886-87.
Rev. W. A. Campbell, D. D., Richmond, Va. Vice pres., 1891-97.
Philemon Canfield, Hartford, Conn. Director, 1835-37.
Rev. Peter Canouse, Newark, N. J. Director, 1836-37.
Hon. Samuel B. Capen, Boston. Director, 1896-97; Vice pres., 1897-1912;
Representative Director, 1912-14.
Andrew Carnegie, N. Y. C. Vice pres., 1908-19.
Rev. D. L. Carroll, Brooklyn. Director, 1830-35.
Joseph Cartland, Newburyport, Mass. Director, 1890-91; Ex. Com., 1891-92.
Mathew Cary, Philadelphia. Director, 1830-35.
Julius Catlin, Hartford, Conn. Director, 1835-37.
Hon. Jonathan Chace, Providence. Vice pres., 1890-1912.
Pres. Paul A. Chadbourne, Williamstown, Mass. Vice pres., 1876-85.
H. B. Chamberlain, Denver, Col. Vice pres., 1889-98.
Joseph R. Chandler, Philadelphia. Director, 1829-44.
Walter Channing, M. D., Boston. Ex. Com., 1841-47, 1849-50.
William E. Channing, D. D., Boston. Vice pres., 1839-43.
Rev. J. K. Chase, Holden, Rowley, Mass. Ex. Com., 1878-82.

Leverett M. Chase, Roxbury, Mass. Director, 1900-01; Ex. Com., 1900-01.

Rev. Ebenezer Cheever, Newark, N. J. Director, 1836-37.

W. W. Chester, N. Y. C. Director, 1828-35.

Rev. John W. Chickering, Brunswick, Me. Director, 1835-87.

George W. Chipman, Boston. Ex. Com., 1884-85.

R. M. Chipman, N. Y. C. Corresponding Secretary, 1833-34; Director, 1835-37.

Mrs. E. A. Christ, Orlando, Fla. Director, 1918-19.

Hon. William Claflin, Boston. Vice pres., 1872-81. Governor Mass.

Rev. Francis E. Clark, South Boston. Director, 1886-88; Vice pres., 1888-90, 1910-27.

Rev. Frank G. Clark, Gloucester, North Woburn, West Medford, Mass., Plymouth, N. H. Director, 1885-96; Vice pres., 1896-1910.

Hon. S. Reuben Clark, Jr., Washington. Representative Director, 1913-16.

Rev. Dorus Clarke, D. D., Boston. Vice pres. 1872-84; Ex. Com., 1875-82.

Rev. Rufus W. Clarke, Boston. Director, 1852-57; Ex. Com., 1852-57.

Dr. Philander P. Claxton, Washington, Univ. of Ala., Tulsa, Okla. Ex. Com., 1917-24; Hon. Vice pres., 1914-16; Director 1924- .

Dr. B. S. Cleaveland, Detroit. Director, 1836-44.

Edward H. Clement, Boston, Cambridge, Brookline, Mass. Vice pres., 1895-1909; Director 1908-11.

Charles D. Cleveland, LL. D., Philadelphia. Vice pres., 1863-70.

Dr. Stephen B. Cleaveland, Cincinnati. Director, 1828-30.

Thomas Cock, M. D., N. Y. C. Director, 1835-43; Vice pres., 1843-44.

Rev. Joseph S. Cogswell, Windham, N. H., Portland, Standish, Me., Ashburnham, Mass., Walpole, N. H., South Windham, Dummerston, Vt., Colchester, Conn. Director, 1885-92; Vice pres., 1892-1911.

Rev. Charles F. Cole, Jamaica Plain. Director, 1902-11; Ex. Com., 1903-05; Vice pres., 1911-13; Hon. Vice pres., 1914-19.

Rev. D. S. Coles, M. D., East Saugus, Wakefield, Mass. Ex. Com., 1882-91; Director, 1891-92; Vice pres., 1892-1911.

Isaac Collins, Philadelphia. Vice pres., 1839-64.

Henry Colman, Boston. Ex. Com., 1841-42.

Rev. J. B. Cone, Rancho, Texas. Director, 1871-72.

Rev. Salmon Cone, Colchester, Conn. Director, 1829-35.

J. W. Converse, Boston. Director, 1877-87.

Rev. Joseph Cook, Boston. Director, 1876-87, 1892-93; Vice pres., 1891-1901.

Jay Cooke, Philadelphia. Director 1872-75.

Oliver D. Cooke, Hartford, Conn. Director, 1828-33.

T. B. Cooledge, Lawrence, West Medford, North Woburn, Mass. Director, 1871-92; Vice pres., 1892-95.

Hon. Peter Cooper, N. Y. C. Vice pres., 1875-83.

William Knowles Cooper, Washington. Representative Director, 1912-16; Ex. Com., 1917-22, Director, 1916-17.

Melvin Copeland, Hartford, Conn. Director, 1835-38; Ex. Com., 1835-37.

Joseph A. Copp, D. D., Chelsea, Mass. Ex. Com., 1860-70; Director, 1861-70; Vice pres., 1865-66.

William M. Cornell, D. D., LL. D., Boston. Director, 1889-90; Ex. Com., 1875-89; Vice pres., 1890-91.

Jasper Corning, Charleston, S. C., Philadelphia. Director 1829-37.

Senora Angela O. C. de Costa, Buenos Aires, Brussels. Vice pres., 1907-13; Hon. Vice pres., 1913-20; 1922-23.

Samuel E. Coues, Portsmouth, N. H. Vice pres., 1839-41, 1847-54; President, 1841-47.

John M. Crawford, Parkersburg, W. Va. Director, 1927- .

John B. Crenshaw, Richmond, Va. Vice pres., 1886-90.

George Cromwell, Brooklyn. Director, 1883-92; Vice pres., 1892-1911.

Rev. Alpheus Crosby, Boston, Salem, Mass. Director, 1856-74; Ex. Com., 1870-1874.

William B. Crosby, N. Y. C. Vice pres., 1853-65.

George L. Crosman, Portland, Me. Vice pres., 1912-13; Hon. Vice pres., 1913-14; Representative Director, 1914-16; Director, 1916-17.

Rev. William Crowell, Boston. Director, 1847-49; Ex. Com., 1839-49.

Dr. Edward Cummings, Boston. Director, 1918-19.

George Cummings, Boston. Ex. Com., 1872-75.

Frederic Cunningham, Boston. Director, 1904-10; Ex. Com., 1905-10.

Gov. John C. Cutler, Salt Lake City. Vice pres., 1909-12.

Rev. Levi Cutter, Portland, Me. Vice pres., 1839-49.

Charles W. Daniel, Atlanta, Ga. Hon. Vice pres., 1918-21.

Bishop Darlington, Harrisburg, Pa. Hon Vice pres., 1923-27.

Rev. Davis, Philadelphia, Director, 1836-37.

Rev. Gustavus F. Davis, D. D., Hartford, Conn. Director, 1835-37; Ex. Com., 1836-37.

Mrs. Mattie B. Davis, Orlando, Fla., Representative Director, 1914-16.

William Dawes, Oberlin, Ohio. Vice pres., 1843-44.

Nathaniel Dawson, Boston, Director, 1838-39.

Rev. G. L. Demarest, D. D., Manchester, N. H. Vice pres., 1894-1910.

Rev. L. D. Dewey, N. Y. C. Recording and Domestic Secretary, 1830-31; Recording Secretary, 1831-35; Director, 1830-36.

Rev. Thomas De Witt, D. D., N. Y. C. Vice pres., 1846-53. Graduate Union College and Theological Seminary, Dutch Reformed Church.

Tyson S. Dines, Denver, Director, 1927-.

David L. Dodge, N. Y. C. Director, 1828-36; Ex. Com., 1829-35; Treasurer, 1829-1830.

Hon. William E. Dodge, N. Y. C. Vice pres., 1873-83.

Rev. Daniel Dorchester, Washington, Director, 1889-90.

Hon. Frederick Douglas, Washington. Vice pres., 1886-95.

Mrs. Elizabeth Dow, Brookline, Mass. Vice pres., 1892-1902.

Thomas Drown, Boston. Recording Secretary, 1842-44; Ex. Com., 1841-44, 1845-47; Director, 1844-45.

Hon. J. H. Drummond, Portland, Me. Vice pres., 1884-89.

Cornelius T. Dunham, Dorchester, Mass. Recording Secretary, 1882-84; Ex. Com., 1886-92; Director, 1892-96.

Rev. Howard C. Dunham, Winthrop, Mass. Office Agent, 1870-71; Acting Corresponding Secretary and Recording Secretary, 1880-83; Corresponding Secretary, 1882-84; Recording Secretary, 1872-83; Recording Secretary and Office Agent, 1884-86; Director, 1886-91; Vice pres., 1891-1906.

Rev. J. P. Durbin, D. D., N. Y. C. Vice pres., 1852-53.

Rev. Calvin Durfee, South Dedham, Mass., Director, 1844-52.

Prof. Samuel T. Dutton, N. Y. C. Director N. Y.- N. J. Department, 1912-17; Representative Director, 1912-16; Ex. Com., 1916-18; Director, 1911-17. Columbia University.

Henry Dwight, Geneva, N. Y. Vice pres., 1846-58.

Rev. Louis Dwight, Boston. Director, 1843-44; Ex. Com., 1844-45.

Rev. L. R. Eastman, Boston. Director, 1865-71; Ex. Com., 1865-71; Vice pres. 1876-80.

Hon. Dorman B. Eaton, N. Y. C. Honorary Counsel, 1892-1900; Vice pres., 1892-1900.

Anna B. Eckstein, Boston. Director, 1905-11.

Rev. Ansel D. Eddy, Newark, N. J. Director, 1836-44.

Rev. David H. Ela, D. D., Boston, Chelsea, Cambridgeport, Natick, Hudson, Mass. Ex. Com., 1886-94; Director, 1892-1902.

Hon. Samuel J. Elder, Boston. Representative Director, 1914-16; Director, 1916-17.

F. M. Ellis, D. D. Boston, Baltimore. Director, 1883-90.

Hon. William W. Ellsworth, Hartford, Conn. Director, 1835-38; Ex. Com., 1835-1837; Vice pres., 1839-55.

Rev. Brown Emerson, D. D., Salem, Mass. Director, 1837-47.

Ralph Emerson, D. D., Andover, Mass. Director, 1834-36, 1837-44; Ex. Com., 1837-38. Graduate Yale, Andover. Prof. Andover.

S. Hopkins Emery, D. D., Taunton, Mass., Bridgeport, Conn. Assistant Secretary, 1871-72; Director, 1872-93; Vice pres., 1893-1901.
Samuel Emlen, Philadelphia. Vice pres., 1886-87.
Hon. John J. Esch, Washington, Director, 1827-. M. C. I. C. C. Commissioner.
Hon. Charles W. Fairbanks, Indianapolis. Hon. Vice pres., 1914-18. Vice Pres. United States.
J. P. Fairbanks, St. Johnsbury, Vt. Vice pres., 1855.
Allen Farquhar, Sandy Springs, Md. Ex. Com., 1916-20.
James E. Farwell, Boston. Ex. Com., 1875-92; Director, 1892-96.
W. H. P. Faunce, Providence. Hon. Vice pres., 1919-. Pres. Brown Univ.
Francis Fellowes, Hartford, Conn. Director, 1835-38; Ex. Com., 1835-37; Recording Secretary, 1835-37.
Hon. Samuel Fessenden, LL. D., Portland, Me. Vice pres., 1849-69. Graduate Dartmouth. Member Mass. legislature, Maine legislature; probate judge.
Hon. David Dudley Field, N. Y. C. Vice pres., 1890-94.
John Field, Boston, Director, 1847-77; Ex. Com., 1847-70, 1875-76; Treasurer, 1847-70.
J. Worcester Field, Boston. Director, 1877-89.
George A. Finch, Washington, Ex. Com., 1920-22; Hon. Vice pres., 1923-27.
Everett O. Fisk, Boston. Director, 1894-96; Vice pres., 1896-1913; Hon. Vice pres., 1924-27.
Hon. Richard Fletcher, Boston. Vice pres., 1839-44.
B. O. Flower, Brookline, Mass. Vice pres., 1895-1911.
George E. Fogg, Portland, Maine. Director, 1918-19.
Rev. Henry W. Foote, Boston. Director, 1877-85.
Mrs. J. Malcolm Forbes, Milton, Mass. Vice pres., 1911-13; Hon. Vice pres., 1913-23; Representative Director, 1914-16; Director, 1908-17.
D. S. Ford, Boston. Vice pres., 1889-90; Director, 1890-91.
John H. De Forest, D. D., Sendai, Japan. Vice pres., 1908-11.
Hon. John B. Foster, Bangor, Maine. Vice pres., 1884-1908.
Hon. John W. Foster, Washington. Vice pres., 1908-13; Hon. Vice pres., 1913-1918.
Bishop R. S. Foster, Boston. Vice pres., 1877-90.
Rev. Orin Fowler, Plainfield, Conn., Fall River, Mass. Director, 1829-36.
Rev. Alexander G. Fraser, N. Y. C. Recording Secretary, 1829-30; Corresponding Secretary Southwest District, 1829-30; Director, 1829-34; Ex. Com., 1829-30.
Hon. Theodore Frelinghuysen, Newark, N. J. Director, 1836-37; Vice pres., 1839-62; President, 1846-47.
Thomas Gaffield, Boston. Director, 1855-56, 1863-89, 1891-92; Ex. Com., 1855-56, 1870-71, 1889-91; Vice pres., 1892-1901.
Rev. T. H. Gallaudet, Hartford, Conn. Director, 1833-36; Ex. Com., 1835-37; Corresponding Secretary, 1835-37.
Rev. Ezra S. Gannett, D. D., Boston. Director, 1839-47; Ex. Com., 1839-44.
Pres. Harry A. Garfield, Williamstown, Mass. Director, 1927-. President Williams.
Philip C. Garrett, Philadelphia. Vice pres., 1878-1906. U. S. Indian Commissioner.
Merrill E. Gates, LL. D., Amherst, Mass., Washington. Vice pres., 1896-1913; Hon. Vice pres., 1913-14. President Amherst.
William P. Gest, Philadelphia. Hon. Vice pres., 1919-.
Rev. H. C. Gibbons, Philadelphia. Vice pres., 1887-88.
P. R. Gifford, Providence. Ex. Com., 1890-91.
Lyman Gilbert, West Newton, Mass. Ex. Com., 1847-50; Director, 1848-50.
Rev. Simeon Gilbert, D. D. Chicago. Vice pres., 1886-88.
Timothy Gilbert, Boston. Director, 1854-60, 1862-66.
F. B. Gilman, Cambridge. Director, 1884-85; Ex. Com., 1885-87; Auditor, 1885-1890.
John T. Gilman, Exeter, N. H. Director, 1828-29. Governor, N. H.
P. S. Gilmore, Boston. Ex. Com., 1872-73.

Belton Gilreath, Birmingham, Ala. Vice pres., 1908-13.
Edwin Ginn, Boston. Director, 1901-03; Vice pres., 1903-13; Hon. Vice pres., 1913-14.
Hon. Charles W. Goddard, Portland, Me. Director, 1872-85; Vice pres., 1885-1889. Judge.
Leroy A. Goddard, Chicago. Director, 1911-12; Representative Director, 1912-14.
J. Going, D. D., N. Y. C., Granville, Ohio. Director, 1834-36, 1837-44.
Wilbur F. Gordy, Hartford, Conn. Representative Director, 1914-16; Director, 1916-19.
John Gove, Boston, Director, 1854-66.
Moses Grant, Boston. Director, 1844-54; Ex. Com., 1842-44.
Frederick T. Gray, Boston, Ex. Com., 1841-42.
Maria Freeman Gray, Oakland, Cal. Vice pres., 1902-12.
Samuel Greele, Boston. Vice pres., 1843-62; Ex. Com., 1853-62.
Dr. Thomas Edward Green, Chicago. Hon. Vice pres., 1914-19; Ex. Com., 1918- ; Director, 1924-.
W. A. Greene, Malden, Mass. Vice pres., 1888-89.
William P. Greene, Norwich, Conn. Director, 1828-36.
Benjamin Greenleaf, Bradford, Mass. Director, 1852-65; Ex. Com., 1850-65.
Simon Greenleaf, LL. D., Portland, Me., Cambridge, Mass. Director, 1828-36; Vice pres., 1839-53. Author of Greenleaf's Arithmetics.
Henry M. Greenough, Boston. Ex. Com., 1886-87.
Rev. David Gregg, Boston. Ex Com., 1888-90; Vice pres., 1890-91.
Thomas S. Grimke, Charleston, S. C. Director, 1829-30, 1832-34. Judge.
John Griscom, LL. D., Providence. N. Y. C. Director, 1829-36.
Dr. Sidney L. Gulick, N. Y. C. Representative Director, 1915-16; Director, 1916-19.
William H. V. Hackett, Portsmouth, N. H. Director, 1843-48.
Hiram Hadley, Chicago. Director, 1871-76.
Hiram Hadley, Mesilla Park, N. Mex. Hon. Vice pres., 1913-23.
Rev. Edward Everett Hale, D. D., Roxbury. Vice pres., 1873-92, 1893-1909; Director, 1892-93.
Hon. George S. Hale, Boston. Honorary Counsel, 1892-97; Director, 1892-93.
Dr. James J. Hall, Atlanta, Ga. Representative Director, 1914-16; Director, 1916-19; Director South Atlantic States Department, 1912-18.
Rev. John Hall, D. D., N. Y. C. Vice pres., 1893-94.
Andrew Halliburton, Portsmouth, N. H. Director, 1831-36; Vice pres., 1839-44.
Hon. Alpheus Hardy, Boston. Director, 1872-88.
Hon. Thomas N. Hart, Boston. Vice pres., 1891-1905.
A. H. Haskell, Boston. Director, 1862-63.
Walter Hastings, Boston. Ex. Com., 1872-75.
Bishop Gilbert Haven, D. D., Boston. Director, 1871-73.
Hon. H. P. Haven, New London, Conn. Director, 1875-76.
Hon. Nathaniel A. Haven, Portsmouth, N. H. Director, 1828-31.
Samuel Haven, Dedham, Roxbury, Mass. Vice pres., 1843-48.
Rev. D. C. Haynes, Boston. Financial Secretary, 1873-74.
Rev. J. Emory Haynes, Boston. Ex. Com., 1888-89.
Isaac P. Hazard, Newport, R. I. Director, 1876-79.
Hon. Rowland Hazard, Providence. Vice pres., 1890-99.
Dwight B. Heard, Phoenix, Ariz. Director, 1927- .
D. C. Heath, Boston. Director, 1892-93; Auditor, 1880-96.
John Hemmenway, Minneapolis. Vice pres., 1886-99.
Alexander Henry, Philadelphia. Director, 1828-36.
Rev. C. S. Henry, Hartford, Conn. Director, 1835-37.
Hon. Walter L. Hensley, Washington, Farmington, Iowa. Director, 1916-17; Ex. Com., 1916-21.
Rev. S. E. Herrick, Boston. Ex. Com., 1873-75..
Scott F. Hershey, LL. D., Boston, Newtonville, Hyde Park, Mass., Wooster,

Ohio, Newcastle, Pa., Angola, Ind. Director, 1895-1905; Ex. Com., 1896-1905; Vice pres., 1905-13; Hon. Vice pres., 1913-16.

L. P. Hickok, D. D., LL. D., Schenectady, N. Y., Amherst, Mass. Vice pres., 1866-71.

Daniel Hill, Richmond, Ind. Vice pres., 1886-90.

Hon. David Jayne Hill, Washington. Director, 1924- ; Vice pres., 1924-, Ex. Com., 1927-.

Rev. Thomas Hill, D. D., Portland, Me. Director, 1889-92.

Hon. David K. Hitchcock, Newton, Mass. Director, 1873-77, 1892-94; Ex. Com., 1879-92; Vice pres., 1894-96.

Hon. E. R. Hoar, Concord, Mass. Vice pres., 1872-73.

Pres. L. L. Hobbes, Guilford College, N. C. Representative Director, 1914-16. Director, 1916-17.

Prof. B. C. Hobbs, Indianapolis. Director, 1870-72.

Rev. Moses D. Hoge, Richmond, Va. Vice pres., 1890-91.

Frank P. Holland, Dallas, Tex. Hon. Vice pres., 1918-23.

Rev. Frederick W. Holland, Rochester, N. Y. Director, 1843-47; Ex. Com., 1849-50.

Hamilton Holt, N. Y. C. Director, 1911-12.

Rev. Mark Hopkins, D. D., LL. D. Williamstown, Mass. Vice pres., 1872-87.

Bishop E. E. Hoss, D. D., Nashville, Tenn., Dallas, Texas, Citra, Fla. Vice pres., 1903-13; Hon. Vice pres. 1913-18.

George W. Hoss, LL. D., Wichita, Kansas. Vice pres., 1903-07.

Hon. H. O. Houghton, Cambridge, Mass. Director, 1890-92; Vice pres., 1892-1906.

Clarence H. Howard, St. Louis. Director, 1927-28.

Prof. George E. Howard, Lincoln, Neb. Hon. Vice pres., 1913-14.

Rev. Rowland B. Howard, Boston. Corresponding Secretary, 1884-92.

Isaac R. Howe, Haverhill, Mass. Director, 1835-37, 1843-44.

Mrs. Julia Ward Howe, Boston. Ex. Com., 1871-72; Director, 1889-1902; Vice pres., 1902-11.

H. C. Howells, Putnam, Ohio. Director, 1835-37.

Hon. John W. Hoyt, Washington. Vice pres., 1894-1912.

William G. Hubbard, New Vienna, Delaware, Columbus, Cleveland, Zanesville, Ohio, Lansing, Mich., Des Moines, Cedar Rapids, Iowa, Goldsboro, N. C., Sandy Lake, Pa. Director, 1870-88; Vice pres., 1888-1913; Hon. Vice pres., 1913-16.

Hon. Charles E. Hughes, N. Y. C. Hon. Vice pres., 1919-23.

Prof. William I. Hull, Swarthmore, Pa. Director, 1911-17; Representative Director, 1912-14; Ex. Com., 1916-17.

Rev. Heman Humphrey, D. D., Amherst. Director, 1836-37.

Rev. F. D. Huntingdon, Cambridge, Mass. Director, 1853-65; Ex. Com., 1853-1856.

Dr. Charles Cheney Hyde, Washington, N. Y. C. Ex. Com., 1921-23; Hon. Vice pres. 1823. Prof. Columbia University.

Charles H. Hyde, Pierre, S. Dak. Director, 1927-28.

J. F. C. Hyde, Newton, Mass. Vice pres., 1880-87.

E. W. Jackson, Boston. Ex. Com., 1845-47, 1849-50.

Galen James, Boston. Director, 1857-63.

Dr. William F. Jarvis, Waltham, Mass. Auditor, 1900-12.

Hon. John Jay, N. Y. C. Vice pres., 1859-94. Minister to Austria-Hungary.

Hon. William Jay, Bedford, N. Y. Vice pres., 1842-48; President, 1848-58.

Rev. Charles E. Jefferson, N. Y. C. Vice pres., 1899-1913; Hon. Vice pres., 1913-1927.

William Jenkins, Providence. Vice pres., 1839-44.

Rev. William Jenks, D. D., Boston. Director, 1836-67; Vice pres., 1864-66. Graduate Harvard. Prof. Bowdoin.

Hon. Reverdy Johnson, Baltimore. Vice pres., 1872-76.

Augustine Jones, Providence, Newton Highlands. Ex. Com., 1871, 1891-92; Director, 1892-1902, 1908-11; Vice pres., 1902-09.

Dr. Jenkin Lloyd Jones, Chicago. Hon. Vice pres., 1913-16.

Samuel M. Jones, Toledo, Ohio. Vice pres., 1903-05.
President David Starr Jordan, Stanford Univ., Cal. Vice pres., 1906-13; Hon. Vice pres., 1913-27.
George H. Judd, Washington. Hon. Vice pres., 1924- .
Rev. D. X. Junkin, Newcastle, Pa. Vice pres. 1871-72.
Rev. F. H. Kasson, Boston. Vice pres., 1887-88.
Hon. Sumner I. Kimball, Washington. Vice pres., 1890-1916.
Tuthill King, Chicago. Vice pres., 1871-86.
Prof. George W. Kirchwey, N. Y. C. Director at Large, 1912-16; President, 1916-17. Prof. Columbia Law School.
B. F. Knowles, Providence, Ex. Com., 1887-90.
William Ladd, Minot, Me. Secretary, 1828-29; Corresponding Secretary for Eastern District and Editor, 1829-30; Secretary for Foreign Correspondence and Editor, 1830-31. General Secretary, 1831-32; General Agent, 1832-37. President and General Agent 1837-41; Director, 1828-36.
Rev. Henry Lambert, West Newton, Mass. Vice pres., 1896-1900.
Rev. William Lamson, D. D., Brookline, Mass. Director, 1871-72.
Rev. D. C. Lansing, D. D., N. Y. C. Director, 1833-36.
L. B. Larkin, Wrentham, Mass. Director, 1843-44.
Hon. Amos A. Lawrence, Boston. Vice pres., 1877-87.
Hon. Edward Lawrence, Charlestown, Mass. Director, 1872-89.
Edward A. Lawrence, D. D., Marblehead, Mass. Director, 1881-84; Ex. Com., 1875-84.
Bishop William Lawrence, Cambridge, Mass. Vice pres., 1894-1913; Hon. Vice pres. 1913-27.
Rev. B. F. Leavitt, Melrose Highlands, Belmont, Mass. Director, 1896-1911.
Rev. H. H. Leavitt, North Andover, Mass. Director, 1856-85; Ex. Com., 1864-1866.
James T. Leavitt, Boston. Director, 1860-63.
Joseph Lee, Boston. Hon. Vice pres., 1920-27.
Eugene Levering, Baltimore. Director at Large, 1912-16; Ex. Com., 1911-17; Director, 1911-12.
William Mather Lewis, Washington. Director, 1927- .
Hon. Heman Lincoln, Boston. Director, 1829-35.
Joshua Lindley, Chatham Co., N. C. Director, 1830-34.
Daniel C. Linscott, Boston. Ex. Com., 1889-90.
Mary A. Livermore, Melrose, Mass. Vice pres., 1894-1905.
Louis P. Lochner, Chicago. Representative Director, 1914-16; Director Central West Department, 1914-16.
Hon. Stephen Longfellow, Portland, Me. Director, 1833-44. M. C.
Hon. J. Loomis, Montpelier, Vt. Vice pres., 1839-44.
Rev. Amasa Lord, Elgin, Ill. Director, 1866-72; Corresponding Secretary and Assistant Treasurer, 1870-71; Western Secretary, 1871-72; Vice pres., 1875-1878.
Eleazer Lord, N. Y. C. Director, 1828-35.
John Lord, South Berwick, Me. Director, 1838-39. Graduate Dartmouth, Andover. Historian.
Rev. Nathan Lord, D. D. Hanover, N. H. Director, 1835-39. President Dartmouth.
Samuel Lord, Portsmouth, N. H. Director, 1837-44.
Ellis Gray Loring, Boston. Director, 1839-54; Ex. Com., 1841-42.
Rev. Charles Lowell, D. D., Boston. Director, 1831-36; Vice pres., 1839-61.
Mrs. Charles Russell Lowell, N. Y. C. Vice pres., 1905-06.
Isaac S. Loyd, Philadelphia. Vice pres., 1839-43.
William H. Luden, Reading, Pa. Hon. Vice pres., 1920-27.
Joseph H. Lumpkin, Lexington, Ga. Vice pres., 1844-47.
Dr. Frederick Lynch, N. Y. C. Representative Director, 1915-16; Director, 1916-19.
George F. Magoun, D. D., Grinnell, Iowa. Vice pres., 1886-96. President Grinnell College.

Rev. Charles H. Malcolm, D. D. Corresponding Secretary, 1876-80.
Rev. Howard Malcolm, D. D., LL. D., Boston, Georgetown, Ky., Philadelphia, Lewisburg. Director, 1832-43; Ex. Com., 1839-40; Vice pres., 1873-74; President, 1861-73; Honorary President, 1874-79.
Rev. J. M. Manning, D. D., Boston. Director, 1875-83.
Theodore Marburg, Baltimore. Vice pres., 1910-12; Representative Director, 1912-16; Director, 1916-17.
Prof. G. N. Marden, Colorado Springs, Col. Vice pres., 1884-90.
Hon. Nathan Matthews, Jr., Boston. Vice pres., 1891-1905.
A. Maxwell, Boston. Director, 1888-89.
Rev. Samuel J. May, Brooklyn, Syracuse, N. Y., Scituate, Lexington, Mass. Director, 1834-47. Vice pres., 1863-66.
Judge May, Lewiston, Me. Director, 1866-75.
Hon. Samuel W. McCall, Washington, Winchester, Mass. Director, 1911-12; Ex. Com., 1911-14; Director at Large, 1912-13; Hon. Vice pres., 1913-24.
P. McGrath, Quincy, Mass. Director, 1876-95.
William B. McKinley, Washington. Ex. Com., 1924-27; Director, 1924-27; Vice pres., 1924-27.
Felix M. McWhirter, Indianapolis. Director, 1927-28.
Rev. Asa Mead, Brunswick, Gorham, Me., East Hartford, Conn. Director, 1829-32.
Edwin D. Mead, Boston. Vice pres., 1900-13; Representative Director, 1913-16.
Mrs. Lucia Ames Mead, Boston. Director, 1899-1911; Vice pres., 1911-12.
Hon. E. T. Meredith, Des Moines, Iowa. Director, 1927- .
Hon. J. Warren Merrill, Cambridge, Mass. Vice pres., 1877-81.
Rev. T. A. Merrill, Middlebury, Vt. Vice pres., 1849-55.
Rev. W. E. Merriman, D. D., Somerville, Mass. Vice pres., 1885-87.
Rev. James B. Miles, Boston. Corresponding Secretary and Assistant Treasurer, 1871-76.
Rev. Alonzo A. Miner, D. D., Boston. Ex. Com., 1886-96; Director, 1892-95. President Tufts.
S. C. Mitchell, LL. D., Columbia, S. C., Richmond, Va., Newark, Del. Vice pres., 1911-13; Hon. Vice pres., 1913-21. President University of S. C.
Hon. Frank W. Mondell, Washington. Ex. Com., 1918- ; Director, 1927-28.
Hon. Andrew J. Montague, Richmond, Va. Ex. Com., 1920-21, 1924-27; President, 1920-24; Director, 1924-27. M. C.
Prof. John Bassett Moore, N. Y. C., Washington. Vice pres., 1907-13; Hon. Vice pres., 1913-21. Prof. Columbia University.
J. K. Moore, N. Y. C. Director, 1834-36; Treasurer, 1834-35.
Mrs. Philip N. Moore, St. Louis. Hon. Vice pres., 1913-24; Director, 1924-25.
Rev. Walter A. Morgan, Washington. Ex. Com., 1923-28; Director, 1924- .
George Maurice Morris, Washington. Director, 1924- . Ex. Com., 1923- .
Henry C. Morris, Chicago. Director, 1916-17, 1918-19, 1924- ; Ex. Com., 1923- .
Samuel Morris, Philadelphia. Vice pres., 1886-90.
Bishop Thomas A. Morris, Springfield, Ohio. Vice pres., 1870-75.
Hon. Edwin P. Morrow, Ky. Director, 1827- .
A. S. Morse, Charlestown, Mass. Director, 1872-81.
Hon. Robert M. Morse, Brookline, Mass. Honorary Counsel, 1908-12.
Hon. Marcus P. Morton, Boston. Vice pres., 1884-85.
William A. Mowry, Ph. D., LL. D., Hyde Park, Salem, Mass. Ex. Com., 1886-1911; Director, 1892-1911; Vice pres., 1911-13; Hon. Vice pres., 1913-16.
Rev. Philip S. Moxom, D. D., Boston, Brookline, Springfield, Mass. Ex. Com., 1891-94; Director, 1893-96; Vice pres., 1896-13; Hon. Vice pres., 1913-24; Director, 1910-11.
Rev. Nathan Munroe, West Bradford, Mass. Director, 1843-44.
Robert I. Murray, N. Y. C. Vice pres., 1888-90.
R. D. Mussey, M. D., Cincinnati. Vice pres., 1839-44.
Ernest Fox Nichols, Hanover, N. H. Vice pres., 1912-13; Hon. Vice pres., 1913-1914. President Dartmouth College.

S. Edgar Nicholson, Washington. Director, 1911-12; Director at Large, 1912-1915.
William Nicholson, M. D., Lawrence, Kansas. Director, 1870-72.
George B. Norman, Newport, R. I. Director, 1878-82.
Rev. Heman Norton, N. Y. C. Director, 1833-36.
Edward Noyes, Boston. Director, 1837-40; Recording Secretary, 1839-40; Ex. Com., 1837-40.
Rev. S. Olin, D. D., Middletown, Conn. Vice pres., 1847-52. President Wesleyan.
Rev. John W. Olmstead, D. D., Boston. Vice pres., 1872-73, 1877-91; Ex. Com., 1873-77. Editor Watchman.
John Owen, Cambridge, Mass. Ex. Com., 1837-44; Director, 1837-43.
Rev. Charles Packard, Cambridge, Mass. Director, 1854-55.
Hon. Robert Treat Paine, Waltham, Mass. Vice pres., 1890-91; President, 1891-1910.
Robert Treat Paine, Boston, Representative Director, 1914-16.
Mrs. Alice Freeman Palmer, Cambridge, Mass. Director, 1899-1900.
Daniel Palmer, Charlestown, Mass. Director, 1872-75.
Hon. Julius A. Palmer, Boston. Director, 1856-62.
William J. Palmer, Colorado Springs. Vice pres., 1902-03.
Rev. Joseph W. Parker, D. D., Cambridge, Newton, Mass. Ex. Com., 1839-70; Director, 1847-70; Vice pres., 1869-72.
Rev. Nathan Parker, D. D., Portsmouth, N. H. Director, 1829-34.
Rev. David Patten, D. D., Boston. Treasurer, 1871-78.
F. M. Patten, Boston. Treasurer, 1879-92.
Rev. James Patterson, Philadelphia. Director, 1835-37.
Rev. Andrew P. Peabody, D. D., LL. D., Portsmouth, N. H., Cambridge, Mass. Director, 1835-43; Vice pres., 1843-76, 1882-93. Editor N. A. Review. Prof. Harvard.
George Foster Peabody, Brooklyn. Vice pres., 1898-1911; Director, 1911-12.
Benjamin D. Peck, Boston, Ex. Com., 1845-47.
Rev. George F. Pentecost, Boston, Ex. Com., 1877-79.
Rev. R. L. R. Perrine, D. D., Auburn, N. Y. Director, 1830-36.
Hon. Amos Perry, Providence, R. I. Vice pres., 1877-1900.
Bliss Perry, Boston. Director, 1905-17. Prof. Harvard.
Anson G. Phelps, N. Y. C. Director, 1828-36; Ex. Com., 1828-35; Vice pres., 1839-53; President, 1847-48.
Rev. Dudley Phelps, Tecumseh, Mich. Director, 1836-37.
Myron Phelps, Lewiston, Ill. Vice pres., 1870-79.
Hon. Jonathan Phillips, Boston. Vice pres., 1839-43.
Hon. S. C. Phillips, Salem, Mass. Vice pres., 1853-58.
Wendell Phillips, Boston. Vice pres., 1881-84.
Henry Pickering, Boston. Director, 1902-08; Ex. Com., 1902-08.
Rev. Bradford K. Pierce, D. D., Boston. Director, 1873-89. Editor Zion's Herald.
Hon. Henry L. Pierce, Boston. Vice pres., 1875-84.
L. H. Pillsbury, Derry, N. H. Vice pres., 1887-1913; Hon. Vice pres., 1913-27.
Rev. Ebenezer Porter, D. D., Andover, Mass. Director, 1829-34. President Andover.
Rockwell Harmon Potter, Hartford, Conn. Ex. Com., 1916-17.
Hon. J. H. Powell, Henderson, Ky. Vice pres., 1900-08.
Lewis C. Pray, Boston. Ex. Com., 1844-47.
Hon. John Prentiss, Keene, N. H. Vice pres., 1864-73.
Elwyn C. Preston, Woburn. Director, 1907-08.
Rev. Israel W. Putman, Portsmouth, N. H. Director, 1829-35.
William L. Putman, Portland, Me. Vice pres., 1889-1913; Hon. Vice pres., 1913-18; Honorary Counsel, 1892-1912. Judge.
Hon. Josiah Quincy, Boston, Quincy. Honorary Counsel, 1892-1912.
Gerard Ralston, Philadelphia. Director, 1828-35.
Jackson H. Ralston, Washington, Palo Alto, Cal. Ex. Com., 1911-24; Director, 1911-12, 1924- ; Director at Large, 1912-16; Vice pres., 1917-.

Arthur Ramsay, Washington, Southern Pines, N. C. Ex. Com., 1917-24; Director, 1924- .
Franklin Rand, Boston. Director, 1856-62.
Robert Rantoul, Beverly, Mass. Vice pres., 1843-59.
Judge Robert F. Raymond, Newton Center, Mass. Director, 1910-12.
Edwin Reed, Cambridge, Mass. Vice pres., 1884-85, 1886-87; Ex. Com., 1885-86.
J. Edgar Rhoads, Wilmington, Del. Ex. Com., 1917-18.
James E. Rhoads, LL. D., Bryn Mawr, Pa. Vice pres., 1893-95.
Hon. Alexander H. Rice, Boston. Vice pres., 1875-85. Governor Mass.
William Rice, Boston. Ex. Com., 1849-50.
Rev. Daniel Richards, Somerville, Mass. Director, 1885-86; Recording Secretary and Office Agent, 1886-90; Office Agent, 1890-91.
Hiram W. Ricker, Poland, Maine. Director 1927-.
Hon. George E. Roberts, Chicago, Washington. Vice pres., 1910-11; Director, 1911-12; Director at Large, 1912-16; Ex. Com., 1911-15.
Thomas A. Robertson, Rockford, Ill. Director, 1886-92; Vice pres., 1892-1902.
Andrew Robeson, New Bedford, Mass. Director, 1837-44.
Samuel Rodman, New Bedford, Mass. Director, 1869-85.
Dean Henry Wade Rogers, New Haven, Conn., N. Y. C. Vice pres., 1910-13; Hon. Vice pres., 1912-27.
Dean William P. Rogers, Cincinnati. Director, 1911-12.
Hon. Elihu Root, N. Y. C. Hon Vice pres., 1923-28.
Robert C. Root, San Francisco, Pacific Coast Agent, 1908-12; Director, Pacific Coast Department, 1912-18; Director, 1918-19.
Prof. J. C. Rostan, N. Y. C. Director, 1831-33; Secretary for Foreign Correspondence, 1831-33.
William Rotche, New Bedford, Mass. Vice pres., 1839-51.
Rodney W. Roundy, Hartford, Conn. Representative Director, 1913-14.
Rev. L. C. Rouse, Grinnell, Iowa. Director, 1866-67.
Prof. Leo S. Rowe, Philadelphia. Representative Director, 1914-15. Professor University of Pennsylvania.
A. C. Russell, Chicago. Director, 1871-72.
Charles H. Russell, Newport, R. I. Vice pres., 1877-82.
Hon. C. T. Russell, Cambridge, Mass. Ex. Com., 1872-76.
Hon. C. T. Russell, Jr., Cambridge, Mass. Vice pres., 1891-1903.
Thomas H. Russell, Boston. Ex. Com., 1871-73; Auditor, 1872-73; Treasurer, 1893-1910.
William W. Russell, N. Y. C. Director, 1828-36.
Hon. Fletcher Ryland, Proctorsville, Vt. Vice pres., 1856-59.
Daniel Safford, Boston. Director, 1843-56.
Hon. Leverett Saltonstall, Brookline, Mass. Vice pres., 1890-91.
M. H. Sargent, Boston. Director, 1875-85.
Rev. James Saul, D. D., Philadelphia. Director, 1886-88.
Edward Watts Saunders, Washington, Richmond, Va. Ex. Com., 1919-22.
Barthold Schlesinger, Brookline, Mass. Director, 1893-1901; Ex. Com., 1894-1901.
Mrs. Frederic Schoff, Philadelphia. Hon. Vice pres. 1913-27.
D. C. Scofield, Elgin, Ill. Vice pres., 1870-75; Director, 1875-77.
Hon. James Brown Scott, Washington. Vice pres., 1908-13; Hon. Vice pres., 1913-.
Sylvester F. Scovel, D. D., Wooster, Ohio. Vice pres., 1904-11. Pres. Wooster University.
Francis B. Sears, Boston. Ex. Com., 1910-11; Treasurer, 1910-11.
Robert Sedgwick, N. Y. C. Director, 1828-36; Ex. Com., 1834-35.
Julius H. Seelye, Amherst, Mass. Vice pres., 1876-90. President Amherst.
Mrs. Mary Wright Sewall, Indianapolis, Allston, Mass. Vice pres., 1899-1912.
Rev. Daniel Sharp, D. D., Boston. Director, 1836-41; Vice pres., 1853-54.
Hon. James Sheafe, Portsmouth, N. H. Director, 1828-30.
Hon. William E. Sheldon, West Newton, Mass. Director, 1887-88, 1892-1900; Ex. Com., 1888-1900; Auditor, 1896-1900.
George Shepard, Bangor, Me. Director, 1866-68.

John Sherman, Washington. Vice pres., 1893-99; Hon. Vice pres., 1899-1901.
U. S. S.
William H. Short, N. Y. C. Representative Director, 1912-16; Director, 1916-17.
F. L. Siddons, Washington. Ex. Com., 1916-21. Justice Supreme Court, D. C.
Bishop Matthew Simpson, Philadelphia. Vice pres., 1876-85. M. E.
Charles Sisson, Providence. Director, 1918-19.
Hon. James L. Slayden, Washington, San Antonio, Texas. Director at Large,
1913-16; Director, 1916-17; Ex. Com., 1914-20; President, 1917-20; Vice pres.,
1920-24.
Hon. Jacob Sleeper, Boston. Vice pres., 1873-77, 1885-89; Ex. Com., 1876-85.
Paul Sleman, Washington. Ex. Com., 1920-25; Director, 1924-25.
W. F. Slocum, Colorado Springs. Hon. Vice pres., 1914-16. President Colorado
College.
Albert K. Smiley, Mohonk Lake. Vice pres., 1907-13.
Rev. Charles B. Smith, West Medford, Mass. Ex. Com., 1885-1902; Director,
1892-1901.

Edwin Burritt Smith, Chicago. Vice pres., 1901-06.
Franklin W. Smith, Boston. Ex. Com., 1877-84.
Frederic A. Smith, Malden, West Medford, Mass. Director, 1890-93, 1900-07.
Hon. Gerritt Smith, Peterborough, N. Y. Vice pres., 1839-75.
George H. Snelling, Boston, Ex. Com., 1841-42.
D. F. Snow, Boston. Treasurer, 1878-79.
Rev. Charles G. Sommers, N. Y. C. Director, 1830-34; Ex. Com., 1830-31.
Rev. Charles Spear, Boston. Director, 1843-44.
Homer B. Sprague, Ph. D. West Newton, Mass. Director, 1903-08; Ex. Com.,
1905-08.

Mrs. Ruth H. Spray, Salida, Col., Vice pres., 1899-1913; Hon. Vice pres., 1914-27.
Gov. William H. Spry, Salt Lake City. Vice pres., 1912-13; Hon. Vice pres.,
1913-14, 1917-18.
John Stafford, Orange Co., N. C. Director, 1829-36.
Theodore Stanfield, N. Y. C. Ex. Com., 1921-; Director, 1924-.
Senator Leland Stanford, Palo Alto, Cal. Vice pres., 1893-94.
Pres. Edmund Stanley, Wichita, Kansas. Hon. Vice pres., 1913-16.
Rev. G. W. Stearns, Acton, Middleboro, Jamaica Plain, Gloucester, Mass. Ex.
Com., 1891-94; Director, 1892-1908.
Rev. William A. Stearns, D. D., LL. D., Amherst, Mass. Vice pres., 1872-76.
**Rev. Rufus P. Stebbins, D. D., Leominster, Boston, Woburn, Cambridge, New-
ton Center, Mass., Ithaca, N. Y. Director, 1837-47, 1857-60; Ex. Com., 1847-
1854, 1882-86; Vice pres., 1871-86. President Meadville Theological School.**
E. B. Stedman, Hartford, Conn. Director, 1835-37.
Thomas Sterling, Washington. Hon. Vice pres., 1923-27. U. S. S.
Abel Stevens, D. D., LL. D., Brooklyn. Director, 1871-90.
Edward Stevens, Columbia, Mo. Hon. Vice pres., 1918-27.
Mrs. L. M. N. Stevens, Portland, Me. Vice pres., 1898-1913; Hon. Vice pres.,
1913-14.

Alvan Stewart, Utica, N. Y. Director, 1834-44; Vice pres., 1844-47.
Rev. W. F. Stewart, Chicago. Director, 1871-72.
J. H. Stickney, Baltimore. Vice pres., 1886-93.
W. C. Stimpson, Boston. Director, 1852-53.
**Rev. Jay T. Stocking, Washington, Upper Montclair, N. J. Ex. Com., 1914- ;
Director, 1924- ; Director at Large, 1914-15.**
Charles Stoddard, Boston. Director, 1837-46.
Lewis T. Stoddard, Boston. Director, 1837-43, 1849-59, 1863-66; Ex. Com.,
1837-59; Recording Secretary, 1841-42.

Solomon Stoddard, Middlebury, Vt. Director, 1837-44.
Rev. A. L. Stone, Boston. Director, 1852-58; Ex. Com., 1855-56.
William W. Stone, Boston. Director, 1837-46, 1848-49.
Moorfield Storey, Brookline, Boston. Honorary Counsel, 1898-1912.
William W. Story, Rome, Italy. Vice pres., 1892-96.

Rev. Baron Stowe, D. D., Boston. Director, 1839-47, 1859-70; Ex. Com., 1841-1844, 1859-70; Vice pres., 1854-70.
Rev. Calvin E. Stowe, D. D., Cincinnati, Andover, Mass. Director, 1835-44; Vice pres., 1844-47; 1853-63. Graduate Bowdoin, Andover. Prof. Bowdoin, Lane, Andover.
Silas H. Strawn, Chicago, Director, 1827-.
George H. Stuart, Philadelphia. Vice pres., 1873-90.
Russell Sturgis, Boston. Ex. Com., 1878-85.
Bradford Sumner, Boston. Ex. Com., 1841-44; Director, 1844-56.
Charles Sumner, LL. D., Boston. Ex. Com., 1837-38; 1841-44; 1847-54; Director, 1837-42, 1844-54; Vice pres., 1853-74. U. S. S.
Ephraim Swan, Boston. Ex. Com., 1876-83.
David S. Taber, N. Y. C. Vice pres., 1883-1902.
William H. Taft, New Haven, Conn. Vice pres., 1913-20. President U. S.
Daniel S. Tallcott, D. D., Bangor, Me. Director, 1875-76; Vice pres., 1875-84.
Charles Tappan, Boston. Ex. Com., 1841-44; Director, 1844-56.
John Tappan, Boston. Director, 1828-36; Vice pres., 1839-71.
Lewis Tappan, N. Y. C. Director, 1829-47; Ex. Com., 1834-35; Vice pres., 1866-73.
Rev. Edward M. Taylor, Cambridge, Mass. Vice pres., 1904-11.
Hon. Henry W. Temple, Washington. Ex. Com., 1922- ; Director, 1924- .
Prof. J. B. Thayer, Cambridge, Mass. Director, 1892-93; Honorary Counsel, 1892-93.
William W. Thayer, Concord, N. H. Representative Director, 1912-16; Director, 1916-19.
Pres. M. Carey Thomas, Bryn Mawr, Pa. Vice pres., 1902-13; Hon. Vice pres., 1913-26.
Rev. Reuen Thomas, D. D., Brookline, Mass. Director, 1893-1905; Vice pres., 1905-08.
Rev. George W. Thompson, Stratham, N. H. Director, 1867-90.
Thomas Thompson, Jr., Boston. Director, 1837-47; Ex. Com., 1837-38, 1840-41; Recording Secretary, 1837-38.
Rev. James Thurston, Boston, Ex. Com., 1841-45.
Rev. Charles F. Thwing, Cambridge, Mass., Minneapolis, Cleveland. Director, 1885-88; Vice pres., 1888-1913; Hon. Vice pres., 1913-.
Rev. William P. Tilden, Boston, Ex. Com., 1871-78.
Hon. Edward S. Tobey, Boston. President, 1873-91. Mass. Senate. P. M.
Albert Tolman, Worcester, Mass. Director, 1872-91.
James Tolman, Boston. Director, 1856-69.
Rev. Charles T. Torrey, Albany, N. Y. Ex. Com., 1841-43; Director, 1843-44.
Harold G. Townsend, Chicago. Director Central West Dept., 1916-18; Director, 1916-17.
Rev. Trask, Framingham, Mass. Director, 1836-37.
George Trask, Boston. Ex. Com., 1845-46.
Alfred C. True, Ph. D., Washington. Director, 1911-12.
Rev. Benjamin F. Trueblood, LL. D., Boston, Washington. Corresponding Secretary, 1892-1908; Secretary, 1908-15; Honorary Secretary, 1915-17; Director at Large, 1912-16.
James L. Tryon, Attleboro, Waltham, Boston, Portland, Me. Assistant Secretary, 1908-10; Director New England Department, 1910-18; Director, 1906-1910, 1918-19; Representative Director, 1912-14.
L. Tucker, Boston. Ex. Com., 1850-52.
William Twining, Madison, Ind. Director, 1836-44.
Hon. Dudley A. Tyng, Newburyport, Mass. Director, 1828-30.
Rev. Stephen H. Tyng, D. D., N. Y. C. Vice pres., 1846-56. Editor Episcopal Recorder.
Hezekiah C. Ufford, N. Y. C. Director, 1829-30.
Rev. Thomas C. Upham, D. D., Brunswick, Kennebunkport, Me. Director, 1835-43; Vice pres., 1843-72. Professor Bowdoin.

Rev. Joseph Vail, Brunswick, Me. Director, 1835-37.
Dr. J. W. Van Kirk, Youngstown, Ohio. Representative Director, 1914-15.
James H. Van Sickle, Baltimore. Director, 1911-12.
Rev. C. C. Vanarsdalen, Hartford. Ex. Com., 1835-36; Director, 1835-37.
Robert Vaux, Philadelphia, Director, 1829-36.
George E. Vincent, Minneapolis. Hon. Vice pres., 1914-16. President University of Minnesota.
Robert E. Vinson, Cleveland. Director, 1927-28. President Western Reserve.
Thomas Vose, Boston. Director, 1838-39; Ex. Com., 1837-39.
Hon. Amasa Walker, Boston, North Brookfield, Mass. Director, 1835-37, 1862-1875; Ex. Com., 1837-43, 1845-47, 1849-50, 1862-66; Vice pres., 1839-76. **Massachusetts Secretary of State.**
Gen. Francis A. Walker, Boston. Vice pres., 1892-97. President Mass. Inst. of Tech.
Pres. James Wallace, St. Paul., N. Y. C. Vice pres., 1905-13; Hon. Vice pres., 1914-15.
S. H. Walley, Roxbury, Mass. Director, 1843-44.
Rev. J. T. Walsh, D. D., Newbern, N. C. Director, 1870-72.
John Wanamaker, Philadelphia. Vice pres., 1877-78.
Thomas S. Ward, Boston. Vice president, 1843-45.
Henry Ware, Jr., D. D., Cambridge. Director, 1837-44; Ex. Com., 1838-39; 1841-43. Prof. Harvard Divinity School. Editor Christian Examiner.
Fiske Warren, Boston. Director, 1904-11.
Hon. G. Washington Warren, Boston, Ex. Com., 1872-83.
Bishop Henry W. Warren, Denver, Col. Vice pres., 1885-1913.
S. D. Warren, Boston. Ex. Com., 1872-75.
Hon. Emory Washburn, Cambridge, Greenfield, Mass. Vice pres., 1872-78.
Hon. Israel Washburn, Portland, Me. Vice pres., 1877-84.
Hon. William B. Washburn, Boston, Greenfield. Vice pres., 1875-84.
Booker T. Washington, LL. D., Tuskeegee, Ala. Vice pres., 1905-13; Hon. Vice pres., 1913-16.
Hon. Robert Watchorn, Los Angeles. Representative Director, 1912-16; Director, 1916-17.
Rev. J. B. Waterbury, D. D., Boston. Director, 1847-58; Ex. Com., 1847-55.
Rev. T. T. Waterman, Providence. Director, 1834-36.
Robert Waterson, Boston. Director, 1837-45; Vice pres., 1845-50.
David Watkinson, Hartford, Conn. Treasurer, 1835-36; Director, 1835-38; Ex. Com., 1835-37.
Rev. C. H. Watson, D. D., Arlington, Mass. Director, 1901-07.
William Watson, Hartford. Director, 1835-37; Ex. Com., 1835-37; Treasurer, 1836-37.
Francis O. Watts, Boston. Ex. Com., 1841-47; Director, 1847-52.
Rev. Francis Wayland, D. D., LL. D., Providence. Director, 1834-36. Vice pres., 1839-59, 1861-66; President, 1859-61. President Brown University.
Rev. Arthur L. Weatherly, Lincoln, Neb. Representative Director, 1912-16; Director, 1916-17, 1918-19.
Rev. William R. Weeks, D. D., Newark, N. J. Director, 1836-37; Vice pres., 1839-44.
E. M. P. Wells, Boston. Ex. Com., 1849-50.
J. H. Wells, Hartford. Director, 1835-37.
Kate Gannett Wells, Boston. Director, 1889-1905; Vice pres., 1905-12.
Oscar Wells, Birmingham, Ala. Director, 1927-28.
Herbert Welsh, Philadelphia. Vice pres., 1901-12.
Hon. A. B. Wentworth, Boston, Newtonville, Mass. Ex. Com., 1891-92; Director, 1892-95. Honorary Counsel, 1893-95.
Thomas Weston, Newton. Ex. Com., 1875-77.
Charles F. Whaley, Seattle, Wash. Vice pres., 1910-13.
E. P. Wharton, Greensboro, N. C. Director, 1918-19.
Rev. N. S. Wheaton, Hartford. Director, 1835-37.

D. E. Wheeler, N. Y. C. Secretary for Domestic Correspondence, 1831-33; Director, 1831-35.
James K. Whipple, Boston, New Orleans. Treasurer and Depository, 1837-41; Director, 1839-44; Ex. Com., 1839-42.
S. K. Whipple, Boston. Director, 1856-61; Ex. Com., 1859-60.
Edward White, Washington. Auditor, 1912-16.
Hon. Frank White, Washington. Director, 1927- .
George W. White, Washington. Treasurer, 1911-28; Director at Large, 1912-1916.
Dr. Henry C. White, Athens, Ga. Vice pres., 1912-13; Hon. Vice pres., 1913-16.
James C. White, Boston. Director, 1838-39.
Thomas Raeburn White, Philadelphia. Director, 1911-12; Director at Large, 1912-16.
William Allen White, Topeka. Director, 1927- .
John Greenleaf Whittier, Amesbury, Mass. Vice pres., 1870-92.
George Wigglesworth, Bryn Mawr, Pa. Vice pres., 1902-03.
S. V. S. Wilder, N. Y. C. Director, 1830-36; Ex. Com., 1834-35; Vice pres., 1839-53.
Frances E. Willard, Evanston, Ill. Vice pres., 1894-98.
Sidney Willard, Cambridge, Mass. Director, 1837-56; Ex. Com., 1841-43; Vice pres., 1843-44.
Samuel Willetts, N. Y. C. Director, 1872-83.
Frank F. Williams, Buffalo, N. Y. Representative Director, 1912-16; Director, 1911-19.
Hon. Thomas W. Williams, New London, Conn. Vice pres., 1839-44, 1855-66.
Hon. James F. Wilson, Washington, Fairfield, Iowa. Vice pres., 1886-88, 1892-1895. U. S. S.
Rev. A. E. Winship, Somerville, Mass. Ex. Com., 1884-91; Director, 1891-1903; Vice pres., 1904-13; Hon. Vice pres., 1913-21.
Rev. Hubbard Winslow, Boston. Director, 1835-49; Ex. Com., 1846-47.
Hubbard Winston, Boston. Director, 1838-39.
Hon. Robert C. Winthrop, Brookline, Boston. Vice pres., 1871-95. M. C. U. S. S.
John C. Wood, Germantown, Pa. Director, 1886-91.
Richard Wood, Philadelphia. Vice pres., 1893-1911.
Thomas Wood, Boston. Ex. Com., 1884-91.
Pres. Mary E. Woolley, South Hadley, Mass. Vice pres., 1907-13; Hon. Vice pres., 1913-26.
Theodore D. Woolsey, D. D., LL. D., New Haven. Vice pres., 1872-90. President Yale.
Rev. John Worcester, Newtonville, Mass. Director, 1887-93; Vice pres., 1893-1900.
Joseph E. Worcester, LL. D., Cambridge, Mass. Vice pres., 1856-66.
Rev. Noah Worcester, D. D., Brighton, Mass. Director, 1828-36.
Rev. S. M. Worcester, Boston. Director, 1838-39.
Stanley R. Yarnall, Germantown, Pa. Director, 1911-12.

APPENDIX C

DECLARATION OF RIGHTS AND DUTIES OF NATIONS

ADOPTED BY THE
AMERICAN INSTITUTE OF INTERNATIONAL LAW
AT ITS FIRST SESSION
IN THE CITY OF WASHINGTON, JANUARY 6, 1916,
AND APPROVED AT ONCE BY THE AMERICAN PEACE SOCIETY

Whereas the municipal law of civilized nations recognizes and protects the right to life, the right to liberty, the right to the pursuit of happiness as added by the Declaration of Independence of the United States of America, the right to legal equality, the right to property, and the right to the enjoyment of the aforesaid rights; and

Whereas these fundamental rights, thus universally recognized, create a duty on the part of the peoples of all nations to observe them; and

Whereas according to the political philosophy of the Declaration of Independence of the United States, and the universal practice of the American Republics, nations or governments are regarded as created by the people, deriving their just powers from the consent of the governed, and are instituted among men to promote their safety and happiness and to secure to the people the enjoyment of their fundamental rights; and

Whereas the nation is a moral or juristic person, the creature of law, and subordinate to law as is the natural person in political society; and

Whereas we deem that these fundamental rights can be stated in terms of international law and applied to the relations of the members of the society of nations, one with another, just as they have been applied in the relations of the citizens or subjects of the states forming the society of nations; and

Whereas these fundamental rights of national jurisprudence, namely, the right to life, the right to liberty, the right to the pursuit of happiness, the right to equality before the law, the right to property, and the right to the observance thereof, are, when stated in terms of international law, the right of the nation to exist and to protect and to conserve its existence; the right of independence and the freedom to develop itself without interference or control from other nations: the right of equality in law and before law; the right to territory within defined boundaries and to exclusive jurisdiction therein; and the right to the observance of these fundamental rights; and

Whereas the rights and the duties of nations are, by virtue of membership in the society thereof, to be exercised and performed in accordance with the exigencies of their mutual interdependence expressed in the preamble to the Convention for the Pacific Settlement of International Disputes of the First and Second Hague Peace Conferences, recognizing the solidarity which unites the members of the society of civilized nations; it should therefore be universally maintained by the nations and peoples of the world, that:

I. Every nation has the right to exist, and to protect and to conserve its existence; but this right neither implies the right nor justifies the act of the state to protect itself or to conserve its existence by the commission of unlawful acts against innocent and unoffending states.

II. Every nation has the right to independence in the sense that it has a right to the pursuit of happiness and is free to develop itself without interference or control from other states, provided that in so doing it does not interfere with or violate the rights of other states.

III. Every nation is in law and before law the equal of every other nation belonging to the society of nations, and all nations have the right to claim and, according to the Declaration of Independence of the United States, "to assume, among the powers of the earth, the separate and equal station to which the laws of nature and of nature's God entitle them."

IV. Every nation has the right to territory within defined boundaries and to exercise exclusive jurisdiction over its territory, and all persons, whether native or foreign, found therein.

V. Every nation entitled to a right by the law of nations is entitled to have that right respected and protected by all other nations, for right and duty are correlative, and the right of one is the duty of all to observe.

VI. International law is at one and the same time both national and international; national in the sense that it is the law of the land and applicable as such to the decision of all questions involving its principles; international in the sense that it is the law of the society of nations and applicable as such to all questions between and among the members of the society of nations involving its principles.

APPENDIX D

THE RECOMMENDATIONS OF HABANA

ADOPTED BY THE
AMERICAN INSTITUTE OF INTERNATIONAL LAW
AT ITS SECOND SESSION
IN THE CITY OF HABANA, CUBA, JANUARY 23, 1917.
APPROVED BY THE AMERICAN PEACE SOCIETY, JANUARY 22, 1917.

Whereas the independent existence of civilized nations and their solidarity of interests under the conditions of modern life has resulted in a society of nations; and

Whereas the safety of nations and the welfare of their peoples depend upon the application to them of principles of law and equity in their mutual relations as members of civilized society; and

Whereas the law of nations can best be formulated and stated by the nations assembled for this purpose in international conferences; and

Whereas it is in the interest of the society of nations that international agreements be made effective by ratification and observance on all occasions, and that some agency of the society of nations be constituted to act for it during the intervals between such conferences; and

Whereas the principles of law and equity can best be ascertained and applied to the disputes between and among the nations by a court of justice accessible to all in the midst of the independent Powers forming the society of civilized nations;

Therefore the American Institute of International Law, at its second session, held in the city of Habana, in the Republic of Cuba, on the 23d day of January, 1917, adopts the following recommendations, to be known as its *Recommendations of Habana:*

I.   The call of a Third Hague Conference to which every country belonging to the society of nations shall be invited and in whose proceedings every such country shall participate.

II.   A stated meeting of The Hague Peace Conference which, thus meeting at regular, stated periods, will become a recommending if not a law-making body.

III.   An agreement of the states forming the society of nations concerning the call and procedure of the Conference, by which that institution shall become not only internationalized, but in which no nation shall take as of right a preponderating part.

IV. The appointment of a committee, to meet at regular intervals between the conferences, charged with the duty of procuring the ratification of the conventions and declarations and of calling attention to the conventions and declarations in order to insure their observance.

V. An understanding upon certain fundamental principles of international law, as set forth in the Declaration of the Rights and Duties of Nations adopted by the American Intitute of International Law on January 6, 1916, which are themselves based upon decisions of English courts and of the Supreme Court of the United States.

VI. The creation of an international council of conciliation to consider, to discuss, and to report upon such questions of a non-justiciable character as may be submitted to such council by an agreement of the Powers for this purpose.

VII. The employment of good offices, mediation, and friendly composition for the settlement of disputes of a non-justiciable nature.

VIII. The principle of arbitration in the settlement of disputes of a non-justiciable nature; also of disputes of a justiciable nature which should be decided by a court of justice, but which have, through delay or mismanagement, assumed such political importance that the nations prefer to submit them to arbiters of their own choice rather than to judges of a permanent judicial tribunal.

IX. The negotiation of a convention creating a judicial union of the nations along the lines of the Universal Postal Union of 1906, to which all civilized nations and self-governing dominions are parties, pledging the good faith of the contracting parties to submit their justiciable disputes—that is to say, their differences involving law or equity—to a permanent court of this union, whose decisions will bind not only the litigating nations, but also all parties to its creation.

X. The creation of an enlightened public opinion in behalf of peaceable settlement in general, and in particular in behalf of the foregoing nine propositions, in order that, if agreed to, they may be put into practice and become effective, in response to the appeal to that greatest of sanctions, "a decent respect to the opinions of mankind."

APPENDIX E

SUGGESTIONS FOR A GOVERNED WORLD

ADOPTED BY THE
AMERICAN PEACE SOCIETY
AT ITS NINETY-THIRD ANNUAL MEETING
IN THE CITY OF WASHINGTON, MAY 27, 1921.

The American Peace Society, mindful of the precepts of its founders, precepts which have been confirmed by the experience of the past hundred years, recurs in these days of storm and stress at home and of confusion and discord abroad, to these precepts and its own traditions, and, confessing anew its faith in their feasibility and necessity, restates and resubmits to a hesitant, a suffering, and a war-torn world:

That the voluntary union of States and their helpful co-operation for the attainment of their common ideals can only be effective if, and only so far as, "The rules of conduct governing individual relations between citizens or subjects of a civilized State are equally applicable as between enlightened nations";

That the rules of conduct governing individual relations, and which must needs be expressed in terms of international law, relate to "the enjoyment of life and liberty with the means of acquiring and possessing property, and pursuing and obtaining happiness and safety"; and,

That these concepts which are the very life and breath of reason and justice, upon which the Law of Nations is founded, must be a chief concern of nations, inasmuch as "Justice," and its administration, "is the great interest of man on earth."

Therefore, realizing the conditions which confront the world at the termination of its greatest of wars; conscious that permanent relief can only come through standards of morality and principles of justice expressed in rules of law, to the end that the conduct of nations shall be a regulated conduct, and that the government of the Union of States, as well as the government of each member thereof, shall be a government of laws, and not of men; and desiring to contribute to the extent of its capacity, the American Peace Society ventures, at its ninety-third annual meeting, held in the city of Washington, in the year of our Lord one thousand nine hundred and twenty-one, to suggest, as calculated to incorporate these principles in the practice of nations, an international agreement:

I. To institute Conferences of Nations, to meet at stated intervals, in continuation of the first two conferences of The Hague; and

To facilitate the labors of such conferences; to invite accredited institutions devoted to the study of international law, to prepare projects for the consideration of governments, in advance of submission to the conferences; in order

To restate and amend, reconcile and clarify, extend and advance the rules of international law which are indispensable to the permanent establishment and the successful administration of justice between and among nations.

II. To convoke, as soon as practicable, a conference for the advancement of international law; to provide for its organization outside of the domination of any one nation or any limited group of nations; to which conference every nation recognizing, accepting, and applying international law in its relations with other nations, shall be invited, and in which all shall participate upon a footing of equality.

III. To establish an Administrative Council to be composed of the diplomatic representatives accredited to the government of the State in which the conference for the advancement of international law convenes, which representatives shall, in addition to their ordinary functions as diplomatic agents, represent the common interests of the nations during the interval between successive conferences; and to provide that

The president of the Administrative Council shall, according to diplomatic usage, be the Minister of Foreign Affairs of the country in which the conference convenes;

An advisory committee shall be appointed by the Administrative Council from among its members, which shall meet at short, regular, and stated periods;

The chairman of the advisory committee shall be elected by its members;

The advisory committee shall report the result of its labors to the Administrative Council;

The members of the Administrative Council, having considered the report of the advisory committee, shall transmit their findings or recommendations to their respective governments, together with their collective or individual opinions, and that they shall act thereafter upon such fiindings and recommendations only in accordance with instructions from the governments which they represent.

IV. To authorize the Administrative Council to appoint, outside its own members, an executive committee or secretary's office to perform such duties as the conference for the advancement of international law, or the nations shall from time to time prescribe; and to provide that

The executive committee or secretary's office shall be under the supervision of the Administrative Council;

The executive committee or secretary's office shall report to the Administrative Council at stated periods.

V.   To empower the Administrative Council to appoint other committees for the performance of such duties as the nations in their wisdom or discretion shall find it desirable to impose.

VI.   To furnish technical advisers to assist the Administrative Council, the advisory committee, or other committees appointed by the council, in the performance of their respective duties, whenver the appointment of such technical advisers may be necessary or desirable; with the understanding that the request for the appointment of such experts may be made by the conference for the advancement of international law or by the Administrative Council.

VII.   To employ good offices, mediation, and friendly composition wherever feasible and practicable, in their own disputes, and to urge their employment wherever feasible and practicable, in disputes between other nations.

VIII.   To organize a Commission of Inquiry of limited membership, which may be enlarged by the nations in dispute, to which commission they may refer, for investigation and report, their differences of an international character, unless they are otherwise bound to submit them to arbitration or to other form of peaceful settlement; and

To pledge their good faith to abstain from any act of force against one another pending the investigation of the commission and the receipt of its report; and

To reserve the right to act on the report as their respective interests may seem to them to demand; and

To provide that the Commission of Inquiry shall submit its report to the nations in controversy for their action, and to the Administrative Council for its information.

IX.   To create a Council of Conciliation of limited membership, with power on behalf of the nations in dispute to add to its members, to consider and to report upon such questions of a non-justiciable character, the settlement whereof is not otherwise prescribed, which shall from time to time be submitted to the Council of Conciliation, either by the powers in dispute, or by the Administrative Council; and to provide that

The Council of Conciliation shall transmit its proposals to the nations in dispute, for such action as they may deem advisable, and to the Council of Administration for its information.

X.   To arbitrate differences of an international character not otherwise provided for, and in the absence of an agreement to the contrary, to submit them to the Permanent Court of Arbitration at The Hague, in order that they may be adjusted upon a basis of respect for law; with the understanding that disputes of a justiciable nature may likewise be referred to the Permanent Court of Arbitration, when the parties in controversy prefer to have their differences settled by judges of their own choice, appointed for the occasion.

XI.   To set up an international court of justice with obligatory jurisdiction, to which, upon the failure of diplomacy to adjust their disputes of a justiciable nature, all States shall have direct access; a court whose decisions shall bind the litigating States, and, eventually, all parties to its creation, and to which the States in controversy may submit, by special agreement, disputes beyond the scope of obligatory jurisdiction.

XII. To enlarge from time to time the obligatory jurisdiction of the Permanent Court of International Justice, by framing rules of law in the conferences for the advancement of international law, to be applied by the court for the decision of questions which fall either beyond its present obligatory jurisdiction, or which nations have not hitherto submitted to judicial decision.

XIII. To apply inwardly international law as a rule of law for the decision of all questions involving its principles, and outwardly to apply international law to all questions arising between and among all nations, so far as they involve the Law of Nations.

XIV. To furnish their citizens or subjects adequate instruction in their international obligations and duties, as well as in their rights and prerogatives;

To take all necessary steps to render such instruction effective; and thus

To create that "international mind" and enlightened public opinion which shall persuade in the future, where force has failed to compel in the past, the observance of those standards of honor, morality, and justice, which obtain between and among individuals, bringing in their train law and order, through which, and through which alone, peace between nations may become practicable, attainable, and desirable.

APPENDIX F

THE FOUNDATIONS OF PEACE BETWEEN NATIONS

Adopted by the American Peace Society, November 30, 1925.

THE American Peace Society reaffirms, at this its ninety-seventh annual meeting, its abiding faith in the precepts of its illustrious founders. These founders, together with the men of later times who have shared in the labors of this Society, are favorably known because of their services to the building and preservation of the Republic. Their work for peace between nations must not be forgotten.

Largely because of their labors, the purposes of the American Peace Society have become more and more the will of the world, and opponents of the war system of settling international disputes have reason for a larger hope and a newer courage.

At such a time as this, with its rapidly developing international achievements, it is fitting that the American Peace Society should restate its precepts of a century in the light of the ever-approaching tomorrow.

Peace between nations, demanded by every legitimate interest, can rest securely and permanently only on the principles of justice as interpreted in terms of mutually accepted international law; but justice between nations and its expression in the law are possible only as the collective intelligence and the common faith of peoples approve and demand.

The American Peace Society is not unmindful of the work of the schools, of the churches, of the many organizations throughout the world aiming to advance interest and wisdom in the matters of a desirable and attainable peace; but this desirable, attainable, and hopeful peace between nations must rest upon the commonly accepted achievements in the settlement of international disputes.

These achievements, approved in every instance by the American Peace Society, and in which some of its most distinguished members have participated, have heretofore been—

By direct negotiations between free, sovereign, and independent States, working through official representatives, diplomatic or consular agents —a work now widely extended by the League of Nations at Geneva;

By the good offices of one or more friendly nations, upon the request of the contending parties or of other and disinterested parties—a policy consistently and persistently urged by the United States;

By the mediation of one or more nations upon their own or other initiative—likewise a favorite policy of the United States;

By commissions of inquiry, duty provided for by international convention and many existing treaties, to which the Government of the United States is pre-eminently a contracting party;

By councils of conciliation—a method of adjustment fortunately meeting with the approval of leading nations, including the United States;

By friendly composition, in which nations in controversy accept, in lieu of their own, the opinion of an upright and disinterested third party —a method tried and not found wanting by the Government of the United States;

By arbitration, in which controversies are adjusted upon the basis of respect for law—a method brought into modern and general practice by the English-speaking peoples.

All of these processes will be continued, emphasized, and improved. While justice and the rules of law—principles, customs, practices, recognized as applicable to nations in their relations with one another— frequently apply to each of these methods just enumerated, there remain two outstanding, continuous, and pressing demands:

(1) Recurring, preferably periodic, conferences of duly appointed delegates, acting under instruction, for the purpose of restating, amending, reconciling, declaring, and progressively codifying those rules of international law shown to be necessary or useful to the best interests of civilized States—a proposal repeatedly made by enlightened leaders of thought in the United States.

(2) Adherence of all States to a Permanent Court of International Justice mutually acceptable, sustained, and made use of for the determination of controversies between nations, involving legal rights—an institution due to the initiative of the United States and based upon the experience and practice of the American Supreme Court.

INDEX

348

Buffum, Arnold, 66
Bullard, Artemus, 93
Burdette, Bob, 241
Burke, Hon. John, 312
Burke, Judge Thos., 260
Burnet, Rev. John, 67
Burns, Dr., 127
Burritt, Elihu, 76, 78, 79, 81, 86, 89,
90, 91, 93, 94, 95, 107, 126, 127, 129,
131, 141, 246, 247
Burt, Hon. Thomas, 117, 161
Burton, Theodore E., 185, 225, 242, 243,
246, 259, 272, 310, 312
Bush, George, 25, 26
Bushnell, S. C., 279
Butler, Chas. Henry, 226, 305
Butler, Nicholas Murray, 224, 233
Butler, Wm. Allen, 194
Butterworth, Benjamin, 192

C

Caine, Hall, 191
Call, Dr. Arthur Deerin, Secretary
American Peace Society; Executive-
Secretary American Group of the
Inter-Parliamentary Union; 169, 185,
224, 270, 271, 280, 291, 296, 297, 300,
304, 305, 311, 313, 314
Call, Mrs. Arthur Deerin, 314
Callanan, James, 256
Calvo, Chas., 130, 132
"Calumet", 1831-35, 29, 35, 47
Campbell, Hon. Judge Ceylon, 26
Campbell, Sir Geo., 163, 176
Capen, Samuel B., 189, 201, 218, 224,
229, 231
Carey, Matthew, 25
Carlyle, Thomas, 95
Carnegie, Andrew, 161, 163, 164, 165,
206, 208, 218, 219, 231, 237, 238, 280
Carnegie Endowment, 261, 273, 275,
310
Carnegie Institution, Washington, D.
C., 260
Carnegie Peace Fund, 259-263
Carnot, President, 172
Casimer-Perier, 13
Centennial Celebration of the Society,
Cleveland, 1928, 314
Central American Court of Justice,
217
Chadbourne, Paul E., 140, 141
Chalmers, Thomas, 14
Channing, Wm. Ellery, 11, 42, 46, 82,
220
Channing, Dr. Walter, 73, 81
Chant, Mrs. Laura Ormiston, 152
Chapin, E. H., 93
Chase, Rev. B. A., 136
Chevalier, Michel, 90

Cheever, Rev. George B., 107
Chicago Peace Congress, 1893, 192;
1909, 240
Chicago Peace Society, 278
Chickering, Rev. John W., 37
Childs, Geo. W., 163
Chipman, R. M., 24, 26, 37
Choate, Joseph H., 226
Christian Arbitration and Peace So-
ciety, 193
Church Peace Union, 265
Churchill, Mrs. Annie S., 247
Civil War, Articles by the American
Peace Society, 111-115
Civil War, 111-115
Claflin, William, 140, 141
Clapp, Henry, 88
Clark, Champ, 242
Clark, Dorus, 141
Clark, E. C., 130
Clark, Rev. Francis E., 220
Clark, John B., 218, 224, 237, 297
Clarke, Rev. James Freeman, 83, 91
Clarke, Rev. R. W., 107
Claxton, Dr. P. P., 224, 242, 252, 282,
311
Clay, Henry, 58
Clement, Edward H., 218
Clementi, Canon, 70
Cleveland, Centennial Celebration, 314
Cleveland, C. D., 93
Cleveland, Grover, 155, 163
Cleveland, Judge John B., 280
Cleveland Peace Society, 279
Cleveland, Dr. Stephen B., 25
Cobden, Richard, 66, 89, 90, 92, 93,
94, 95, 96
Cock, Thomas, 37, 42, 66, 67, 69
Codification of International Law
adopted by Senate, 159
Codman, Rev. John, 25
Colfax, 127
Collier, Rev. Joseph A., 109
Collins, Isaac, 66
Collins, Patrick A., 220
"Coming Peace", 152
Conference between states, 1888, legis-
lation and appropriation, 156
Congress of Nations, 50, 53, 55, 59
Connecticut Peace Society, 33, 36, 280
Constitution, Amendments to, 253
Convention at Brussels, 1848, 87
" " Paris, 1849, 92
" " Frankfort, 1850, 92
" " London, 1851, 94
" " Brussels, 1873, 132
Converse, Jas. W., 145
Cook, Joseph, 140, 164, 165, 190, 196,
224
Cooke, H. D., 127

Everett, Wm., 201
Ewart, 66, 94

F

Faider, Ch., 132
Fair, first, held for benefit of peace, 38
Fairbanks, Chas. W., 250
Fairbanks, J. P., 106
Farley, Archbishop, 238
Farwell, J. E., 165
Faunce, Pres. W. H. P., 224, 264, 311
Faure, 176
Fellows, Francis, 36, 37
Female Peace Society, Cincinnati, 11
Ferguson, Munro, 163
Fessenden, Hon. Samuel, 106
Field, David Dudley, 125, 127, 129, 131, 190
Field, John, 78, 106, 123
Field Work, 276
Fillmore, President, 101
Finances, 1842-7, 77; 1856, 104; 1901-06, 256-7; 1912-18, 275
Finch, George A., 308
Finley, J. H., 297
First Peace Society, 1812, 10
Fish, Hamilton, 130
Fish, Stuyvesant, 231
Fishery treaty, 1854, 101
Fisk, Everett O., 190
Fletcher, Hon. Richard, 42
Forbes, Mrs. J. Malcolm, 265
"Force and The League of Nations", 298
Foster, Aaron, 76
Foster, Arthur Wm, 260
Foster, Bp., (M. E.), 165
Foster, John, 11
Foster, Hon. John W., 201, 218, 224, 230, 231, 274
Foulk, Fred B., 272
Foulk, Wm. Dudley, 282, 297
Fox, Austin G., 260
Franks, R. A., 260
Francke, Kuno, 239
Fraser, Rev. Alexander, 26
Frelinghuysen, Theodore, 42, 82, 106
"Friend of Peace" Magazine, 15, 47
Frisbie, Levi, 14
Freck, Charles, 163
Frost, Rufus, S., 160
Frothingham, Rev. Paul Revere, 220
Frye, W. P., 250
Fulk, George, 282
Fuller, Melville W., 201, 212
Fund, Permament Peace, 143-147

G

Gaffield, Thomas, 106, 165
Gage, Lyman J., 192, 201
Gaillaud, 176
Gallaudet, Rev. T. H., 25, 33
Gallitzin, Prince A., 14
Garibaldi, Gen., 124
Garnett, Henry, 93
Garnier, 92, 93, 94, 124
Garrett, John B., 224
Garrett, Philip C., 139, 163, 218, 229, 231
Garrison, Wm. Lloyd, 44
Gates, Merrill E., 125, 190, 201, 224
Geiger, Frankfort, 117
Geneva Peace Society, 13, 24
Gannett, Rev. E. S., 26, 42, 43
Garrett, Dr. Alfred C., 188
Gevers, Baron, 212
Gibbons, Cardinal, 196
Gifford, Rev. O. P., 247
Gifford, D. C., 201, 218, 230
Gilman, John T., 14, 25
Gilmore, P. S., 127
Ginn, Edwin, 172, 218, 219, 231, 263
Girardin, Emile de, 89, 93, 05
Giraud, Ch., 132
Gladstone, Wm., 140
Gobart, B. B., 224
Gobat, Chas. Albert, 173, 182, 225
Goblet, Secretary 176, 198
Goddard, C. W., 131
Goddard, Leroy A., 278
Godin, France, 117
Golay, H., 173
Gompers, Samuel, 206, 208, 220, 231, 238, 239
Gordon Smith, Capt. Gordon, 312
Gore, Christopher, 14
Gould, Jay, 196
Grant, Gen. Fred Dent, 241
Grant, Moses, 107
Grant, U. S., 140
Graves, John Temple, 296
Gray, Judge George, 125, 218, 224, 231
Greele, Samuel, 77, 84
Greeley, Horace, 94
Green, Thos. E., 243, 308, 312
Greene, Rev. S. H., 231
Greenleaf, Benjamin, 107
Greenleaf, Simon, 14, 25, 42, 83, 84
Gregg, Dr. David, 165
Gresham, Walter, 196, 202
Grey, Sir Edward, 233
Griggs, John W., 212
Grimke, Judge Thomas, 25, 26, 34, 35, 52, 82
Griscom, John, 25
Groegg, Geneva, 117

www.ingramcontent.com/pod-product-compliance
Lightning Source LLC
Chambersburg PA
CBHW071234290326
41931CB00038B/2964

* 9 7 8 1 6 3 3 9 1 5 4 5 9 *